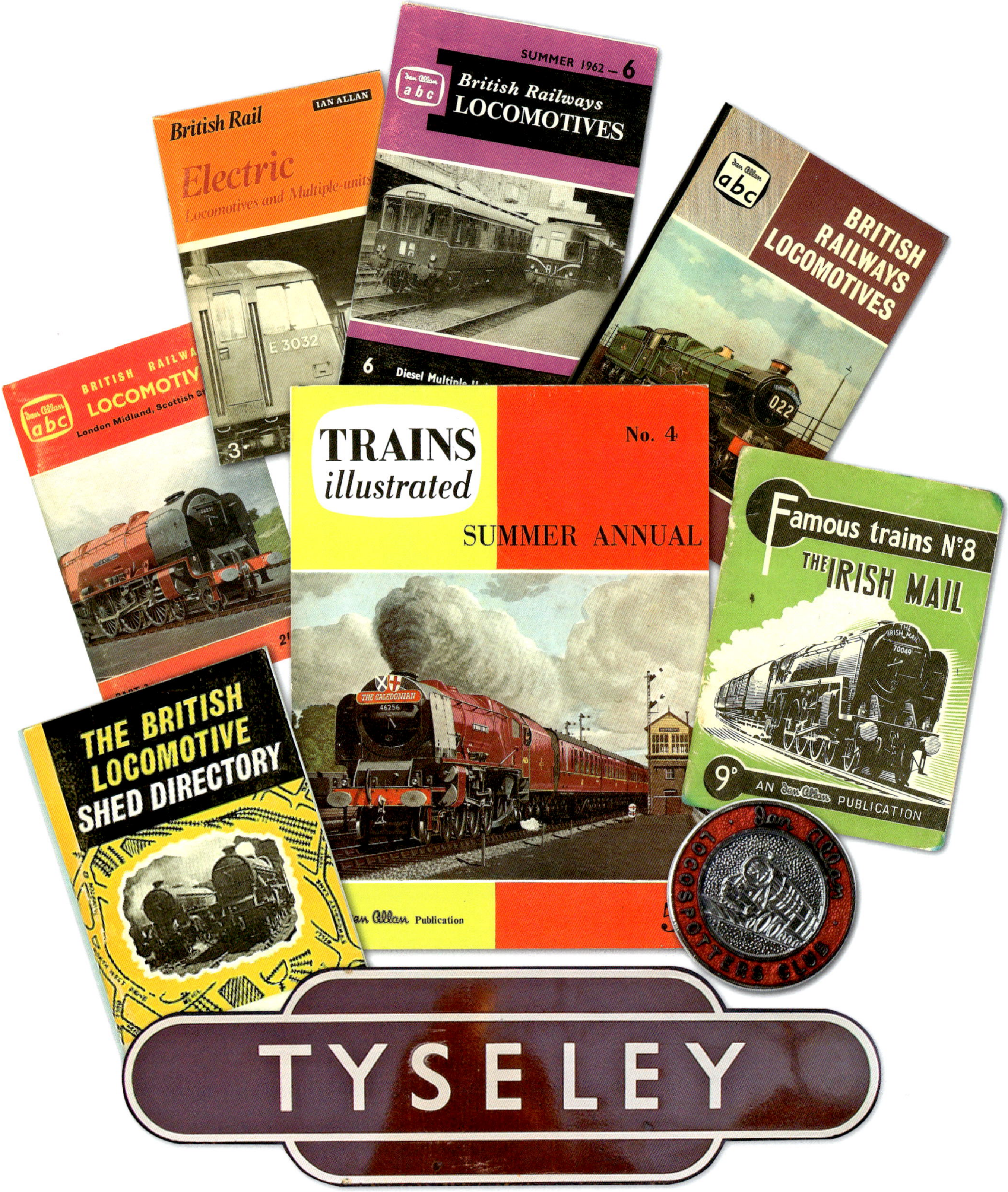
British Rail
IAN ALLAN
Electric
Locomotives and Multiple-units
E 3032
SUMMER 1962 — 6
abc
British Railways
LOCOMOTIVES
BRITISH RAILWAYS LOCOMOTIVES
022
TRAINS illustrated
No. 4
SUMMER ANNUAL
THE CALEDONIAN
46256
Publication
Famous trains N°8
THE IRISH MAIL
70049
9d
AN Ian Allan PUBLICATION
THE BRITISH LOCOMOTIVE SHED DIRECTORY
Ian Allan
LOCOSPOTTERS CLUB
TYSELEY

Sixties Spotting Days Around The Midlands

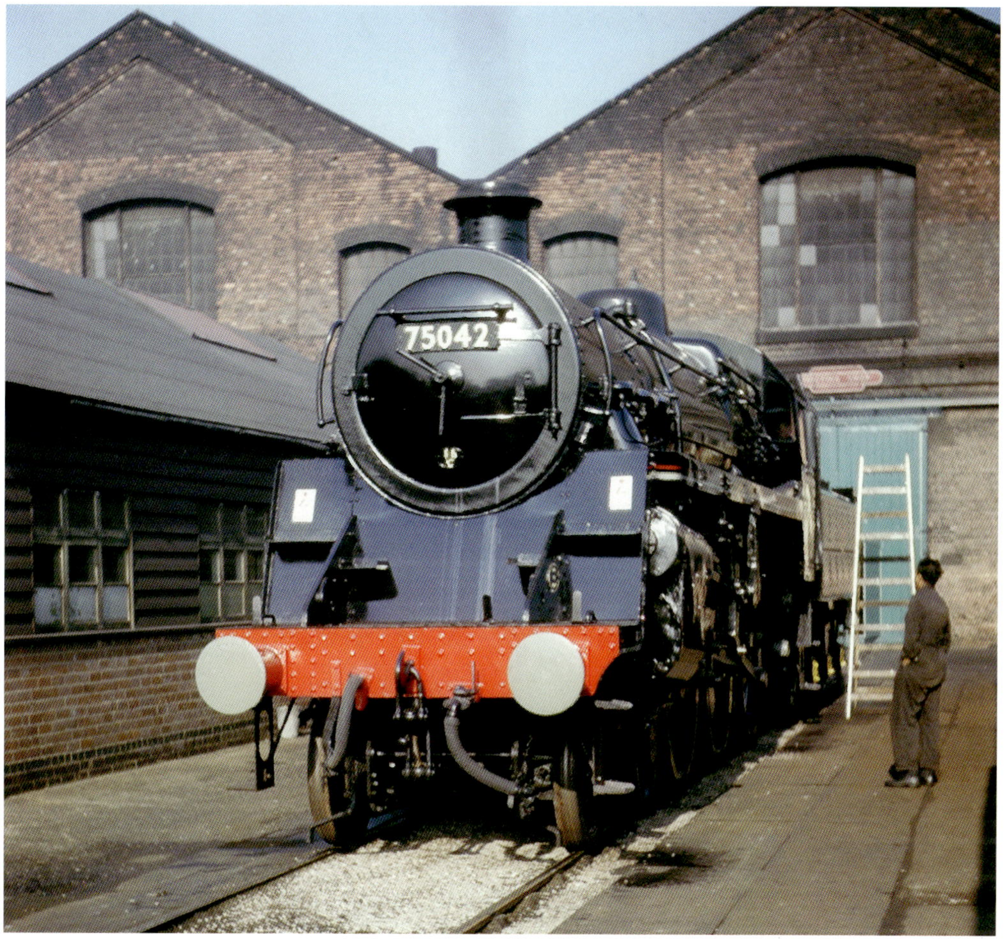

Cover: The last steam locomotive to be repaired at Derby Works, Riddles 4MT 75042 is seen on 20 September 1963 it would leave the works under its own steam later in the day. ***Len Smith***

Kevin Derrick

Strathwood

Sixties Spotting Days Around The Midlands

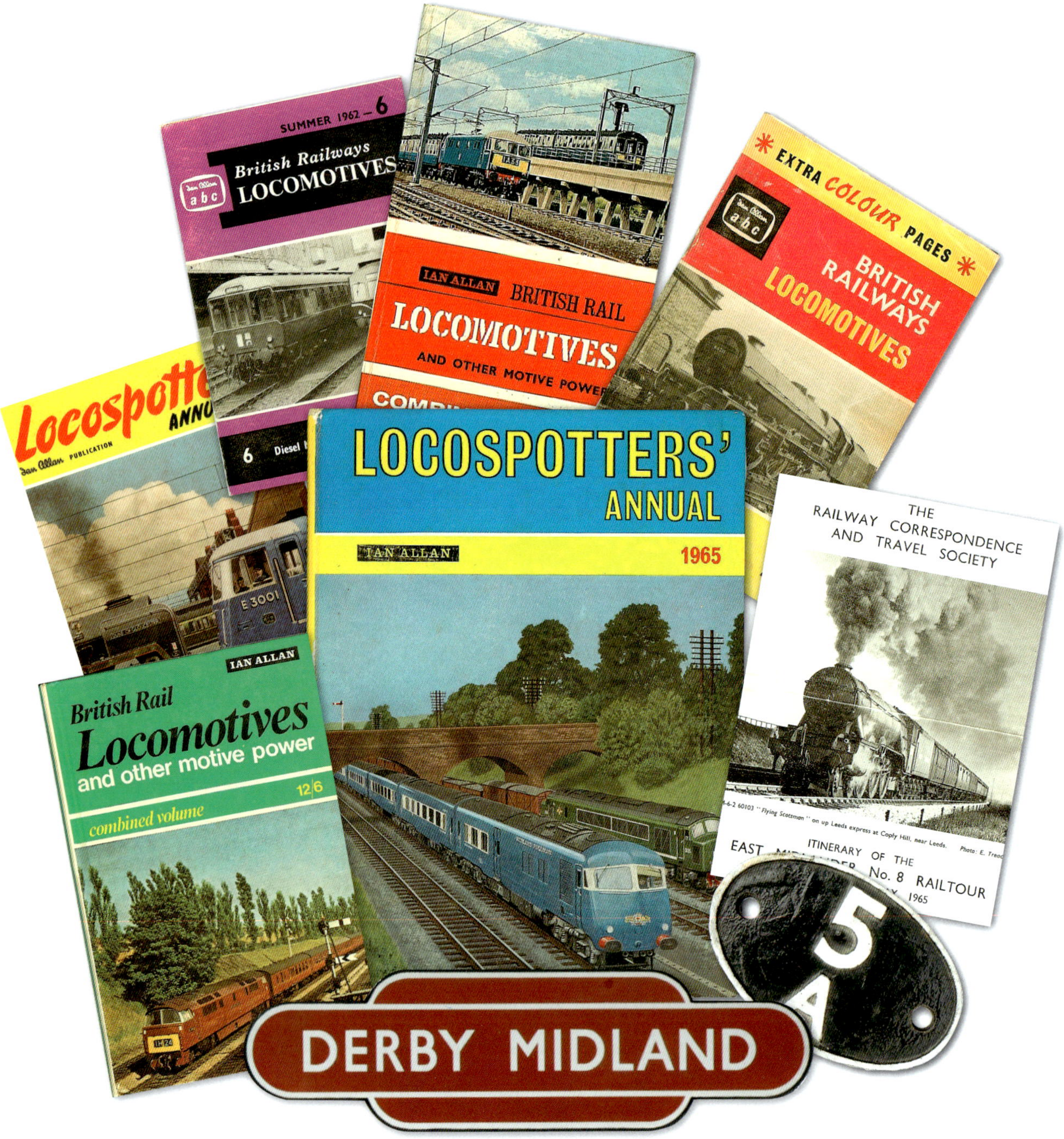

First published 2010

ISBN 1-905276-32-X
ISBN 978-1-905276-32-5

Published by Strathwood Ltd, Glenavon House, Kinchurdy Road, Boat of Garten, Inverness-shire, PH24 3BP. Tel 01479 831139

Contents **Page**

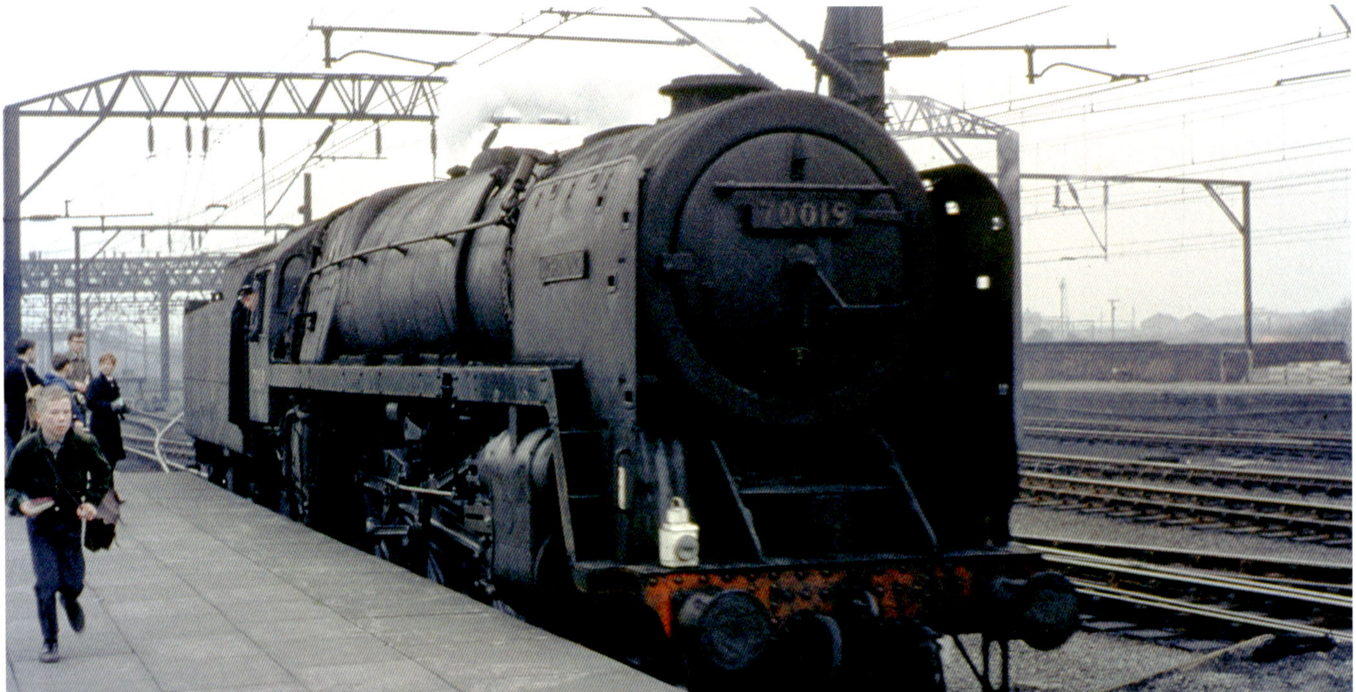

One young spotter fancies his chances of racing 70019 Lightning along the platforms at Crewe during 1965. ***Tim Meredith***

Introduction

The hobby of trainspotting really took off post war thanks to the efforts of Ian Allan and the publishing empire he built. It was supplied with not only the ABC spotters books, but also a number of magazines and reference works to support the interest in not only railways, but for some buses and aircraft too.

During the mid fifties it probably hit its peak with two issues of the ABCs for each region, two Locoshed books and for those who could afford them two Combines a year. This was brought about by both high demand as the print runs were throught to be over 100,000 copies for some of the ABCs, also because of the large numbers of new Standards being built along with other pre-nationalisation types still being constructed as well. Looking back at those high print runs, it can be seen that it was justifiable, as most stations of any size had a prosperous bookstall who would stock copies, most high streets still had a bookshop too. Besides this was an age before television arrived in most homes never mind computer games, as a generation our parents were happy to see us out of the house, and as a rule trainspotters were seen as normal and well behaved within society.

As the sixties dawned many of those who had begun spotting in the fifties were drawn away from the hobby perhaps by the lures of popular music, the opposite sex and what might be considered more grown up interests. Although the numbers in the hobby were perhaps reducing, it was still a major draw to many a youngster. Every month we would see new locomotives arriving albeit mostly diesels and ever increasing numbers of old friends being set aside as change on our railways and within the country as a whole was rampant.

It is a sobering thought that anyone who was at school leaving age at the start of the sixties, is now most likely retired, some may no longer even be with us anymore, sadly. As a child from the late fifties I was too young to appreciate what I saw half the time in the sixties, as a result a lot of pleasure can be realised today in putting these books together, recalling innocent times of the past.

If like us you enjoy a little bit of nostalgia join us in a good wallow again back in time within both the Sixties and Seventies Spotting Days series.

Kevin Derrick
Boat of Garten 2010

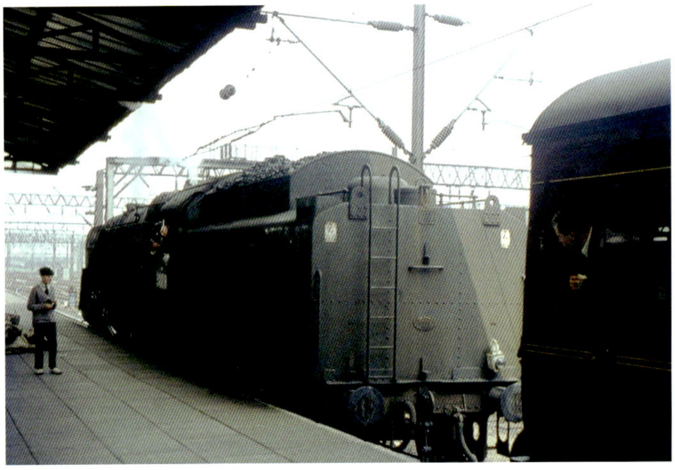

Less frantic activity at Crewe as 70018 Flying Dutchman is caught backing onto an arrival from Euston on 4 June 1965. ***Strathwood Library Collection***

Midland HQ

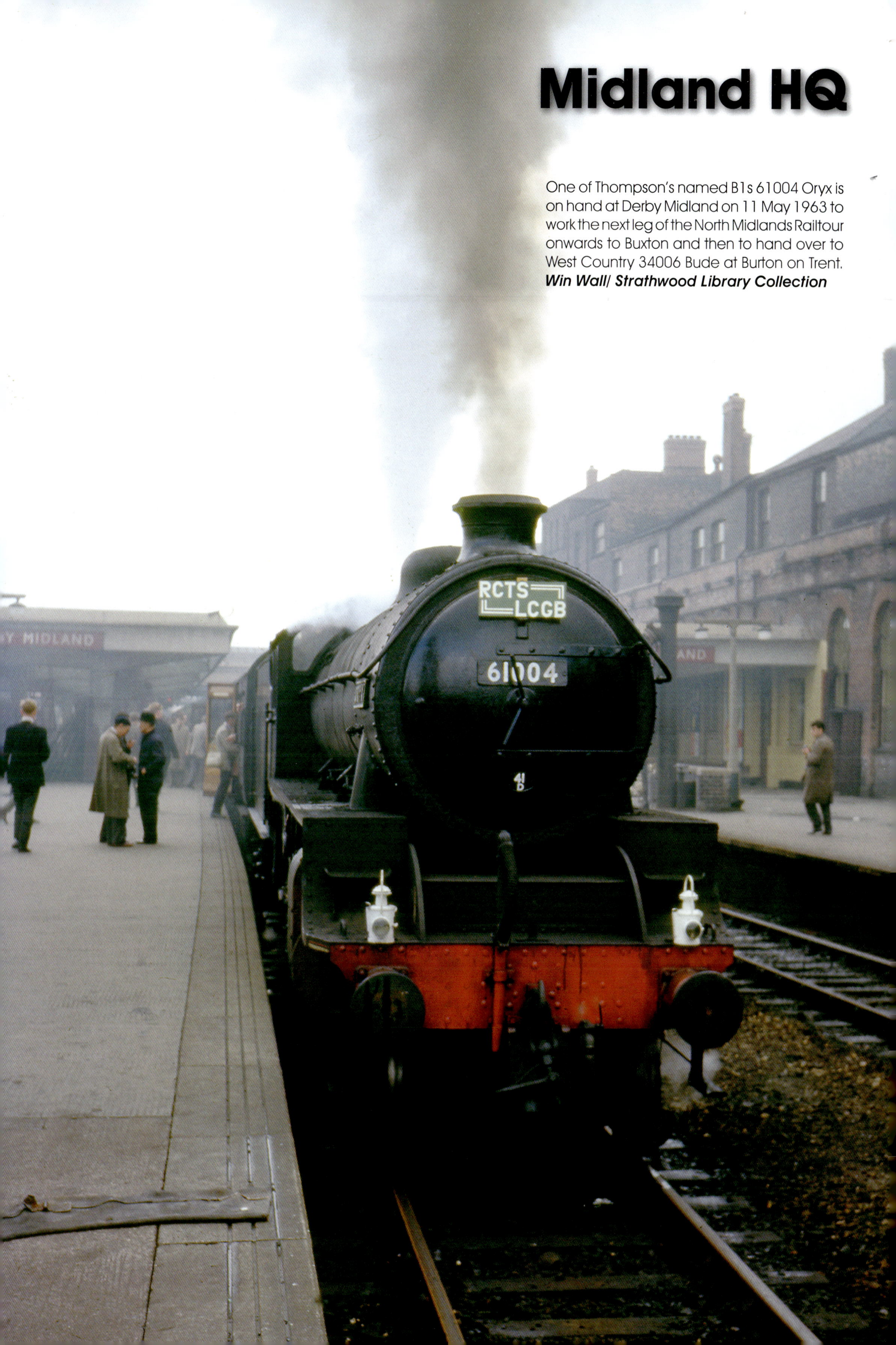

One of Thompson's named B1s 61004 Oryx is on hand at Derby Midland on 11 May 1963 to work the next leg of the North Midlands Railtour onwards to Buxton and then to hand over to West Country 34006 Bude at Burton on Trent. ***Win Wall/ Strathwood Library Collection***

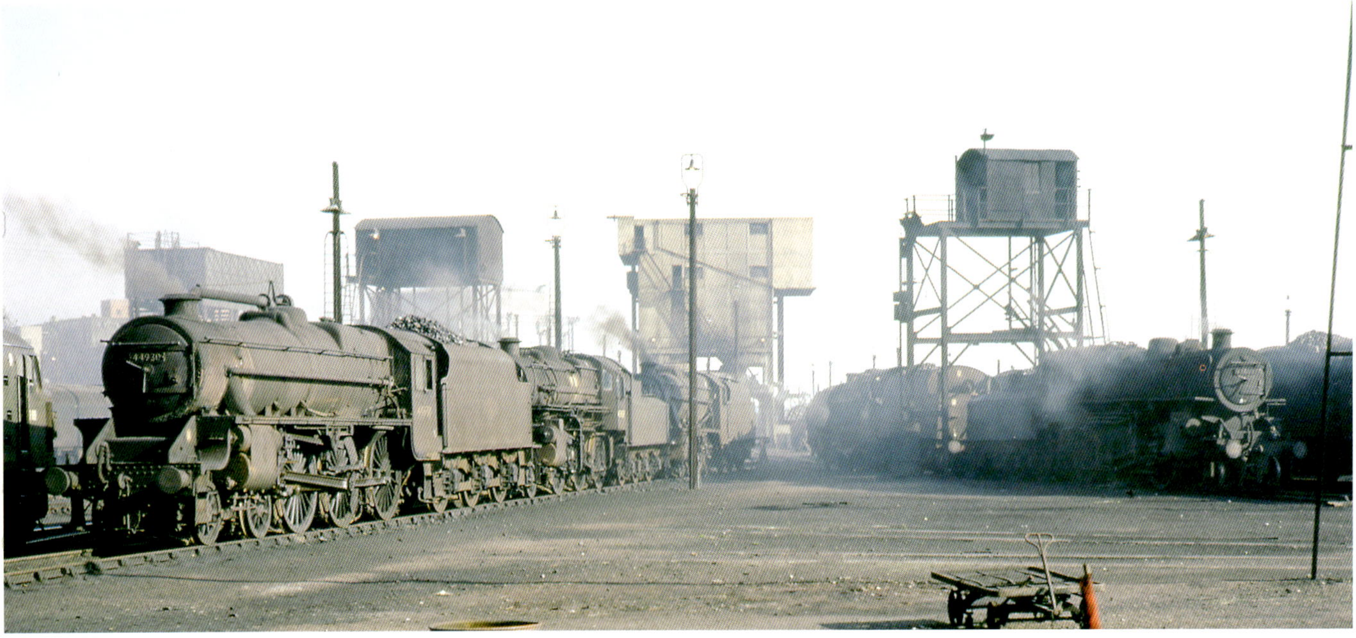

By February 1967 16C Derby was officially closed to steam as of the previous October, however as can be seen things lingered on until March 1967 the month after this view was taken. ***Late Norman Browne/Strathwood Library Collection***

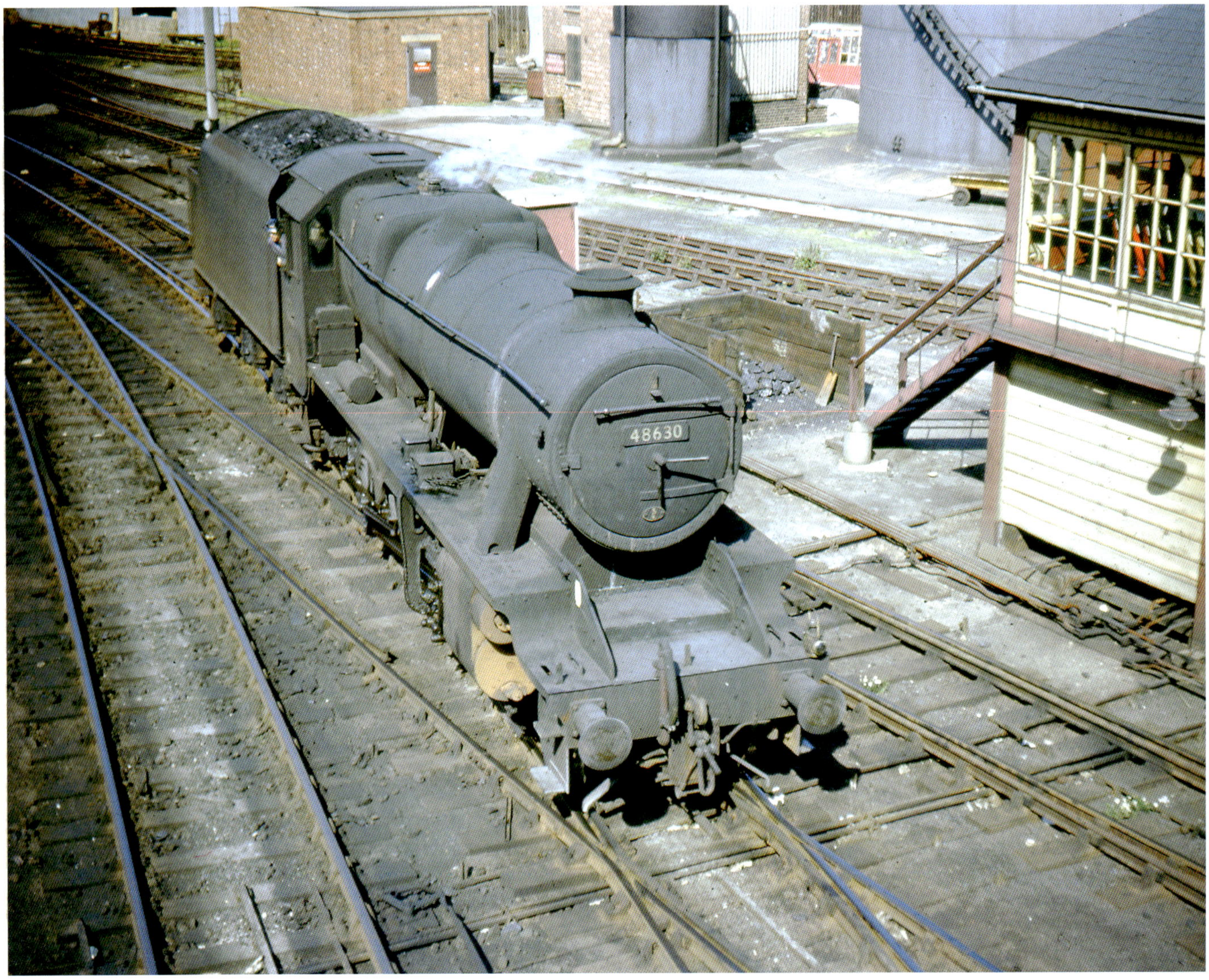

This Stanier 8F 48630 had been among those built at Brighton during 1943 and had just under another year in service when recorded passing light through Derby on 29 August 1964. The Beatles were packing the crowds into venues on tour in America and Manfred Mann had just dislodged the Fab Four and A Hard Day's Night from the top of the charts with Do Wah Diddy Diddy. ***Strathwood Library Collection***

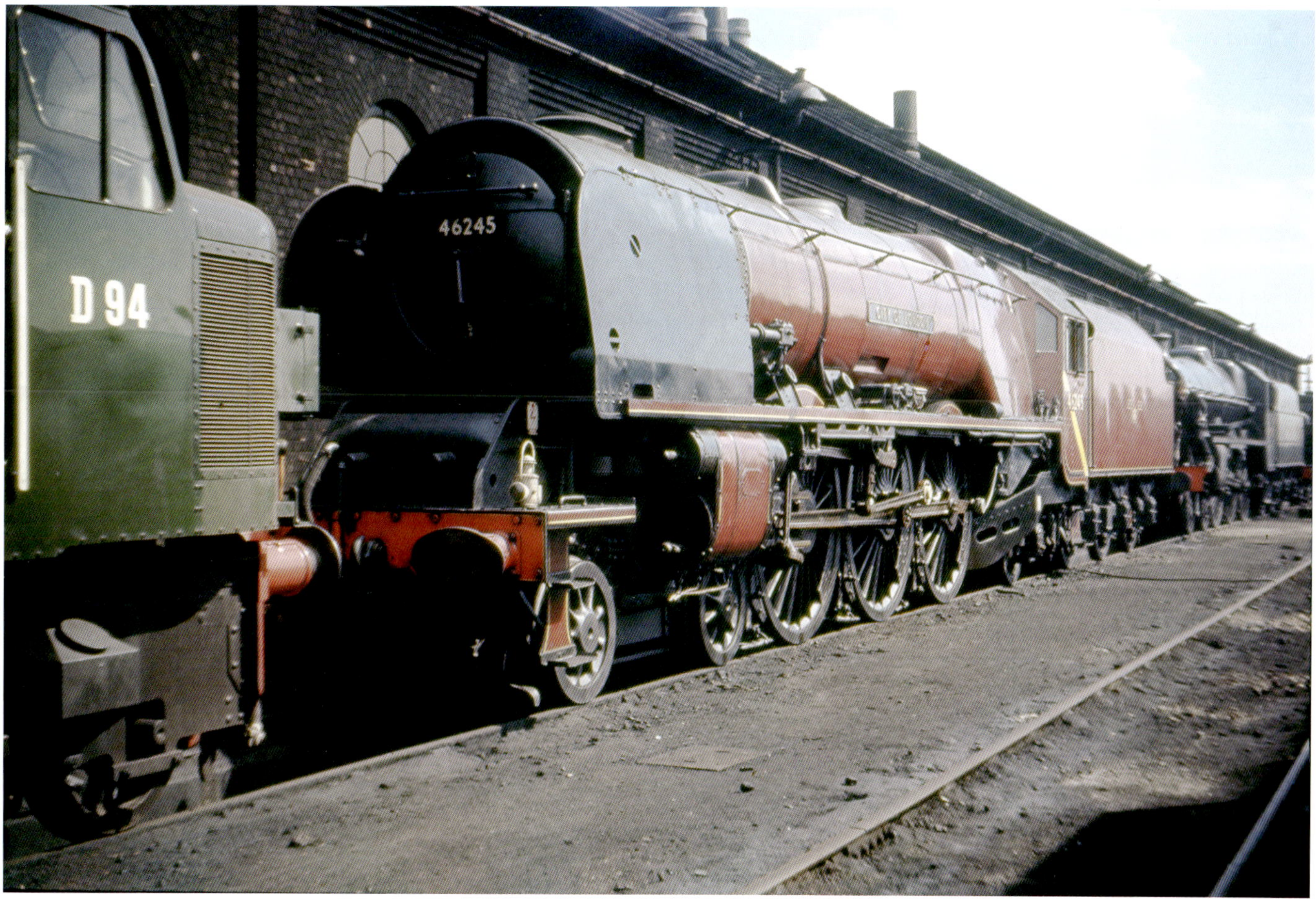

Taken the same time at Derby, alongside the sheds Duchess 46245 City of London was engaged more on specials than the West Coast Main Line which was now the domain of English Electric Type 4s. The once elegent Stanier Pacific would be posted as withdrawn a few weeks later in October 1964 and swiftly cut up just two months afterwards. ***Len Smith***

That visit to Derby's old steam shed in February 1967 brought this chance for a chat alongside Black Five 45268 which would remain in traffic until August 1968. ***Late Norman Browne/Strathwood Library Collection***

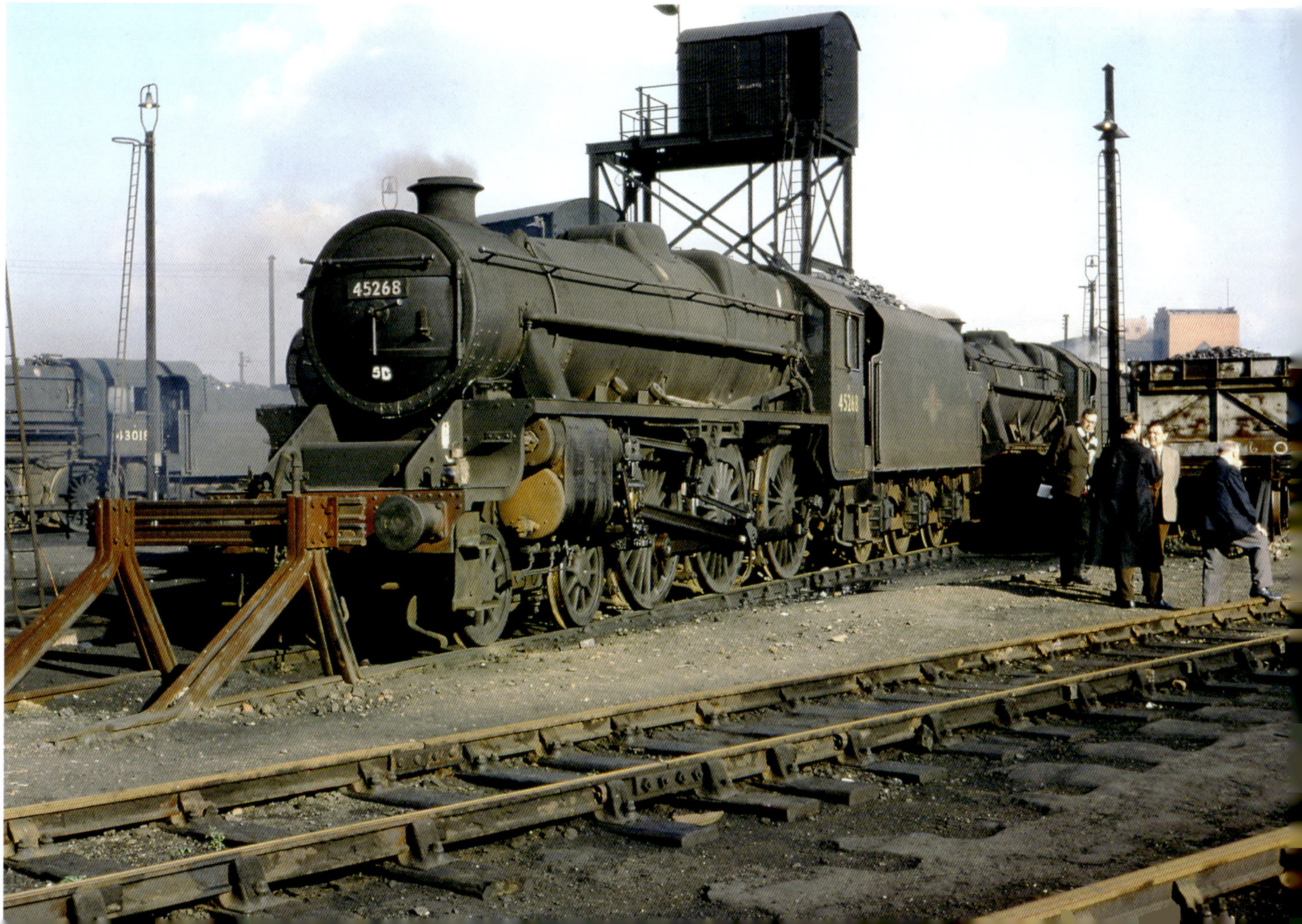

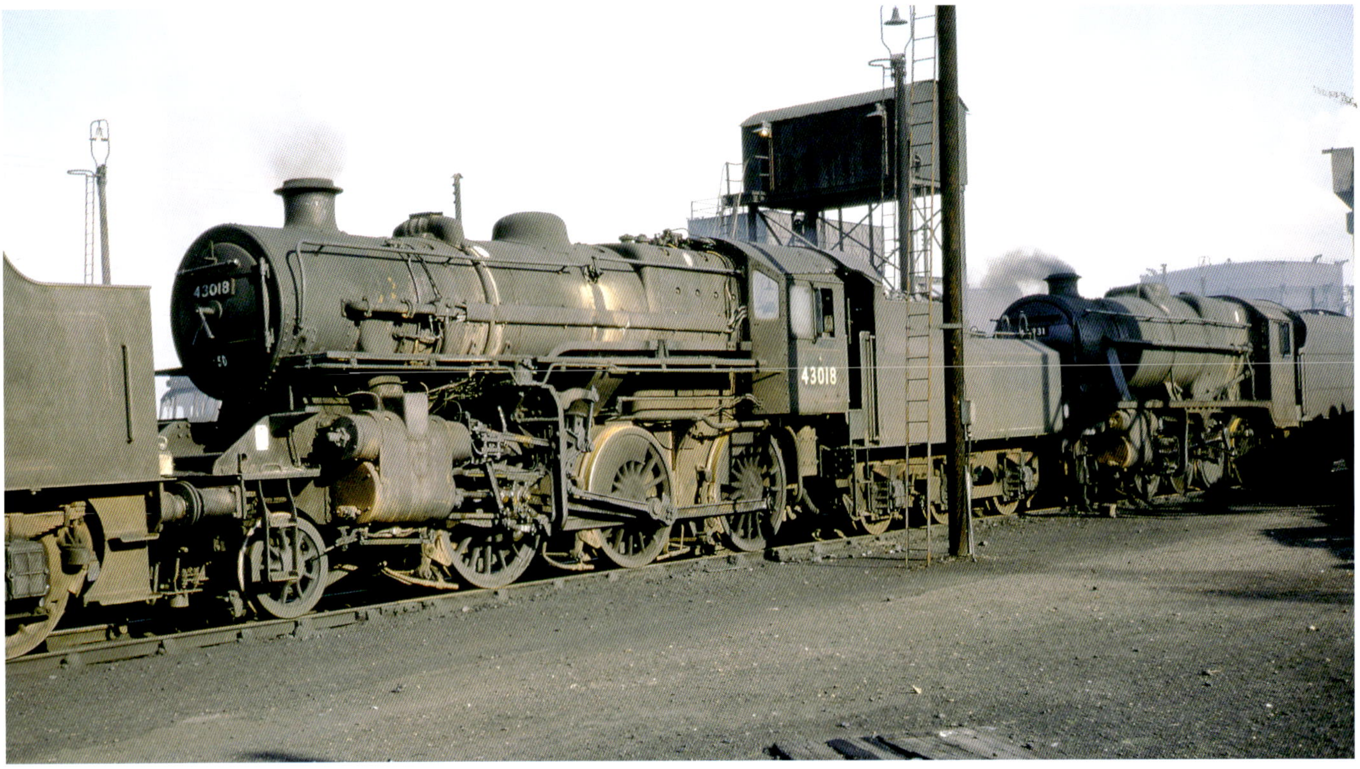

Less fortunate would be this Ivatt Mogul 43018 which was taken out of service in November 1966 a few months before and was being steamed to head off for scrapping we believe in February 1967. ***Late Norman Browne/Strathwood Library Collection***

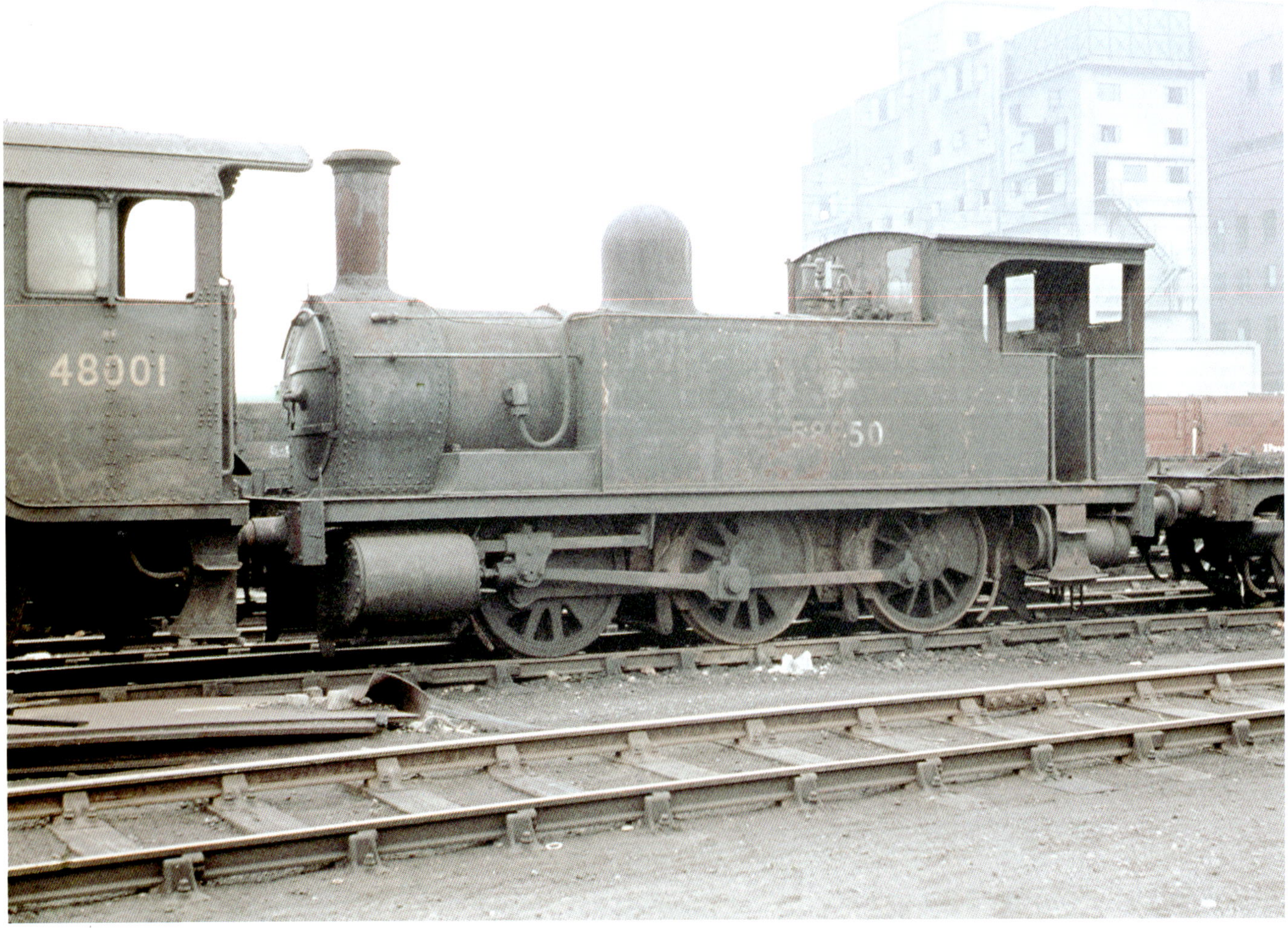

In the summer of 1960 good fortune befell Class 2F 58850 which had been built by the North London Railway in December 1880 and had already outlived its sisters having found work on the Cromford and High Peak line in the Peak District. Arriving at Derby Works it was to be saved for preservation. ***Strathwood Library Collection***

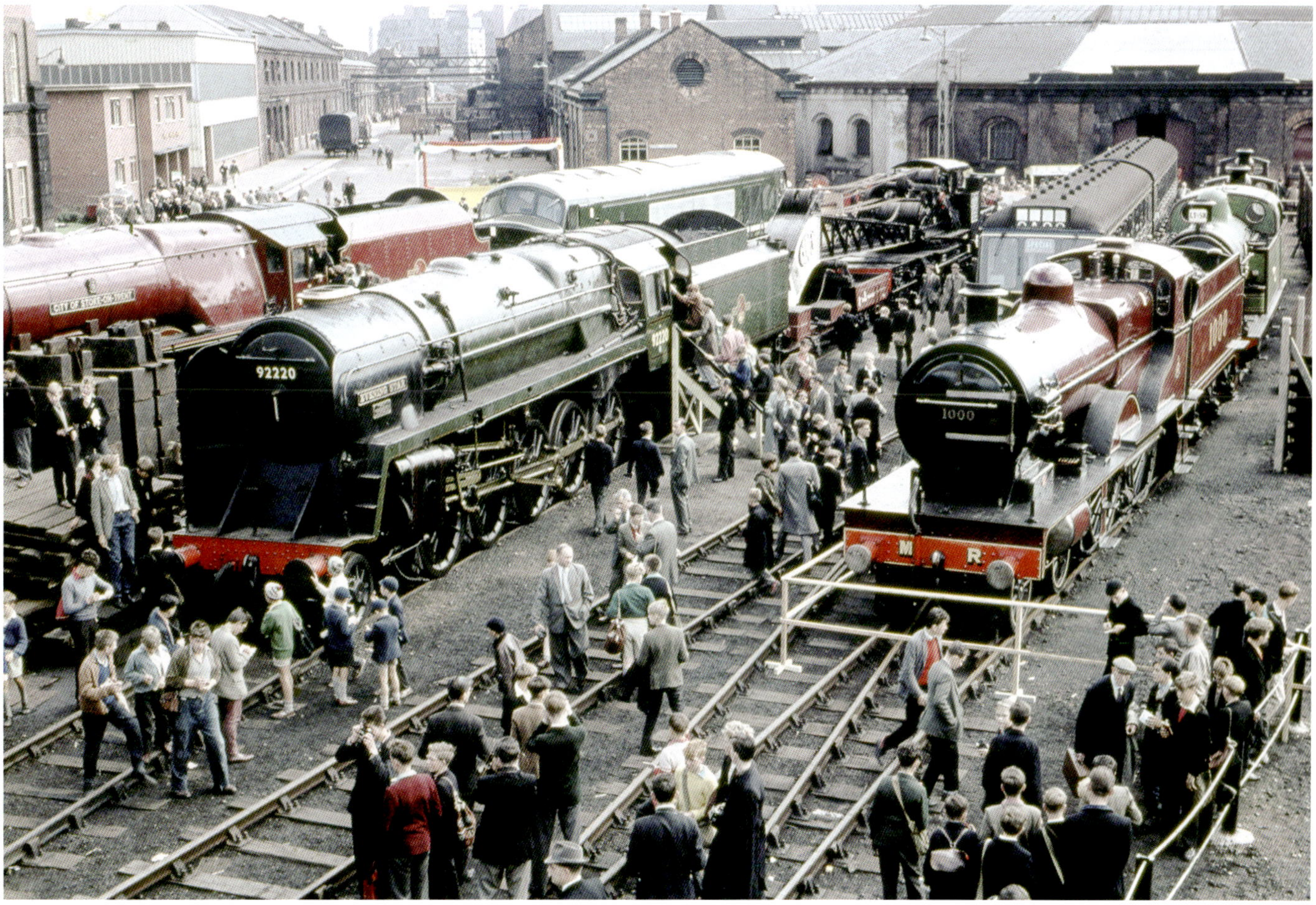

In 1961 Derby Works hosted an Open Day, exhibits seen from the footbridge included 92220 Evening Star and 46254 City of Stoke on Trent. ***Strathwood Library Collection***

Derby steam shed was coded as 17A when this relaxed view was taken in May 1963, the change of code to 16C would take place a few months later in September. ***Win Wall/Strathwood Library Collection***

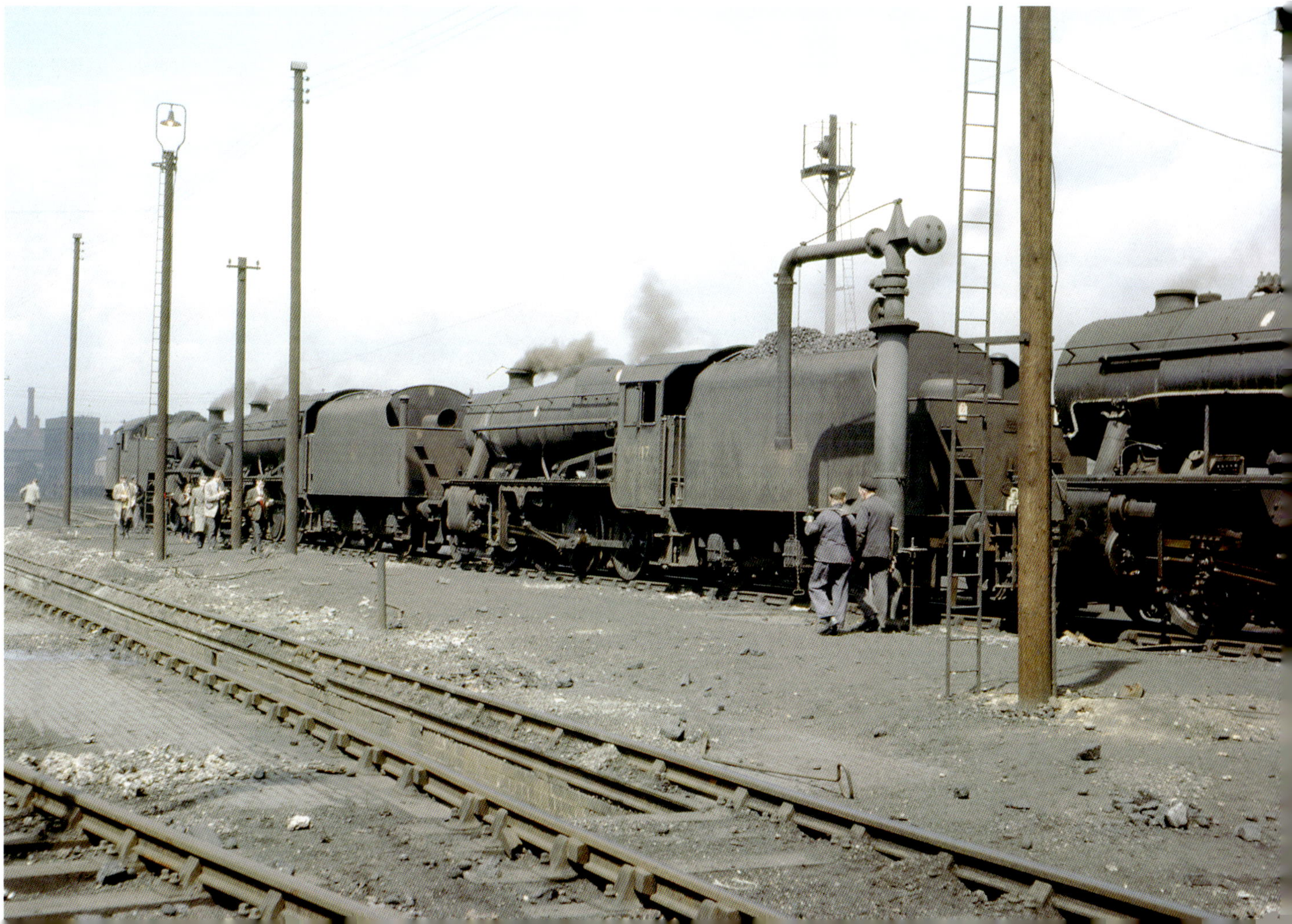

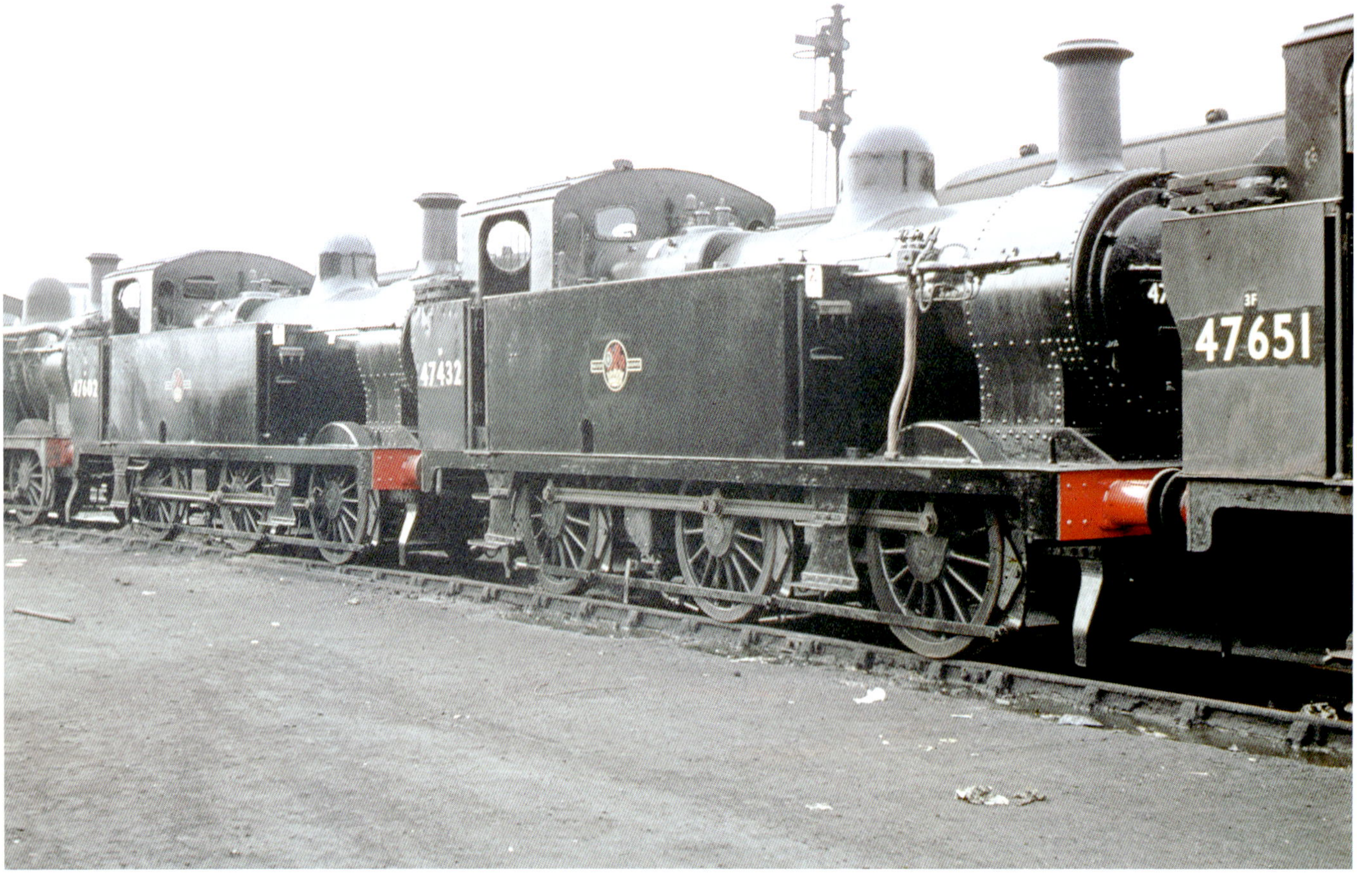

A line up of outshopped Jinties include 47602 and 47432 along with a condensing specimen in 1960, diesel shunters and yard closures would shorten this group's lifespan. ***Strathwood Library Collection***

This Johnson 3F 43612 had been taken out of use in January 1959 and when seen at Derby in early 1961 was days away from the cutters breaking her up. ***John Gill***

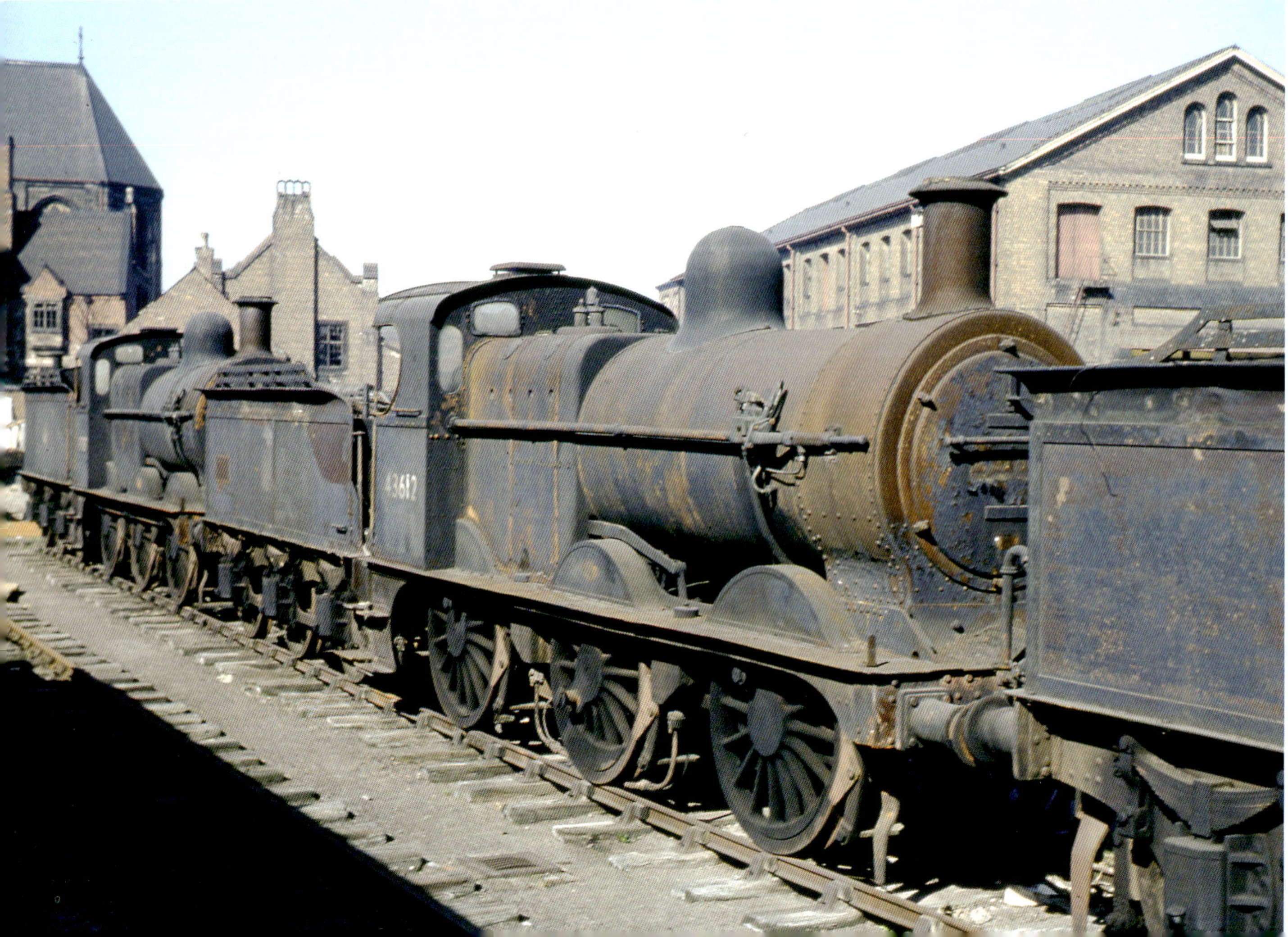

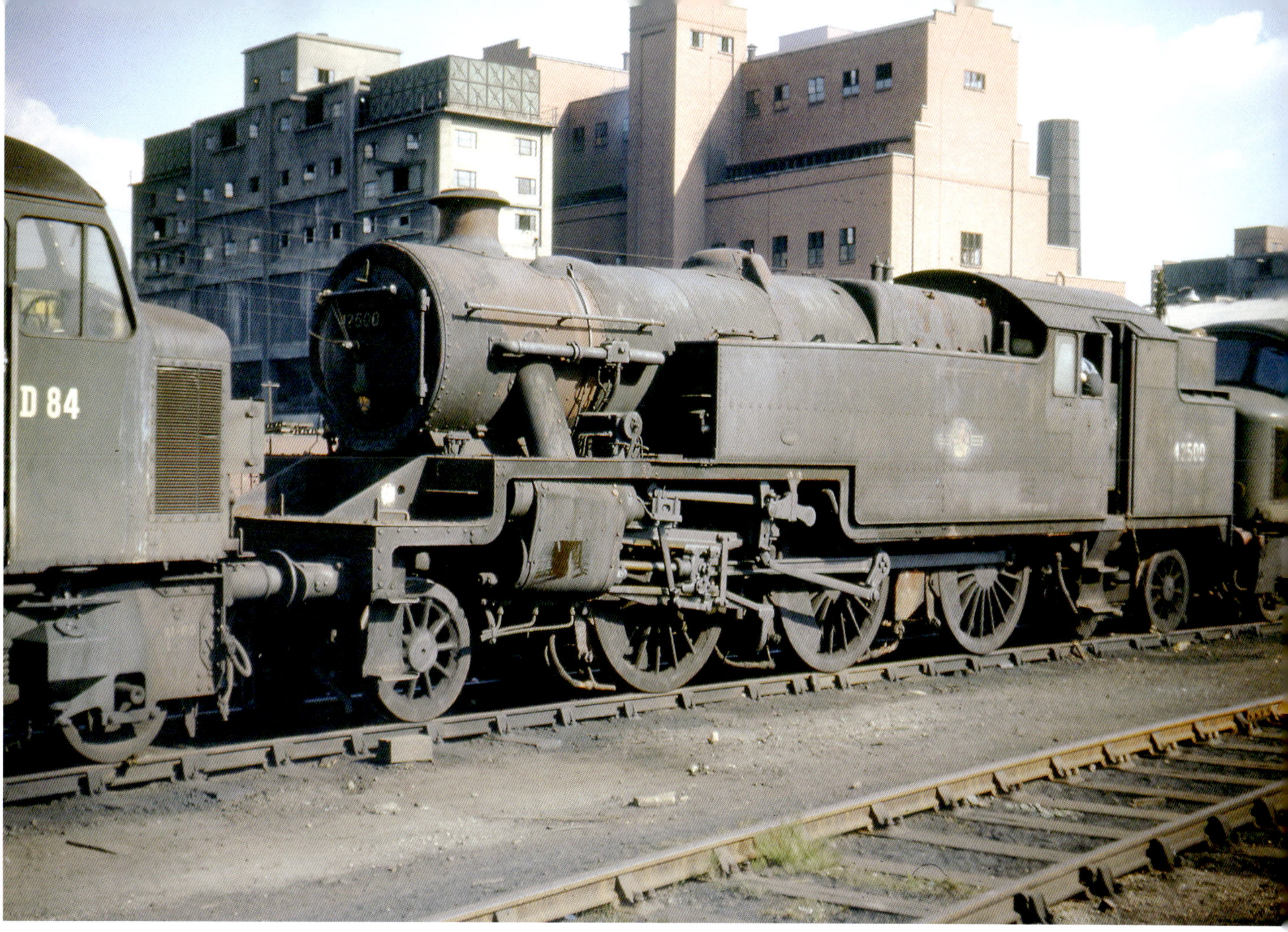

It had been decided to preserve the first built of the Stanier three cylinder Class 4MTs number 42500 when withdrawn in the summer of 1962. Two years later on 29 August 1964 it was sandwiched between a pair of Peaks in Derby Works yard awaiting restoration. ***Strathwood Library Collection***

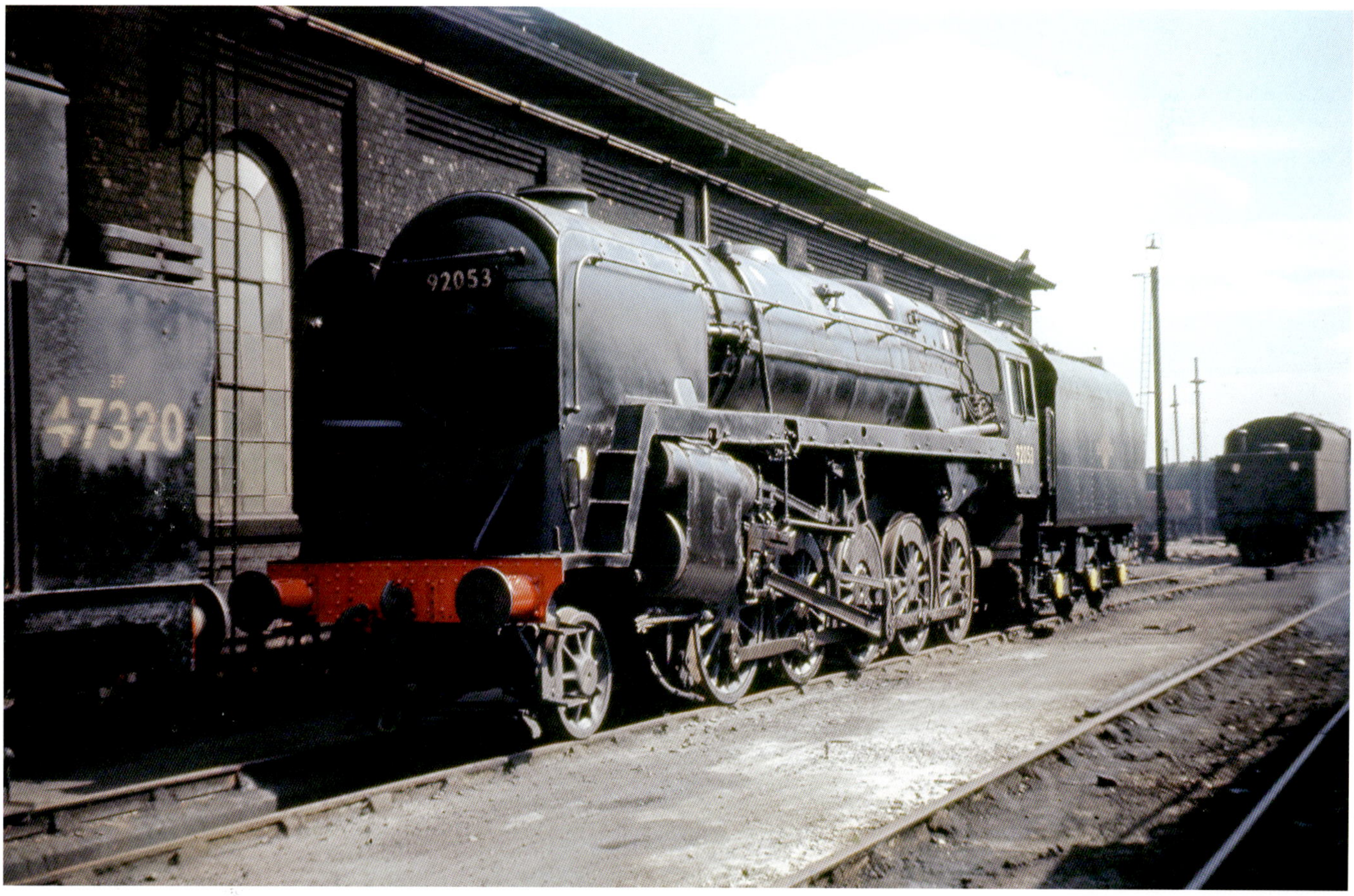

This Class 9F 92053 appears to have had just a quick sole and heel visit to Derby in 1964, certainly little has been invested in a fresh paint job to send it back to work. One of the majority of her class that were built at Crewe, this example just managed to get ten years service in before being withdrawn in February 1966. ***Len Smith***

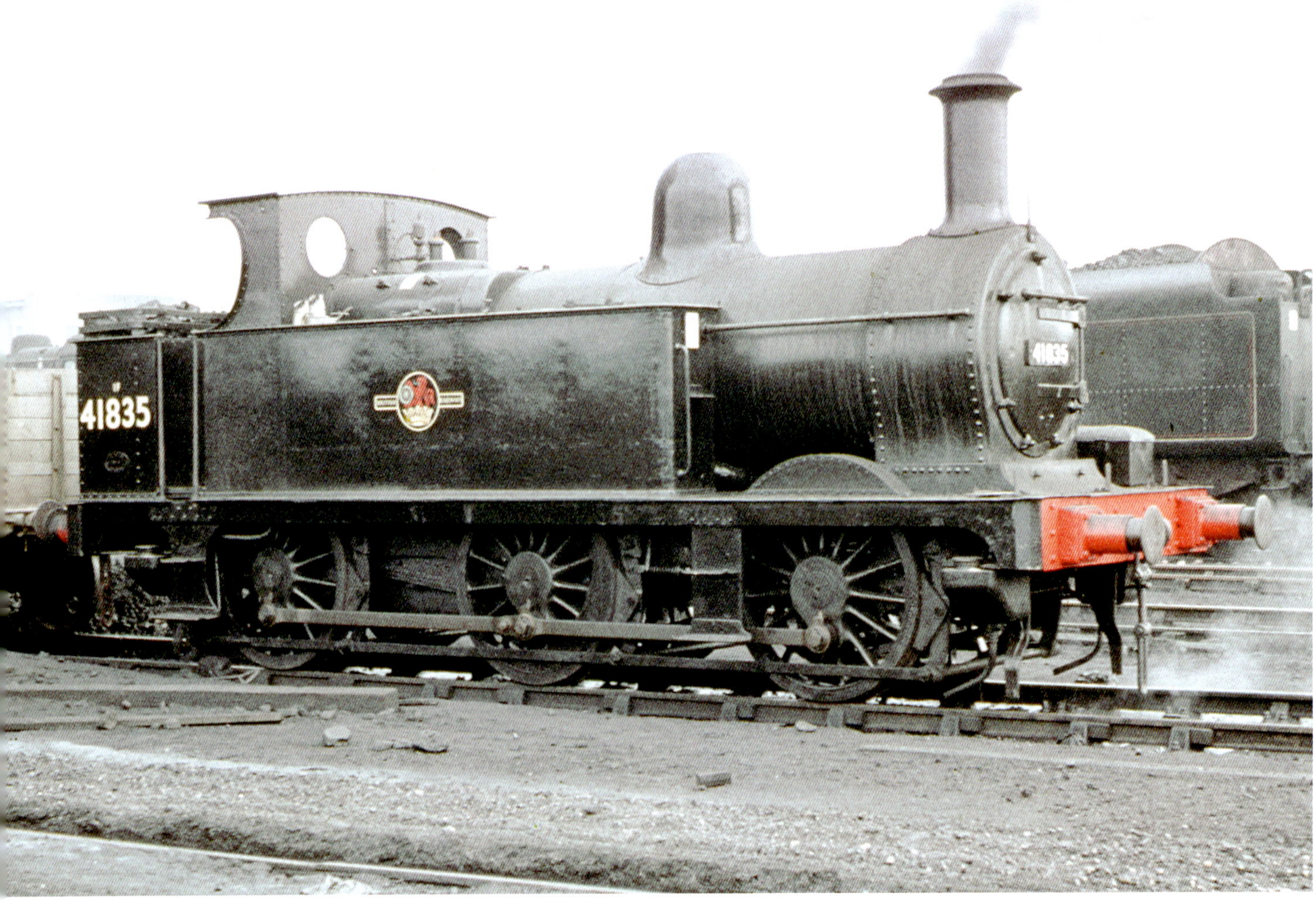

Far better value for the accountants was Johnson 1F half cab 41835 in the shed yard at Derby in 1960, when withdrawn at the close of 1966 she had seventy four years service under her belt. ***Strathwood Library Collection***

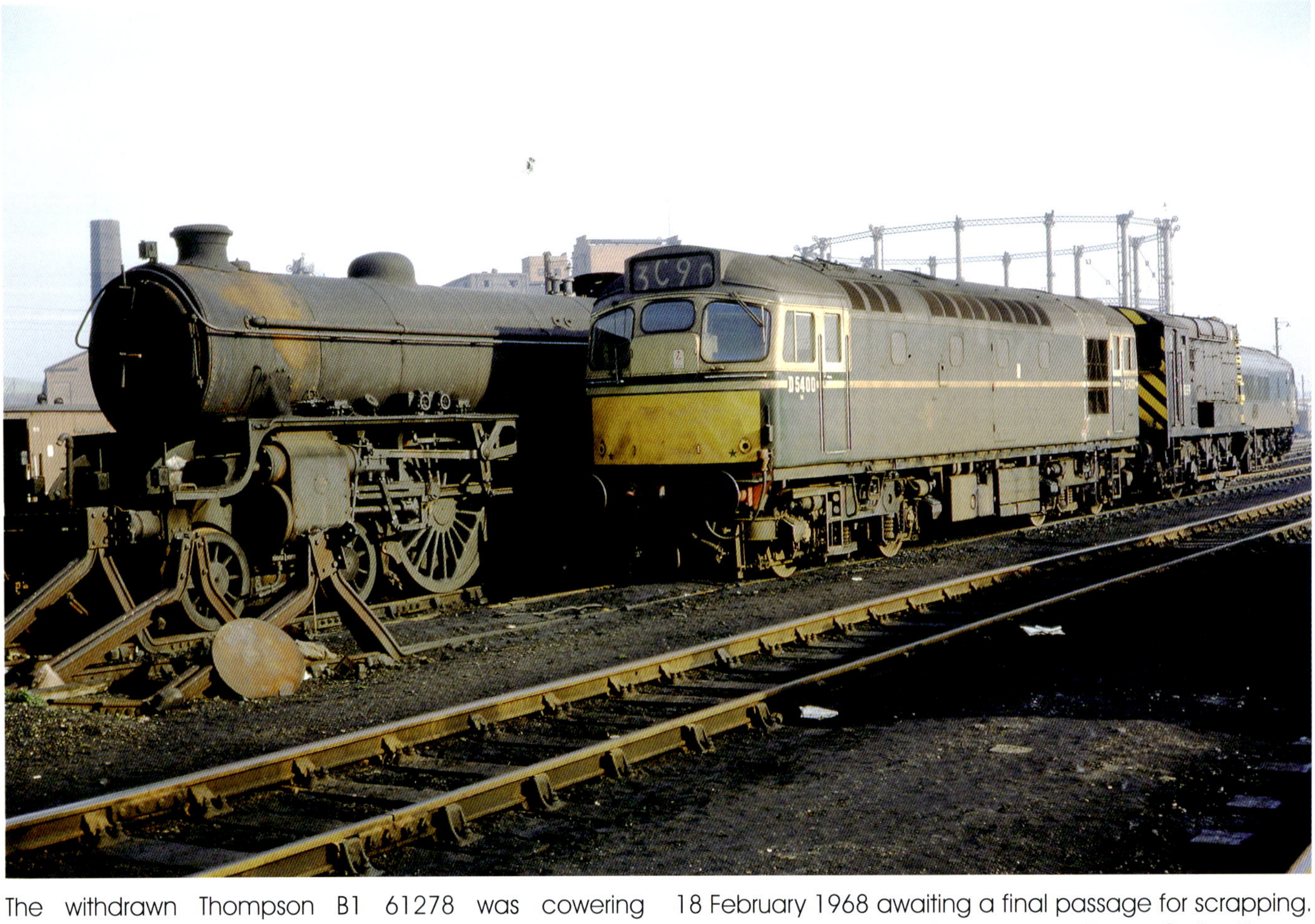

The withdrawn Thompson B1 61278 was cowering behind BRC&W Type 2 D5400 at Derby shed on 18 February 1968 awaiting a final passage for scrapping. ***Late Norman Browne/Strathwood Library Collection***

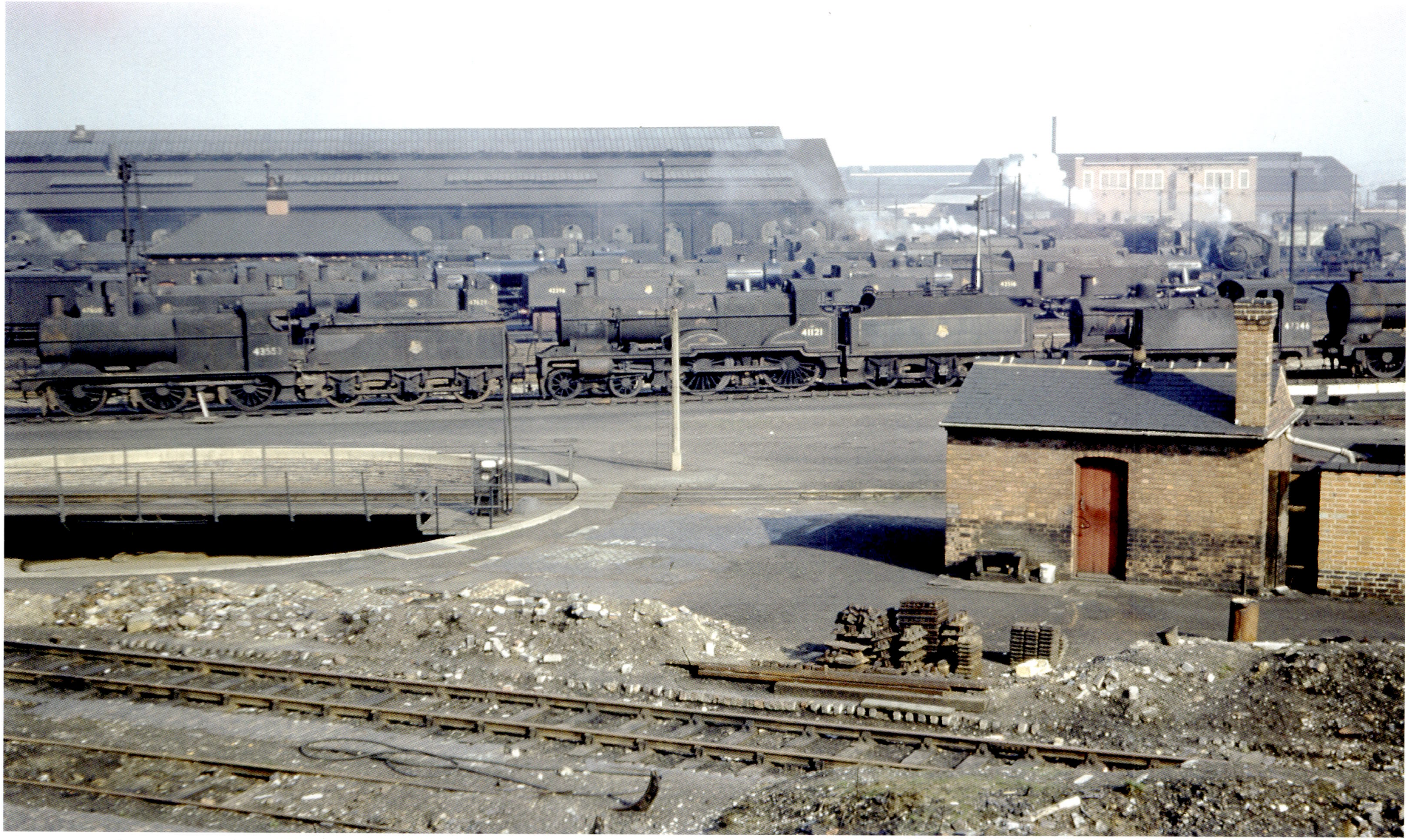

A pleasing vista across the shed yard at Derby on 15 March 1960 shows a number of locomotives whose parentage is easily traceable back to the Midland Railway and Derby Works. ***Frank Hornby***

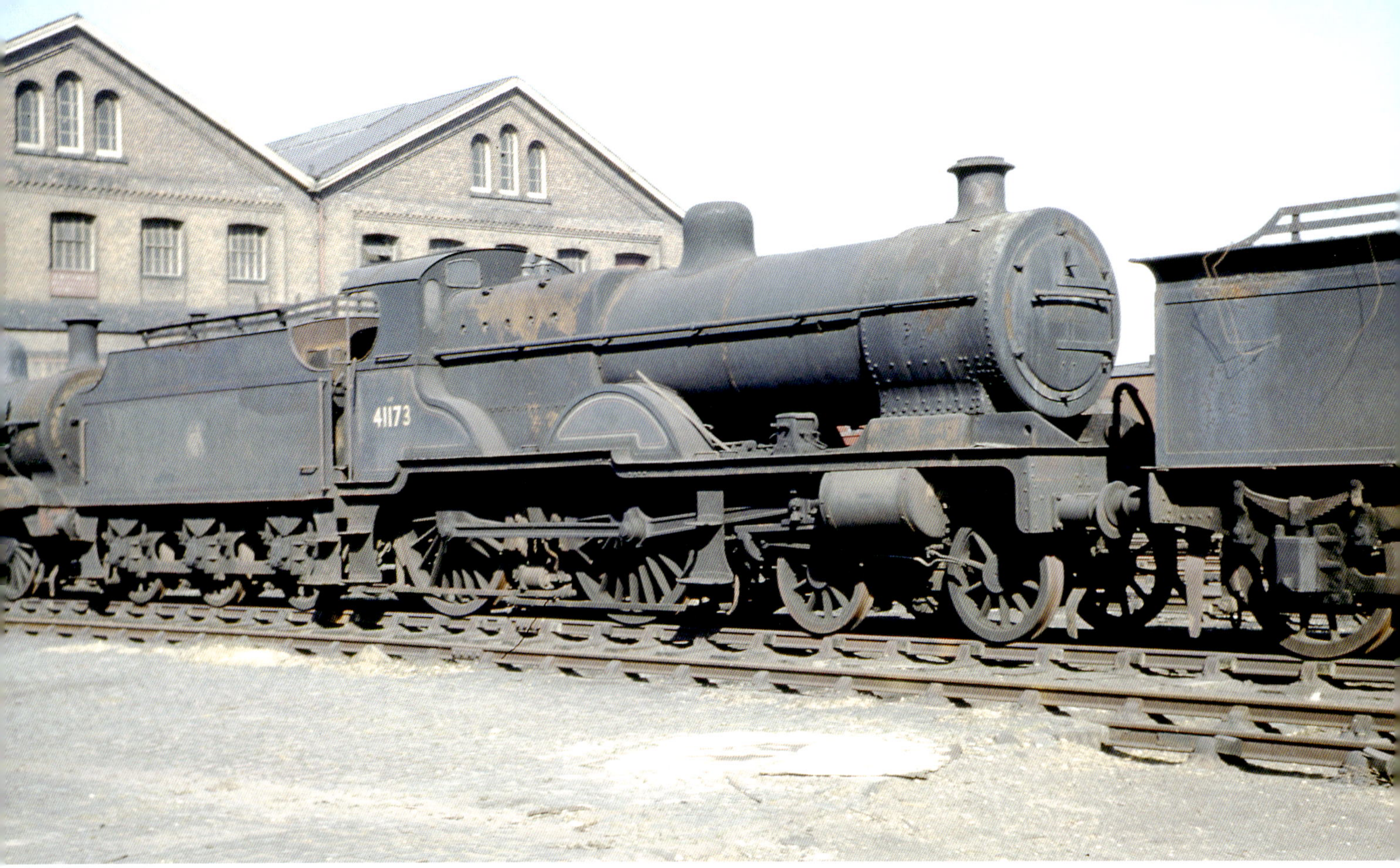

As we have already seen a number of locomotives such as this 1925 Vulcan Foundry built 4-4-0 41173 were gathering back at Derby, not for repairs but for scrapping. ***John Gill***

Although unfortunately this Derby built product from 1914 for the Somerset & Dorset Joint Railway numbered 53801 had arrived for assessment for works repairs but was withdrawn instead in July 1961. ***Strathwood Library Collection***

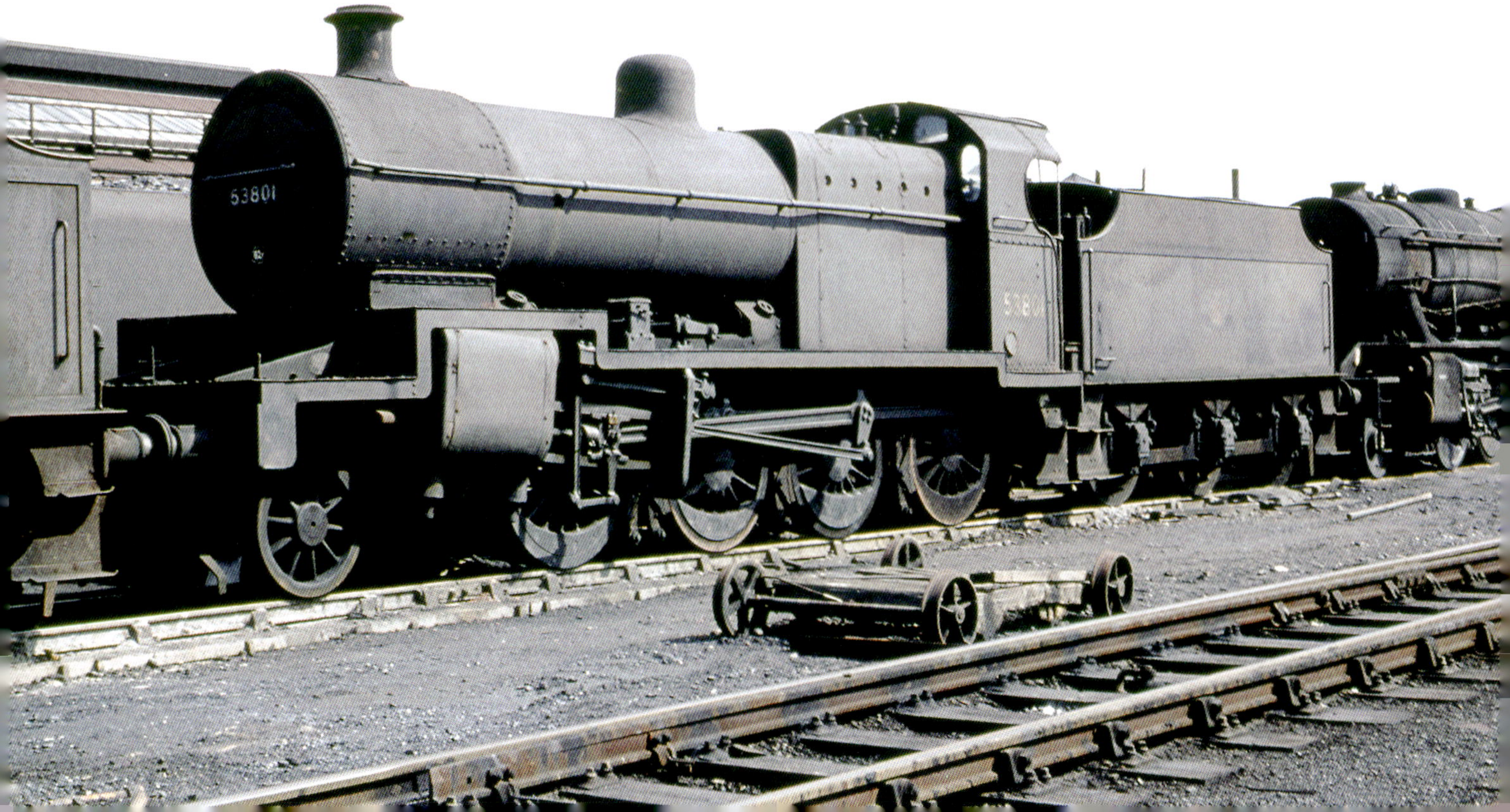

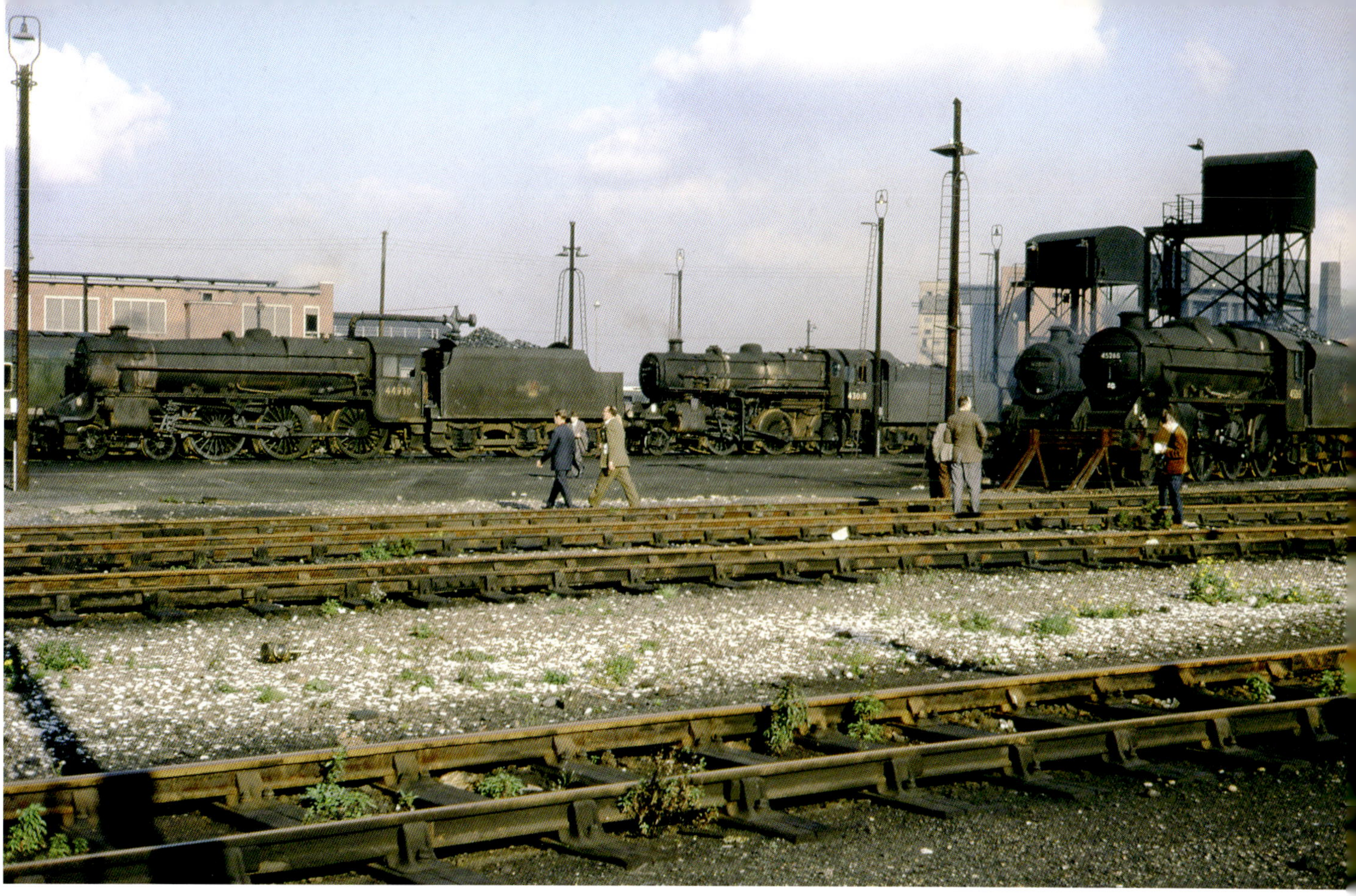

Another view of that visit to Derby's shed in early 1967 shows 43018, 45268 and 44930 whilst inside the works in the background they would be busy overhauling Peaks, diesel shunters and Sulzer powered Type 2s with the last few still being built. Diesel locomotive production here had reached its 1000th example with the release of D7667 a few weeks before this shot was taken. ***Late Norman Browne/Strathwood Library Collection***

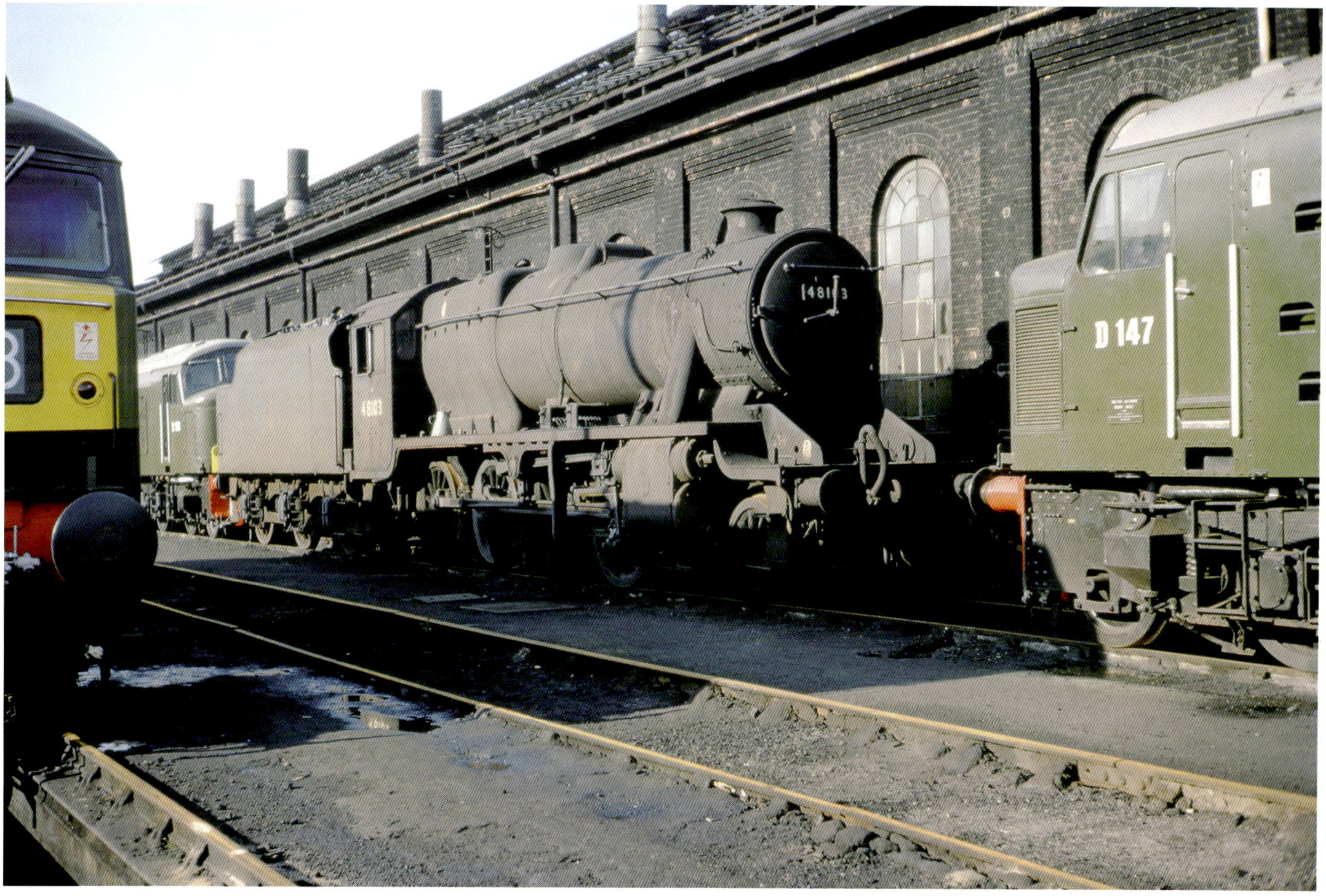

Also here on this day was the withdrawn Stanier 8F 48103 surrounded by Sulzer power awaiting a convenient path to the scrappers which would come a day or two later in February 1967. ***Late Norman Browne/Strathwood Library Collection***

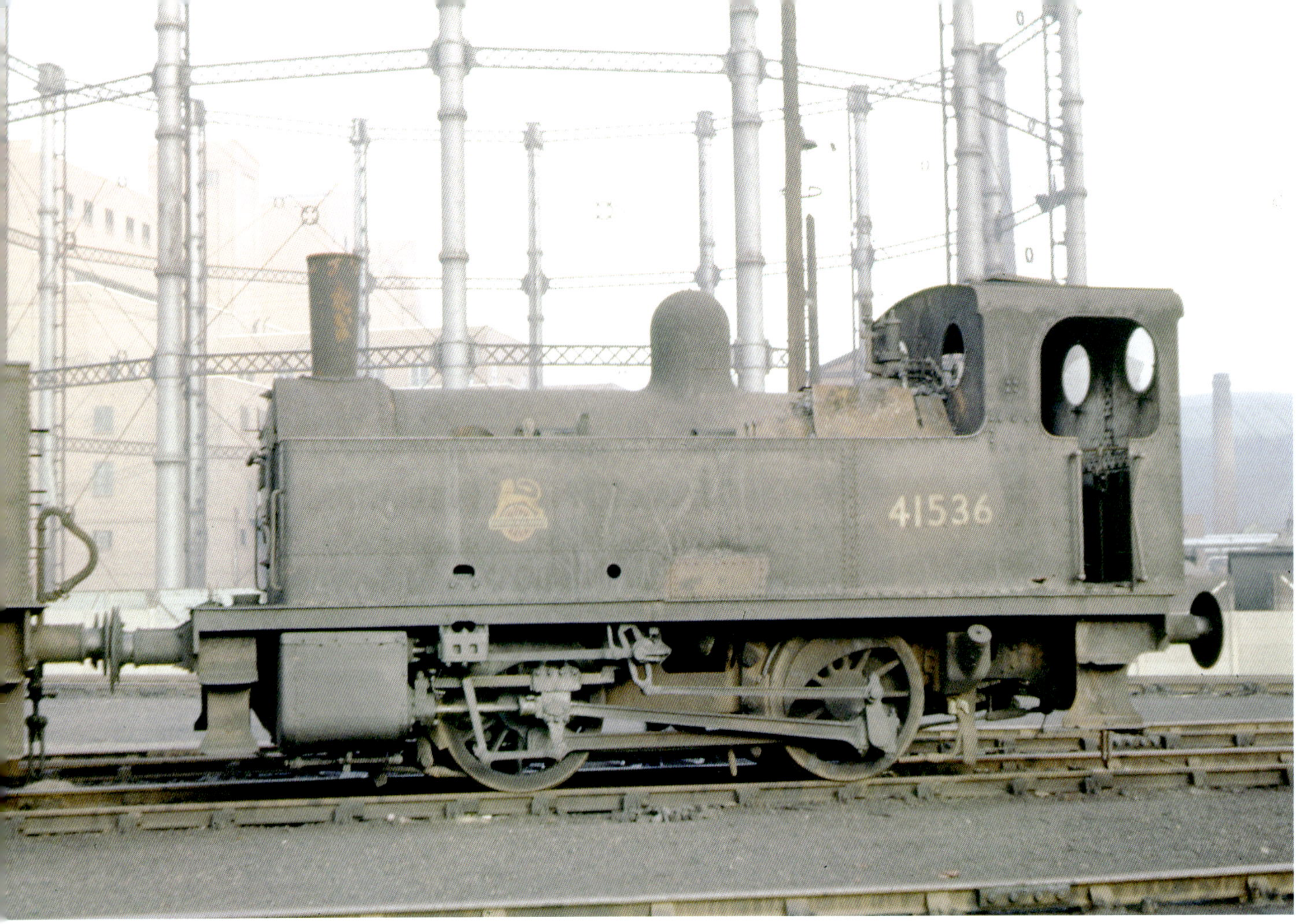

The former Midland Railway had built a number of short wheelbase 0-4-0Ts to work tightly radiused tracks in docks, factories and breweries such as 41536 seen at Derby on 12 February 1961 for scrapping. ***Frank Hornby***

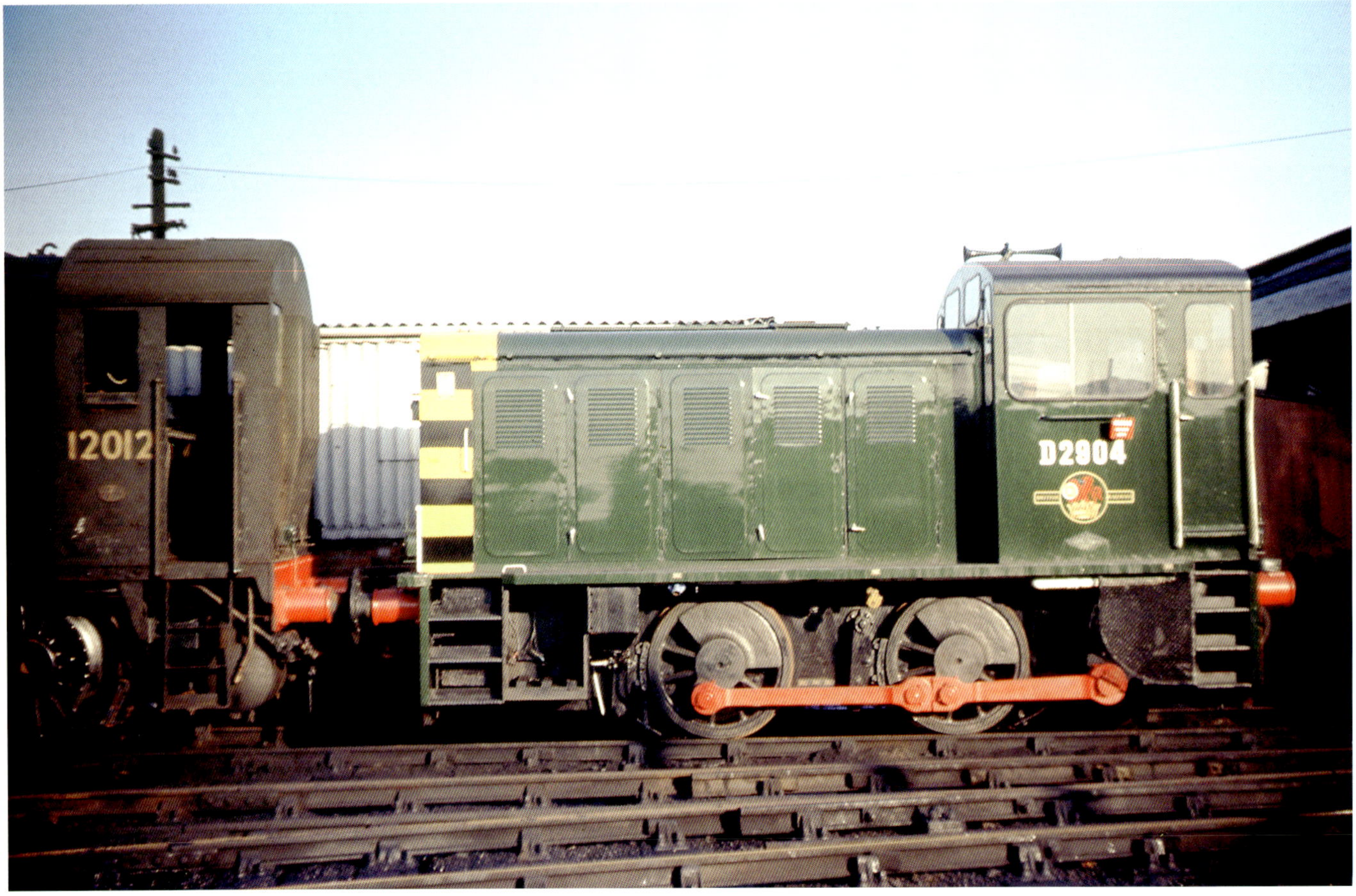

Among the lame duck replacements for work in docks was a batch of North British built diesel shunters including D2904 which was overhauled in 1964, having seen a few years use in the London dockyards. In 1966 it was sent to Wolverton Works to find use hopefully as one of their shunters, it cannot have been popular as it was withdrawn in February 1967 and sent for scrapping after just nine years use. ***Len Smith***

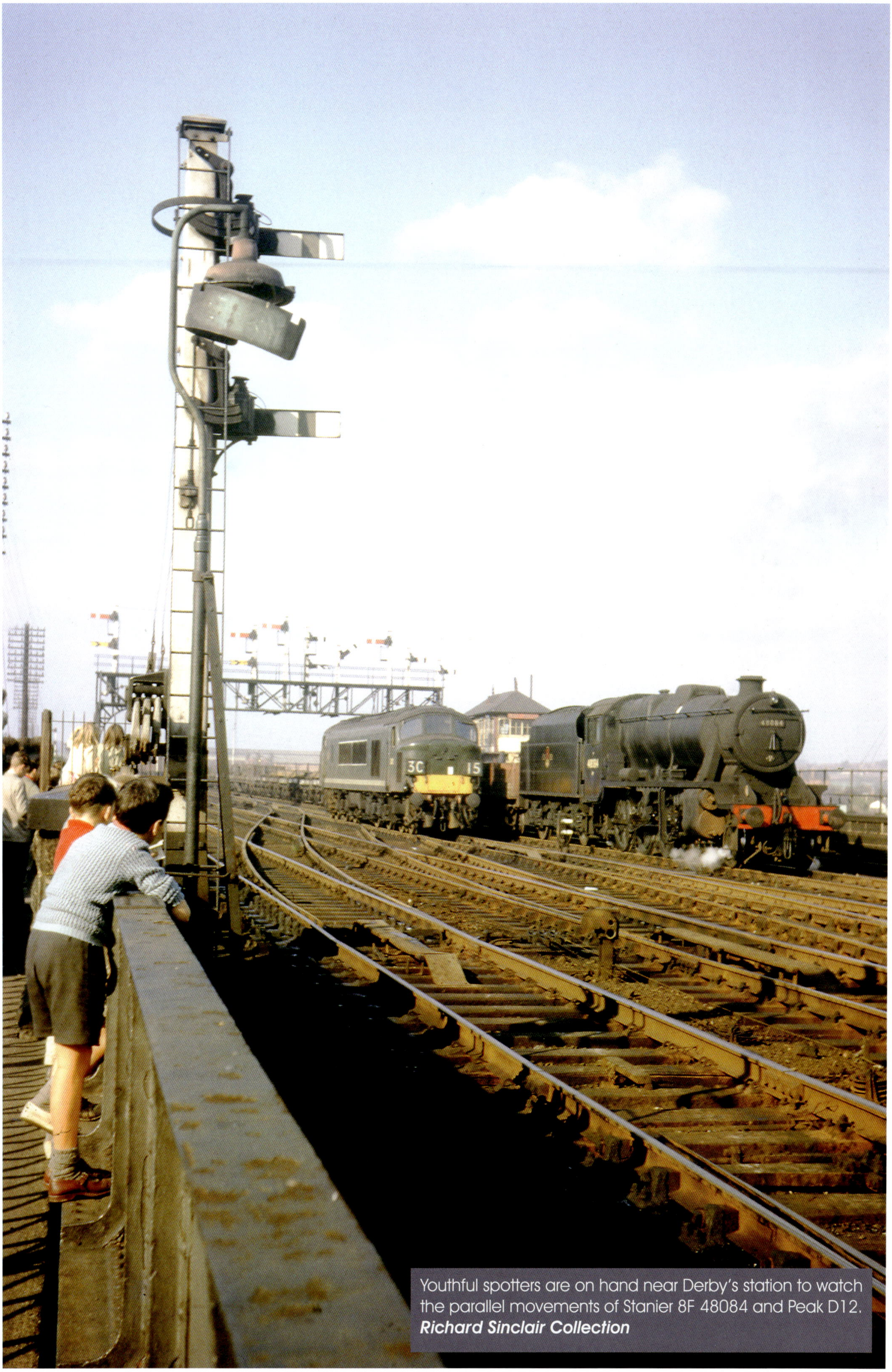

Youthful spotters are on hand near Derby's station to watch the parallel movements of Stanier 8F 48084 and Peak D12. ***Richard Sinclair Collection***

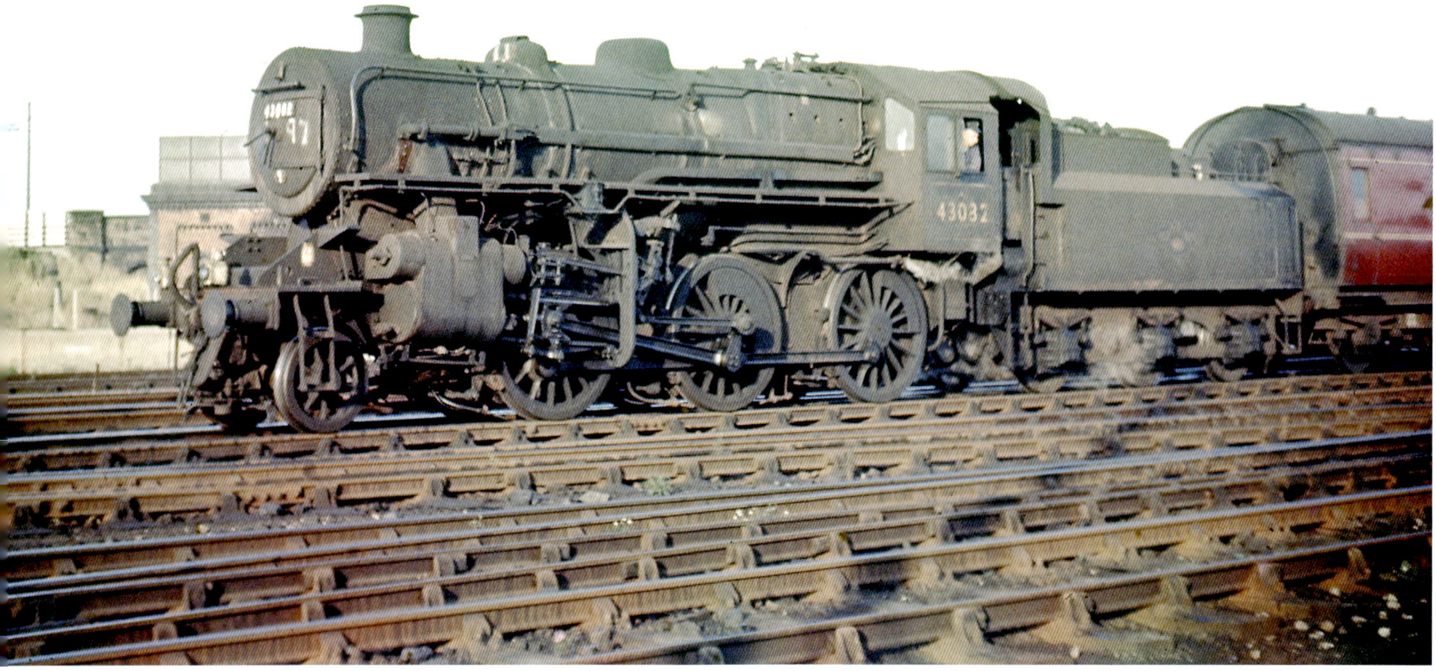

Acting as the Derby station pilot in 1964 was one of the Darlington Works built Ivatt Moguls 43082 shuffling around some ex LMS coaching stock. ***Len Smith***

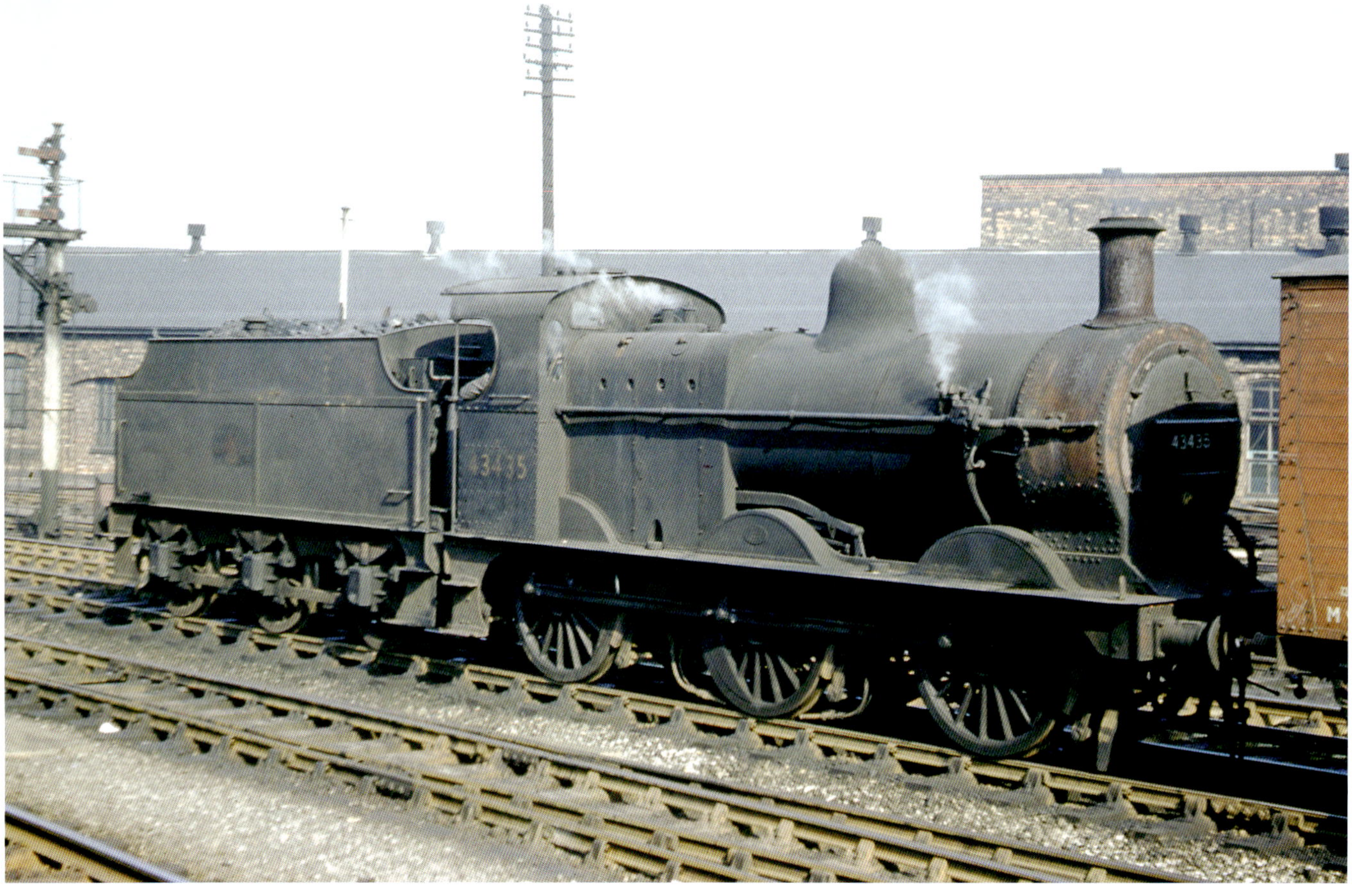

Whilst waiting on the station platforms on 15 March 1960 our camaraman happily thought this Johnson Class 3F 43435 matched with a tender from an LMS built 4F worthy of a picture for posterity. ***Frank Hornby***

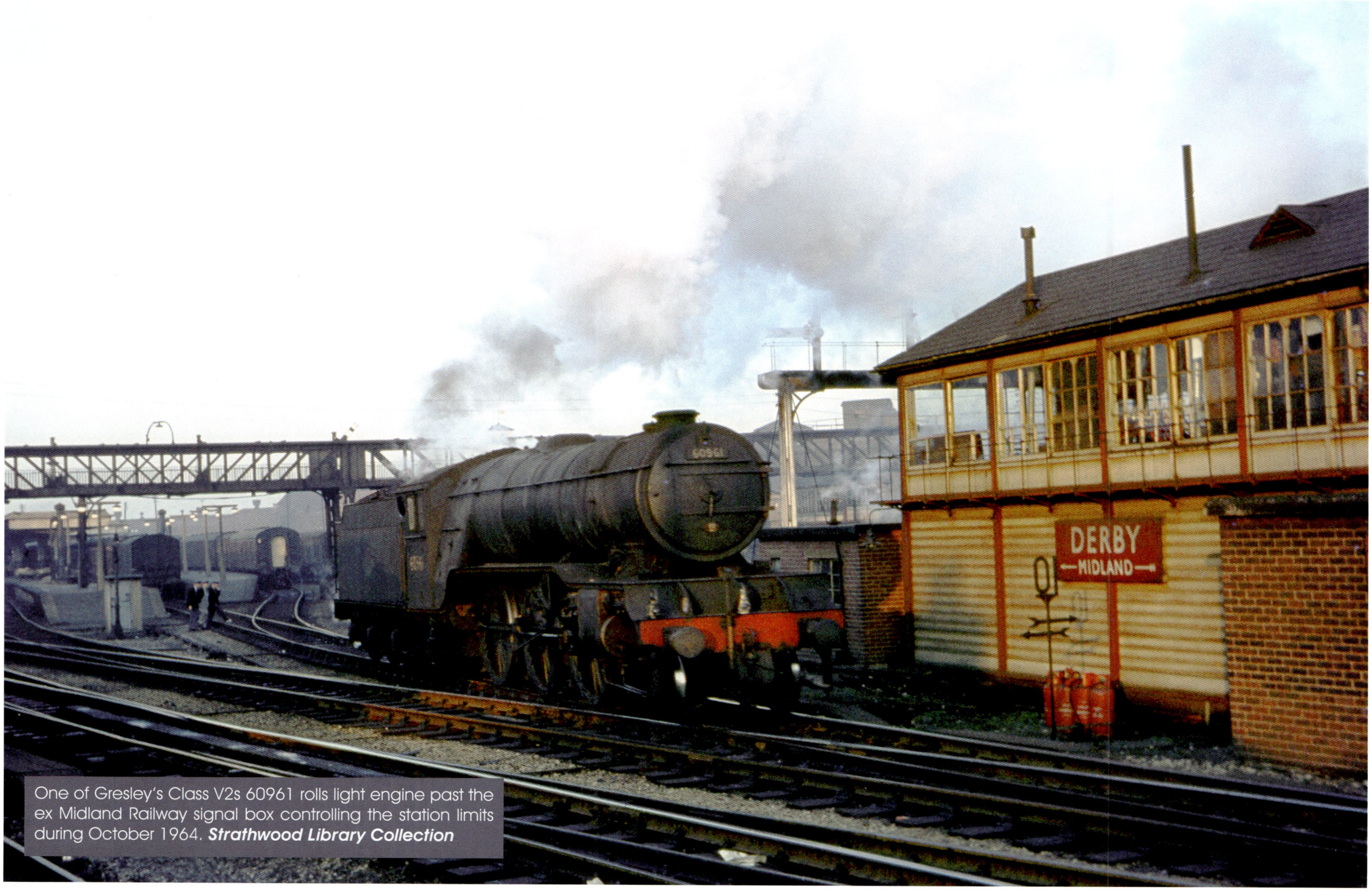

One of Gresley's Class V2s 60961 rolls light engine past the ex Midland Railway signal box controlling the station limits during October 1964. ***Strathwood Library Collection***

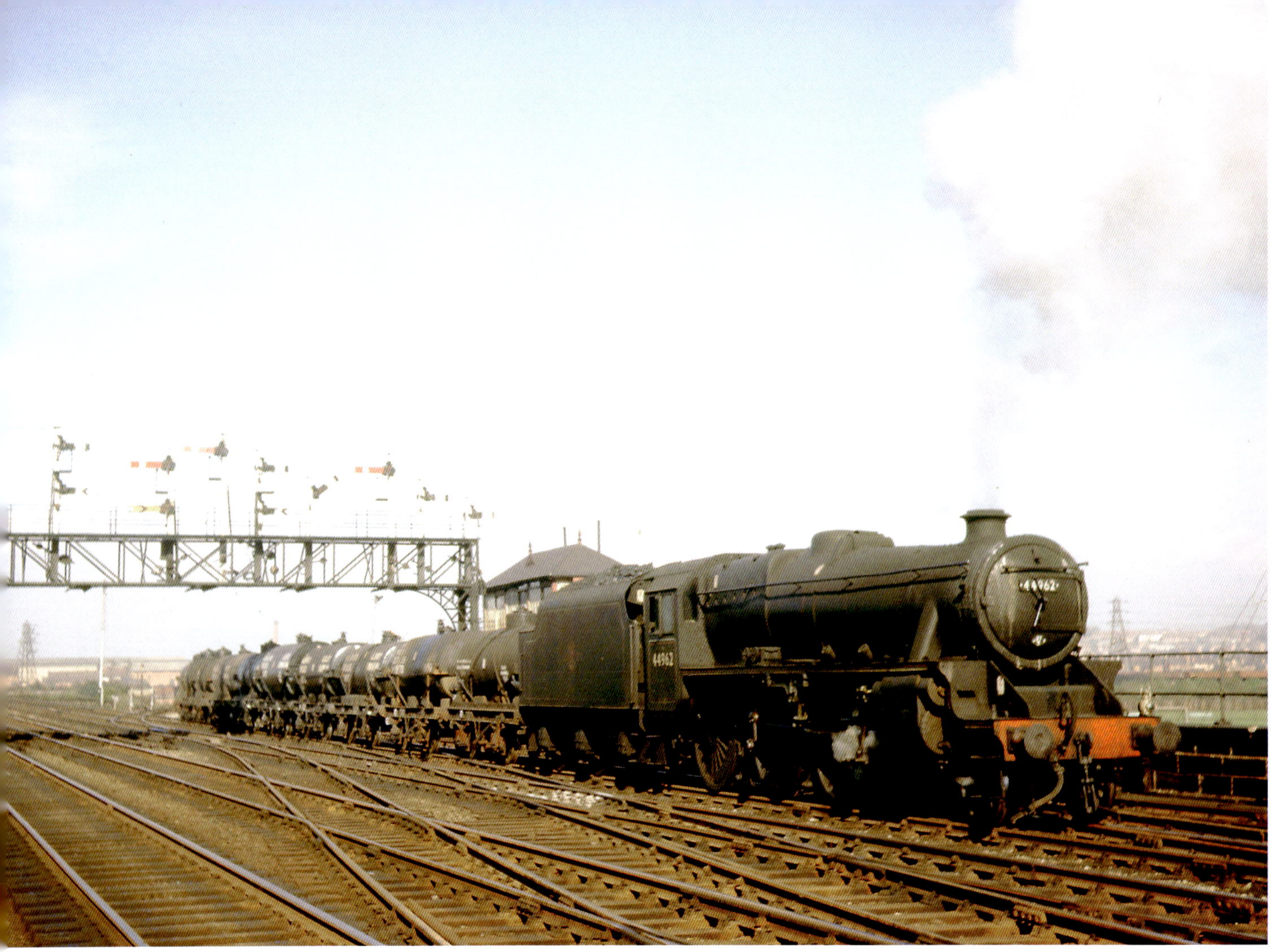

With what appears to be a train of tank wagons used for transporting bi-products from gas works through Derby in 1964 was 44932 from a Horwich batch of Black Fives built in 1945. ***Richard Sinclair Collection***

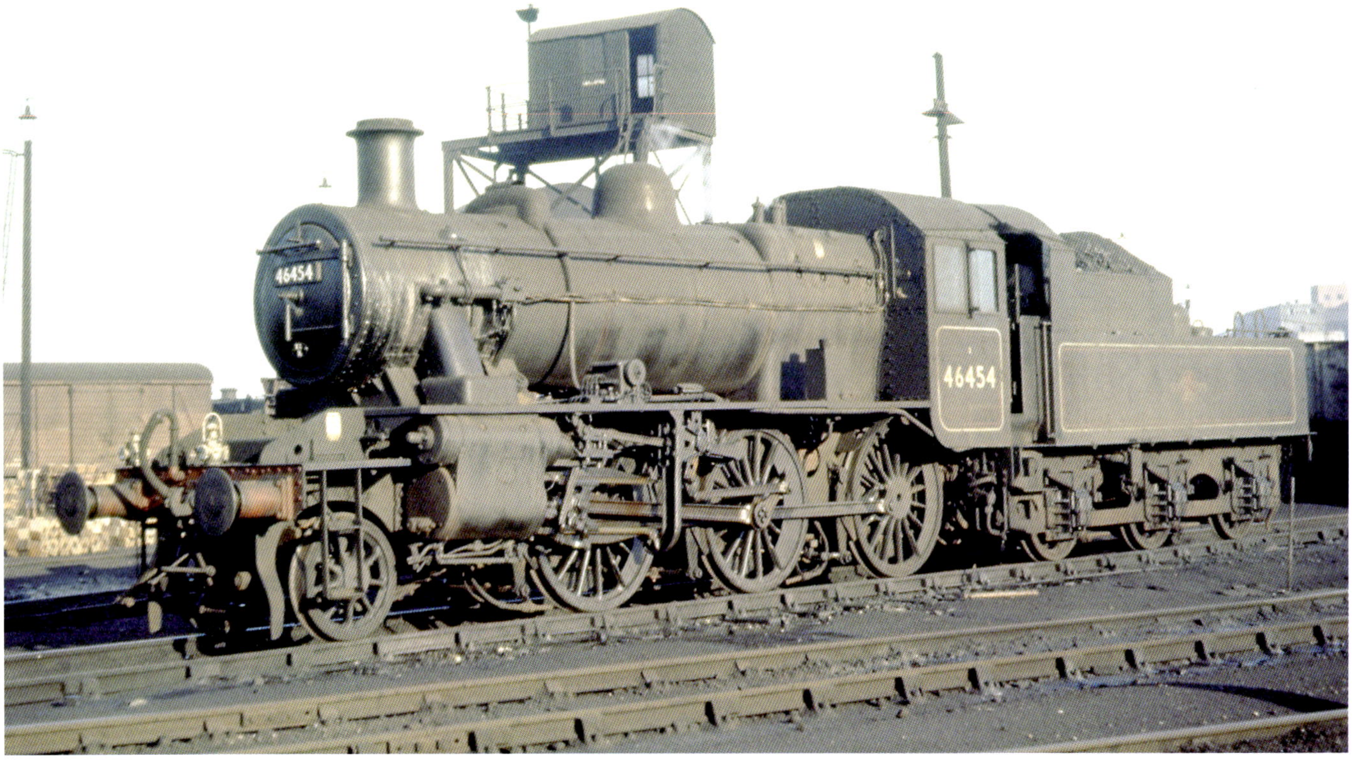

A visit to the shed at Derby on 12 February 1961 yeilded Ivatt 2MT 46454 simmering in the sunshine. Meanwhile this was the day that the very first space craft to be sent to another planet was launched. The Russian built craft bound for Venus had a problem however, although information was sent back from the probe on 19 February 1961 nothing was heard from it afterwards. ***Frank Hornby***

Black Country

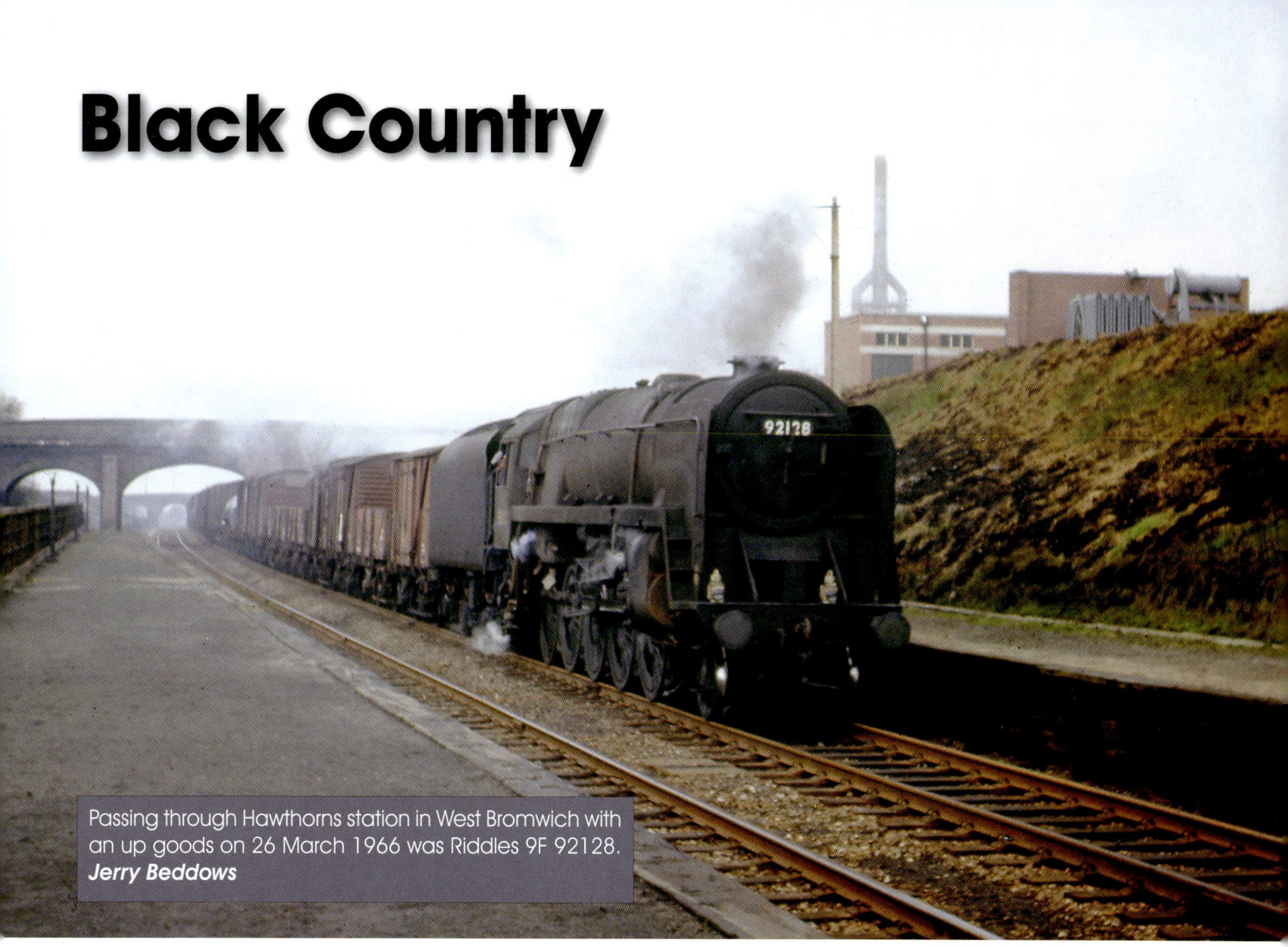

Passing through Hawthorns station in West Bromwich with an up goods on 26 March 1966 was Riddles 9F 92128. ***Jerry Beddows***

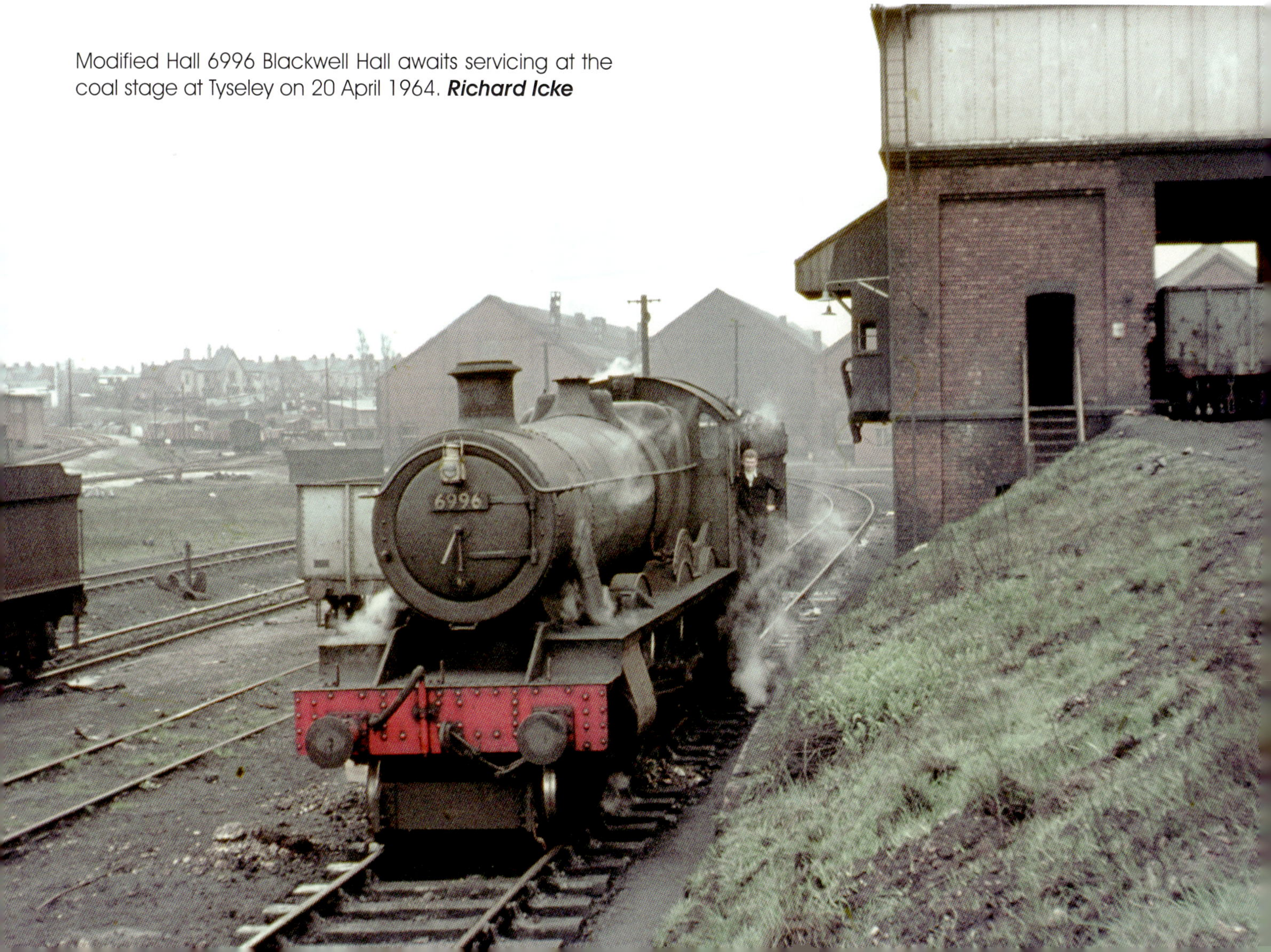

Modified Hall 6996 Blackwell Hall awaits servicing at the coal stage at Tyseley on 20 April 1964. ***Richard Icke***

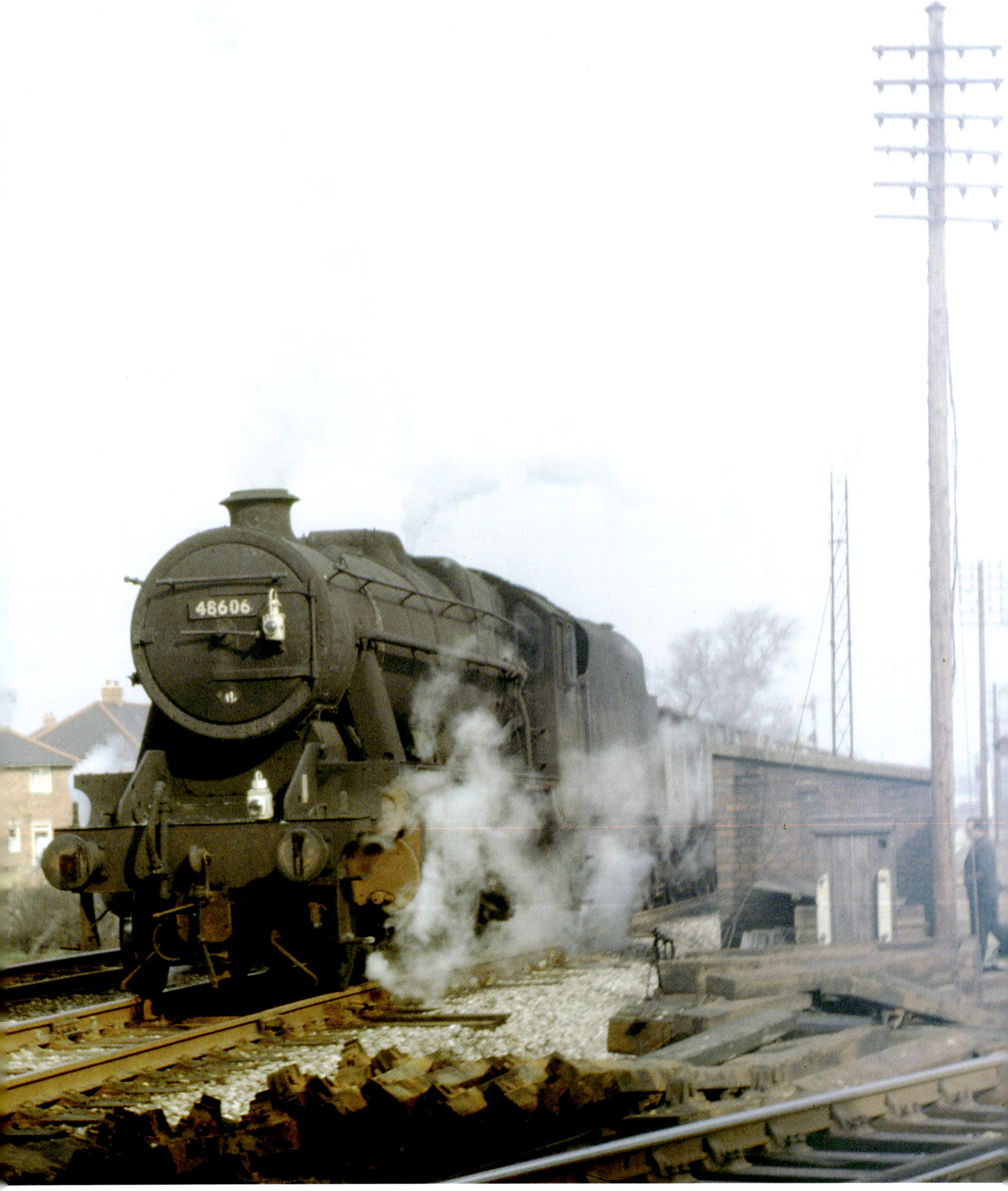

The driver of a Stanier 8F wrestles with his steam sanders on board 48606 with a down goods near Bescot on 29 April 1966 with a train from Burton. Born this day in Barnet in London was one time test cricketer and now television personality Phil Tufnell. ***Jerry Beddows***

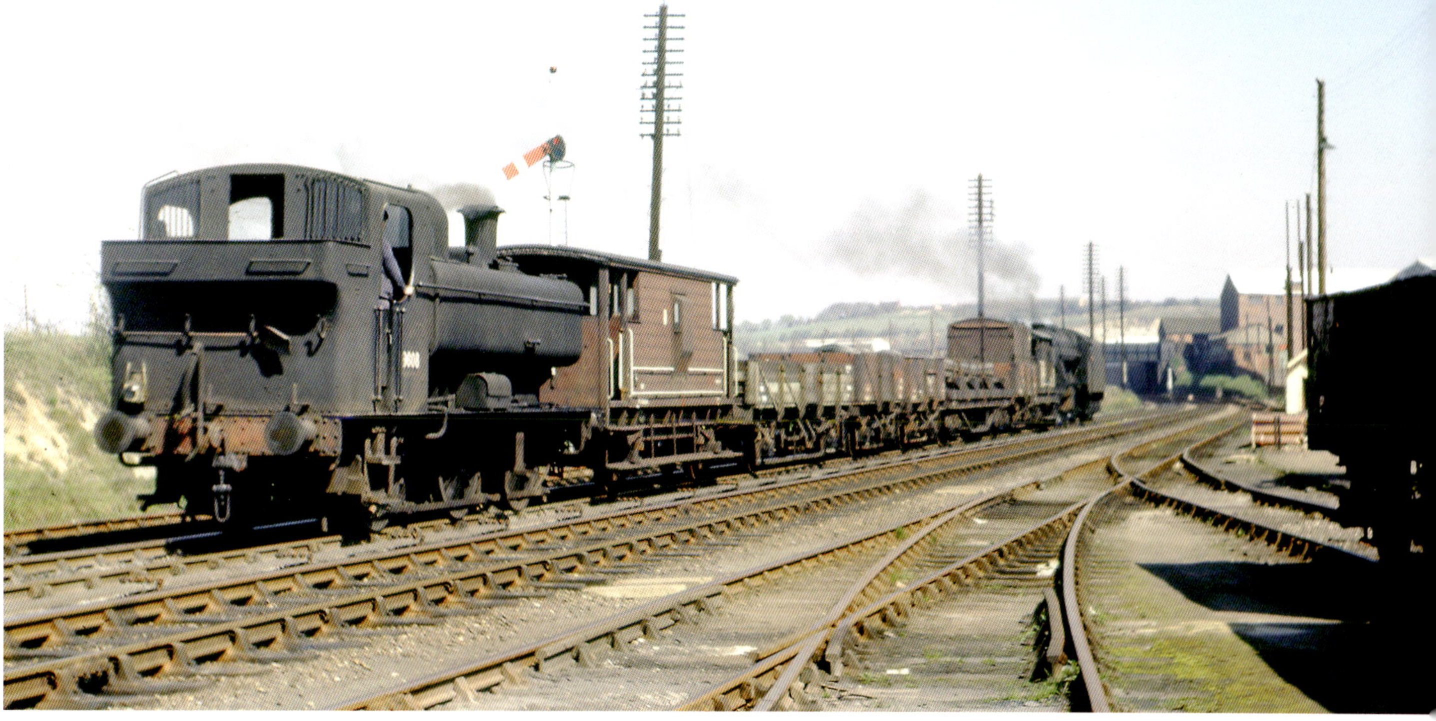

Among the last duties for Pannier Tanks in the Midlands was this banking duty at Old Hill involving 9608, today seen assisting a Black Five from Halesowen in the spring of 1966. ***Jerry Beddows***

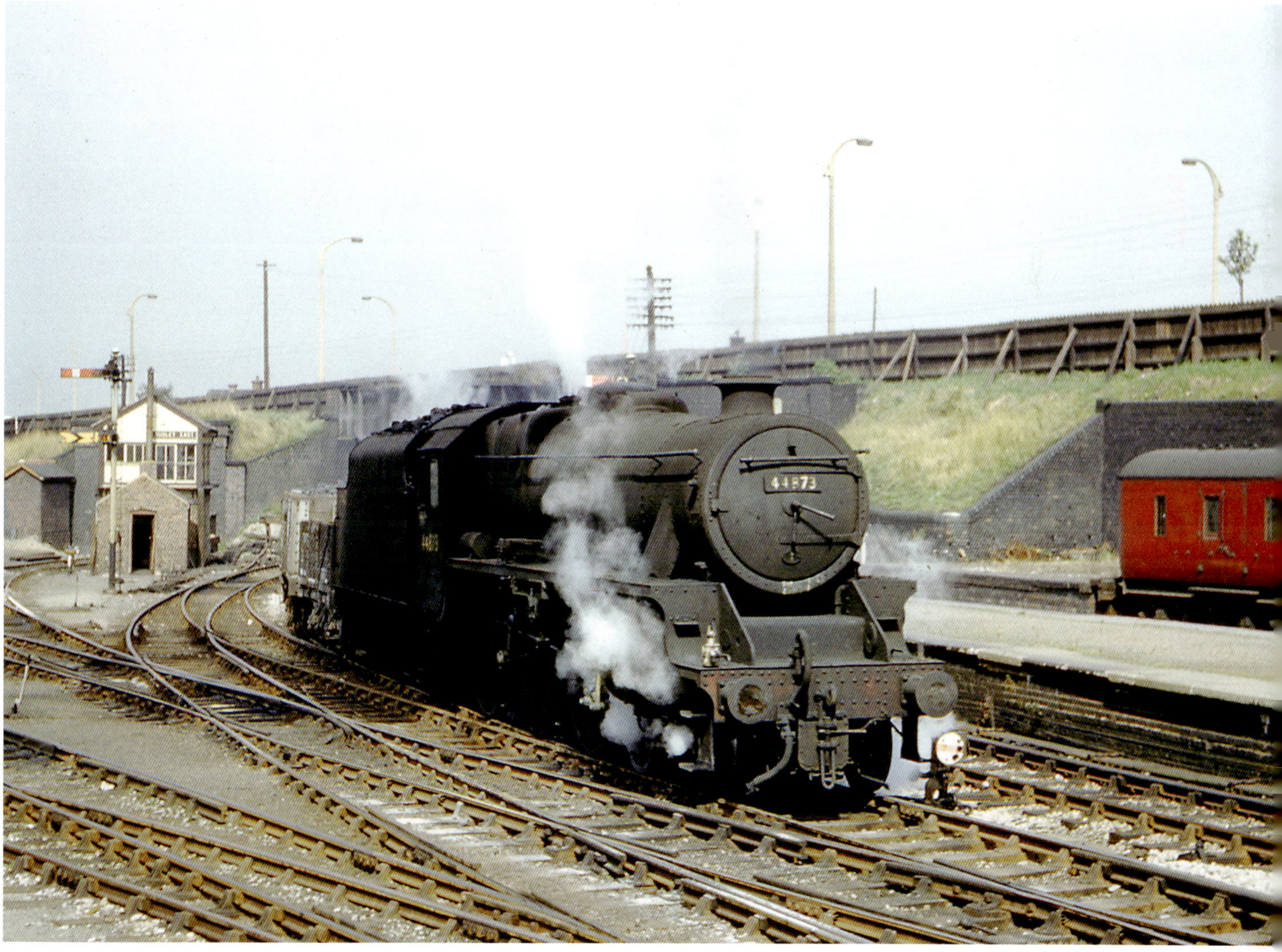

Plodding steadily around the curve in Dudley during 1960 with a goods working was 44873 from the 1945 build at Crewe Works. Dudley is the largest town in the Black Country. For many years the town formed part of an exclave of Worcestershire entirely surrounded by Staffordshire. ***Frank Hornby***

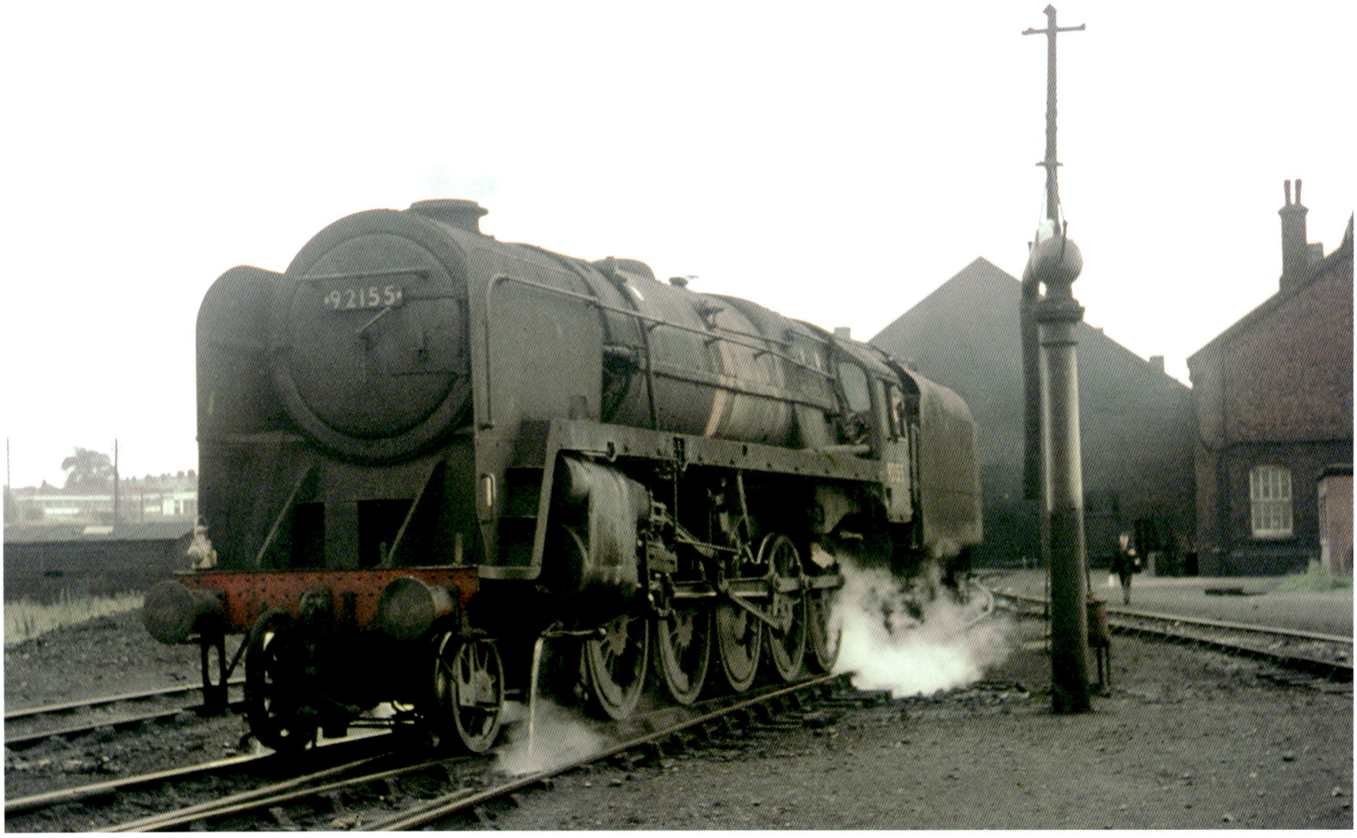

With cylinder drain cocks open Riddles 9F 92155 hisses around the shed yard outside the roundhouse at Oxley on 30 July 1965. ***Dave Down***

More 1966 Pannier activity at Old Hill with 1939 Swindon built 3619 running light back through the station having brought an up goods from Halesowen earlier in the morning. ***Jerry Beddows***

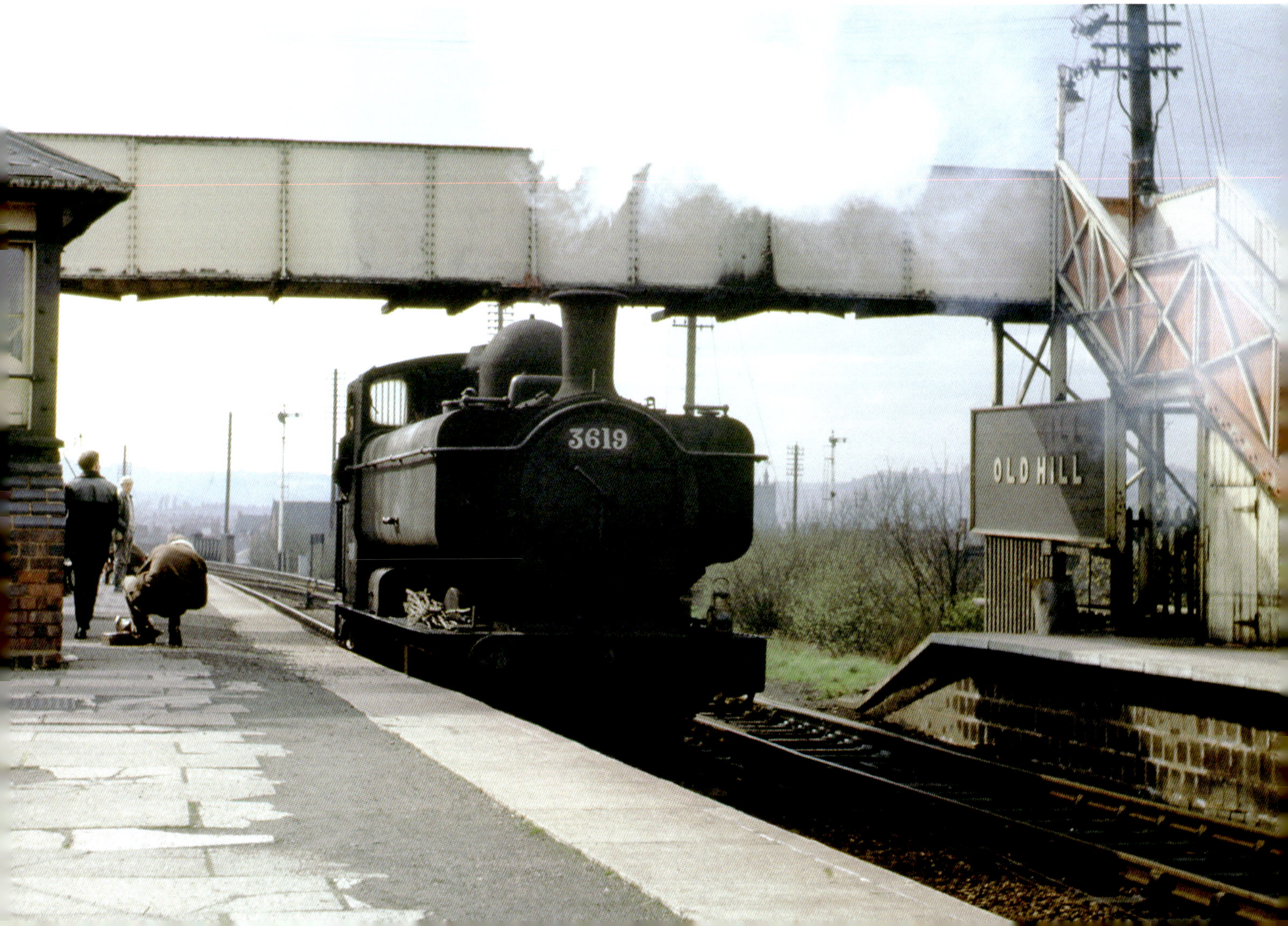

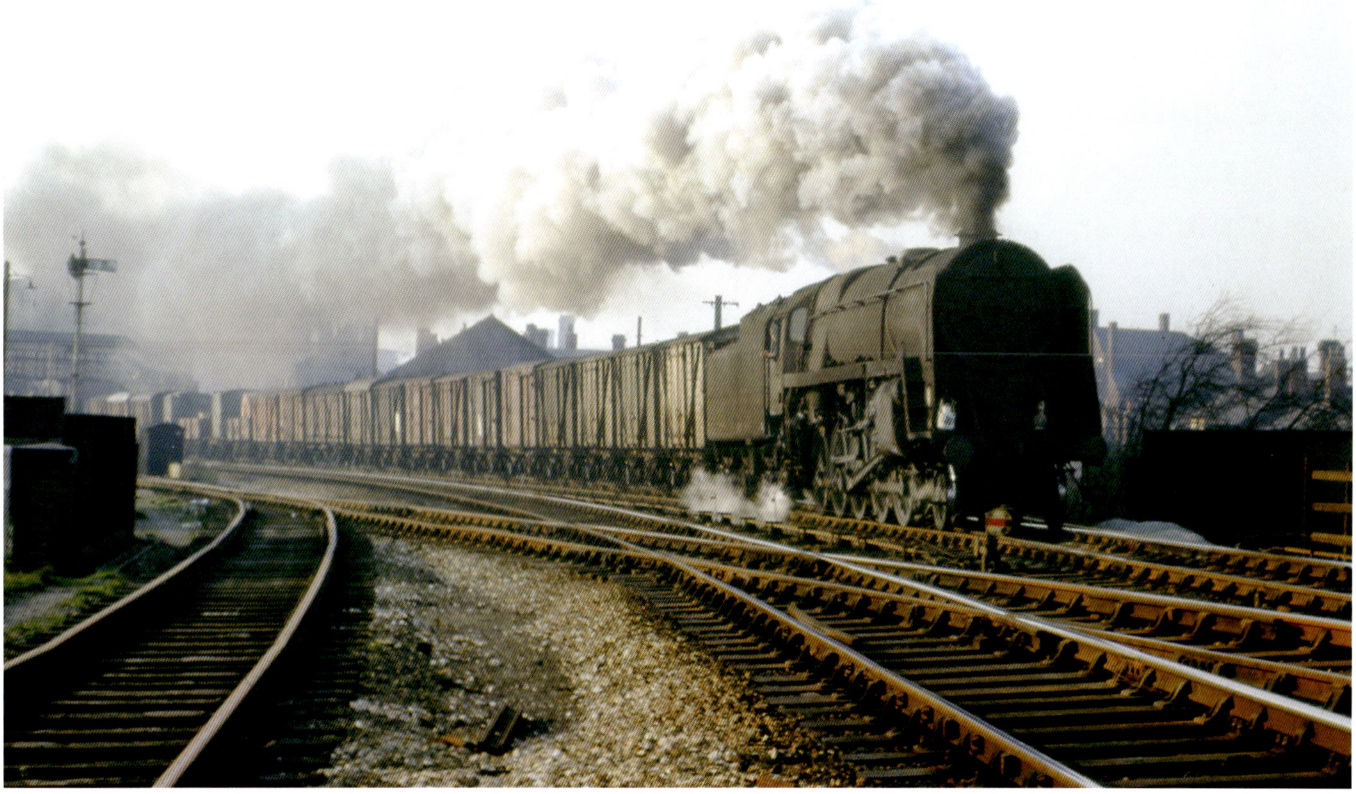

An up goods is brought smartly through Wednesbury behind 92004 on 19 March 1966. ***Jerry Beddows***

A down godds for Dudley shuffles through Old Hill in early 1966 behind Black Five 45285. ***Jerry Beddows***

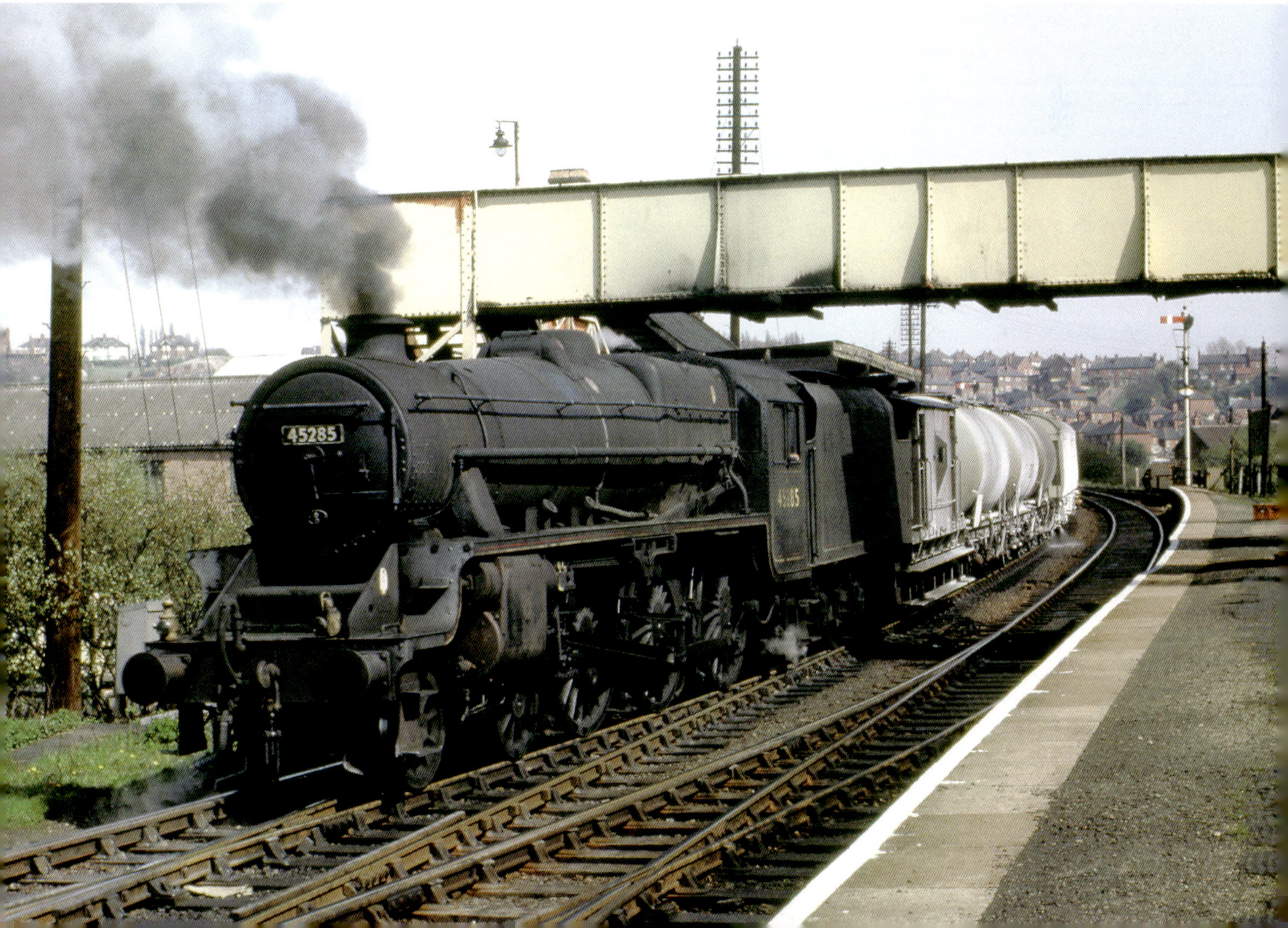

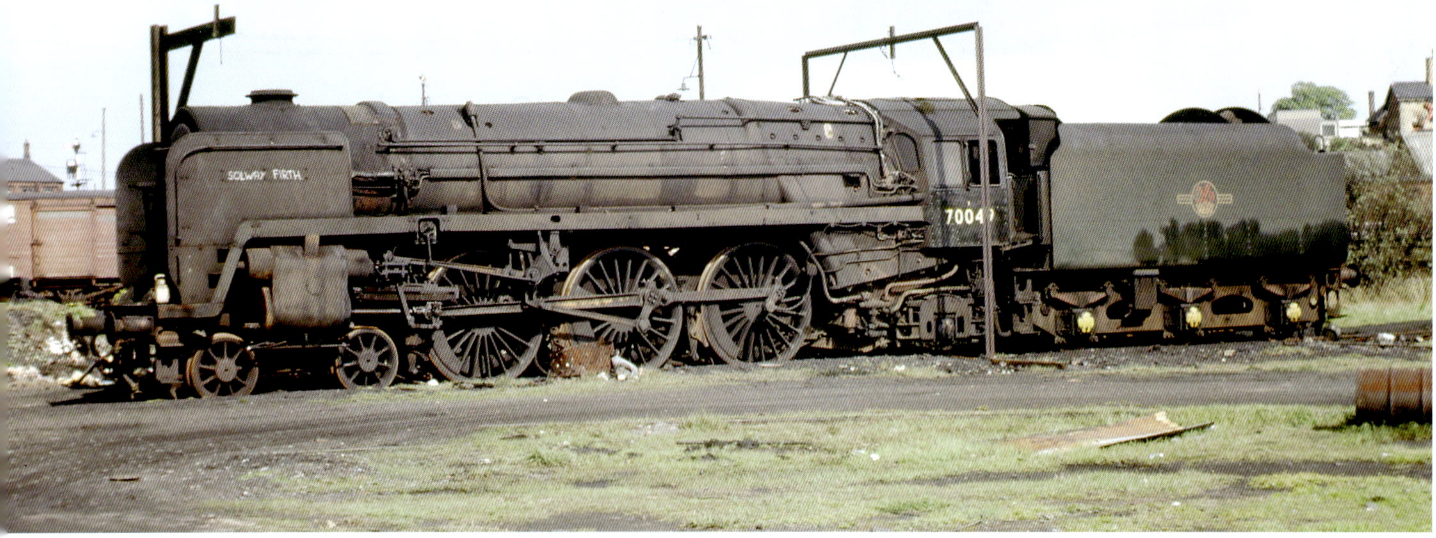

Temprorarily stored at Tyseley was 70049 Solway Firth on 7 May 1967. ***Jerry Beddows***

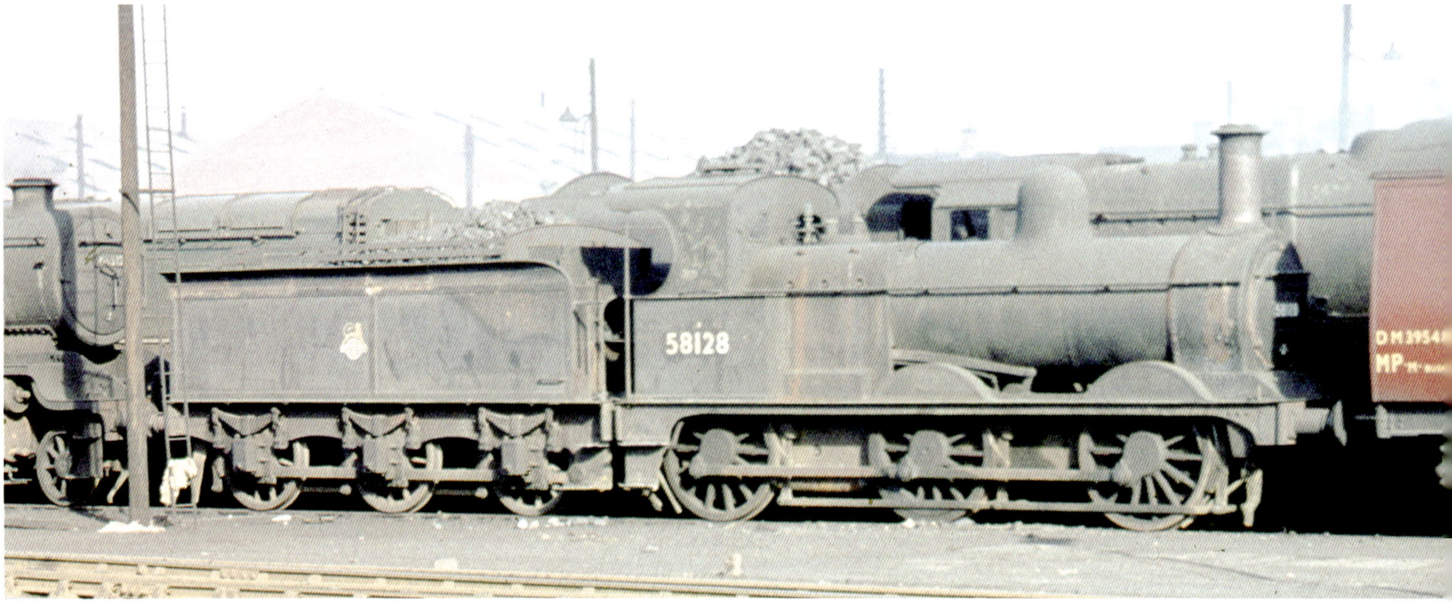

Just one more year to run for Johnson 2F 58128 at Bushbury in 1961. ***Strathwood Library Collection***

Below: A well lime stained Riddles 9F 92235 in June 1965 rests at Tyseley. ***John Gill***

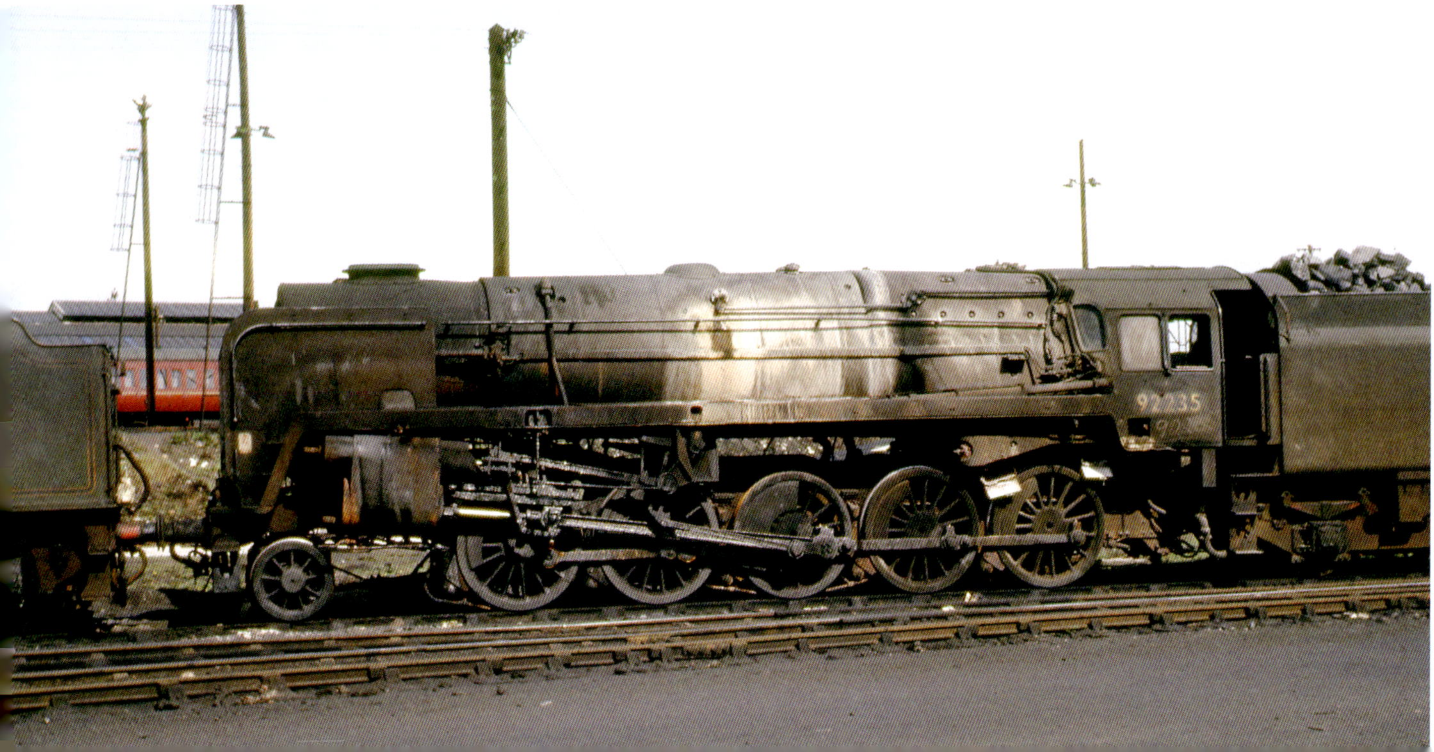

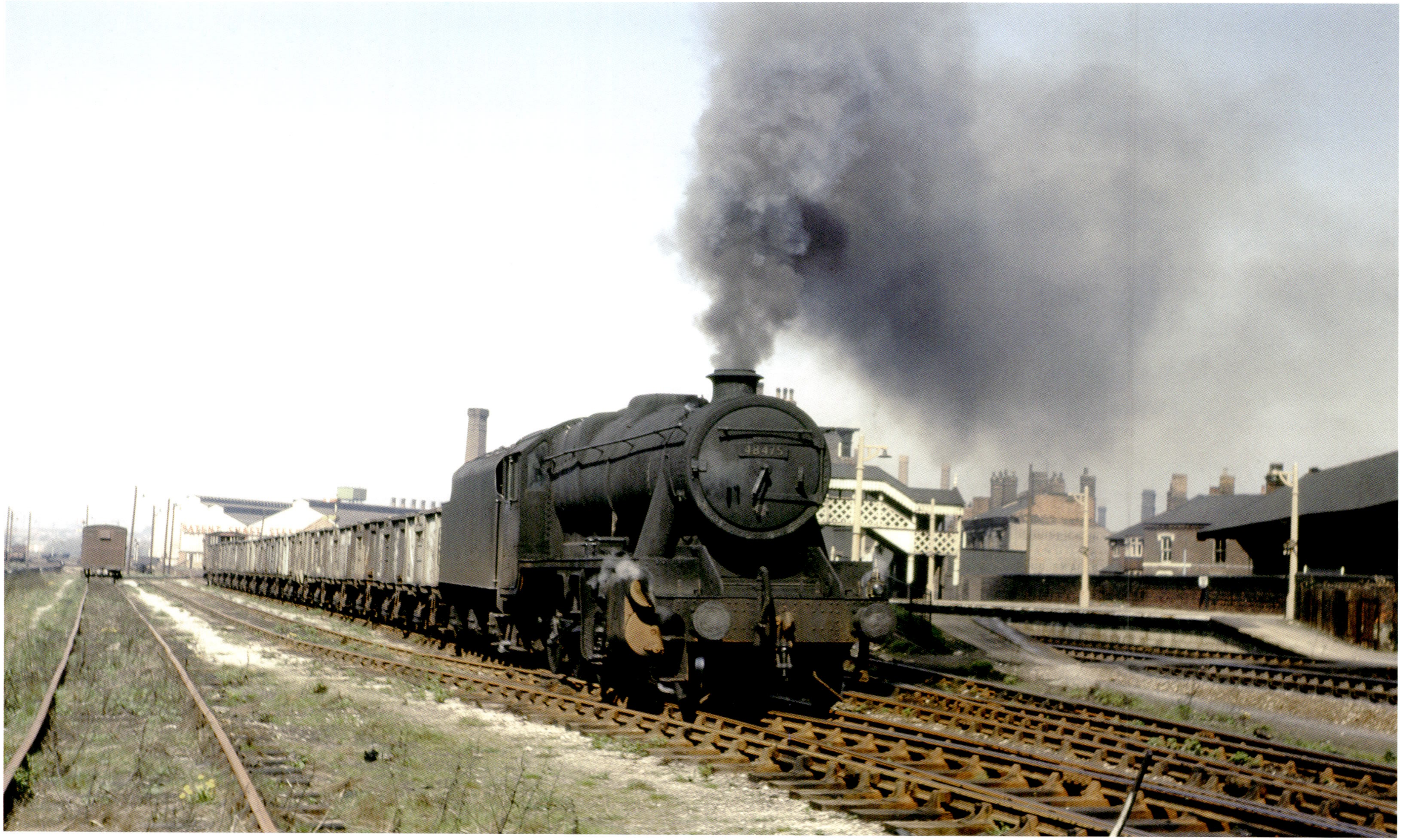

The couplings are pulled out tight again through Wednesbury on 30 April 1966 as the driver of Stanier 8F 48475 opens the regulator further. This was the last year of the Final of the League Cup being held over two both legs home and away, with West Bromwich Albion overhauling West Ham Utd 5-3 on aggregate over the two legs. ***Jerry Beddows***

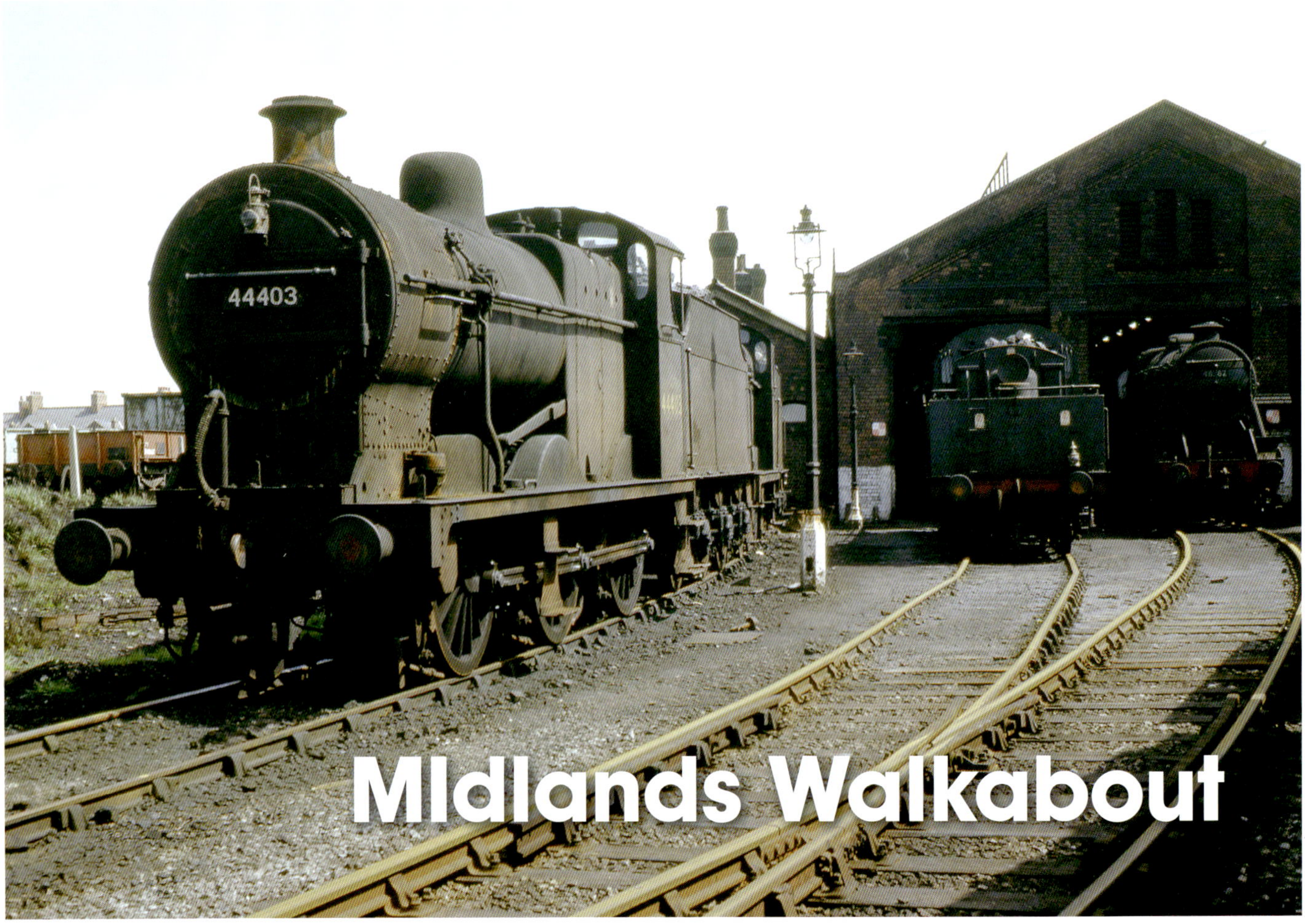

Midlands Walkabout

The shed at Coalville would become diesel only as of February 1965 and would be closed officially on 4 October 1965, although diesels would be stabled here for many years afterwards, and even Open Days held. However in May 1964 a Riddles Mogul and Stanier 8F kept company with Fowler 4F 44403 Coalville on a Sunday in May 1964. ***Win Wall/Strathwood Library Collection***

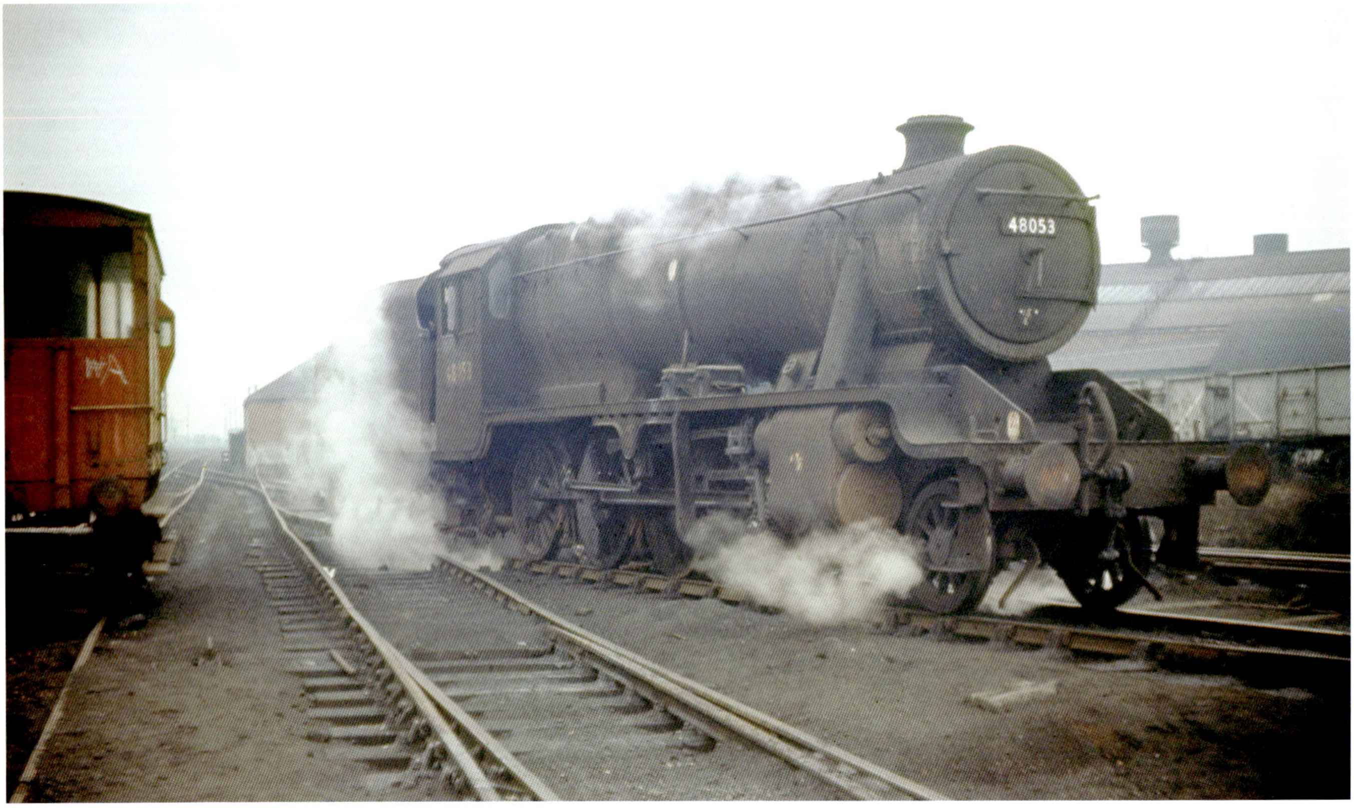

A few months before in the winter air Stanier 8F 48053 made its way onto the shed at Coalville. It would be a year of Mods and Rockers fighting at the seaside and Mary Poppins singing at the cinema. ***Len Smith***

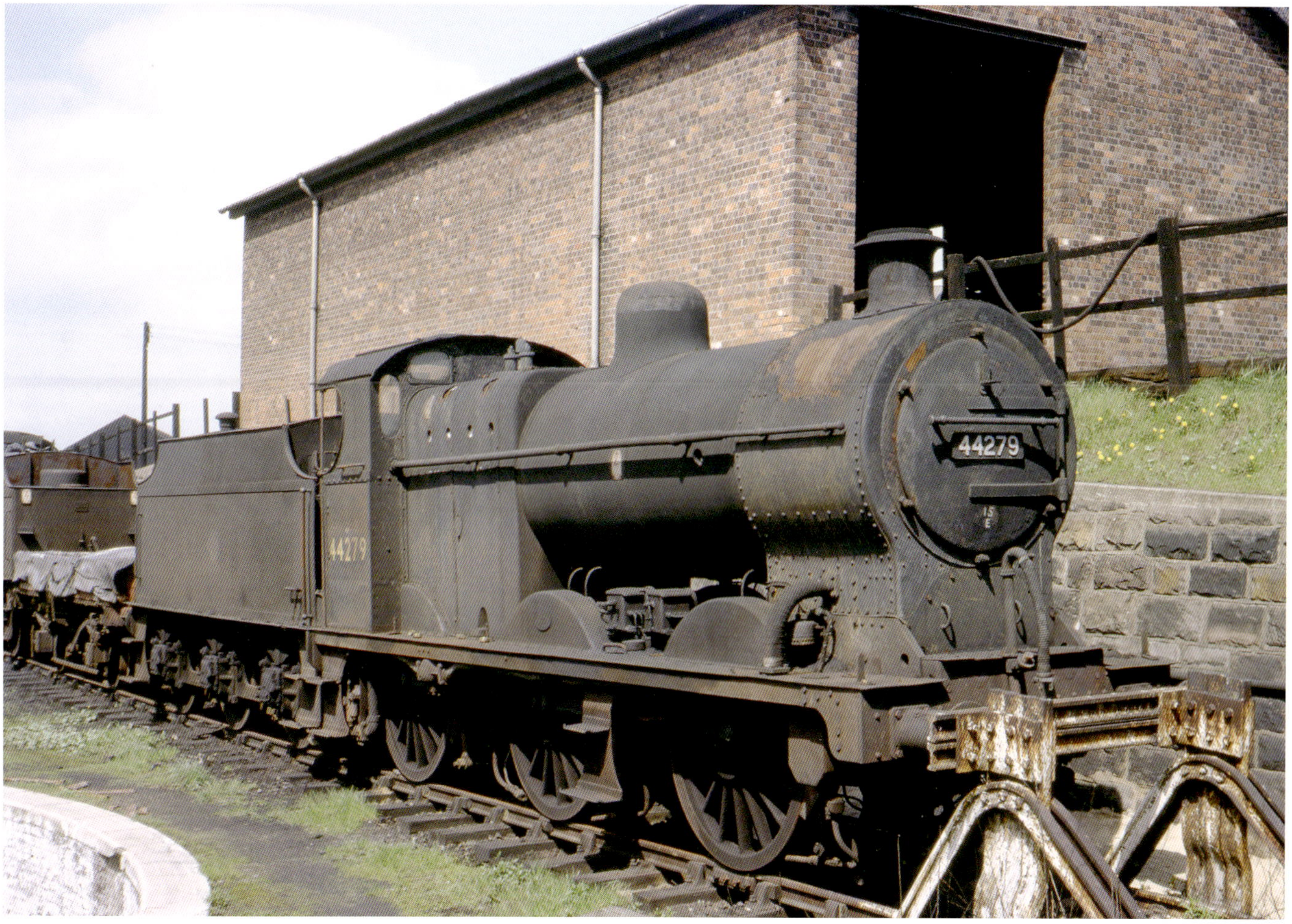

This particular Fowler 4F had been set aside alongside the shed at Coalville after the Christmas and New Year break as 1963 became 1964. It would be the end for 44279 which spent almost a year awaiting its destiny as scrap. ***Win Wall/Strathwood Library Collection***

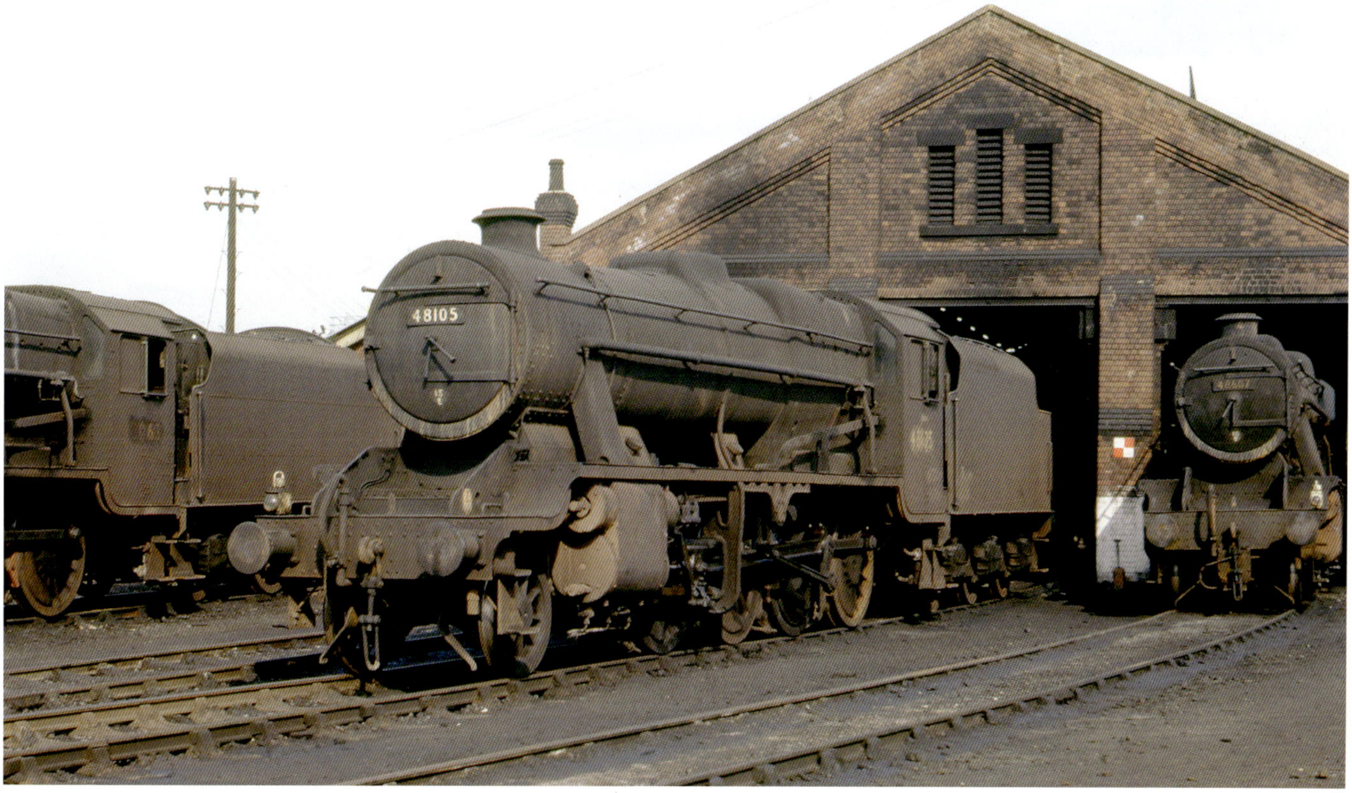

A trio of Stanier 8Fs with 48105 to the fore at Coalville on 2 May 1965, as was so common during the sixties the Beatles were at number one with Ticket to Ride. ***Peter Hutchinson/Strathwood Library Collection***

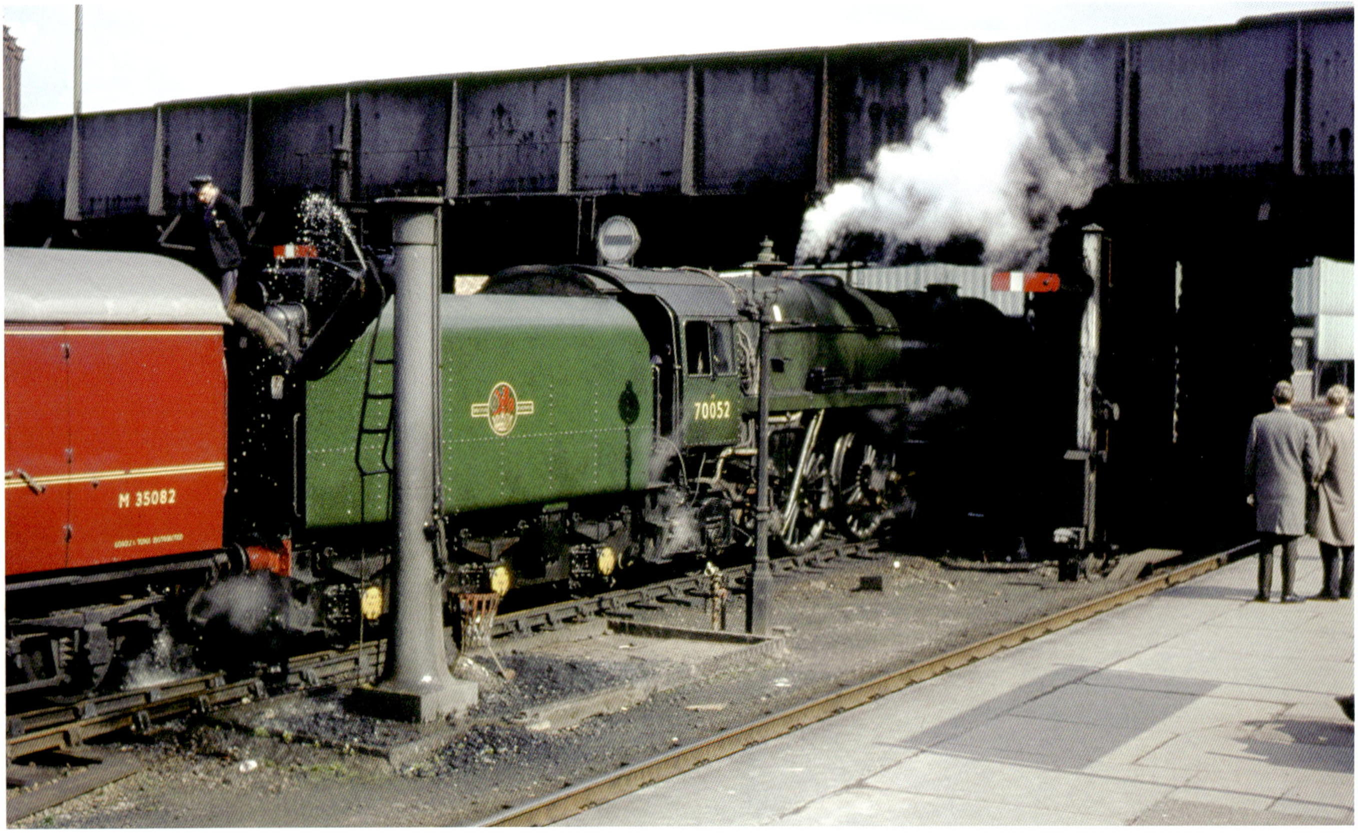

No doubt the fireman keeps his eye on the leak from the bag of the water crane as he fills the tender of Britannia 70052 Firth of Tay working the L.C.G.B Notts and Lincs Railtour on 24 April 1965 during a stop at Leicester Midland. ***Strathwood Library Collection***

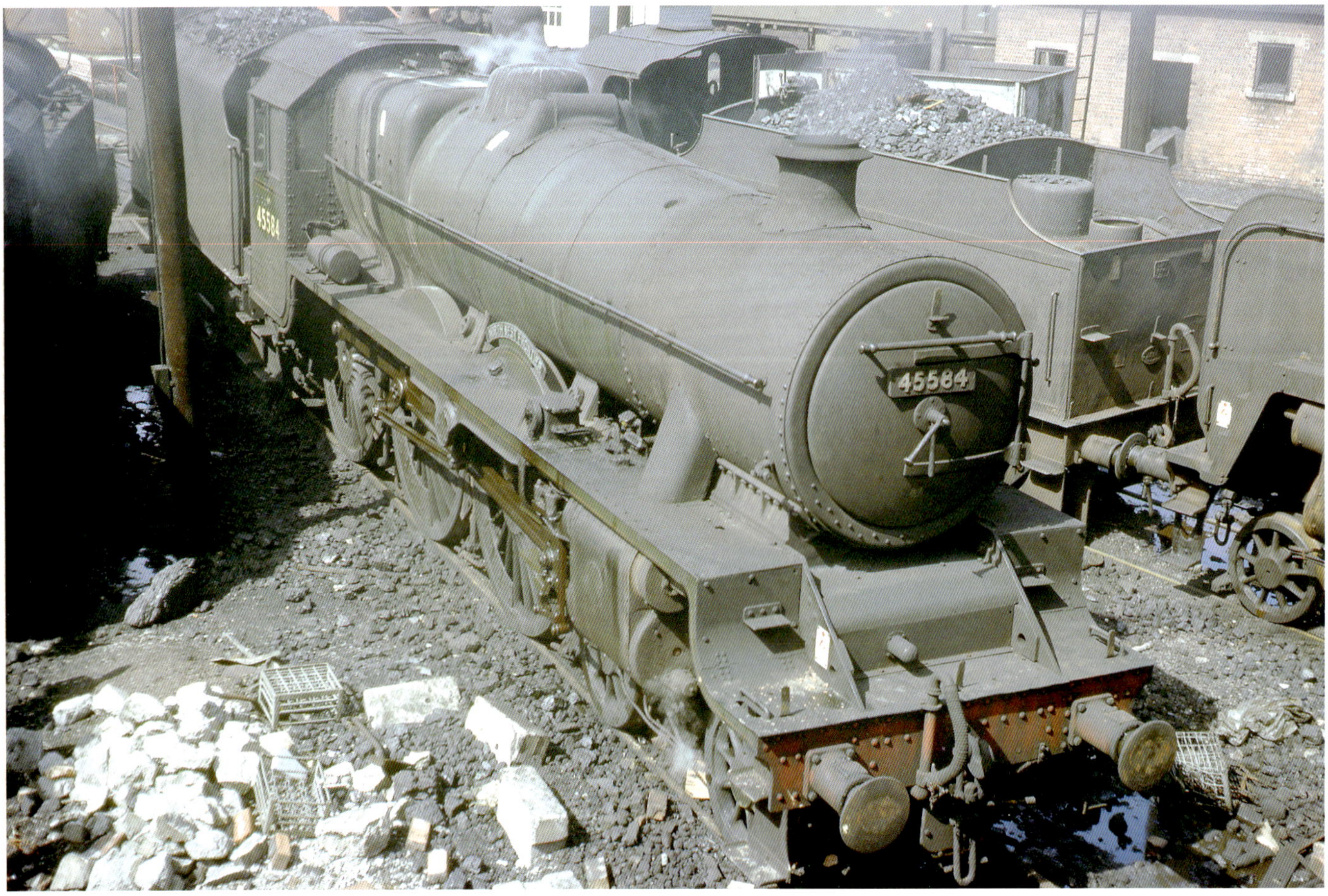

The ground is strewn with debris around Leicester Midland shed during May 1964 as we look down the bank upon Stanier Jubilee 45584 North West Frontier. This was to be a busy year for the Carry On team as they released both Carry on Cleo and Carry on Spying into the country's cinemas. ***Win Wall/Strathwood Library Collection***

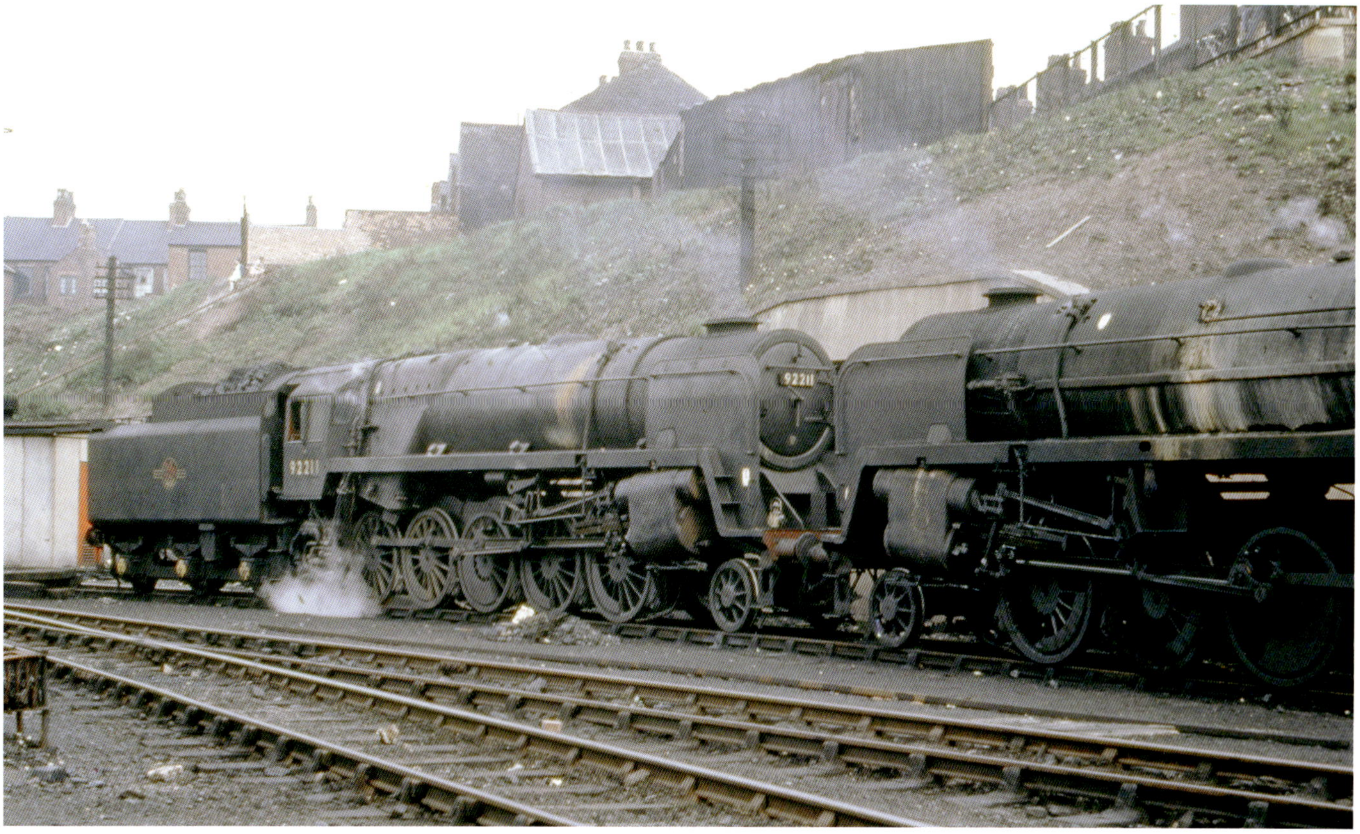

Facing off another Riddles 9F on shed at Leicester on 2 May 1965 was 92211, the shed here had another thirteen months to go with live steam which finished on 13 June 1966. although shed bashers may have seen several steam locomotives stored here after this date as part of the National Collection for a number of years. ***Peter Hutchinson/Strathwood Library Collection***

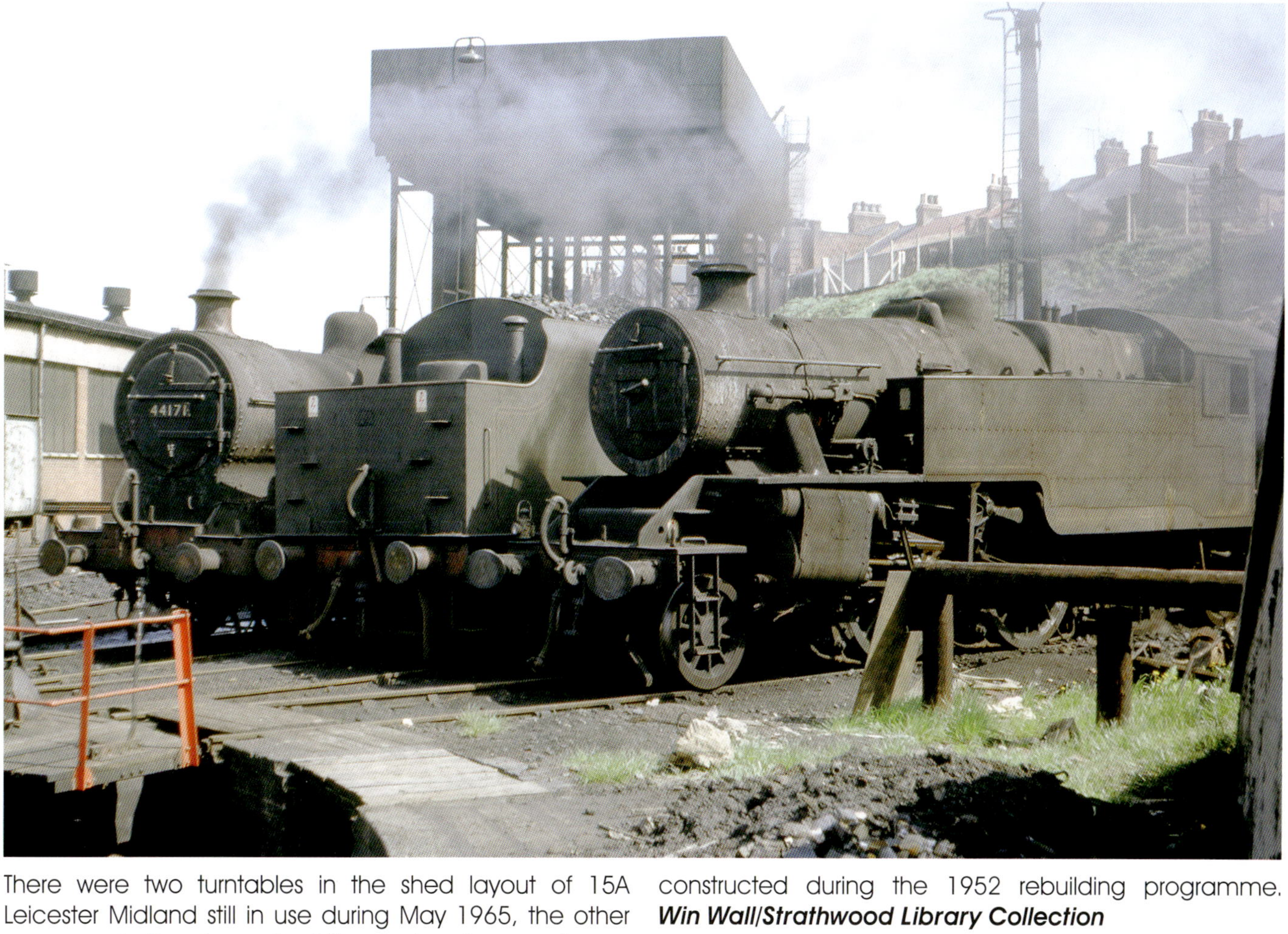

There were two turntables in the shed layout of 15A Leicester Midland still in use during May 1965, the other was open to the elements at the centre of a roundhouse constructed during the 1952 rebuilding programme. ***Win Wall/Strathwood Library Collection***

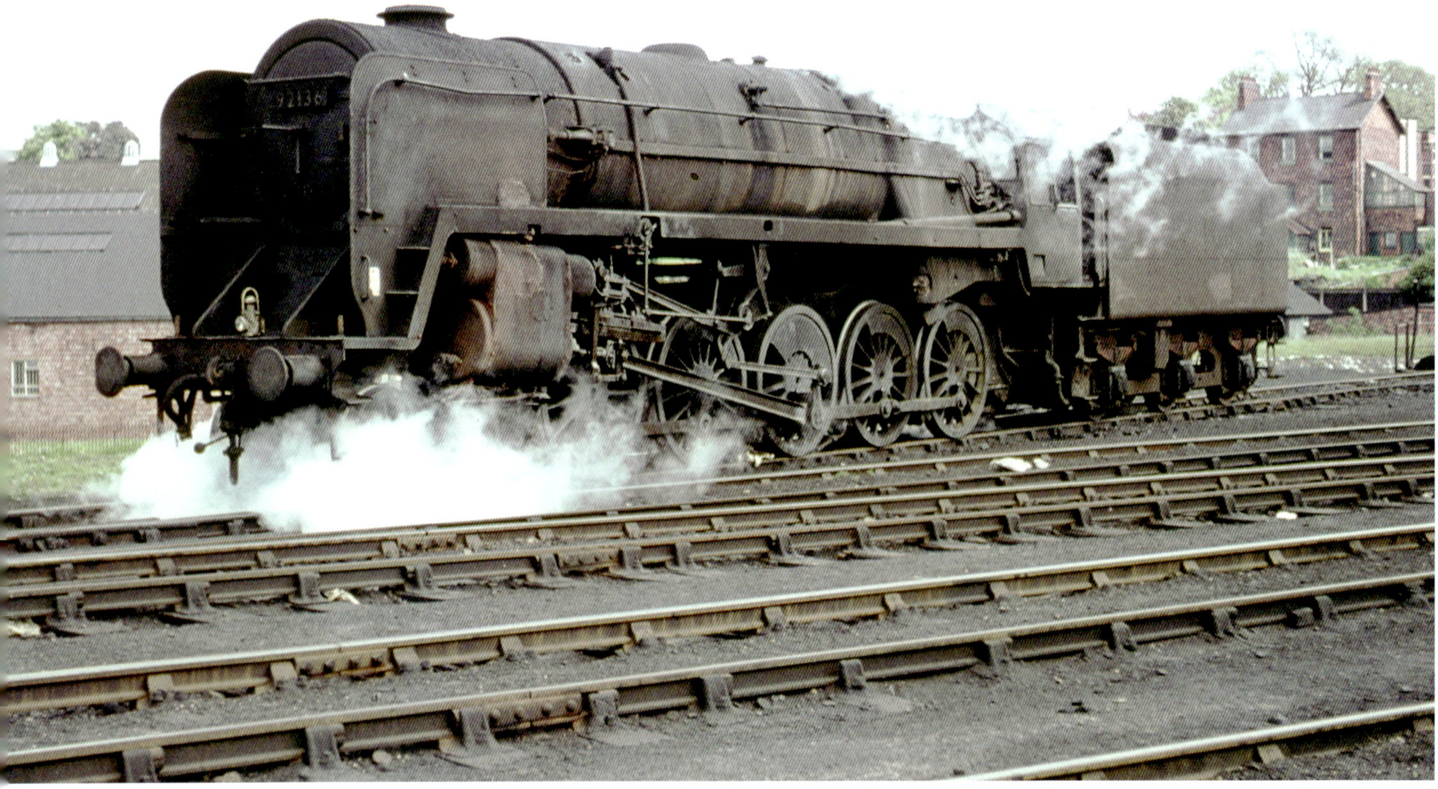

Grubby Riddles 9Fs such as 92136 seen at 15C Kettering on 15 May 1965 were once commonplace, the shed here would close the following month which had prior to 1963 been coded as 15B. ***Strathwood Library Collection***

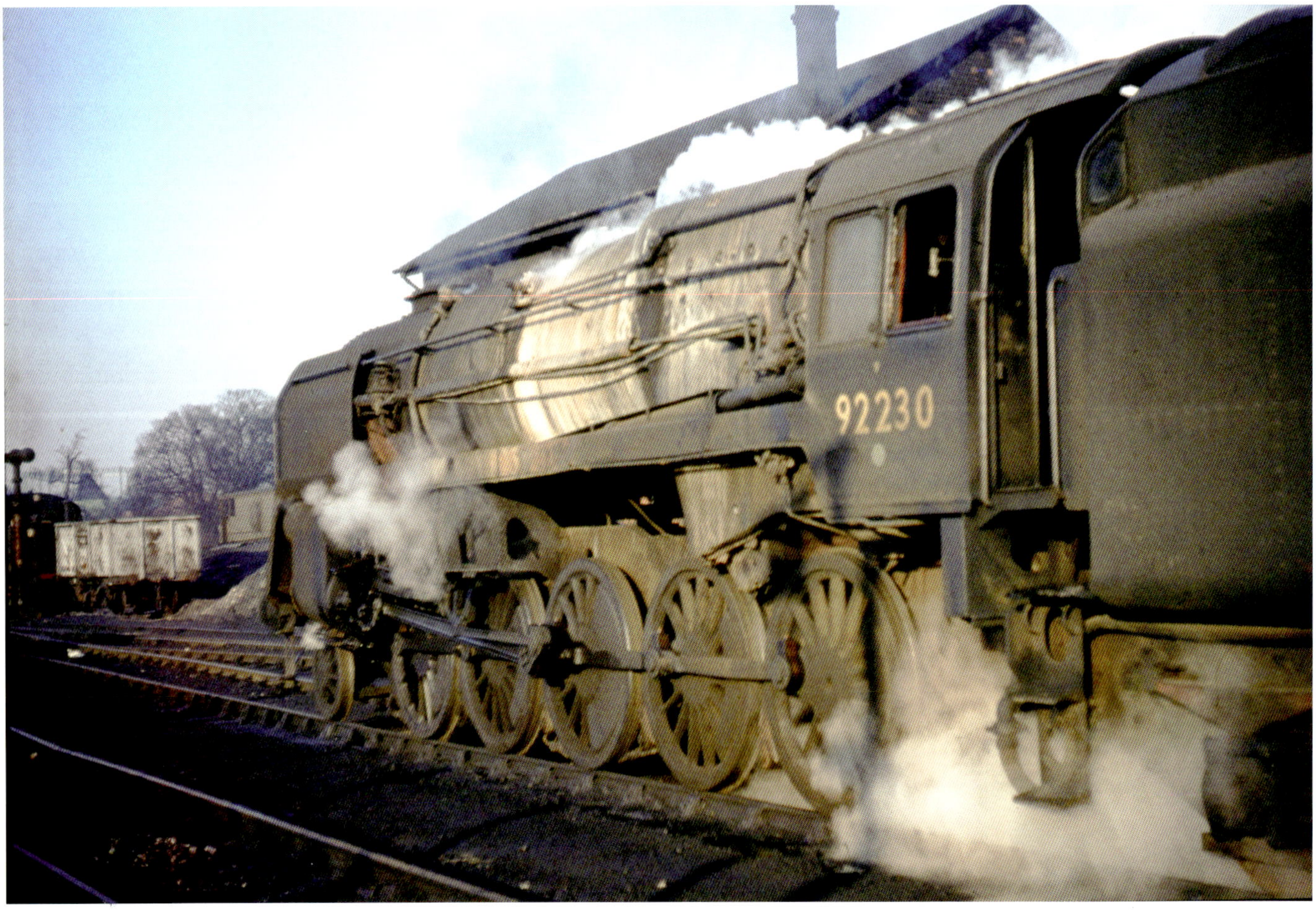

Stayiing at Kettering and more heavy limescale staining, no doubt leading to priming problems was to be seen on Riddles 9F 92230 on 2 January 1965. This modern and powerful 2-10-0 built at Crewe in August 1958 would only manage just over seven years in traffic, such was the desire to despatch assetts to the scrapyard after the politics of the Beeching report. ***Strathwood Library Collection***

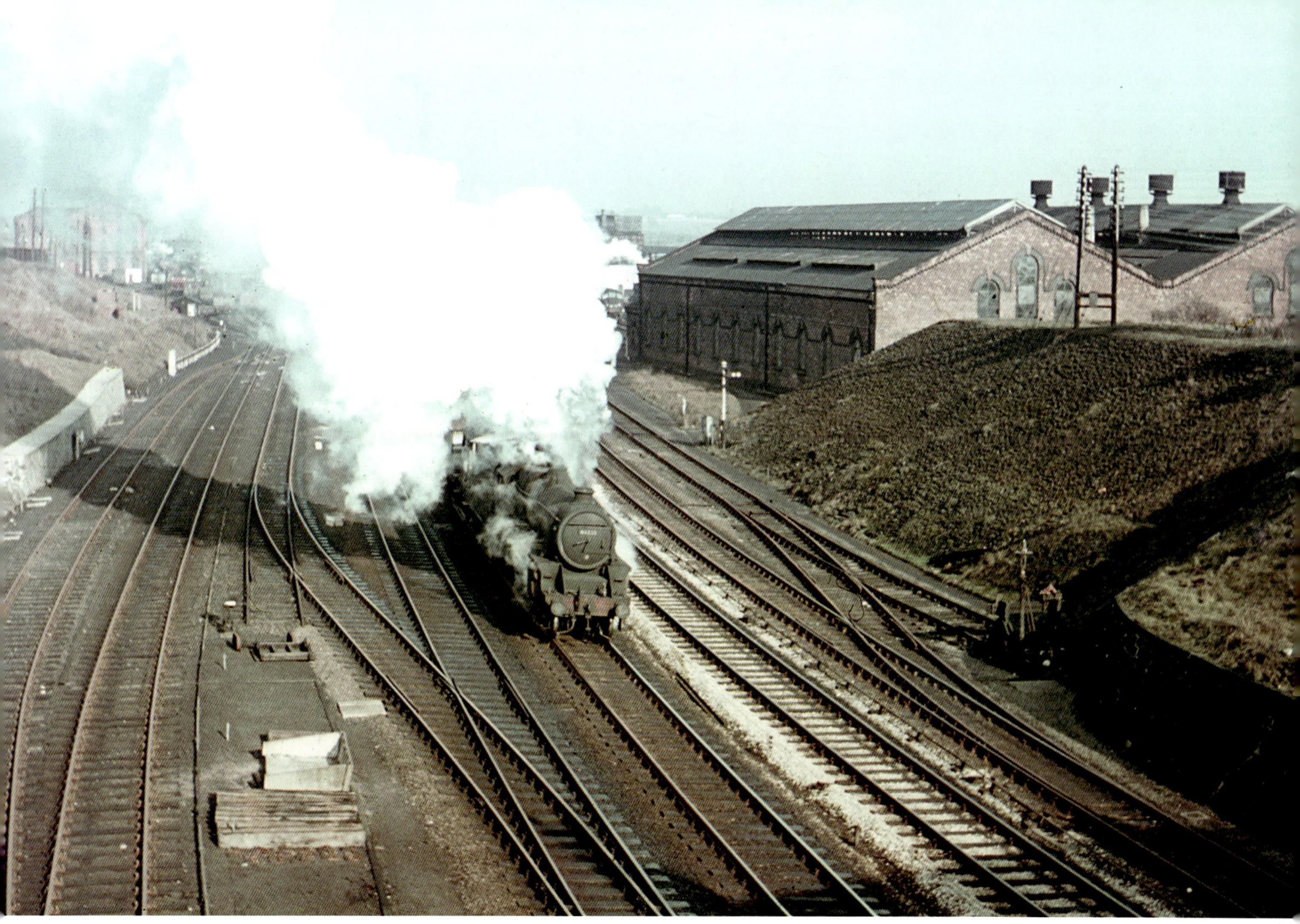

Considering the shed's close proximity to the station at Wellingborough, it seems that the depot has been often negelected in many books previously. In this view we see Black Five 44858 passing the ex Midland Railway engine sheds in the background on 29 January 1965. ***Dave Down***

As steam was being dispatched to private scrapyards during the middle sixties, a small number of cameramen sought out George Cohen's scrapyard at Cransley which started to recieve a goodly number of ex British Railway's steam locomotives, together with a large number of London Transport Underground units. In the winter of 1964 a pair of Ivatt 2-6-2Ts 41228 and 41327 were captured for one last time. ***Strathwood Library Collection***

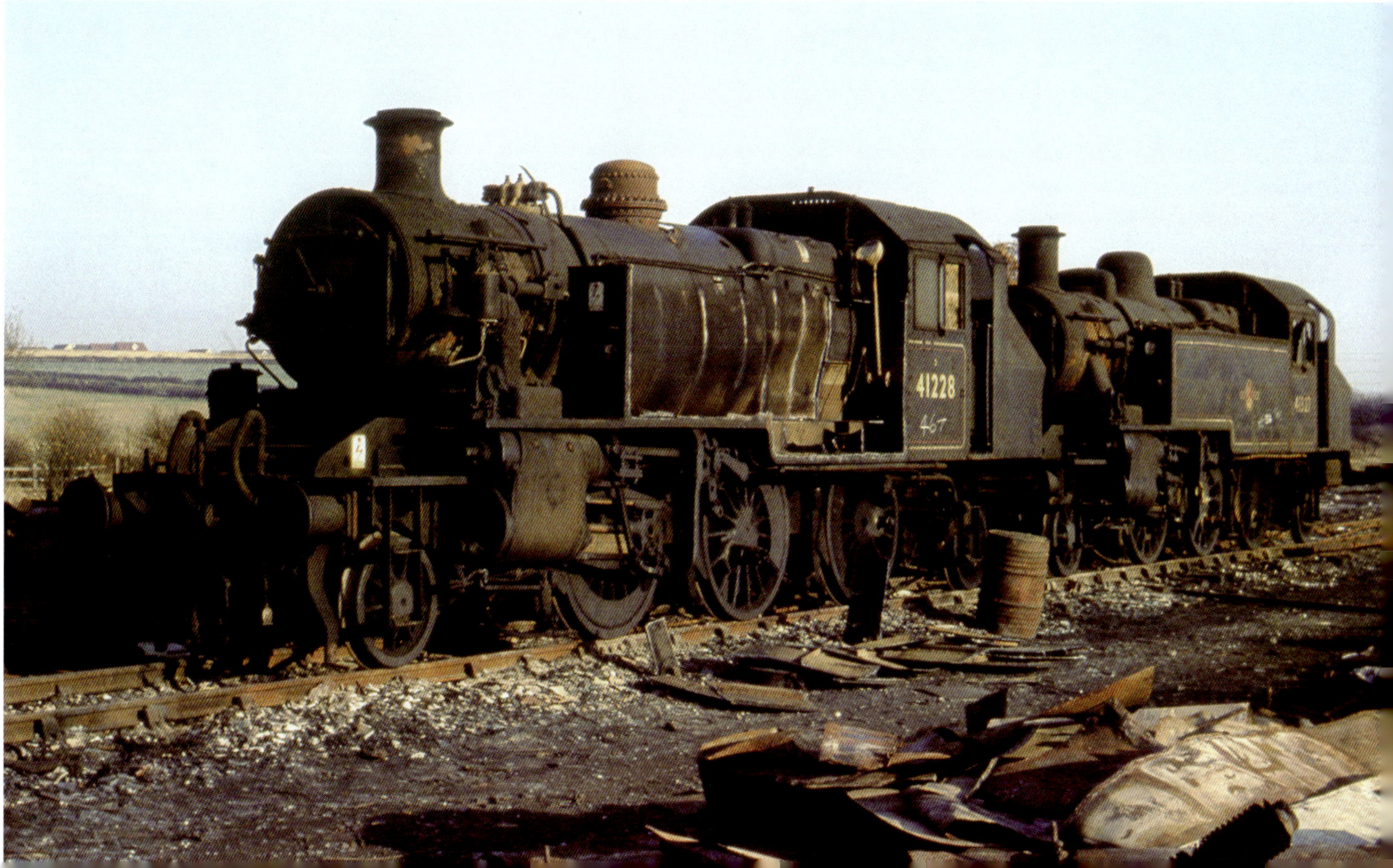

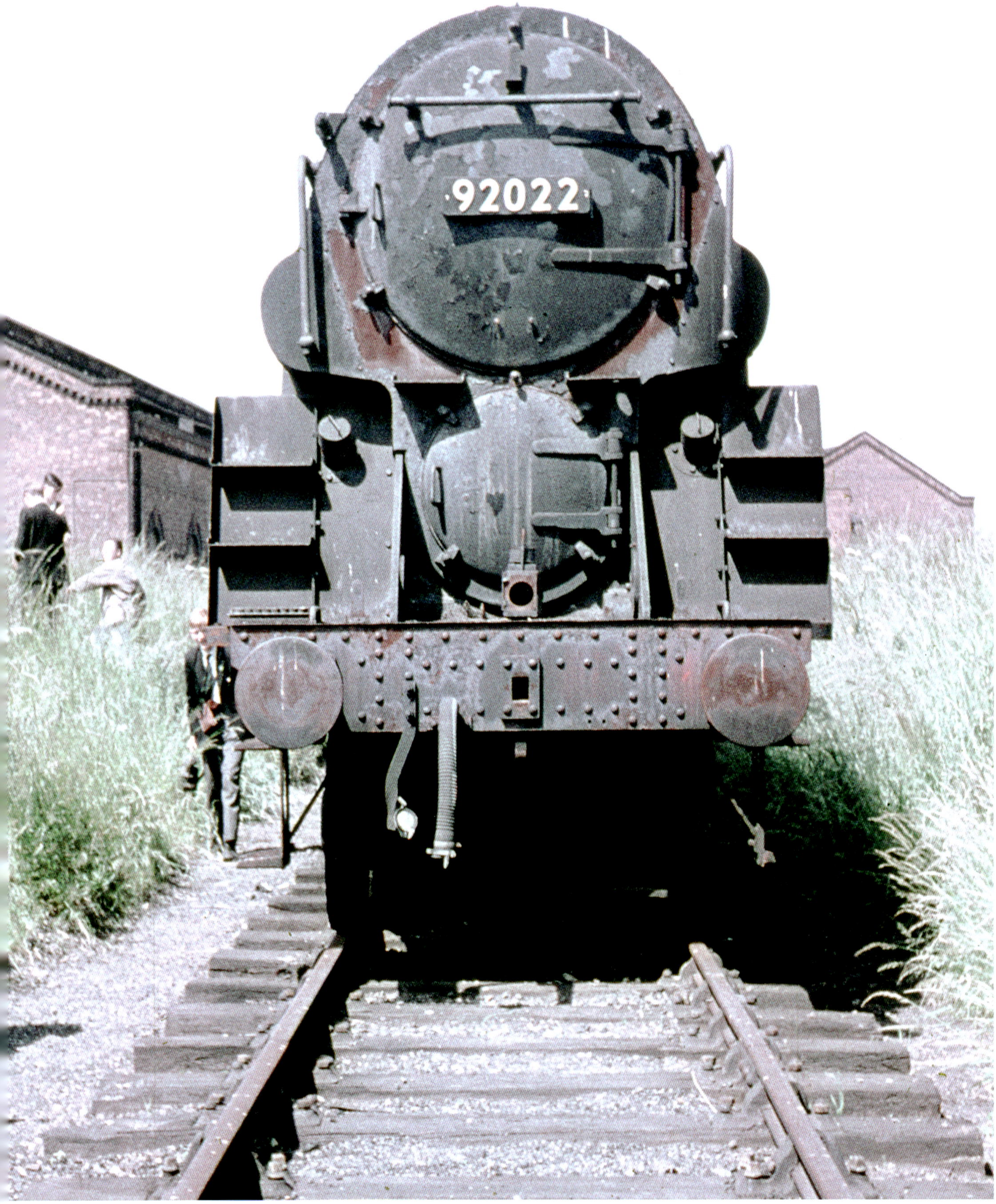

Looking more like a Barry Scrapyard wreck at Wellingborough on 18 June 1961 was Crosti 9F 92022 in store awaiting rebuild back to a conventional locomotive which would happen the following year, to prolong the life of the former 9F as an 8F until November 1967. ***Late Vincent Heckford/Strathwood Library Collection***

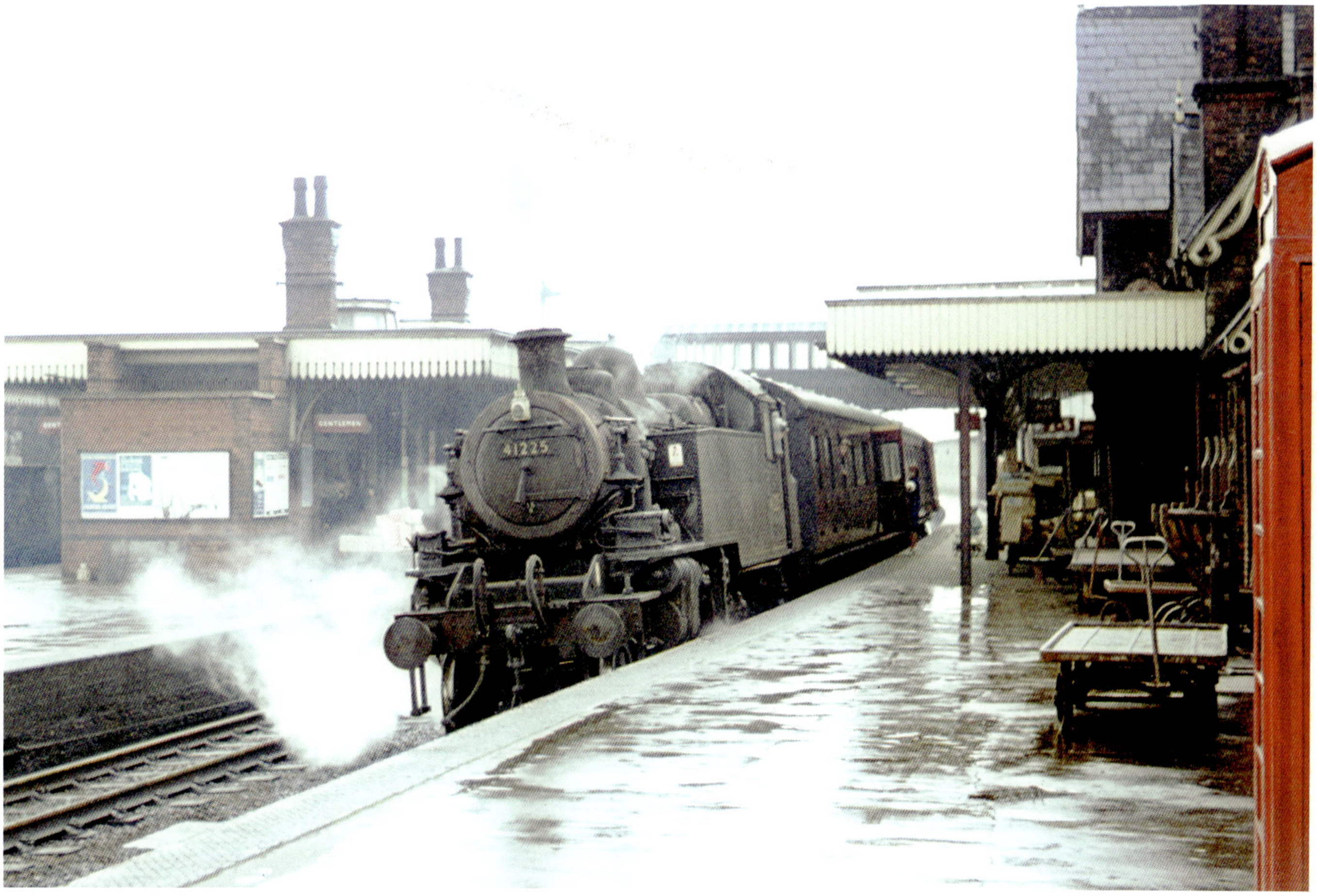

Waiting in the rain with a Northampton service at Wellingborough during 1964 was Ivatt 2MT 41225 which was push and pull fitted. ***Strathwood Library Collection***

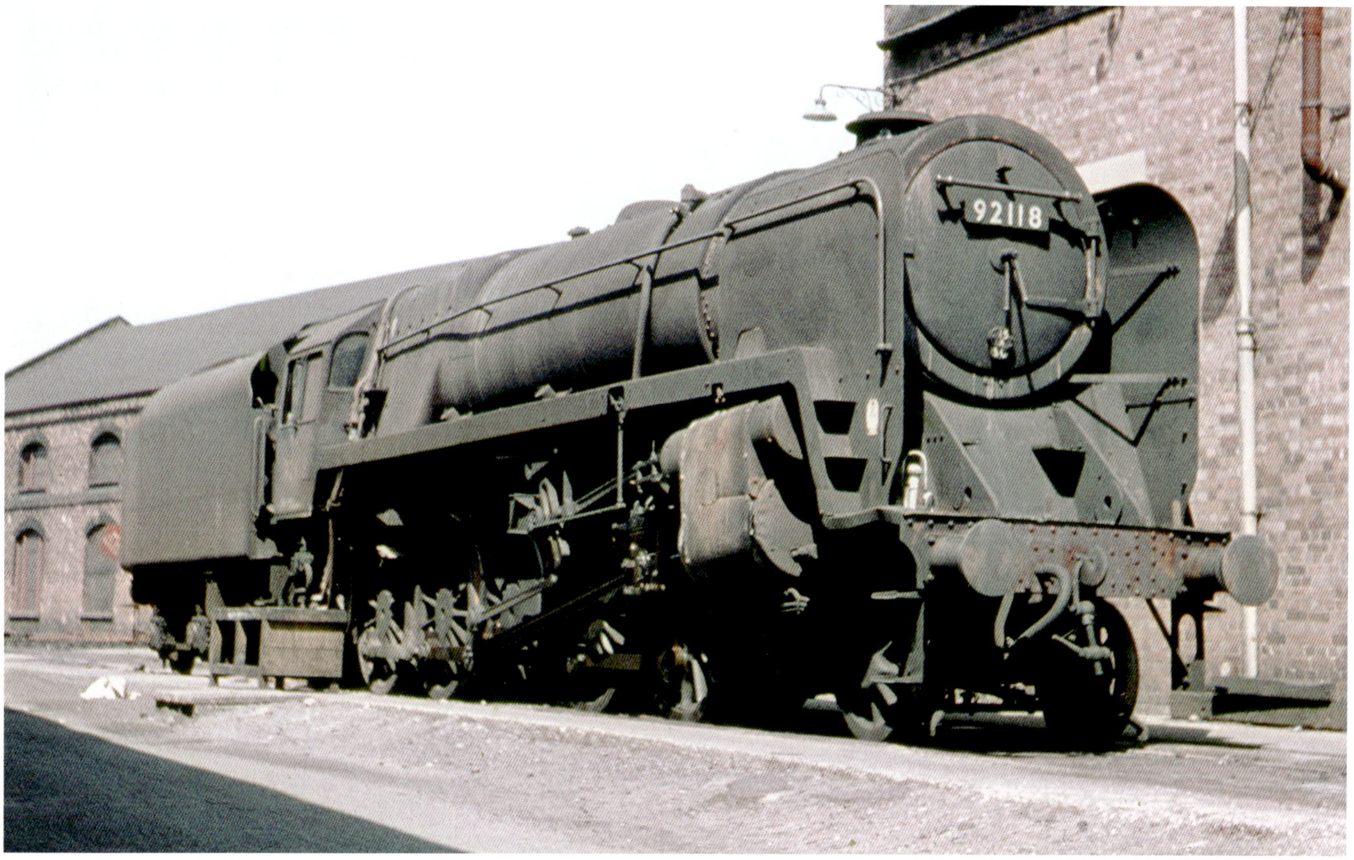

Standing with its original BR1C tender on shed at Wellingborough on 18 June 1961 was 92118, as with a number of other 9Fs it was to change tenders during the mid sixties as locomotives were being patched up to keep them going without visiting works. ***Late Vincent Heckford/Strathwood Library Collection***

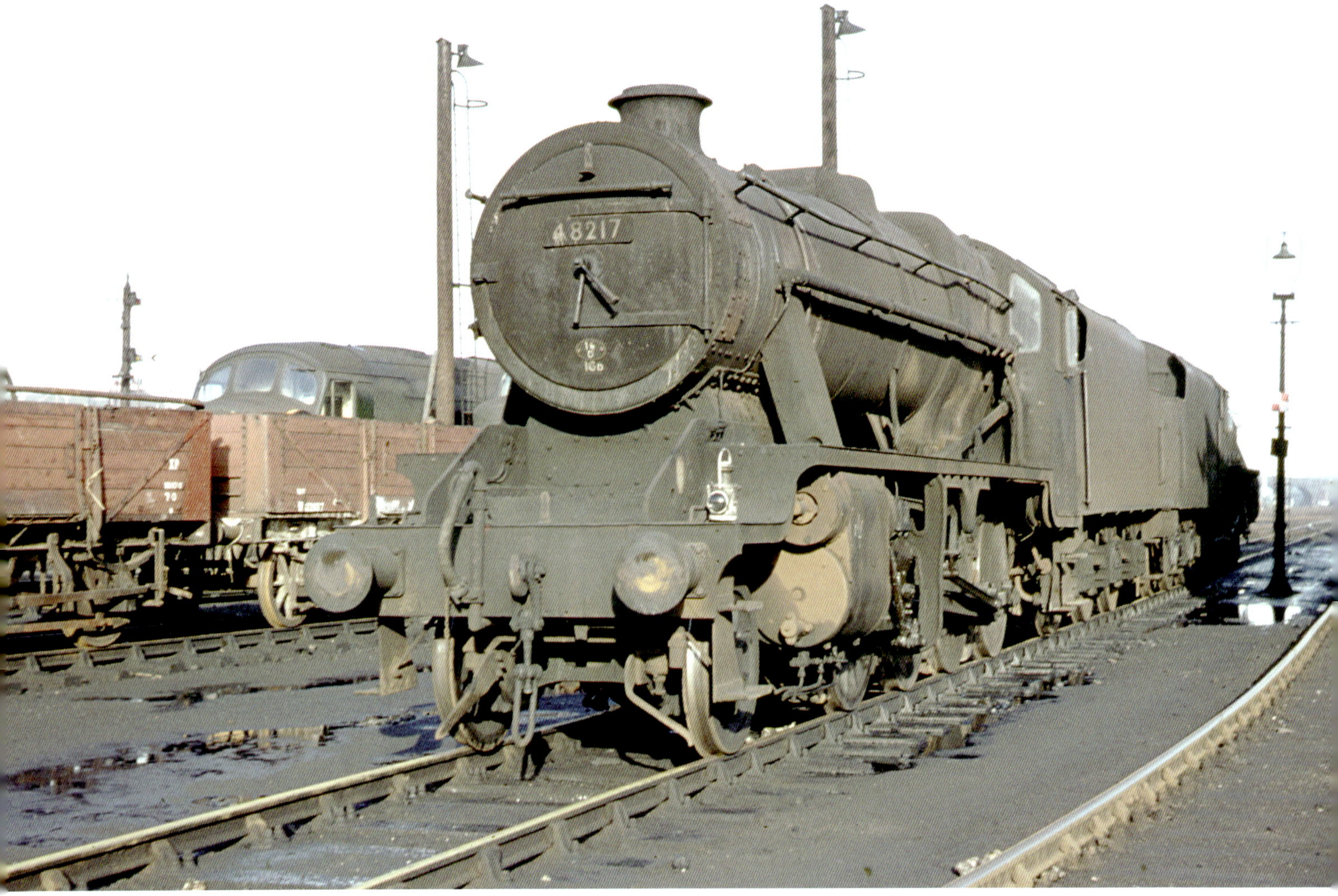

A pair of Peaks can be picked out joining Stanier 8F 48217 on shed at Wellingborough on 17 January 1965. Adding further to the tragedy of the Titanic story that month, Frederick Fleet now aged seventy six, who was a survivor from the White Star sticken liner, who had said at the earlier Inquiry, he could have saved the disaster was found dead, hanged, at his home in Southampton. On April 14, 1912, Mr. Fleet was the night crow's nest lookout on the Titanic and spotted the iceberg which sank her on her maiden voyage. ***Strathwood Library Collection***

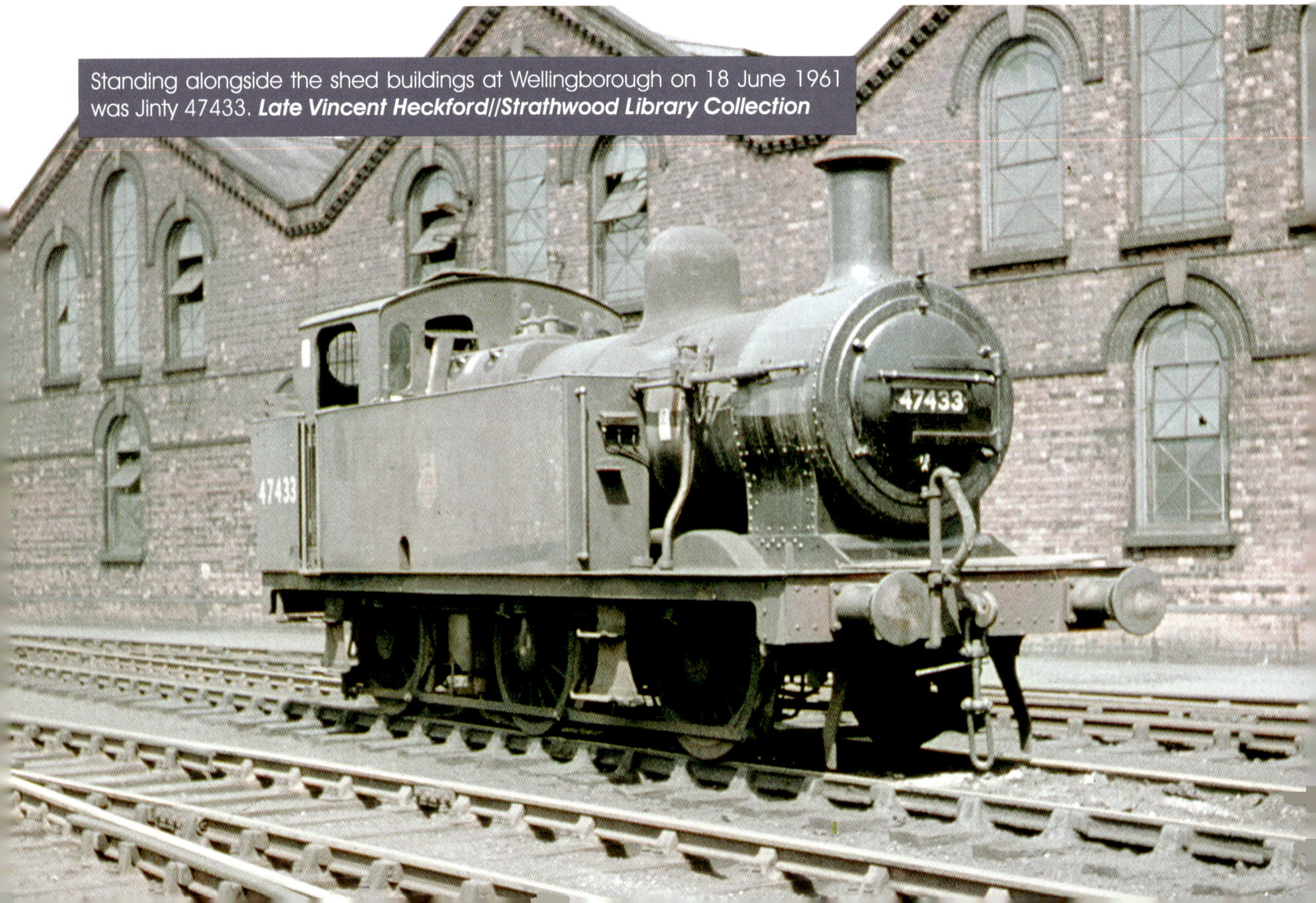

Standing alongside the shed buildings at Wellingborough on 18 June 1961 was Jinty 47433. ***Late Vincent Heckford//Strathwood Library Collection***

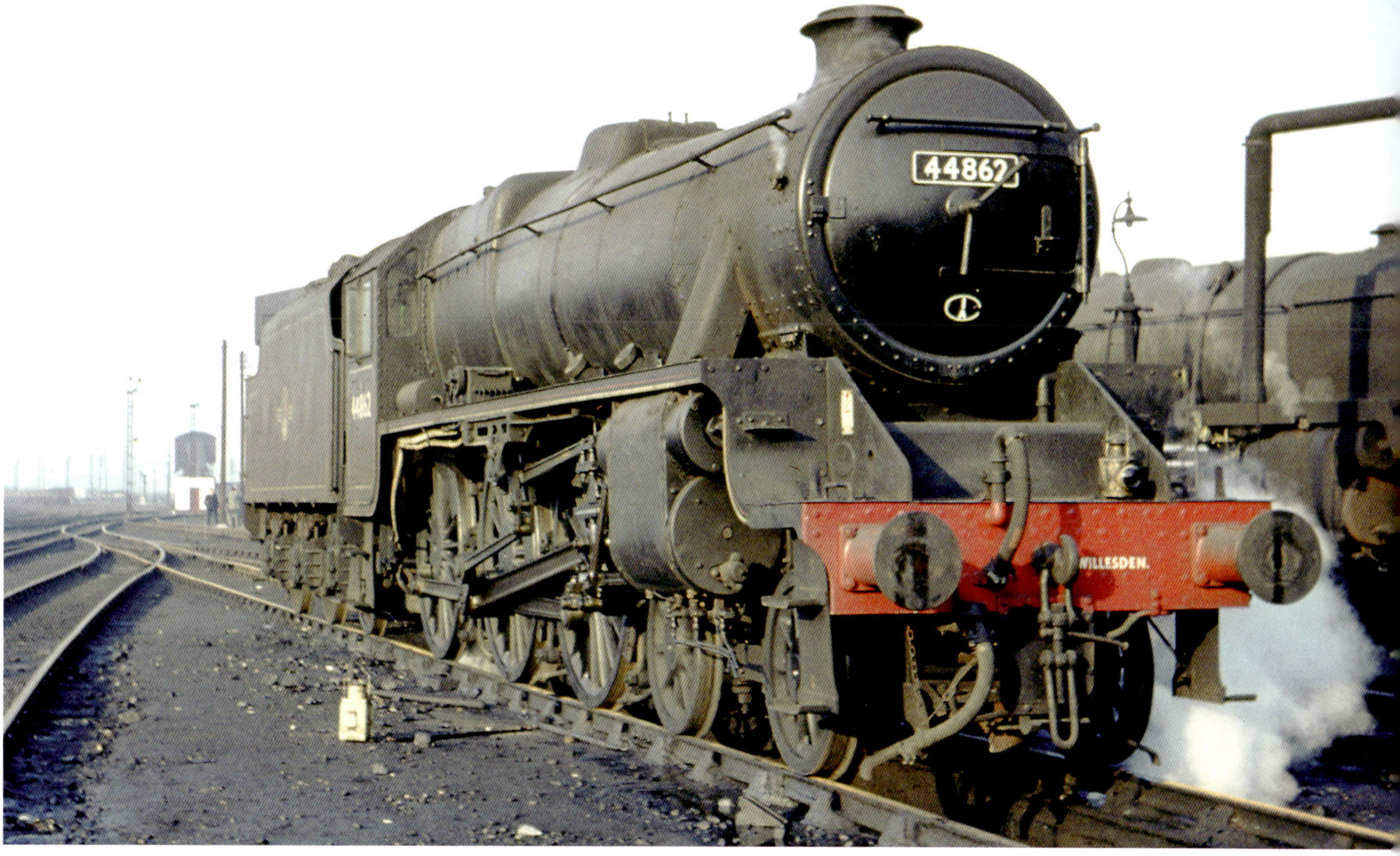

Taken in the sunshine of 7 March 1965 at Wellingborough was Stanier Black Five 44862, whilst The Seekers were to be beat Tom Jones to number one for two weeks with their hit I'll Never Find Another You. ***Winston Cole***

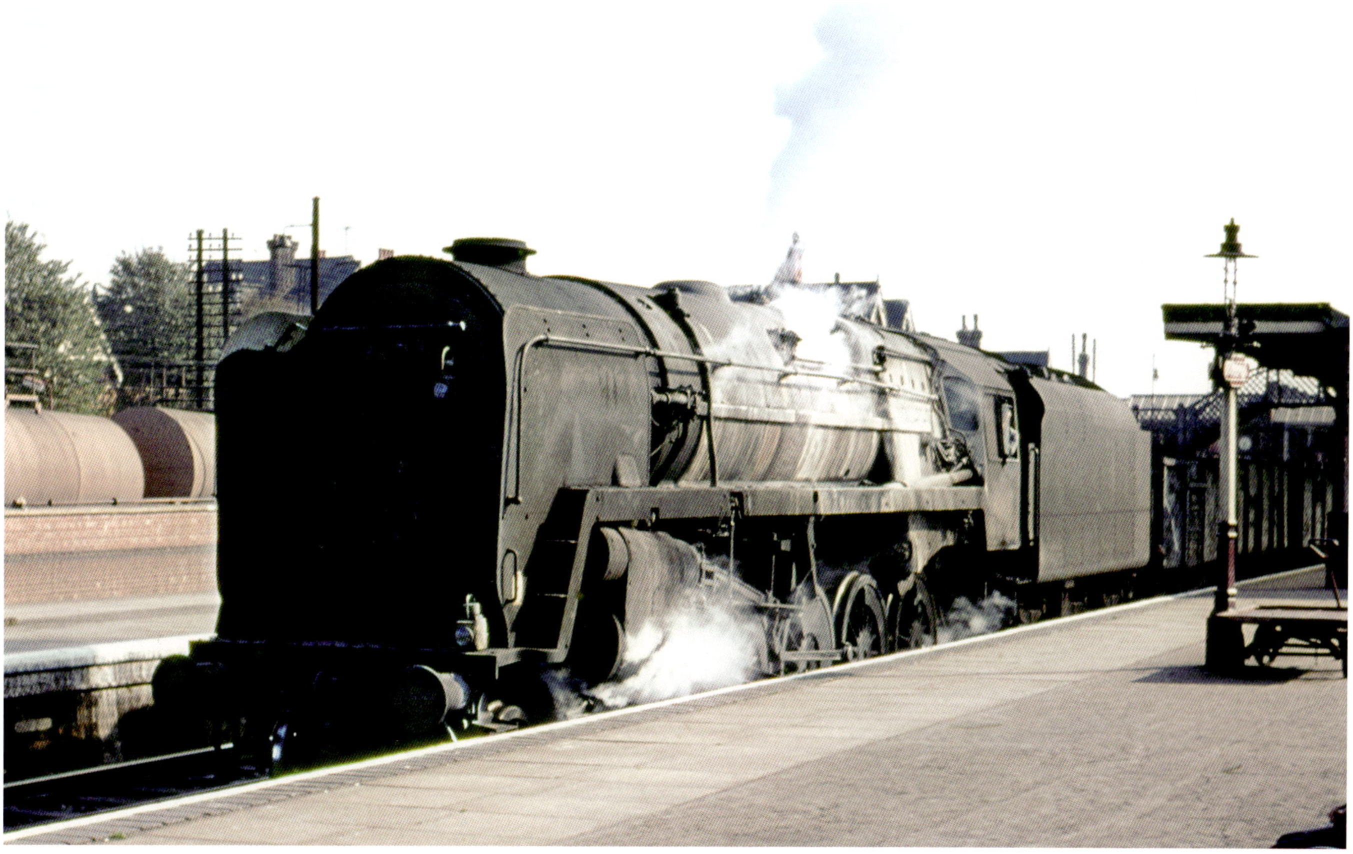

Yet more terrible limescale staining to be witnessed along the boiler casing of Riddles 9F 92113 rumbling through Bedford with a down goods on 3 October 1964. This was the year that the BBC first brought us the adventures of Terry Collier and Bob Ferris in The Likely lads. ***Strathwood Library Collection***

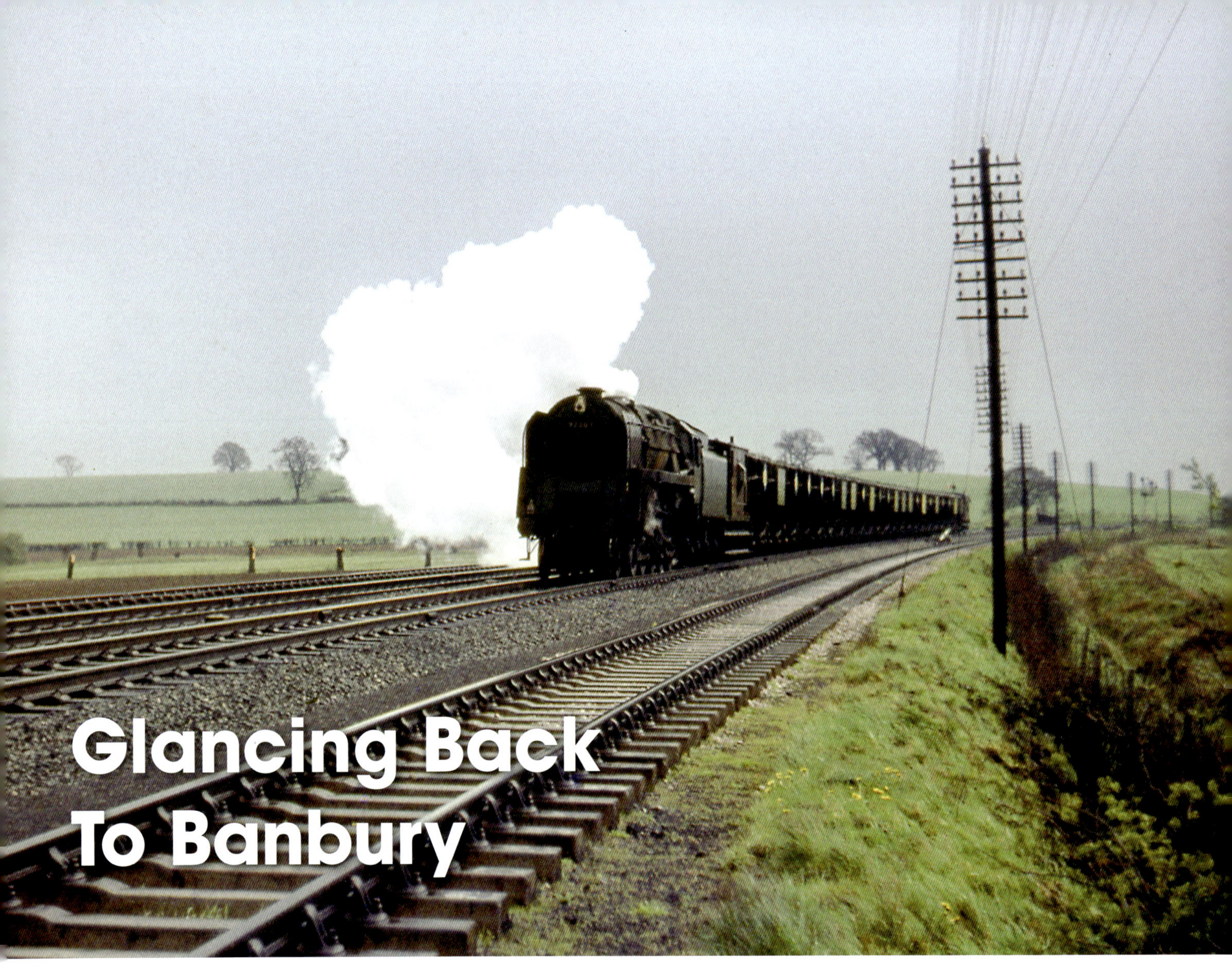
Glancing Back
To Banbury

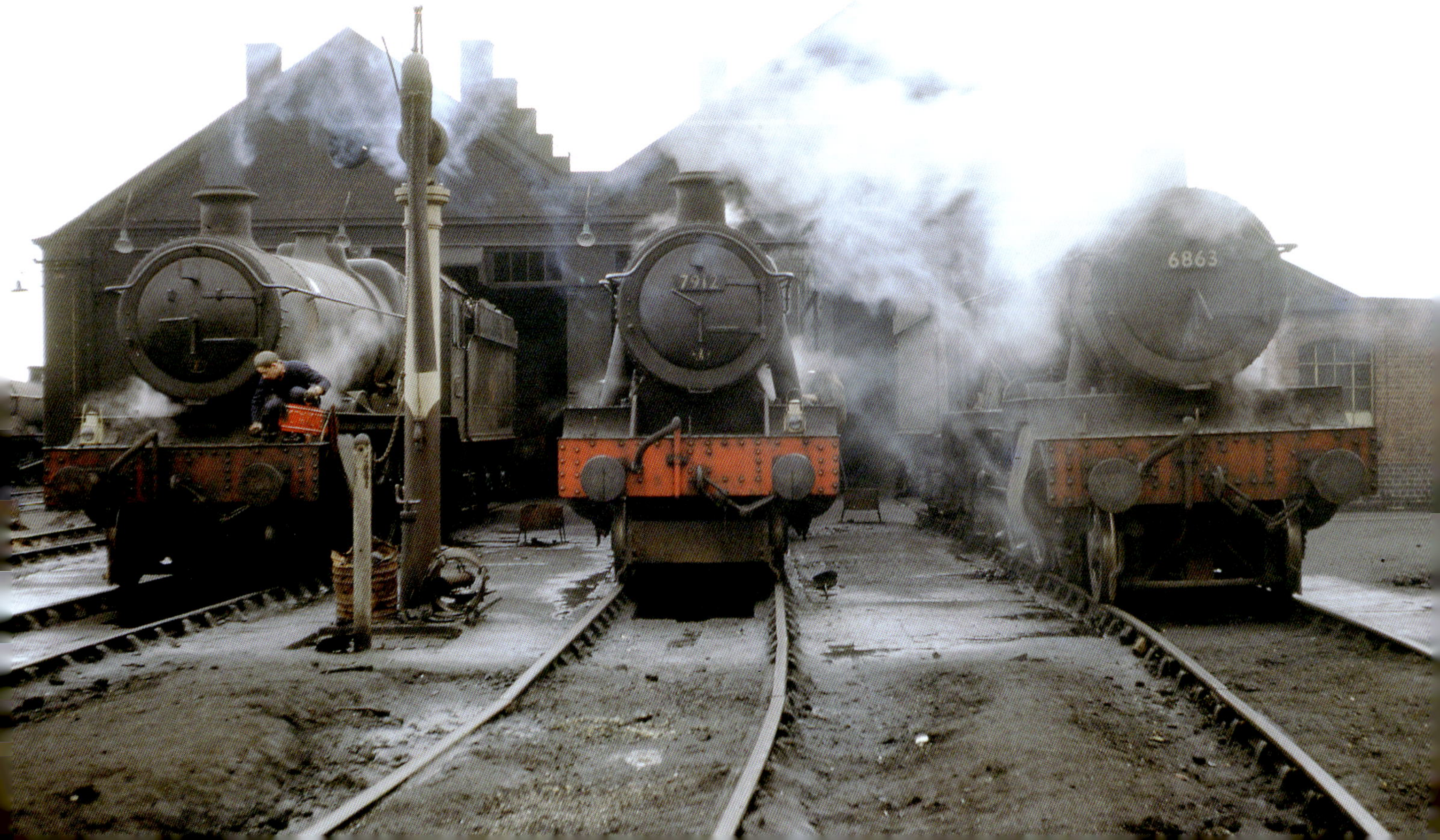
7912
6863

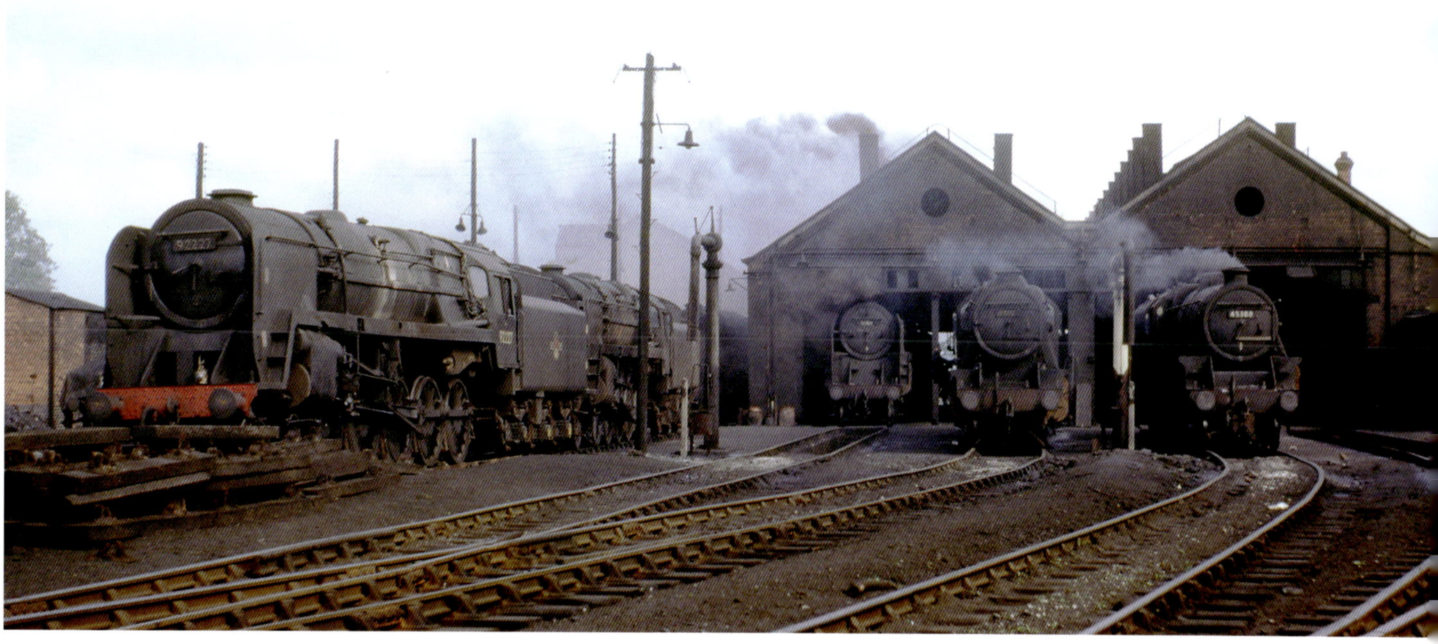

Opposite: Its a drizzly April day in 1965 and Riddles 9F 92203 is near Banbury. ***Strathwood Library Collection***

Opposite: A shed call in February 1964 provides a western trio 6951 Impney Hall, 7912 Little Linford Hall along with 6863 Dolywel Grange. ***Strathwood Library Collection***

The Western Region's influence had gone by 14 May 1966. ***Strathwood Library Collection***

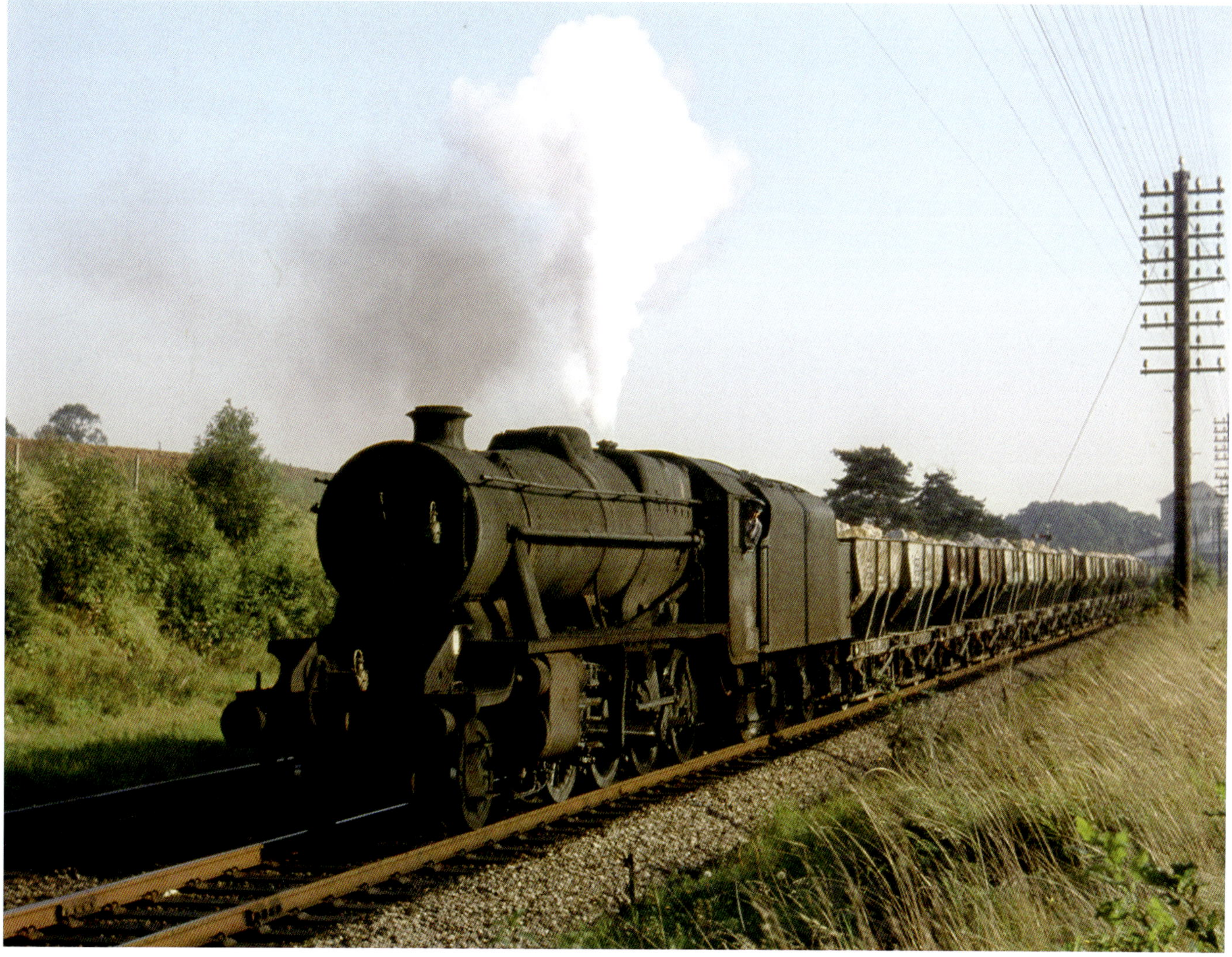

An ore working is hauled by Stanier 8F 48347 near Banbury during September 1965. ***Strathwood Library Collection***

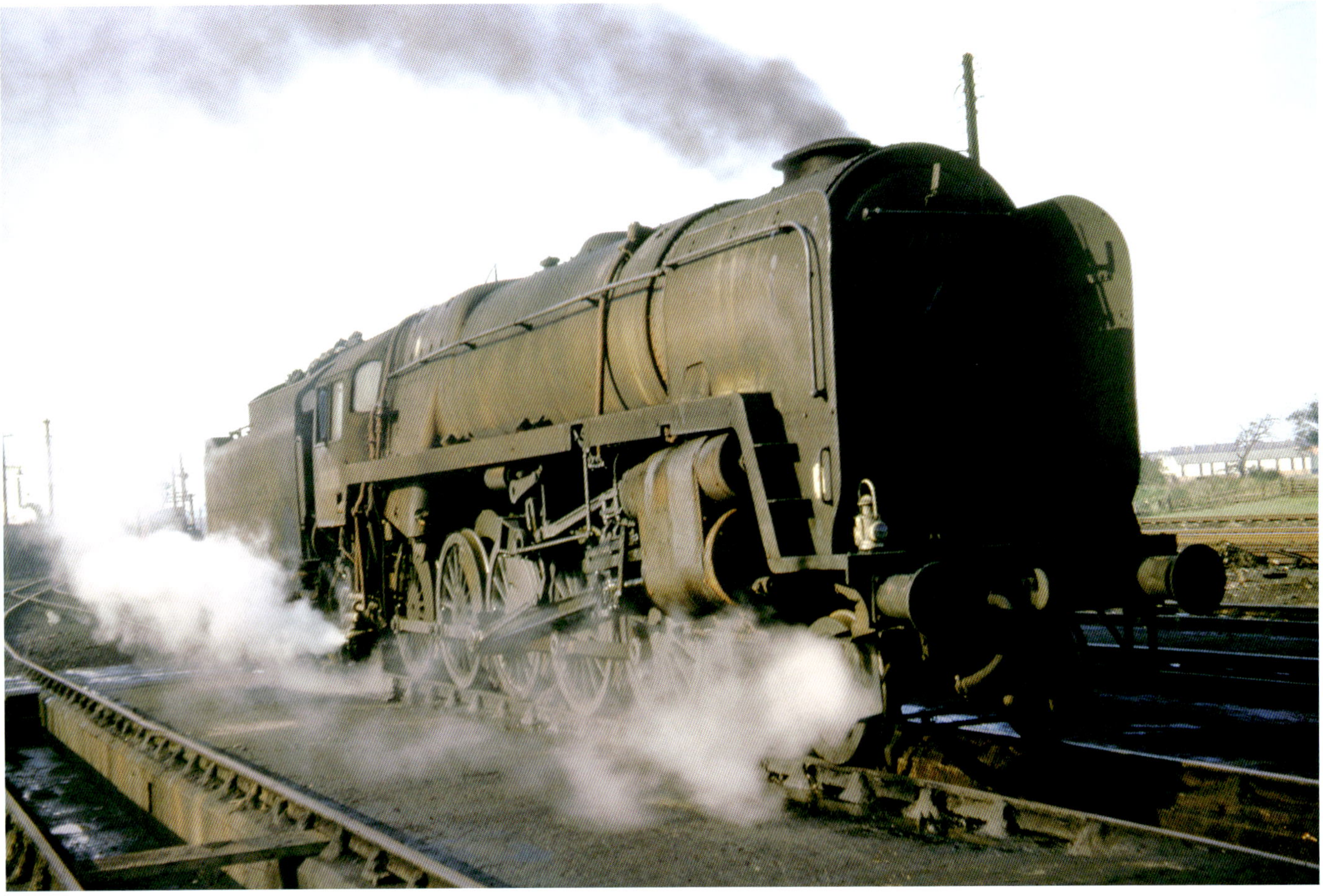

Not really looking like a Black Prince pottering around in Banbury's shed yard on 9 October 1965 was Riddles 9F 92203. ***Michael Beaton***

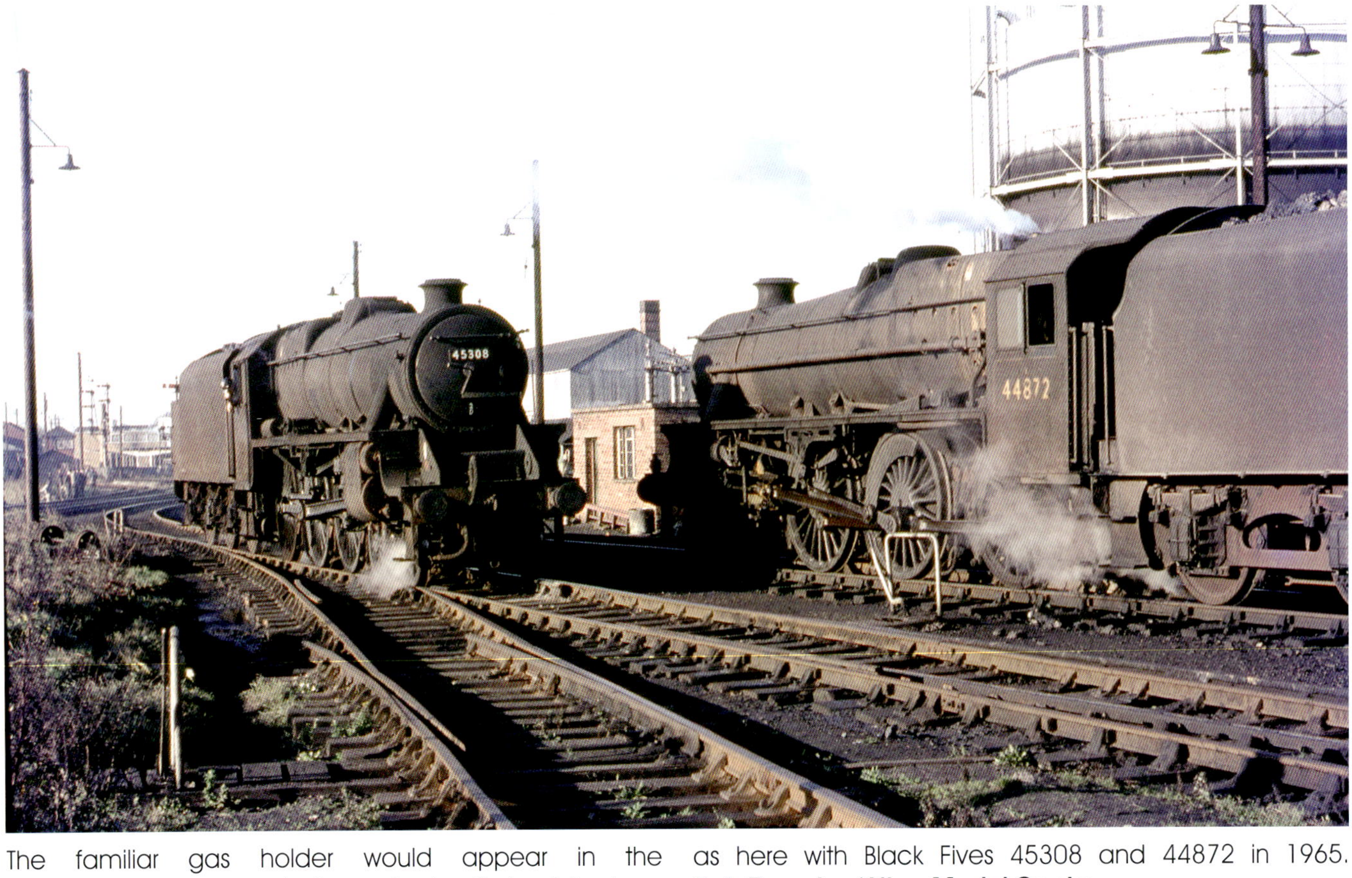

The familiar gas holder would appear in the background to many photographer's efforts at Banbury as here with Black Fives 45308 and 44872 in 1965. ***Bob Treacher/Alton Model Centre***

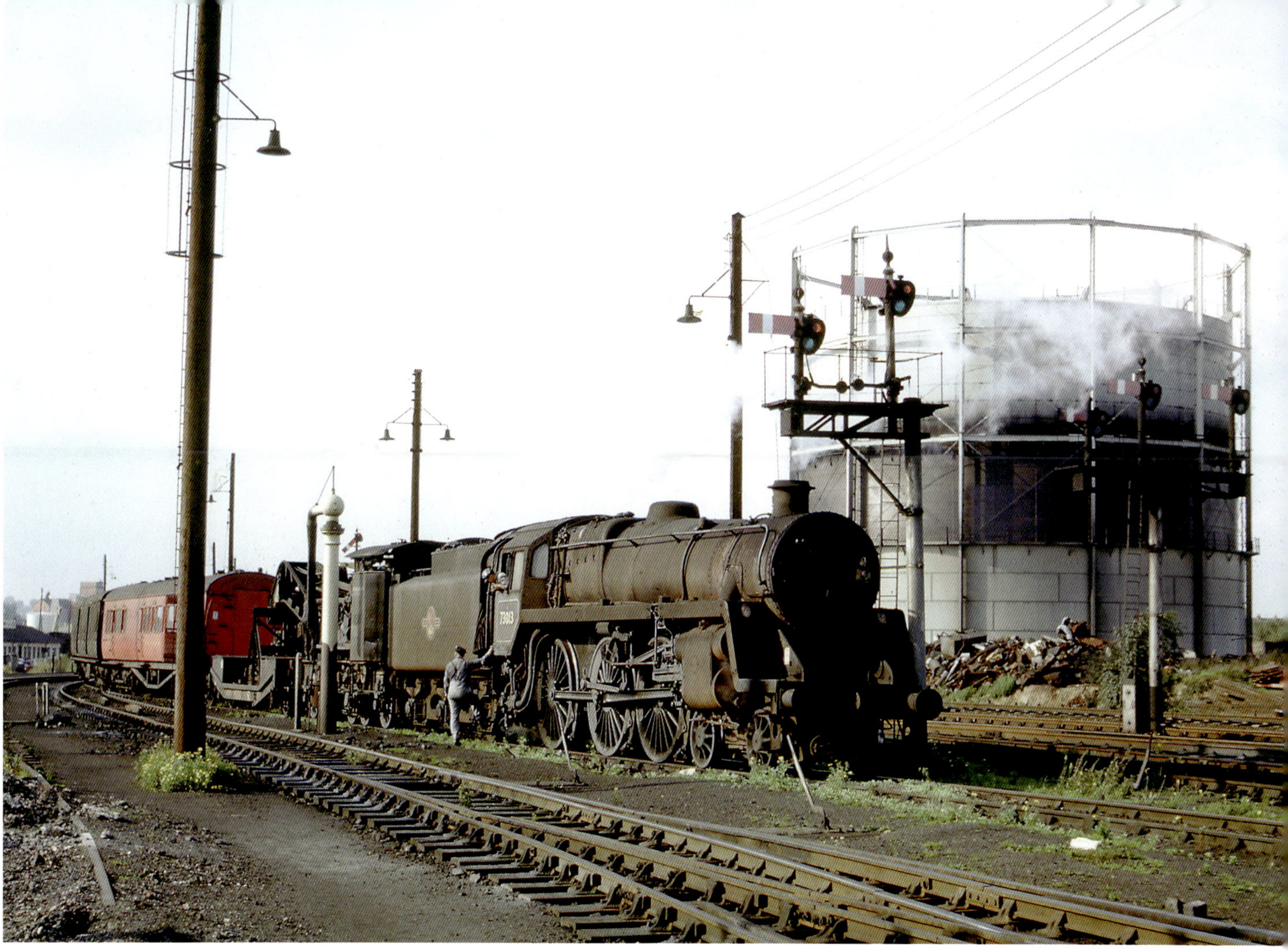

Looks like there may be trouble about in the area as Riddles 5MT 73013 sets about today preparing the Banbury breakdown train for the road once again in 1965. ***Strathwood Library Collection***

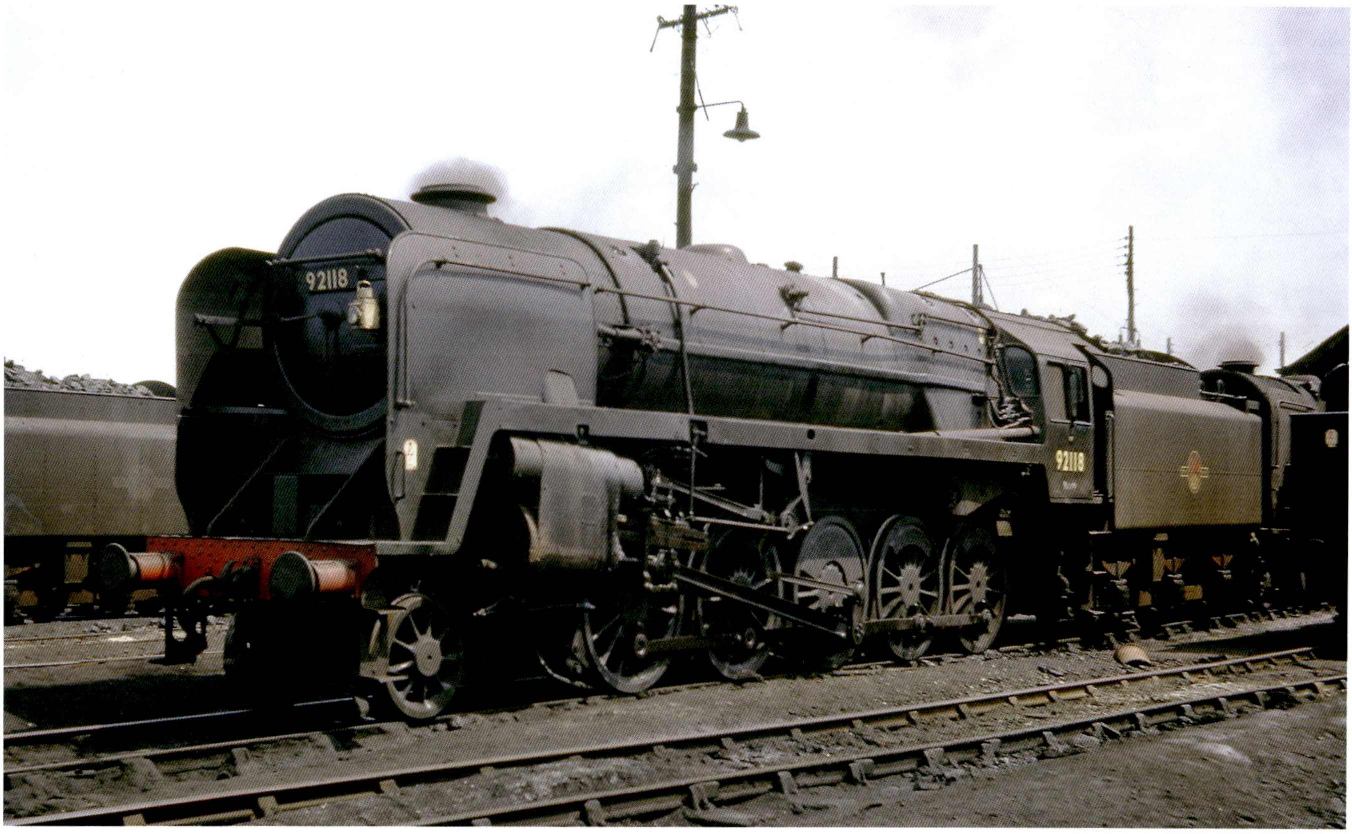

The rostering of Riddles 9Fs such as 92218 from Banbury on iron ore workings from the Oxfordshire Ironstone fields attracted a number of cameramen to the area as here on 23 July 1966. It was Quarter-Finals day in the World Cup and England beat Argentina 1-0 thanks to a Geoff Hurst goal in the seventy eighth minute. ***Michael Beaton***

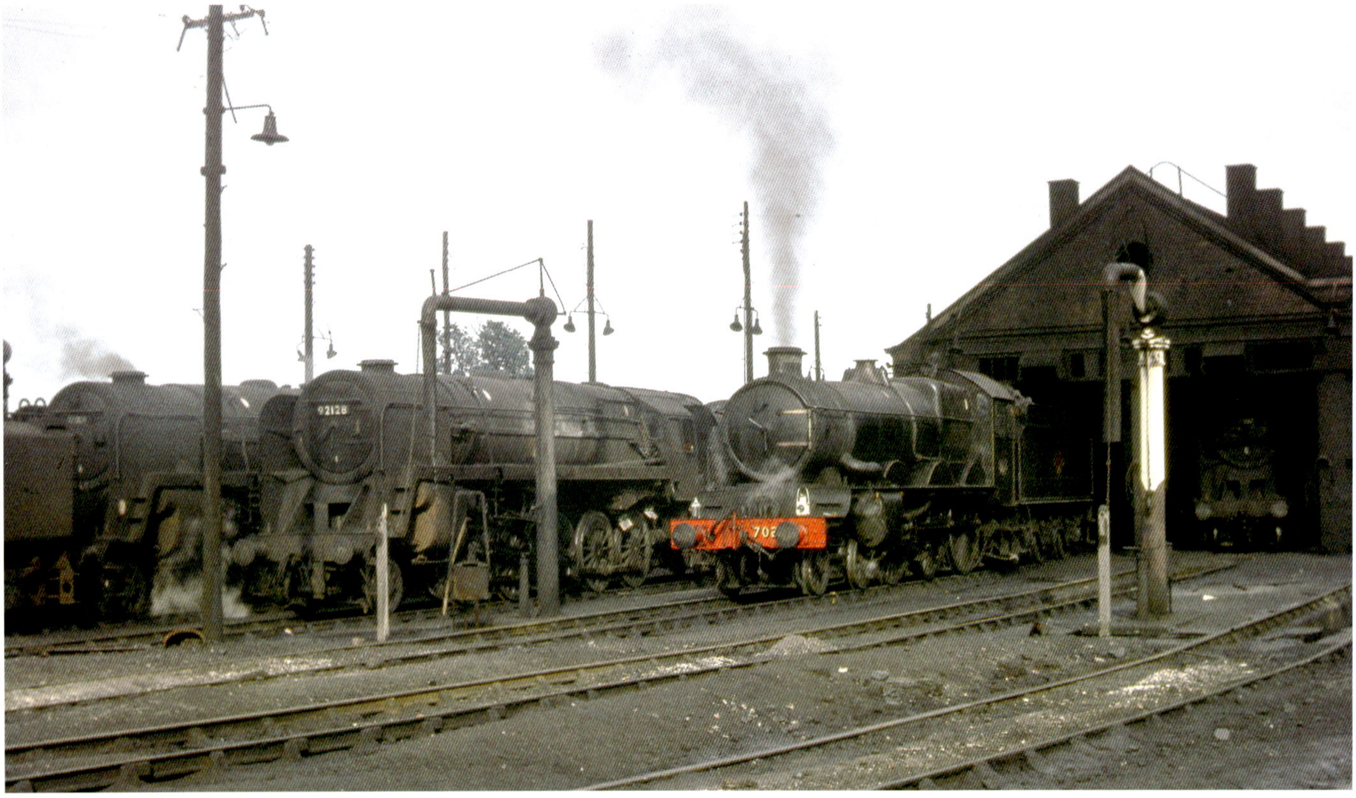

That Western Region flavour was restored again in June 1966 when a slightly workaday 7029 Clun Castle dropped in for servicing at Banbury. Aside from her use on specials at the time she was also sent out on a number of goods workings to keep her fit and active, also no doubt to help pay for her keep. ***Strathwood Library Collection***

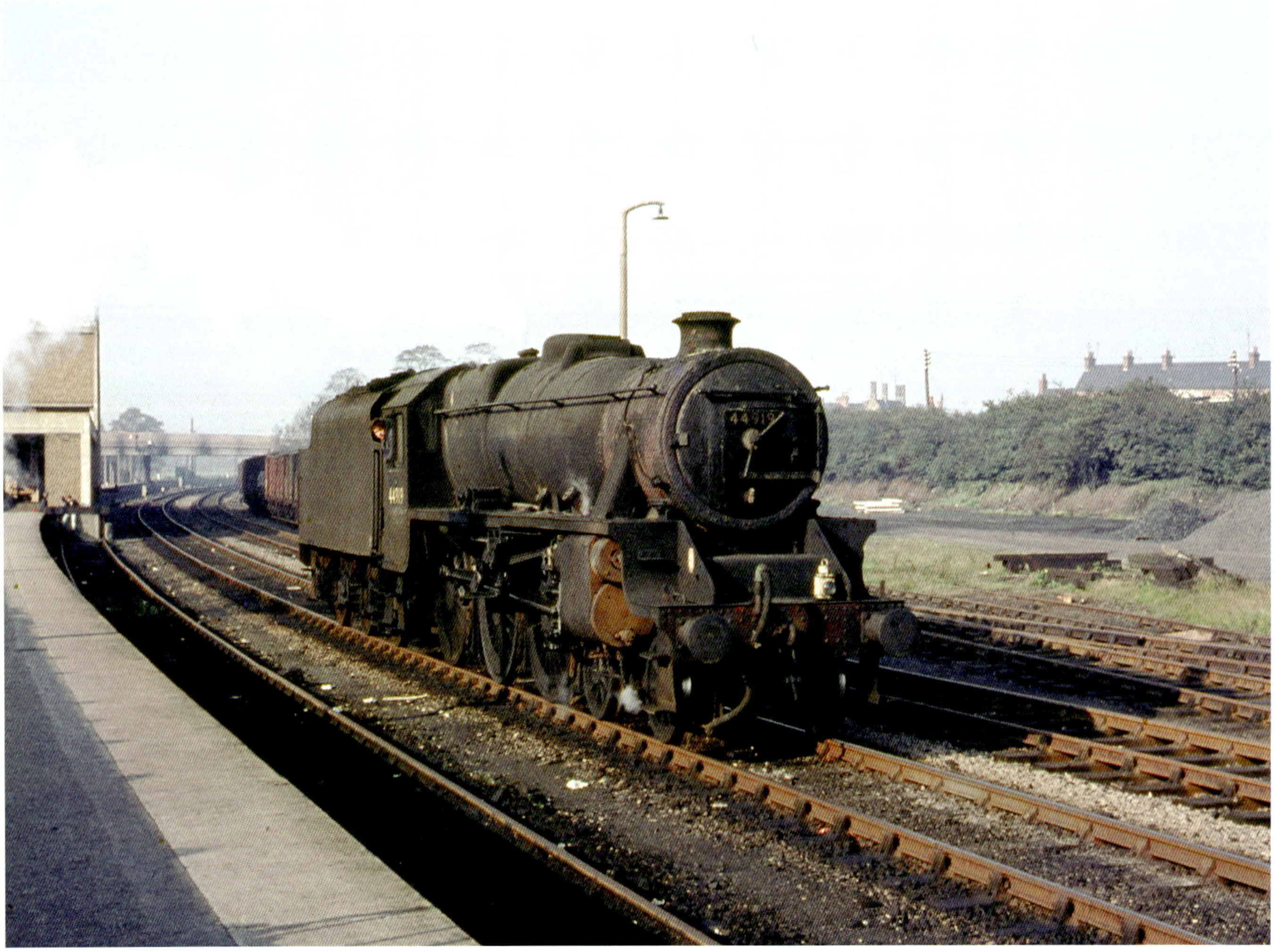

Speeding light engine through Banbury's modernised station in October 1965 was Black Five 44919 in between turns. ***Late Derek Whitnell/Strathwood Library Collection***

Up the Potters

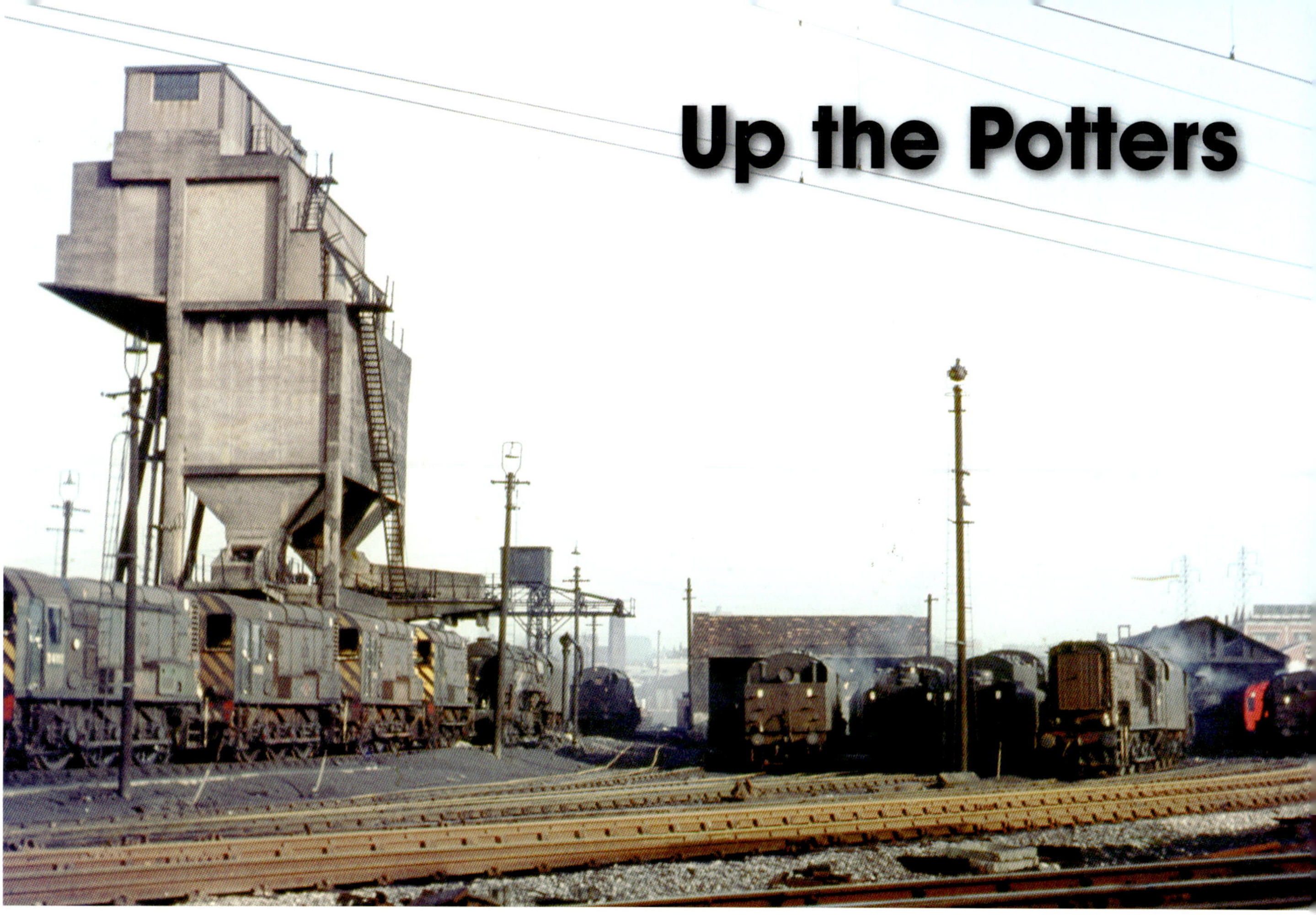

By 9 March 1967 diesel shunters had usurped Stoke's fleet of Jinties. The shed coded as 5D would close to steam a few months later on 7 August and completely in November when all servicing in the area transferred to the diesel depot at Cockshute. ***John Green***

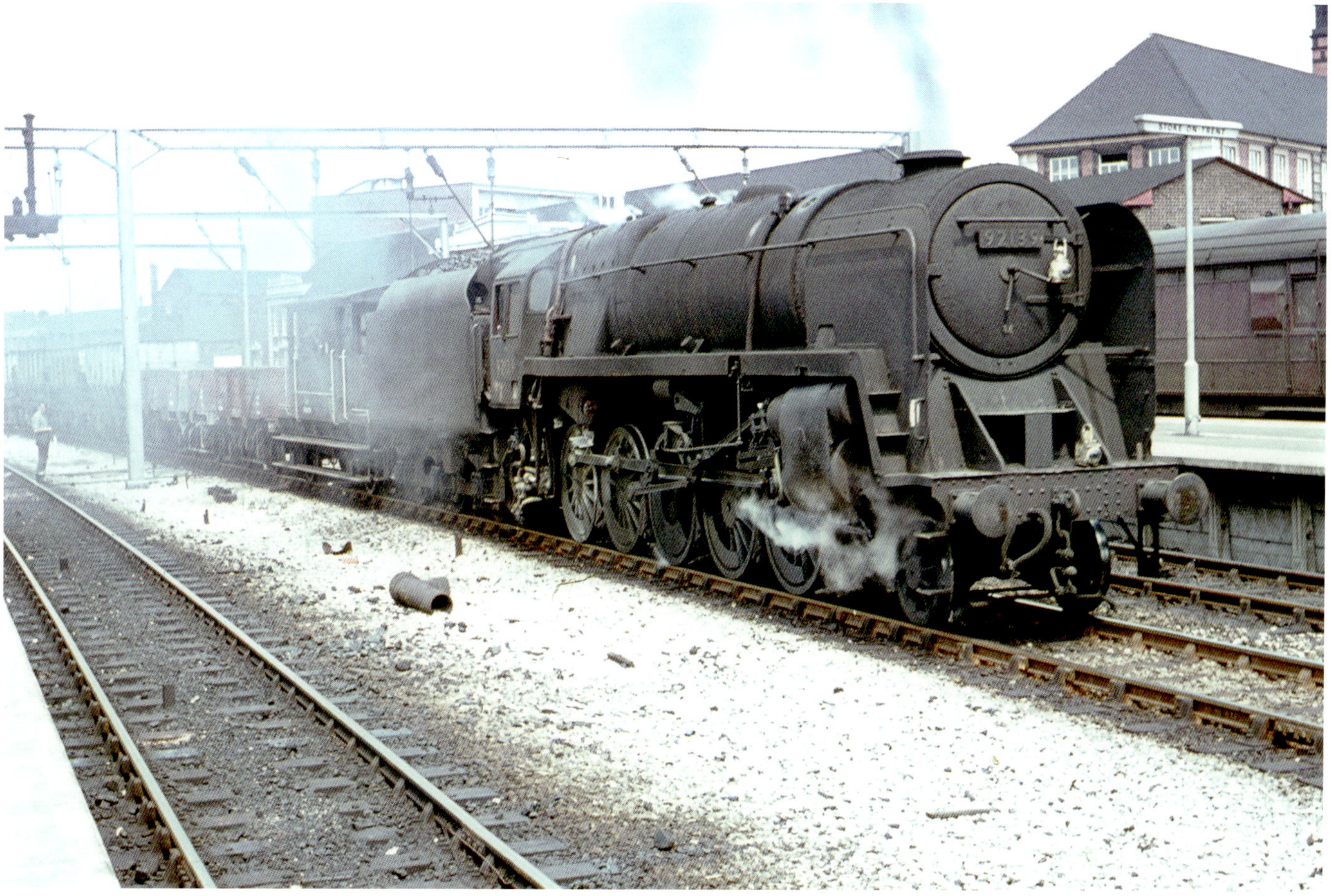

The wiring for the West Coast Main Line electrification including Stoke on Trent is in place in 1966 as Riddles 9F 92139 brings a permanent way train through the city in connection with planting all those gantries as the scheme heads southwards. ***Strathwood Library Collection***

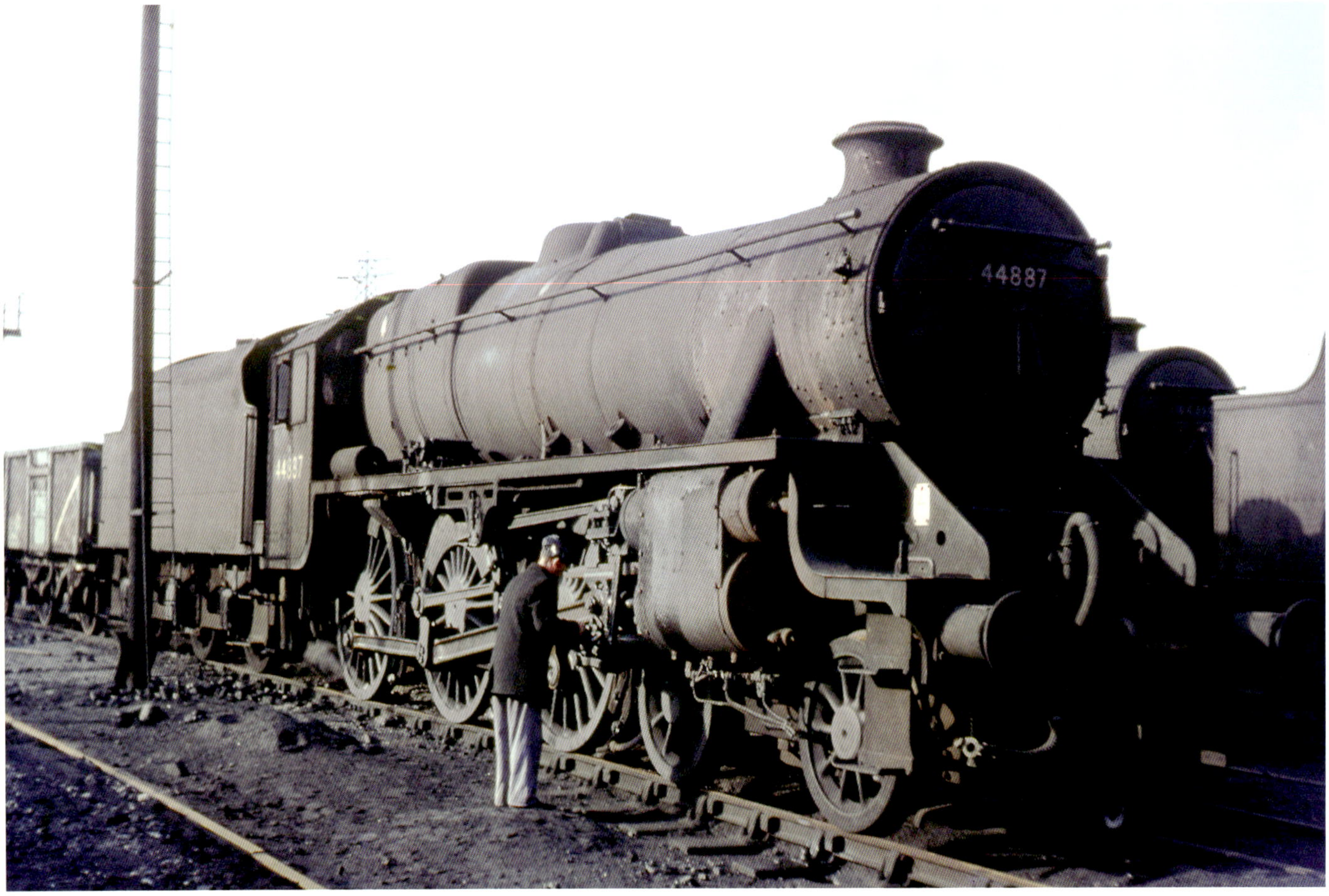

With his coat on against the cold on Sunday 19 March 1967 the driver of Black Five 44887 sets about oiling his steed for the day. Unfortunately an awful amount of oil was spilt this weekend as the huge tanker the Torrey Canyon grounded on the Seven Stones Reef between Lands End and the Islands. She was sailing for Milford Haven with 120,000 tons of Kuwaiti oil, this was the first major oil tanker disaster and sadly not the last. ***John Green***

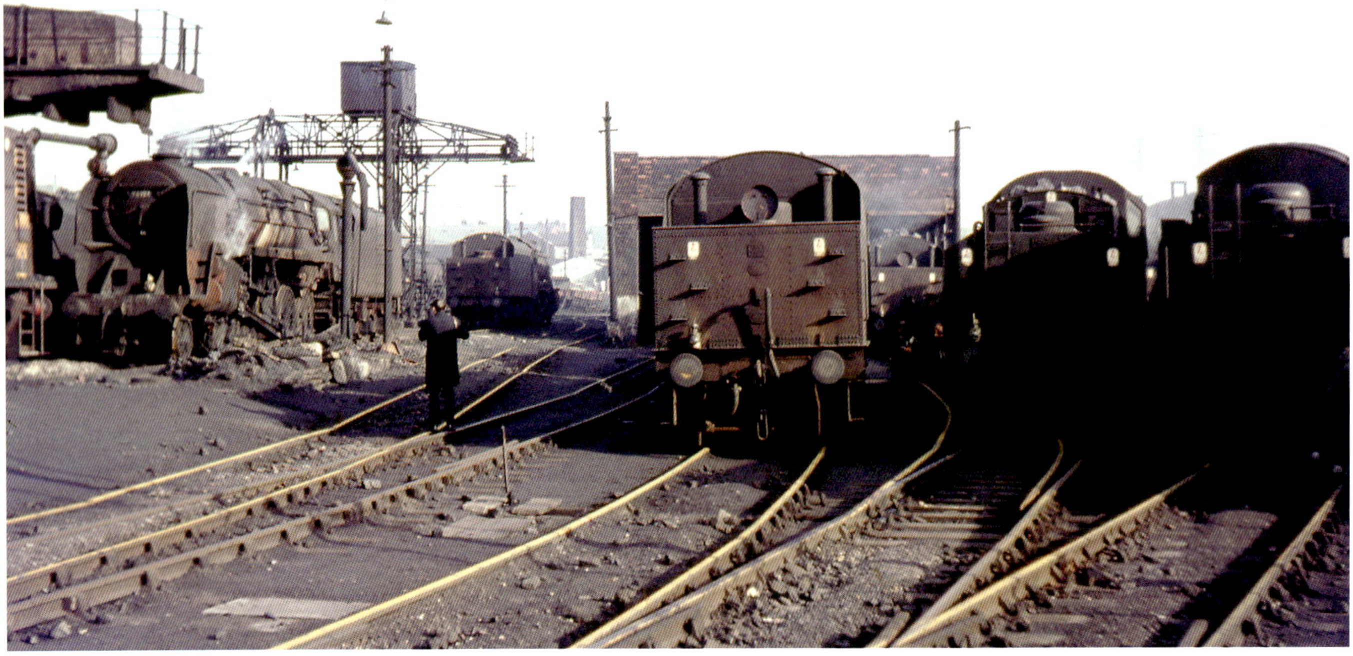

The cramped nature of the shed layout at Stoke seen the same day must have led to incidents involving locomotives colliding in the dark with an atmosphere clouded with smoke, steam and sometimes fog for good measure too. ***John Green***

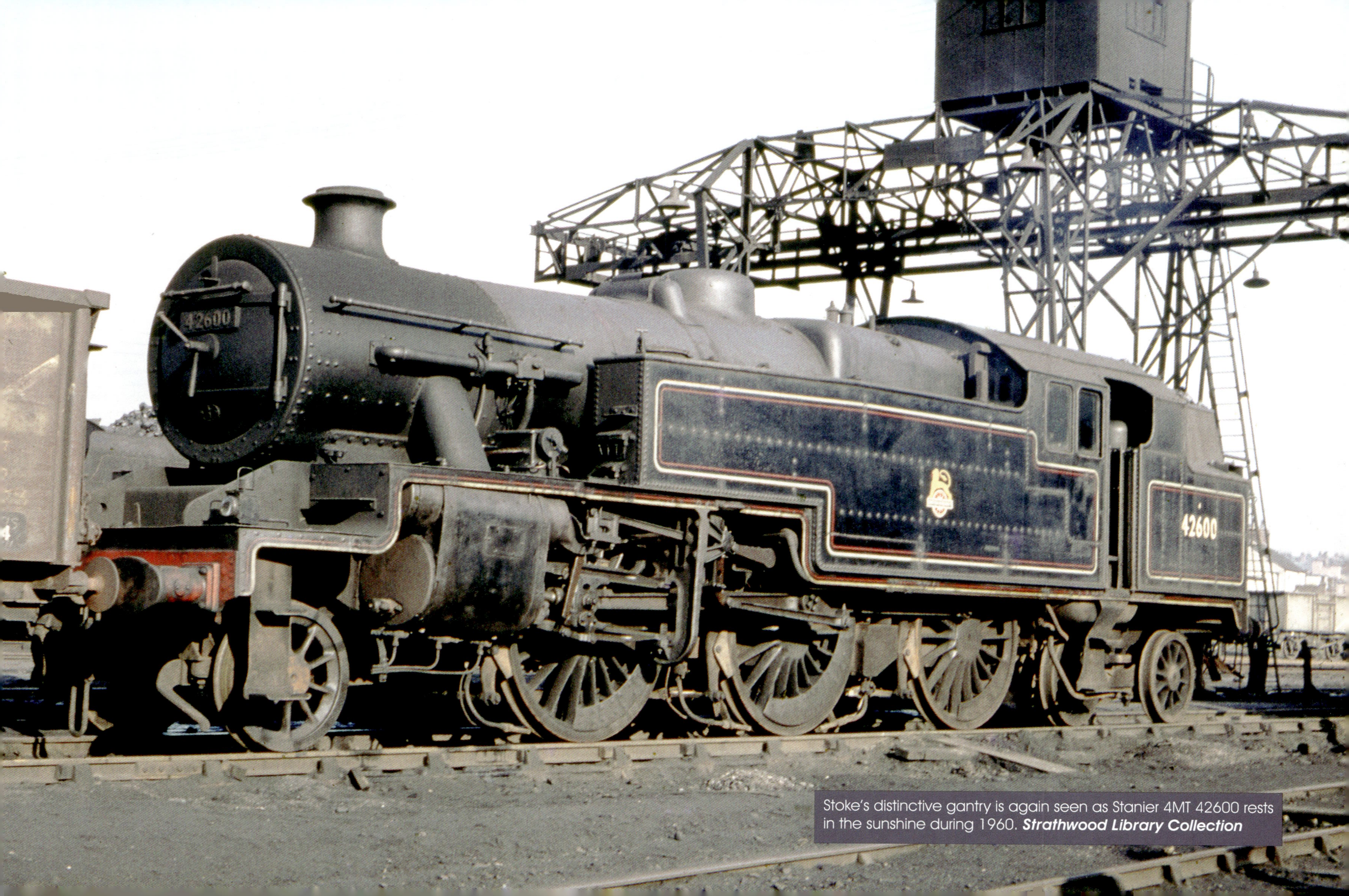

Stoke's distinctive gantry is again seen as Stanier 4MT 42600 rests in the sunshine during 1960. ***Strathwood Library Collection***

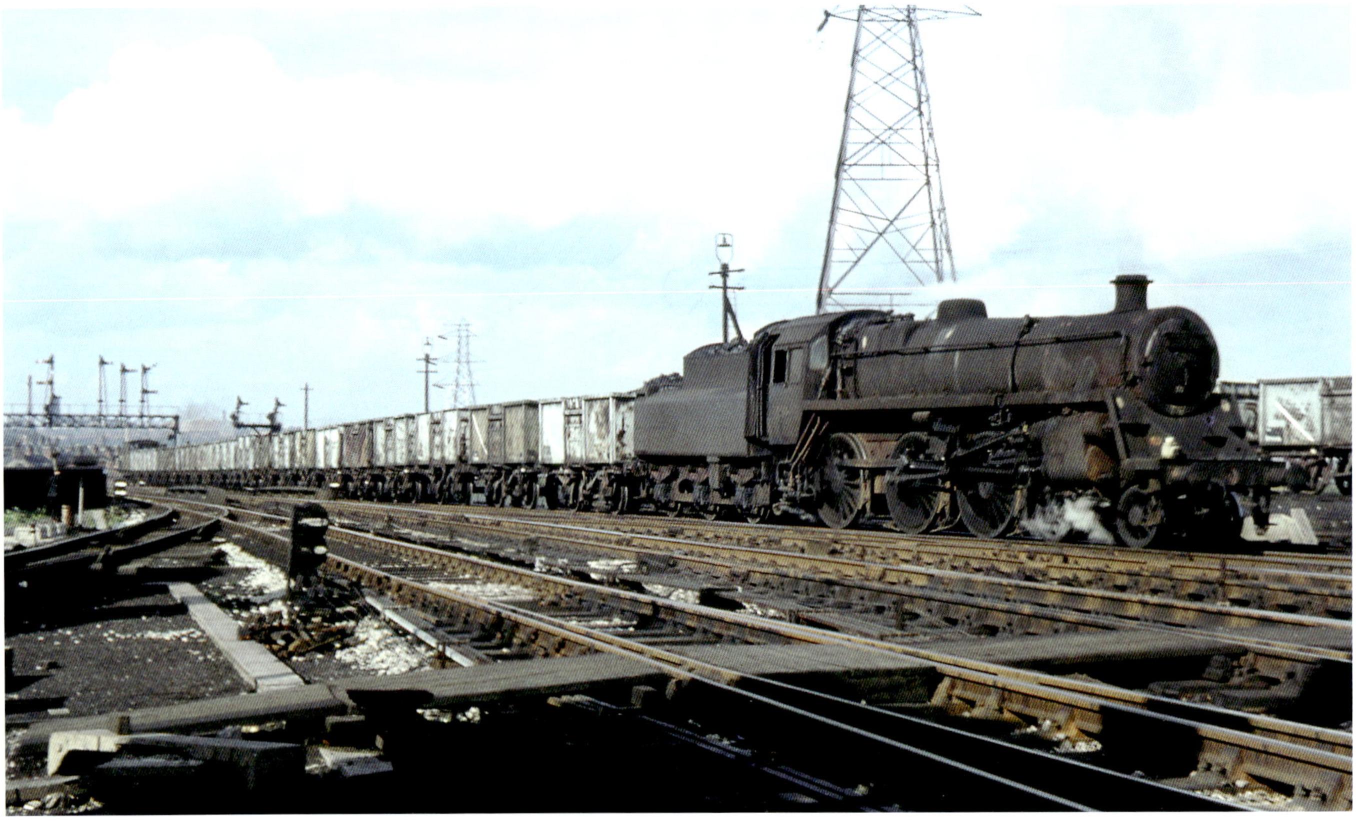

It is a gantry off the National Grid that overhangs Riddles 4MT 75040 bringing coal empties through Stoke in 1966. The six towns which collectively made up the City of Stoke on Trent also once enjoyed a rich coal mining heritage as well as the more obvious one of the potteries. On nationalisation of the coal industry in 1947, around 20,000 men worked in the many pits around Stoke on Trent. ***Winston Cole***

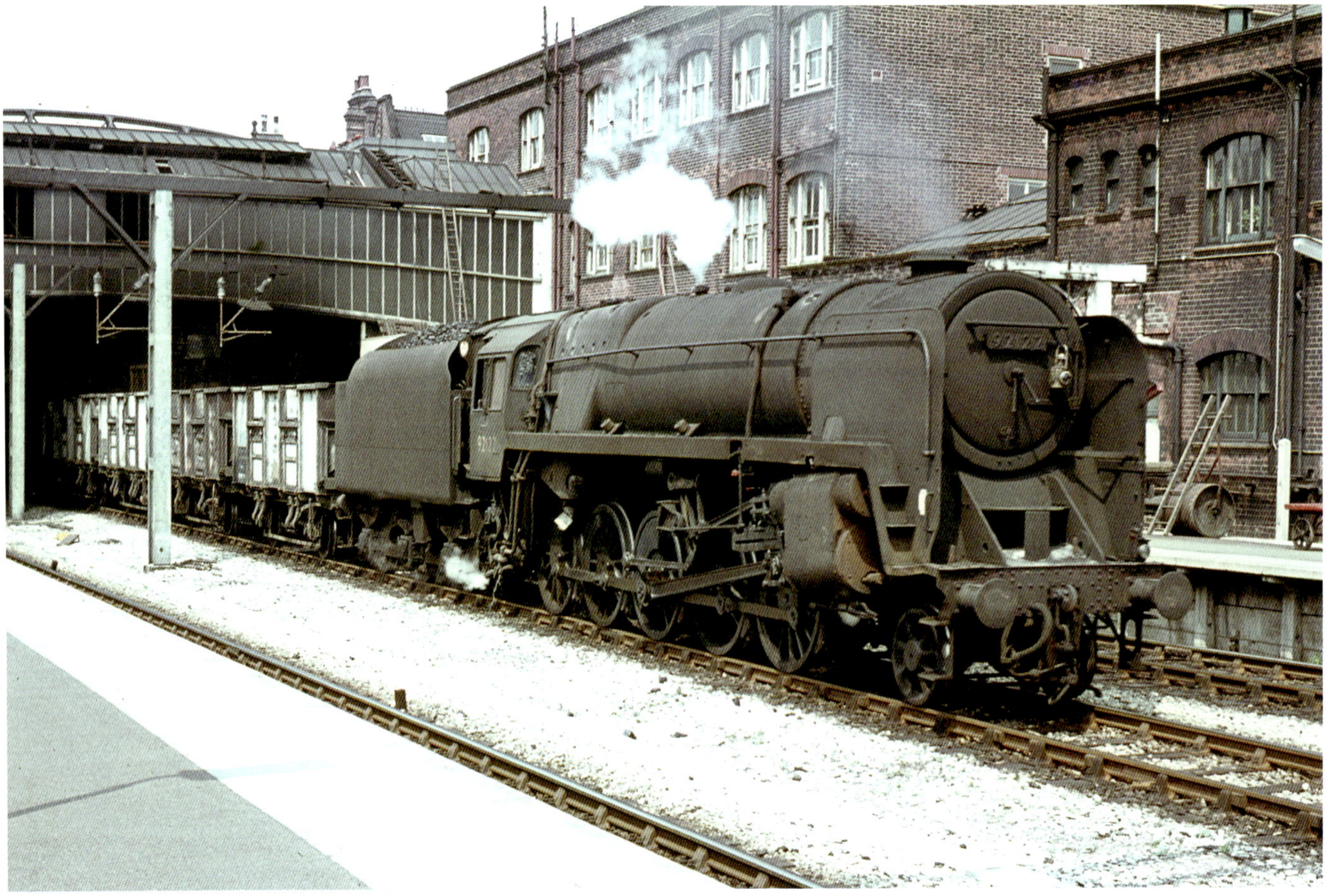

Another coal working for Riddles 9F 92122 bringing empties back through the city's station in 1966 for another load of coal from one of those many coal mines. ***Strathwood Library Collection***

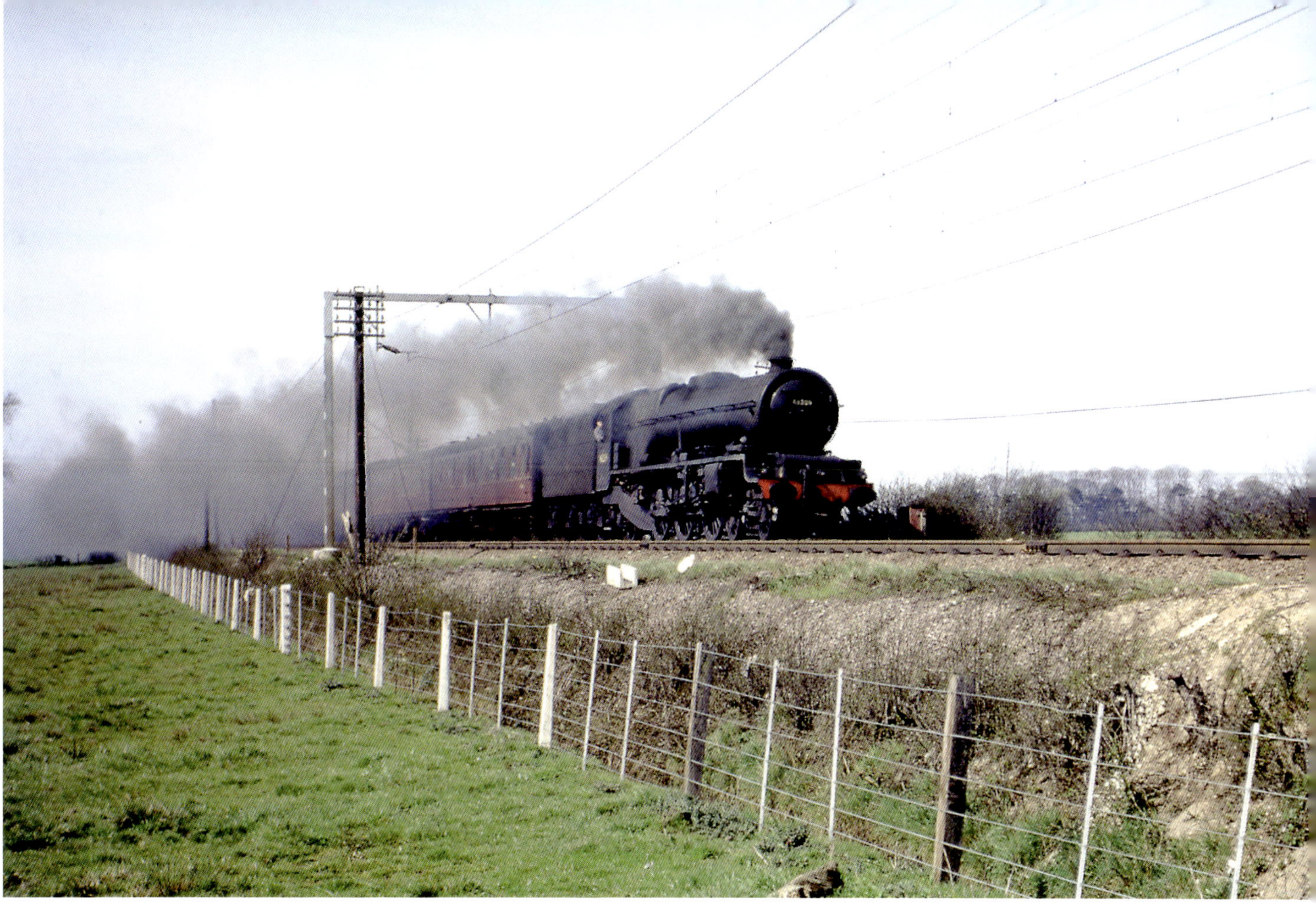

Staying in Staffordshire the electrification gantries were spreading southwards from Crewe in 1962 as Lizzie 46209 Princess Beatrice runs fast near Tamworth in what would be the last spring for the class on the West Coast Main Line, their duties falling to English Electric Type 4s any day now. Their bigger sisters would only manage another year before casualties would be taken again within the Coronations including 46230 Duchess of Buccleuch once more near Tamworth with a lengthy train the same day. ***Both; John Gill***

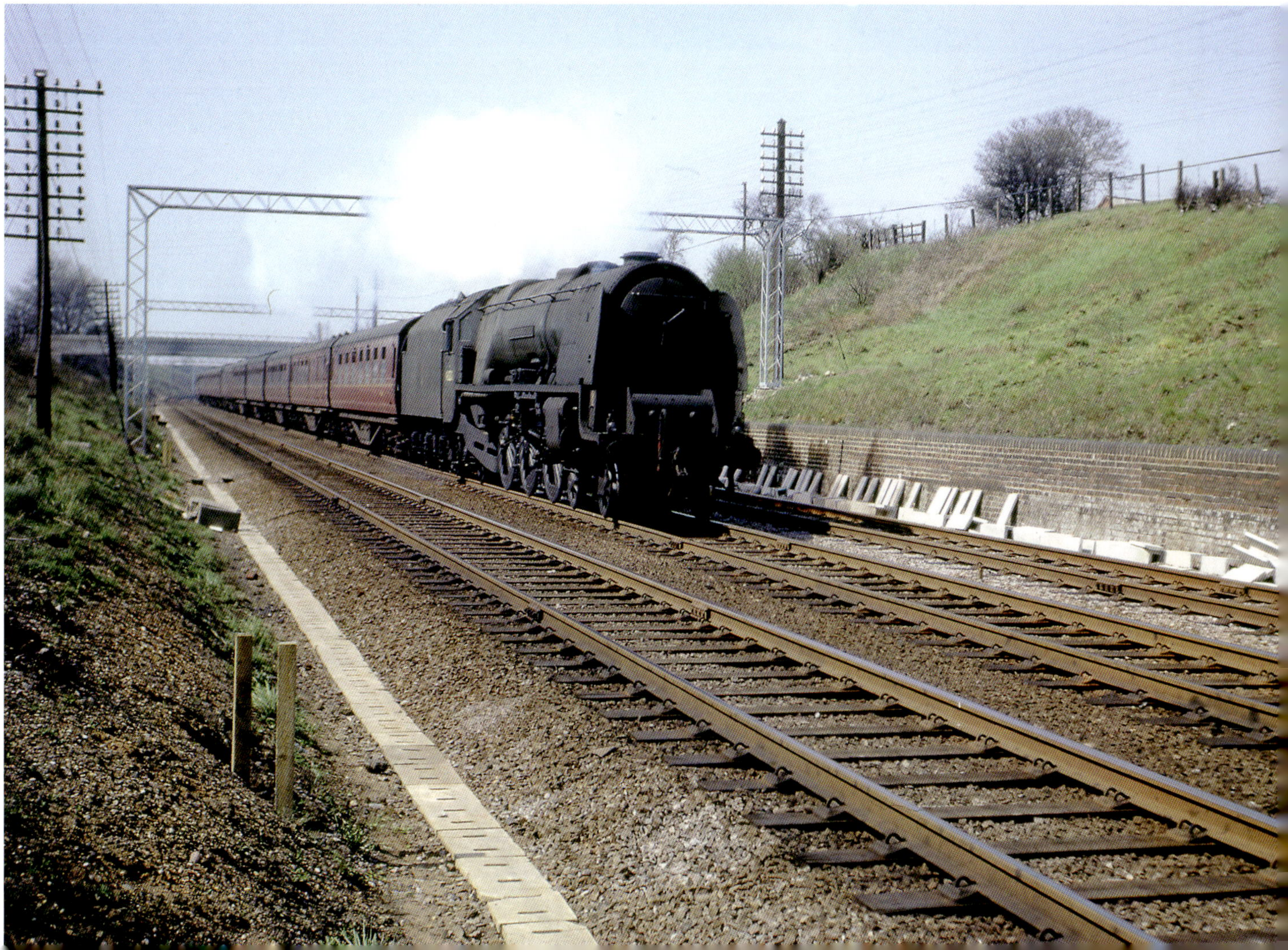

Robin Hood Country

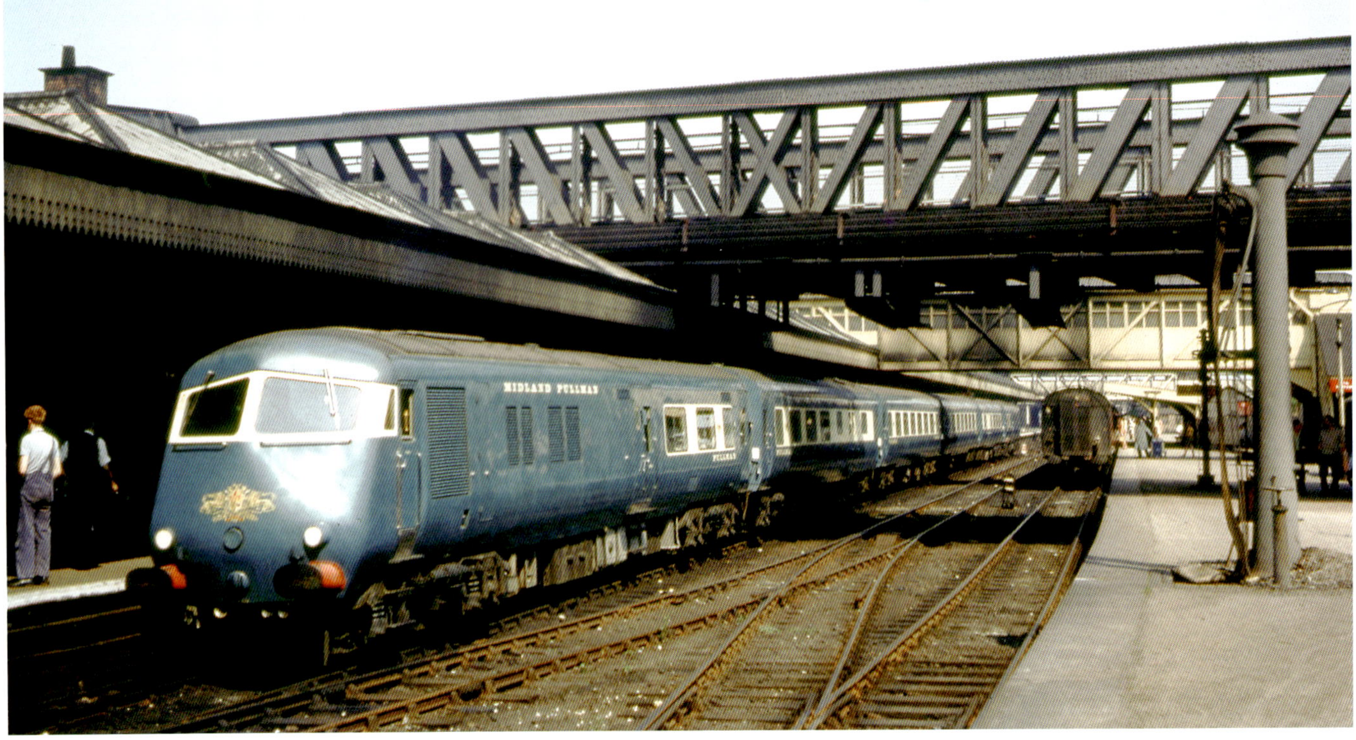

Launched amid great publicity in 1960 the Midland Pullman service ran between Manchester Central and St.Pancras using dedicated six car units as seen here at Nottingham Midland. When launched the service avoided both Derby and Nottingham and only called at Leicester. However by 1964 there was at least a mid-day service that called at the city famed for its lace making. ***Richard Sinclair Collection***

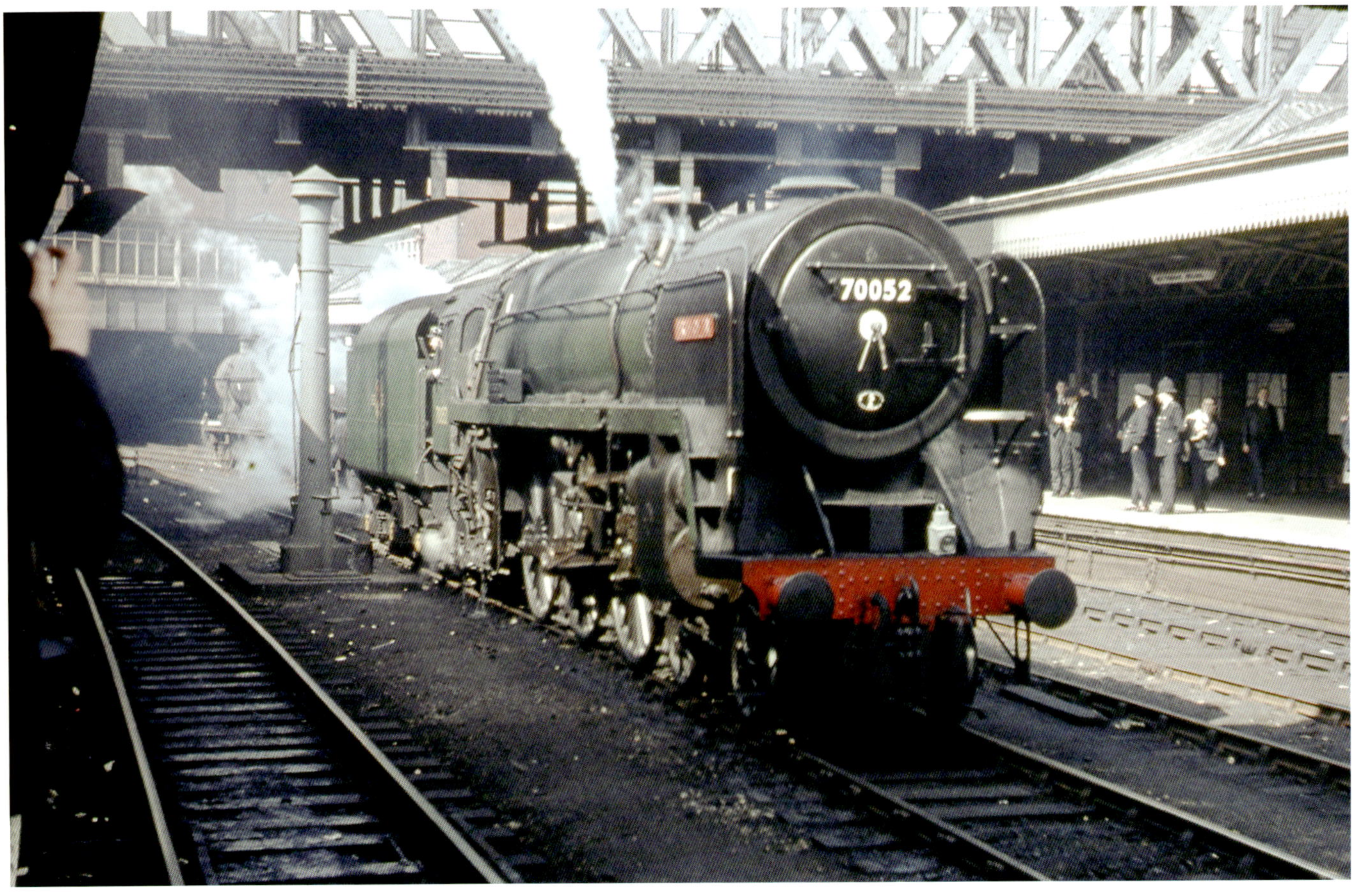

On 24 April 1965 Britannia 70052 Firth of Tay was used for the mainline runs from St.Pancras to Nottingham Midland and back as part of the L.C.G.B. Notts and Lincs Railtour. ***Late Vincent Heckford/Strathwood Library Collection***

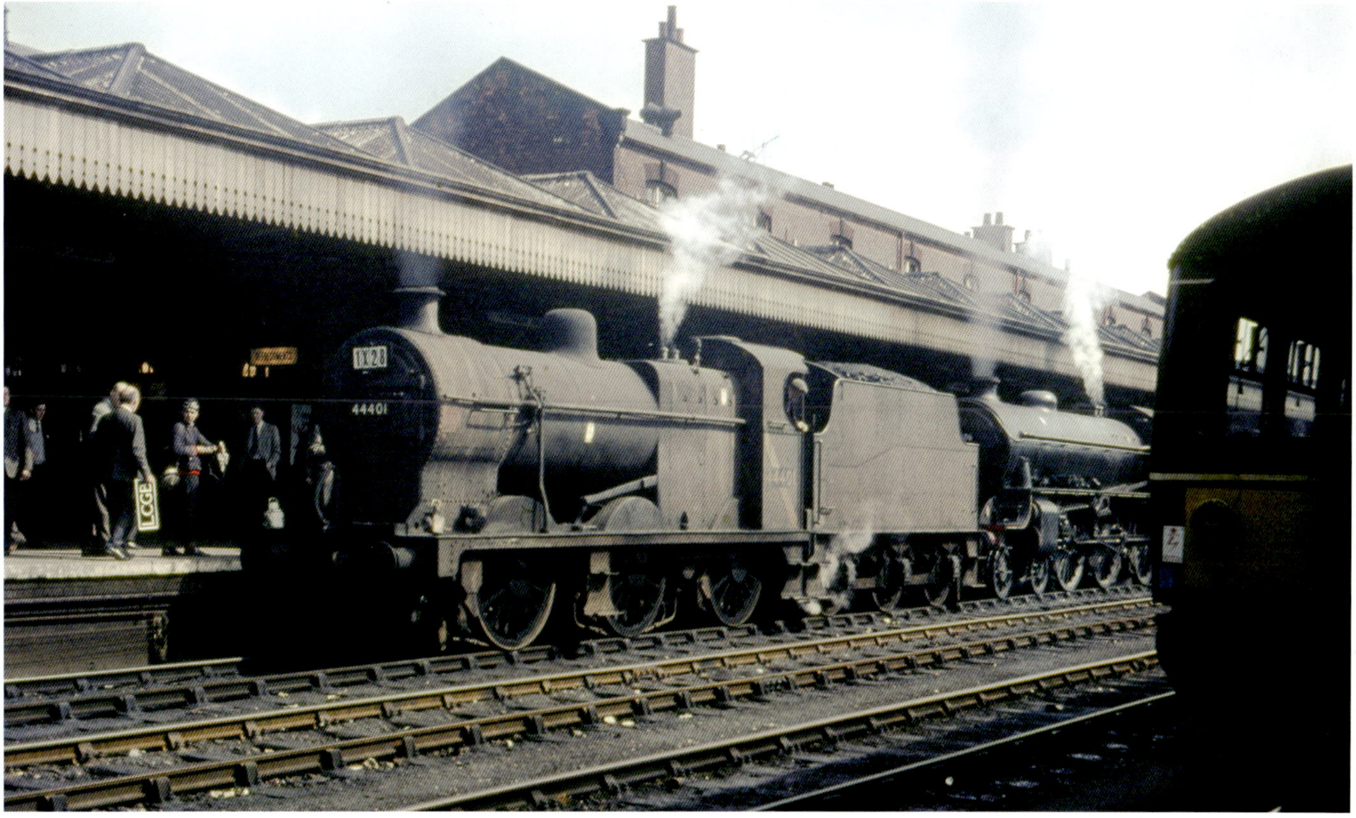

The Riddles Pacific handed over to Fowler 4F 44401 and Thompson B1 61406 as the pair are ready and waiting at Nottingham Midland to head for Shirebrook with the next leg in the late morning. The 4F carries one of the high sided tenders. ***Strathwood Library Collection***

Over at the former Great Central station in the city during 1962 Class O4/8 63873 draws out the couplings again as she gets underway once more through a rain soaked Nottingham Victoria. ***Strathwood Library Collection***

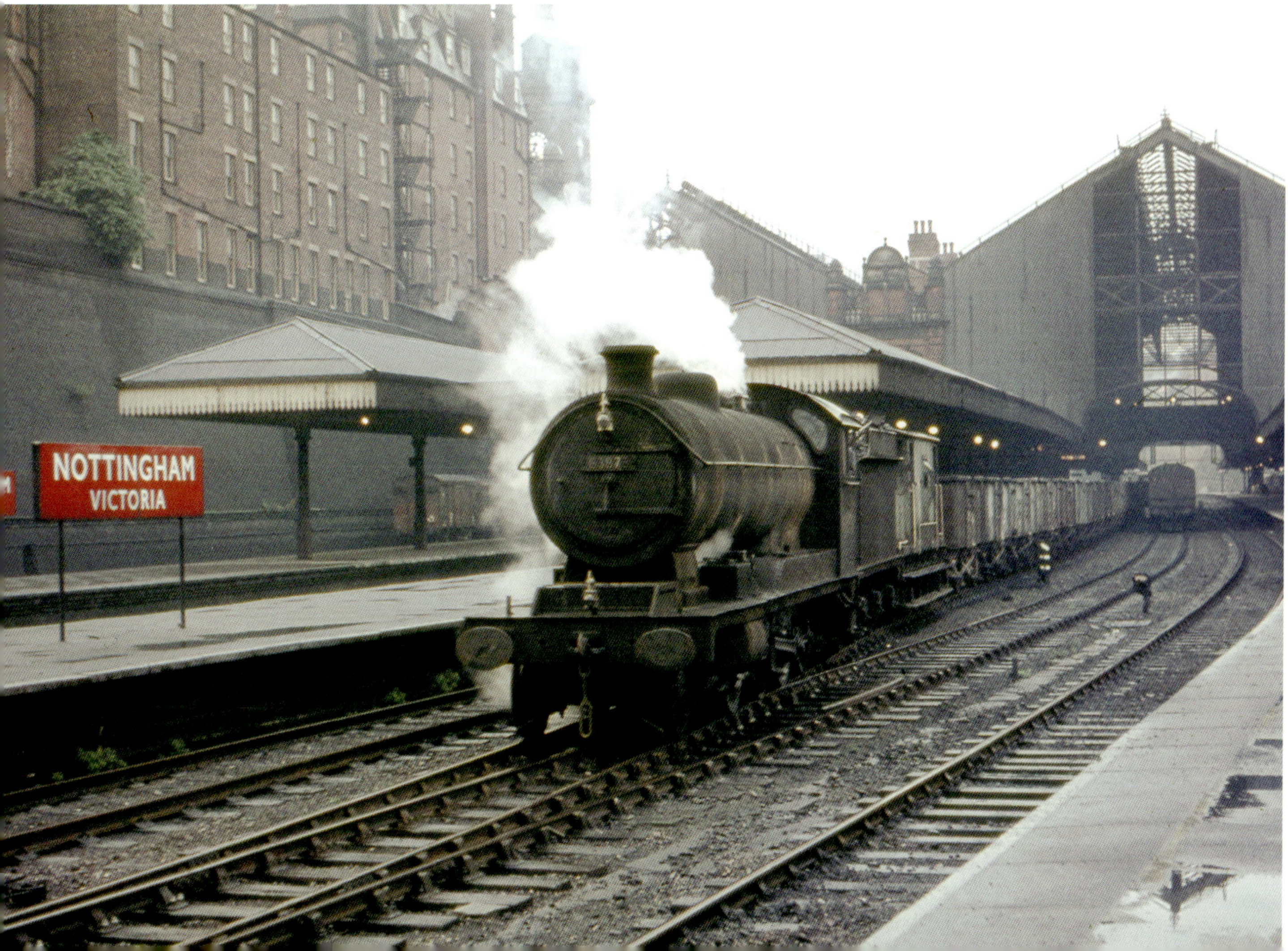

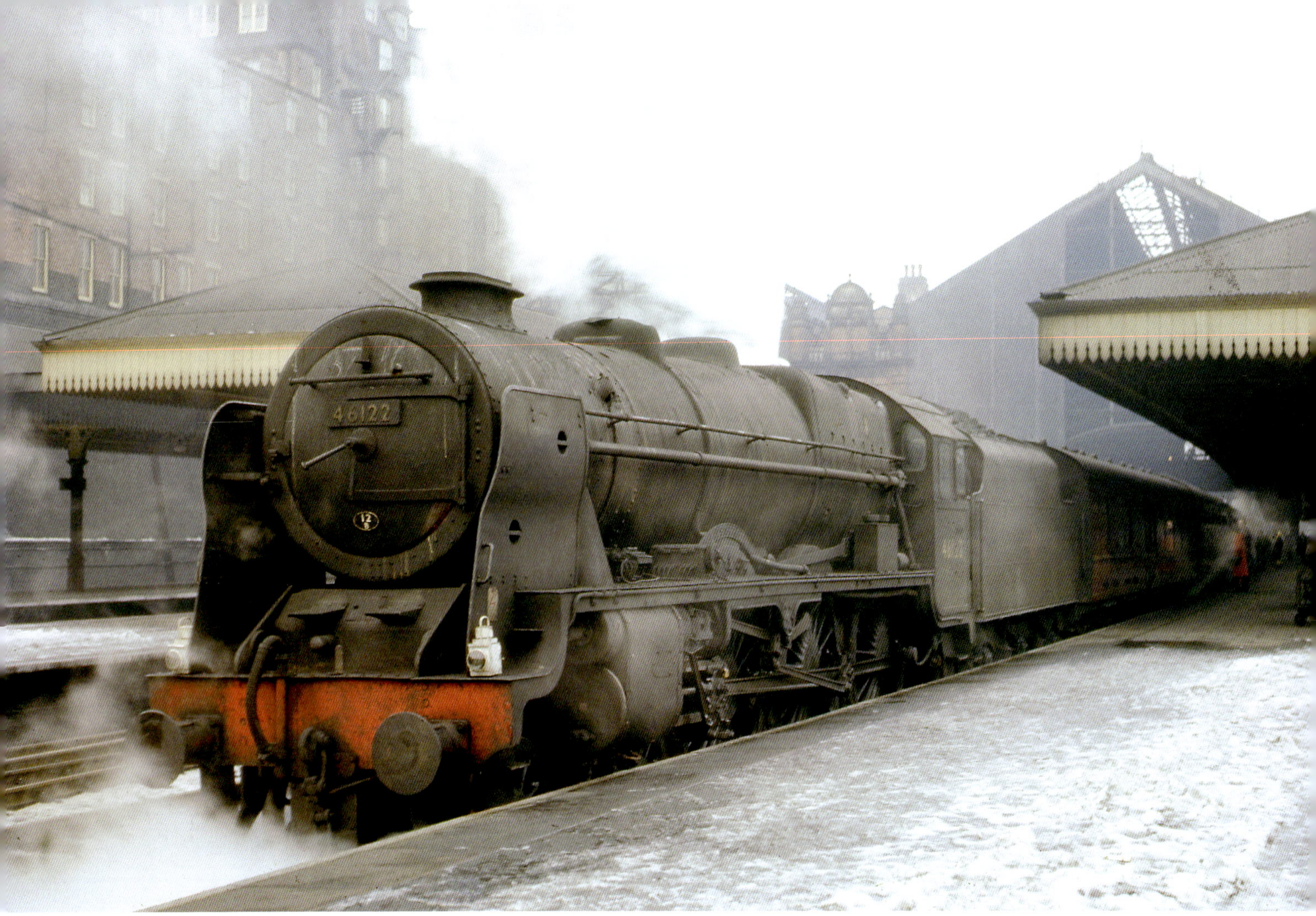

An awful lot has been said about the very harsh winter of 1963 when we see rebuilt Royal Scot 46122 Royal Ulster Rifleman standing at Nottingham Victoria with the 17.15 to Marylebone on an icy January afternoon. ***Win Wall/Strathwood Library Collection***

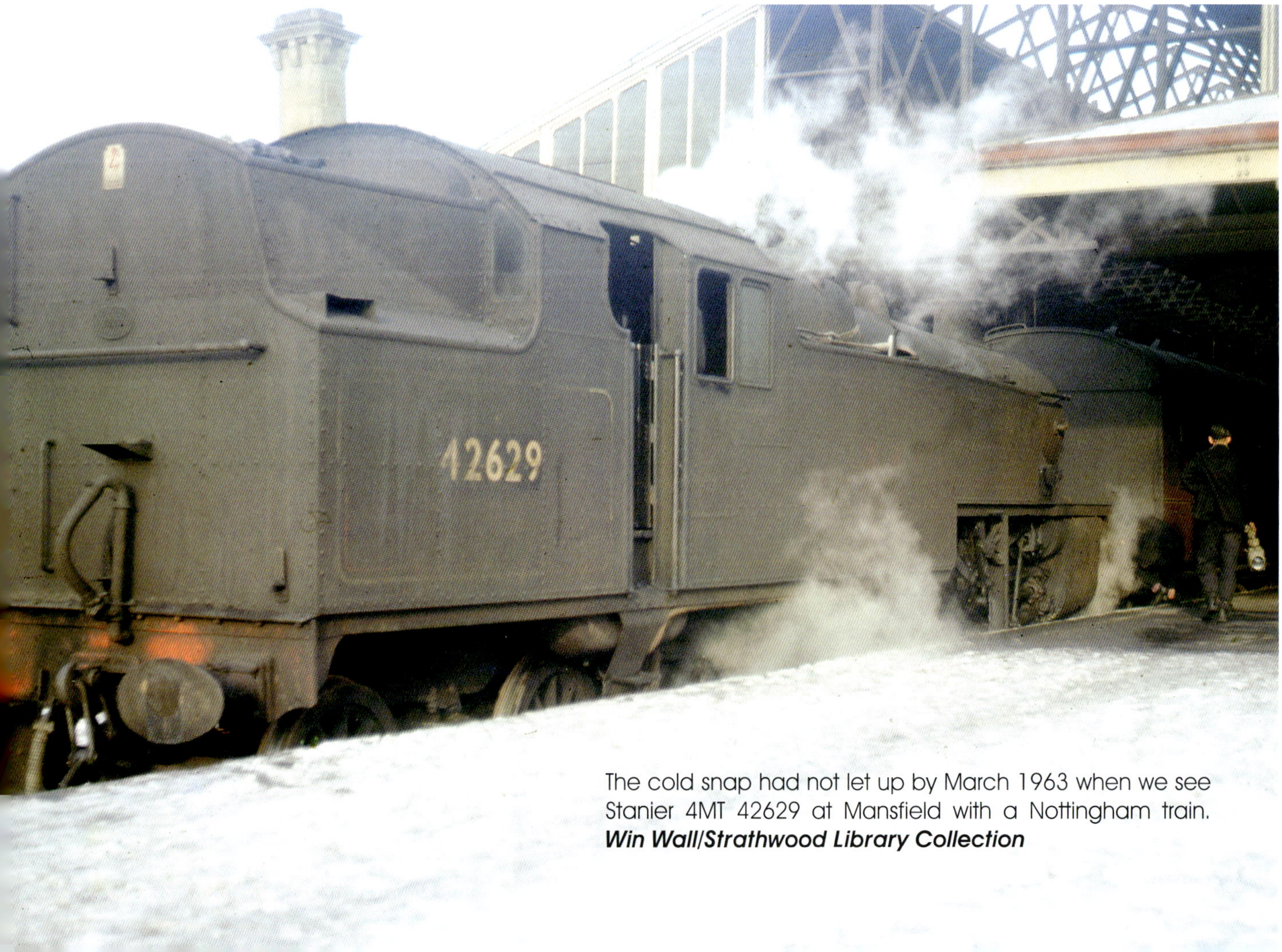

The cold snap had not let up by March 1963 when we see Stanier 4MT 42629 at Mansfield with a Nottingham train. ***Win Wall/Strathwood Library Collection***

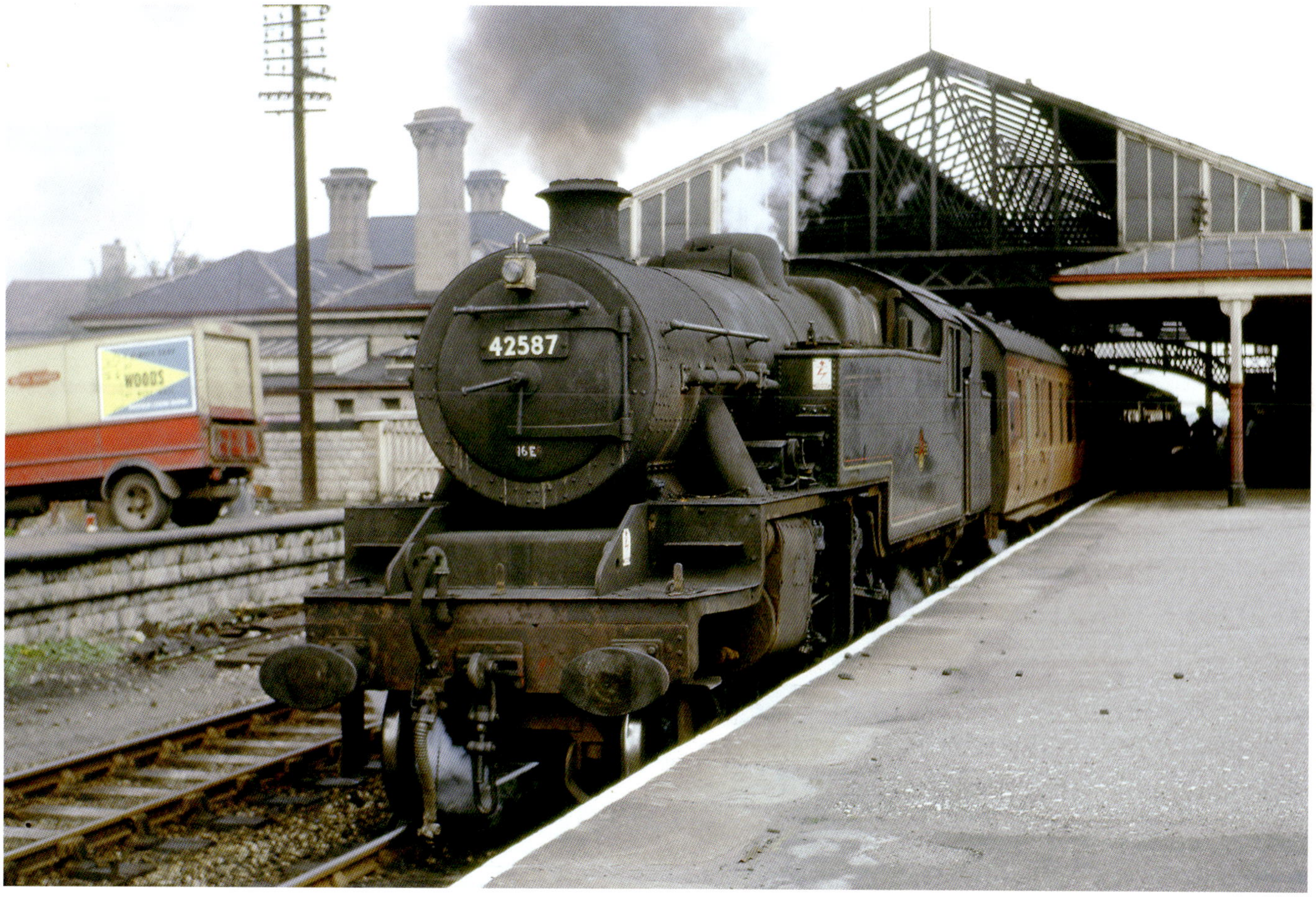

A further visit to Mansfield the year after finds another Stanier 4MT 42587 on a Worksop to Nottingham service. The former Great Central Railway's station had closed in 1956 and the year of this photograpgh 1964 would spell closure for both the former Midland Railway's stations Mansfield Town and Mansfield Woodhouse. ***John Rowe***

Steam was still plentifull at 16E Kirkby in Ashfield in April 1964 although it would be diesel only by November. ***Win Wall/Strathwood Library Collection***

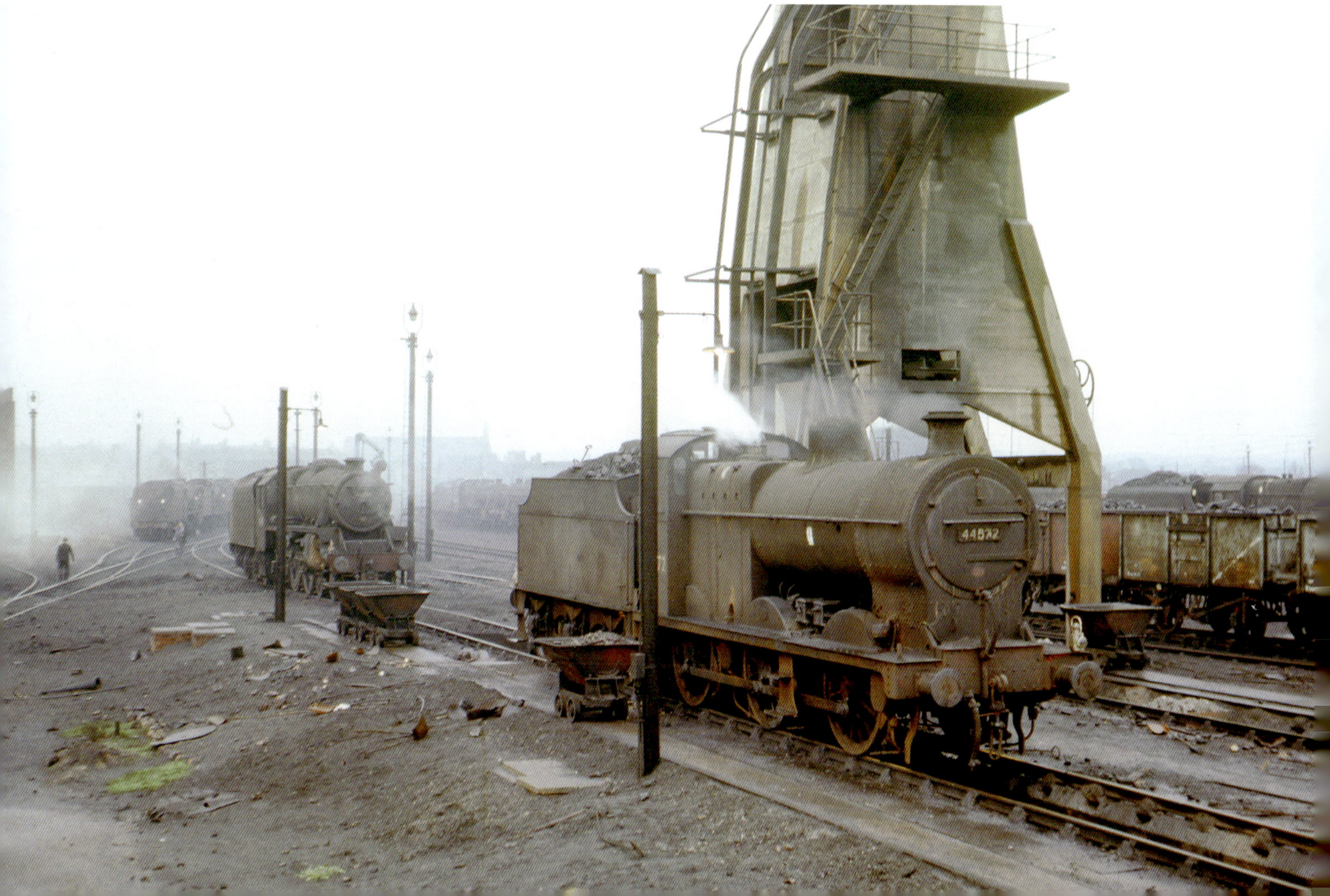

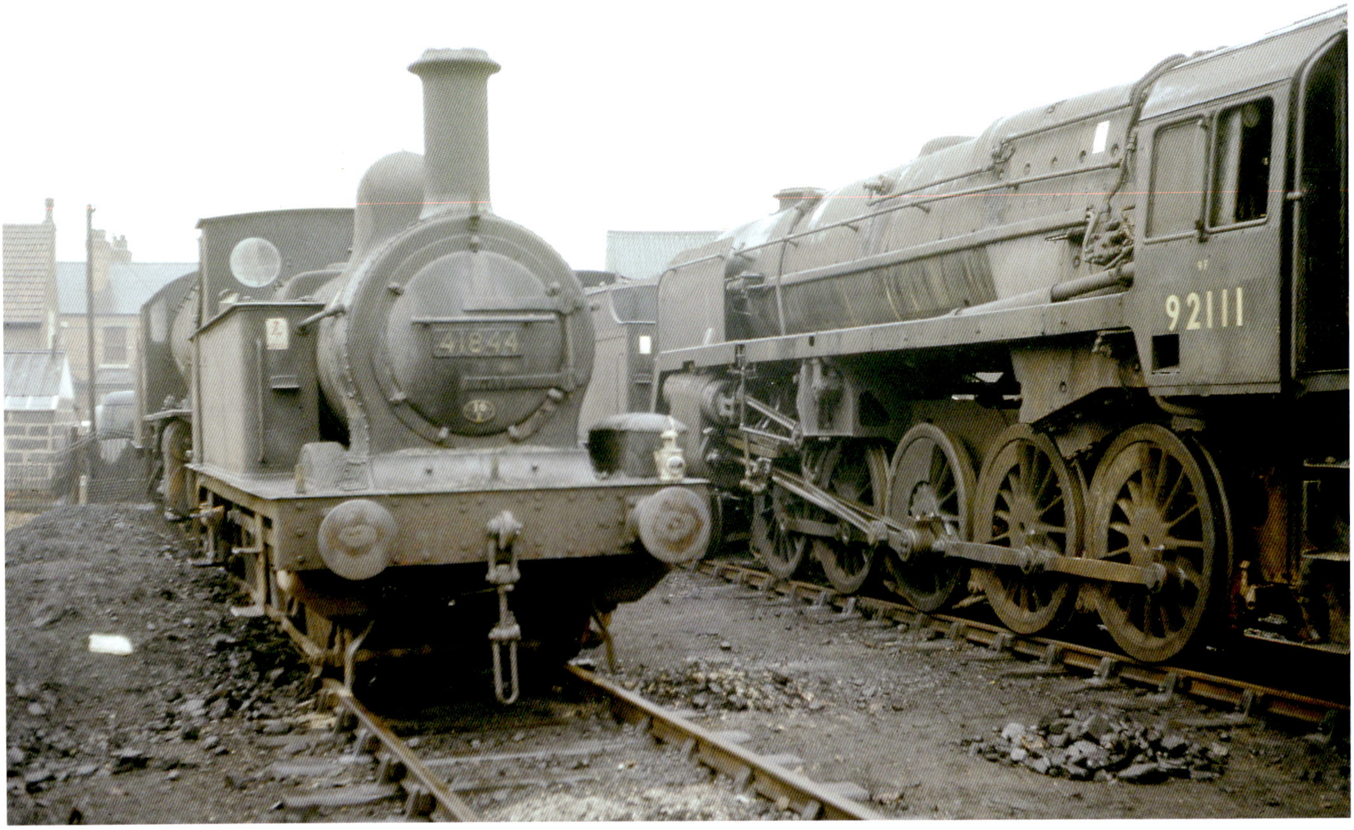

Tucked away at the back of Kirkby in Ashfield shed on 30 March 1964 were Johnson 1F 41844 and Riddles 9F 92111, although the 9F would live on until October 1967, time was running out for the 1892 Vulcan Foundry built 0-6-0T as it was posted as withdrawn in May. ***Win Wall/Strathwood Library Collection***

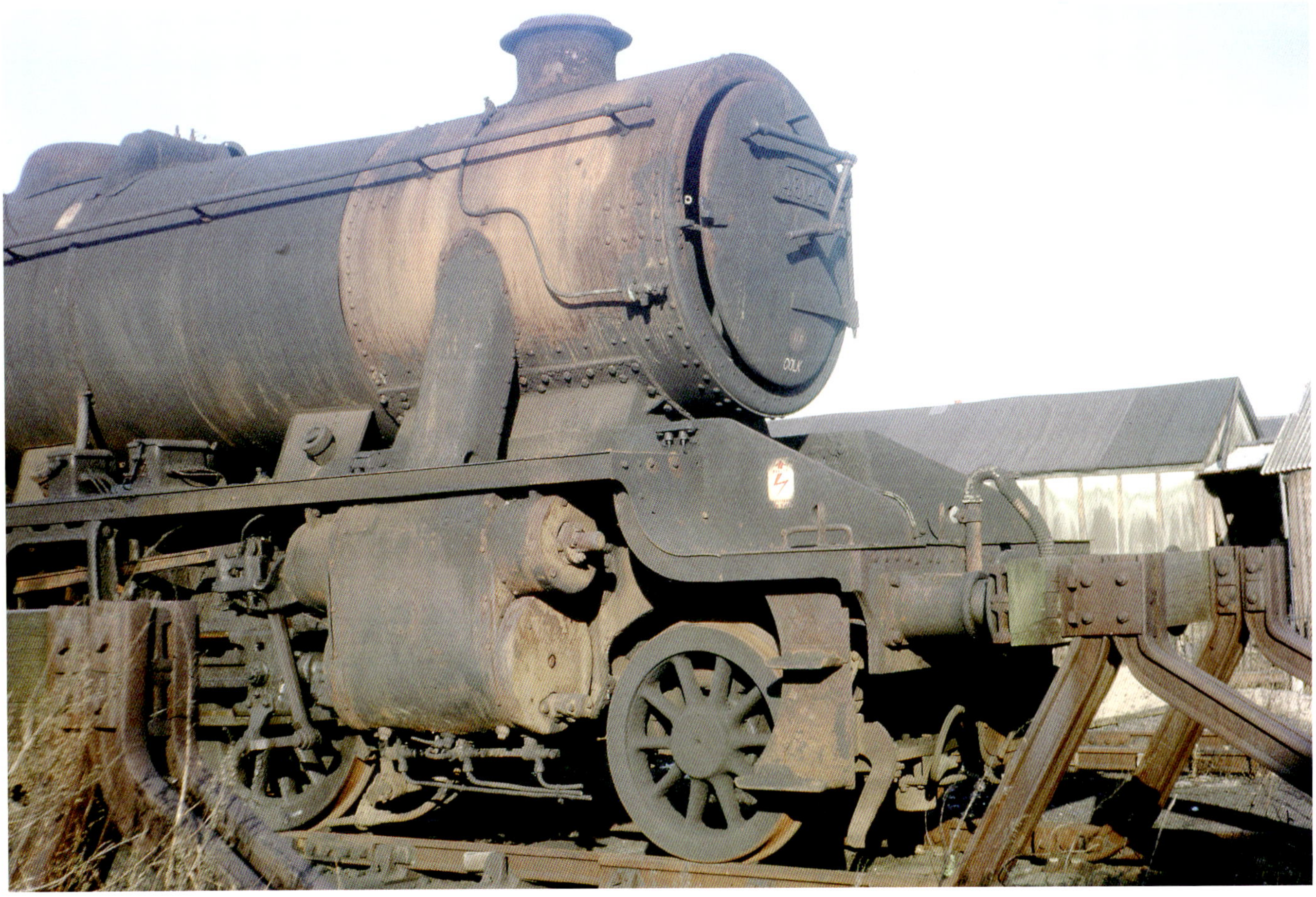

Dumped awaiting a place in front of the scrapmen at Kirkby in Ashfield on 5 March 1967 was Stanier 8F 48142. ***Colin Rodgers/Strathwood Library Coillection***

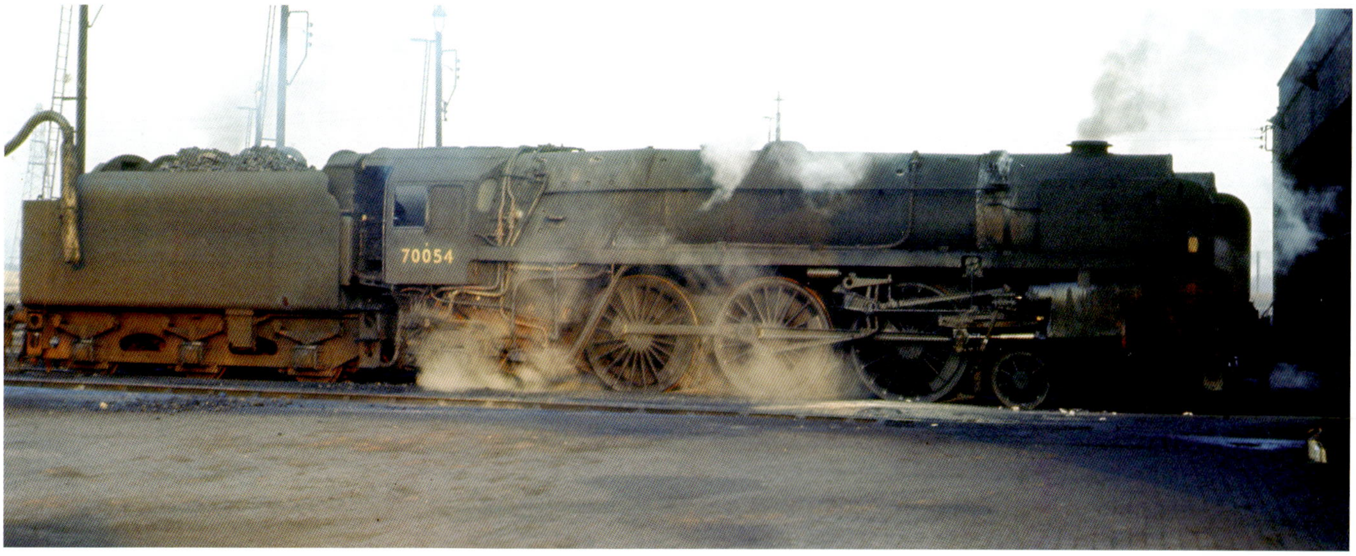

No cleaners are available to smarten up Britannia 70054 Dornoch Firth awaiting its next turn from Annesley depot on 23 October 1965. If you had settled down in front of the fire that evening you may have tuned into the adventures of The Avengers which was still broadcast in black and white, not going over to colour until 1967. ***Win Wall/Strathwood Library Collection***

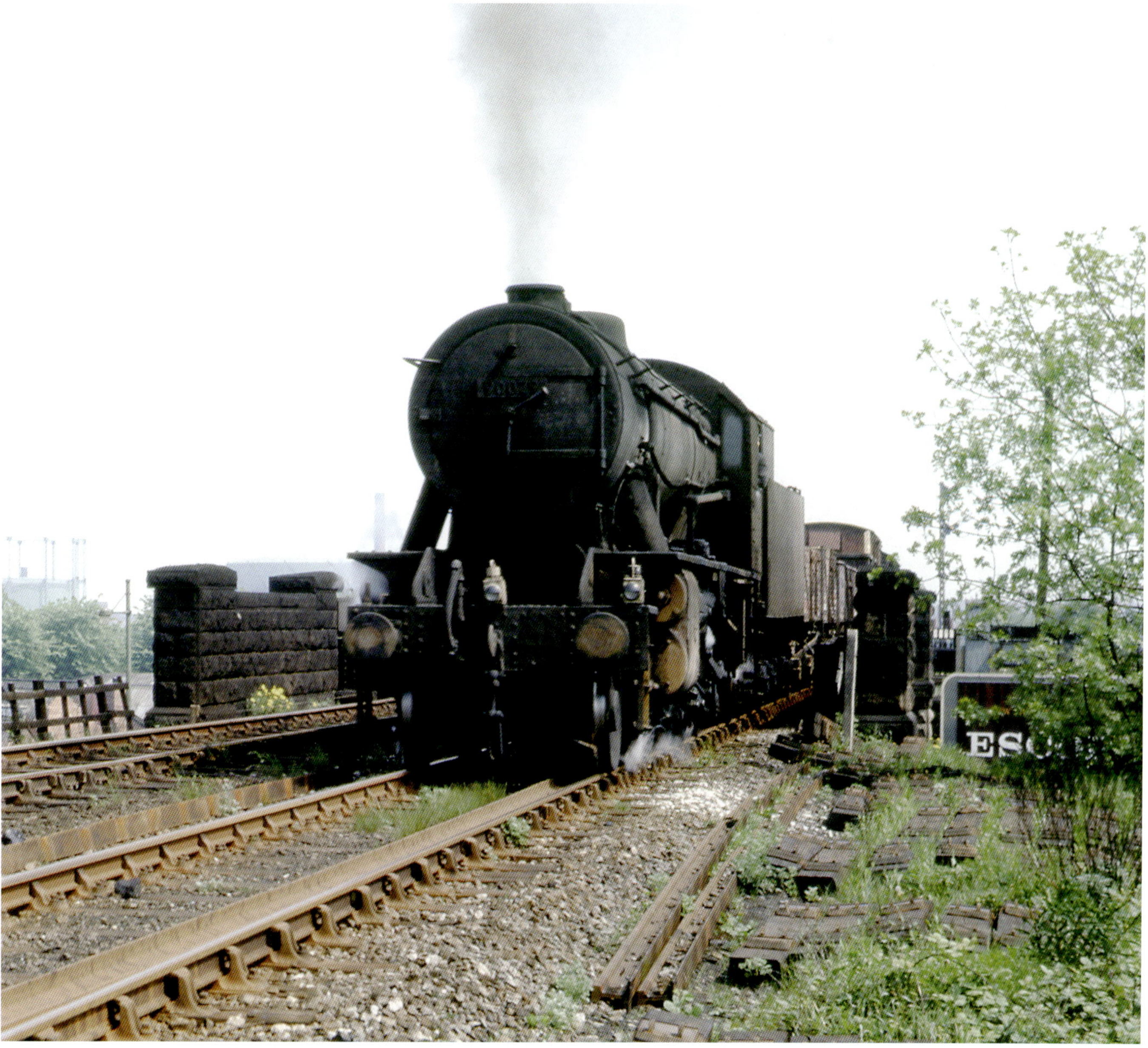

The Austerities could be found everywhere around the Nottingham and Derbyshire coalfields still in June 1964 when we found 90029 clanking through Mansfield on the former Great Central metals with a mixed goods. ***Win Wall/Strathwood Library Collection***

Steam Lives On

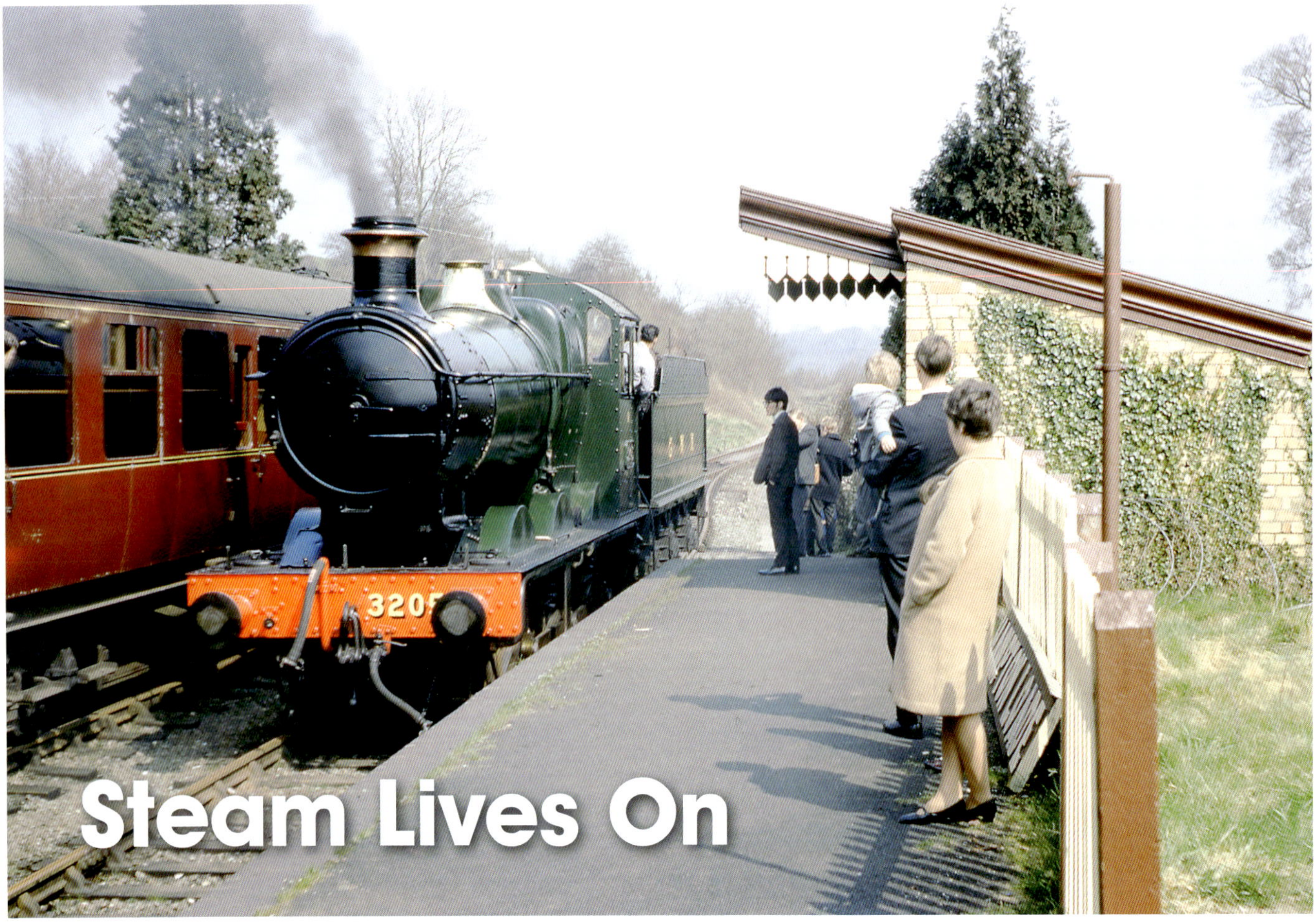

Running round it's train at Hampton Loade on the fledging Severn Valley Railway on 14 April 1968 was the now preserved Collett 0-6-0 3205. ***Jerry Beddows***

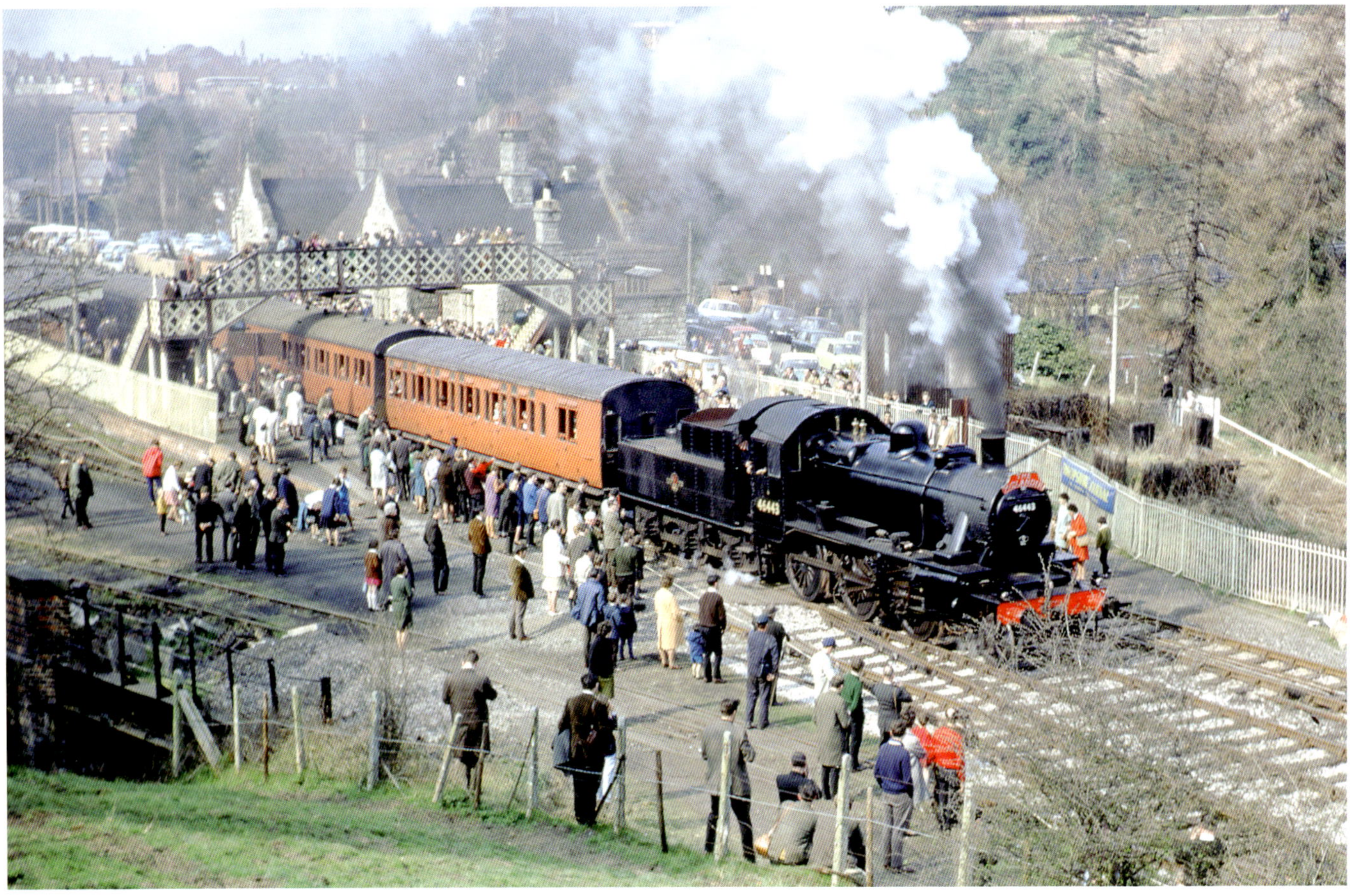

The paintwork of Ivatt Mogul 46443 has been freshened up since arriving on the Severn Valley Railway and she was put to work with enthusiast's trains from Bridgenorth in April 1969. ***John Gill***

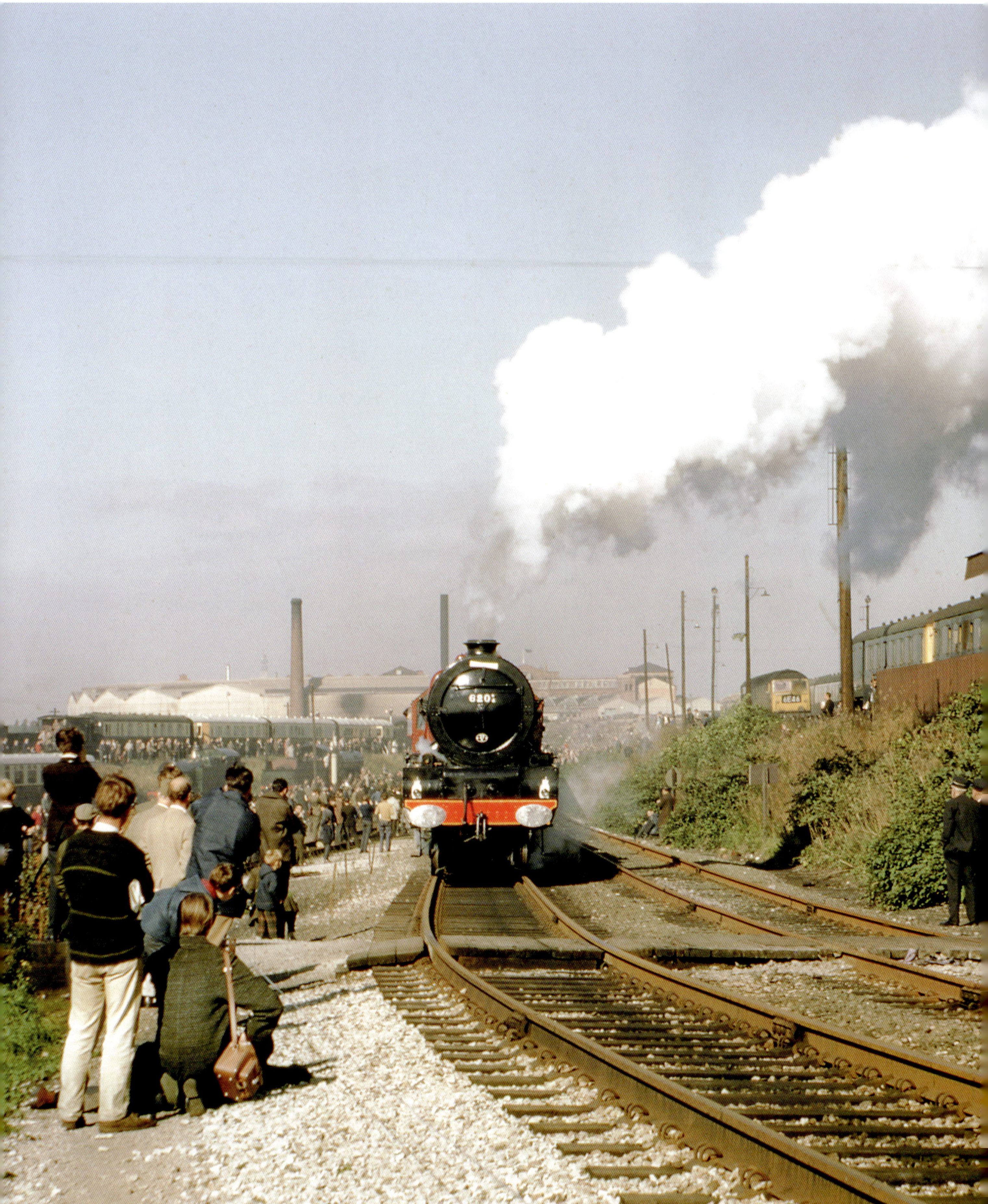

Large crowds turned out in the bright sunshine for an Open Day at Tyseley on 28 September 1969 where the now repainted back into LMS livery 6201 Princess Elizabeth was put to work on shuttles to give visitors the chance to ride behind steam once more. ***Jerry Beddows***

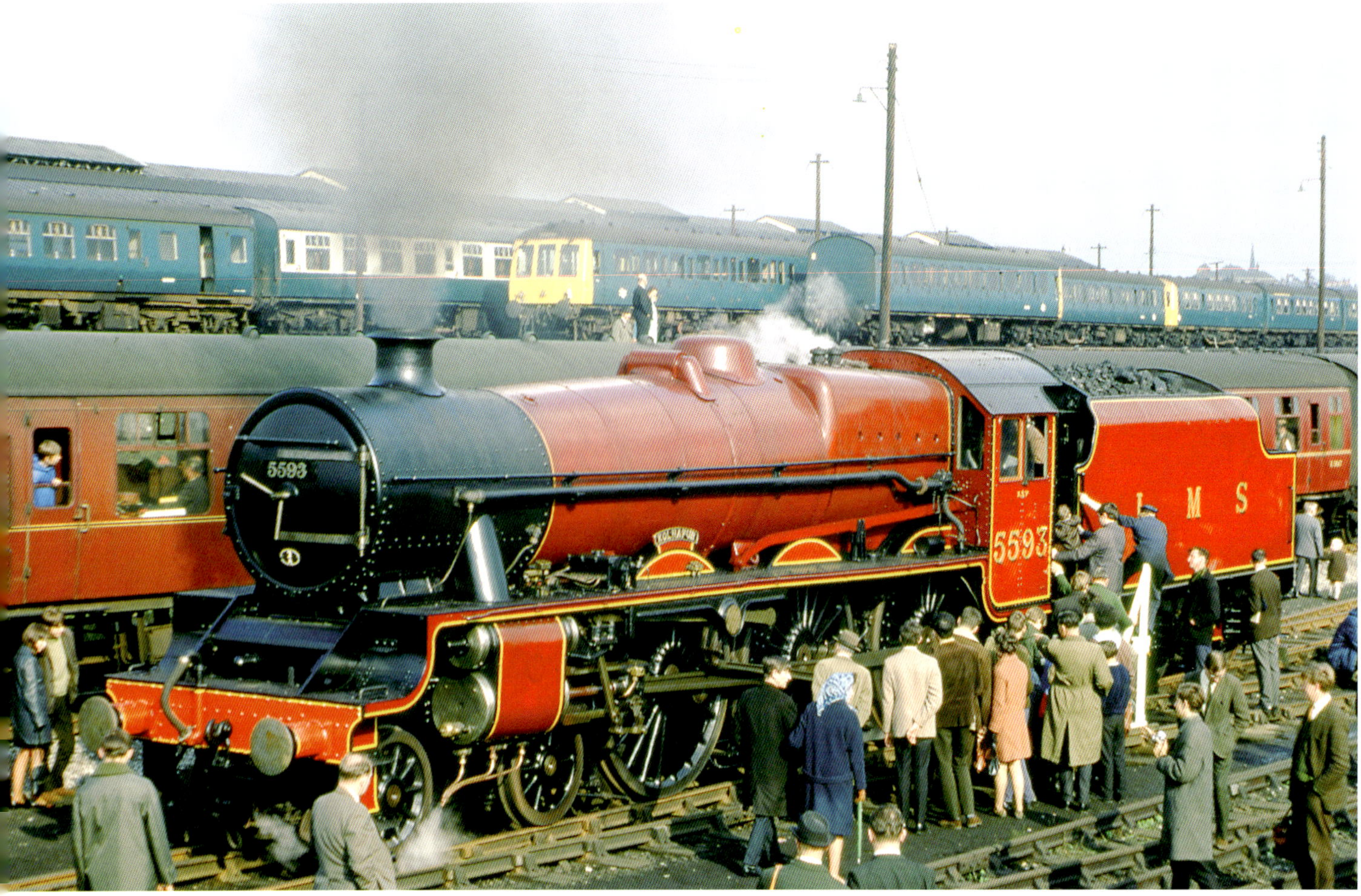

Visitors scramble aboard the cab of Stanier Jubilee 5593 Kolhapur among the rows of DMUs at Tyseley during another Open Day on 4 May 1969. ***Jerry Beddows***

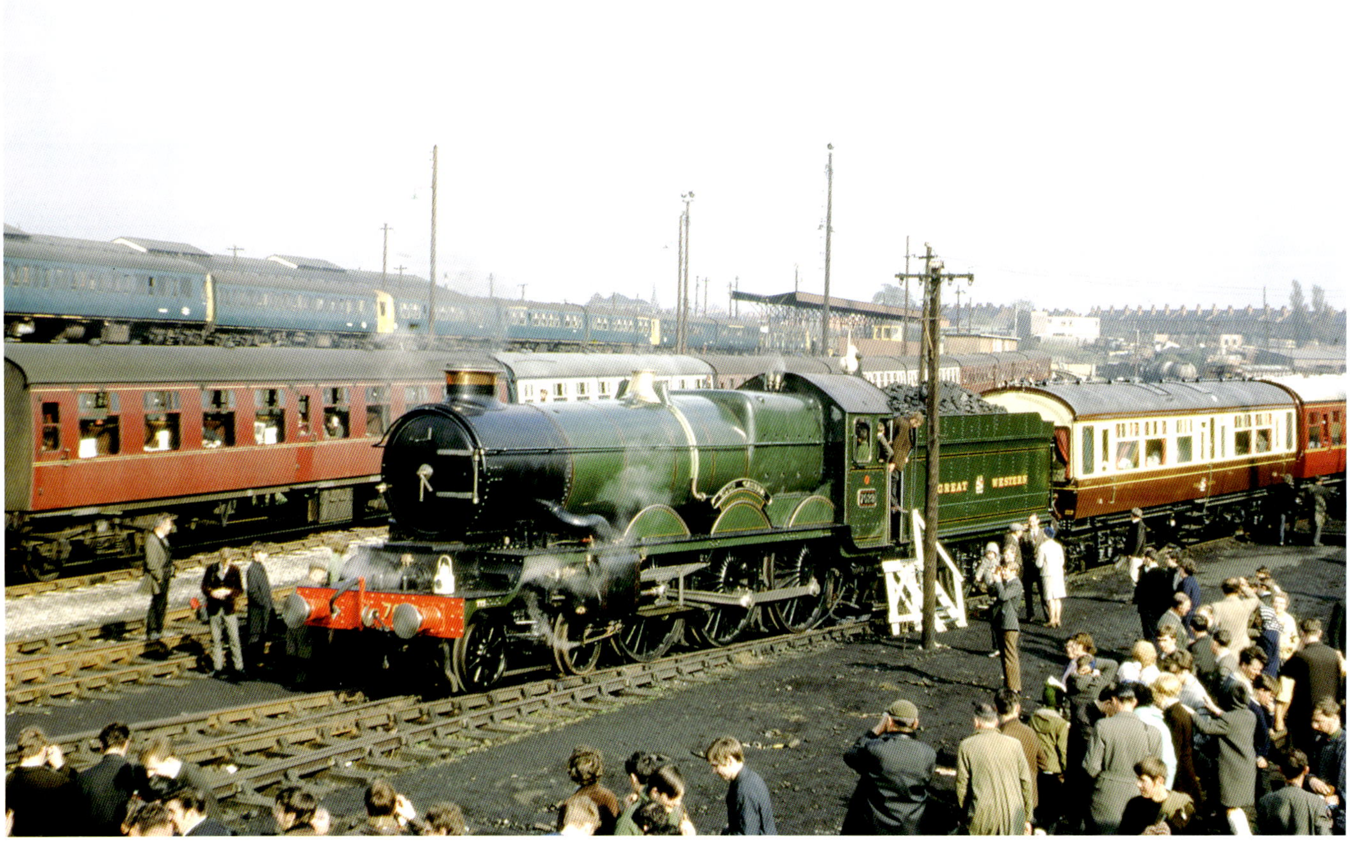

Also engaged in providing rides to the public the same day was Pat Whitehouse's 7029 Clun Castle now resplendent in Great Western livery although the locomotive was not built until 1950 it was the owner's prerogative. ***Jerry Beddows***

South Midlands Medley

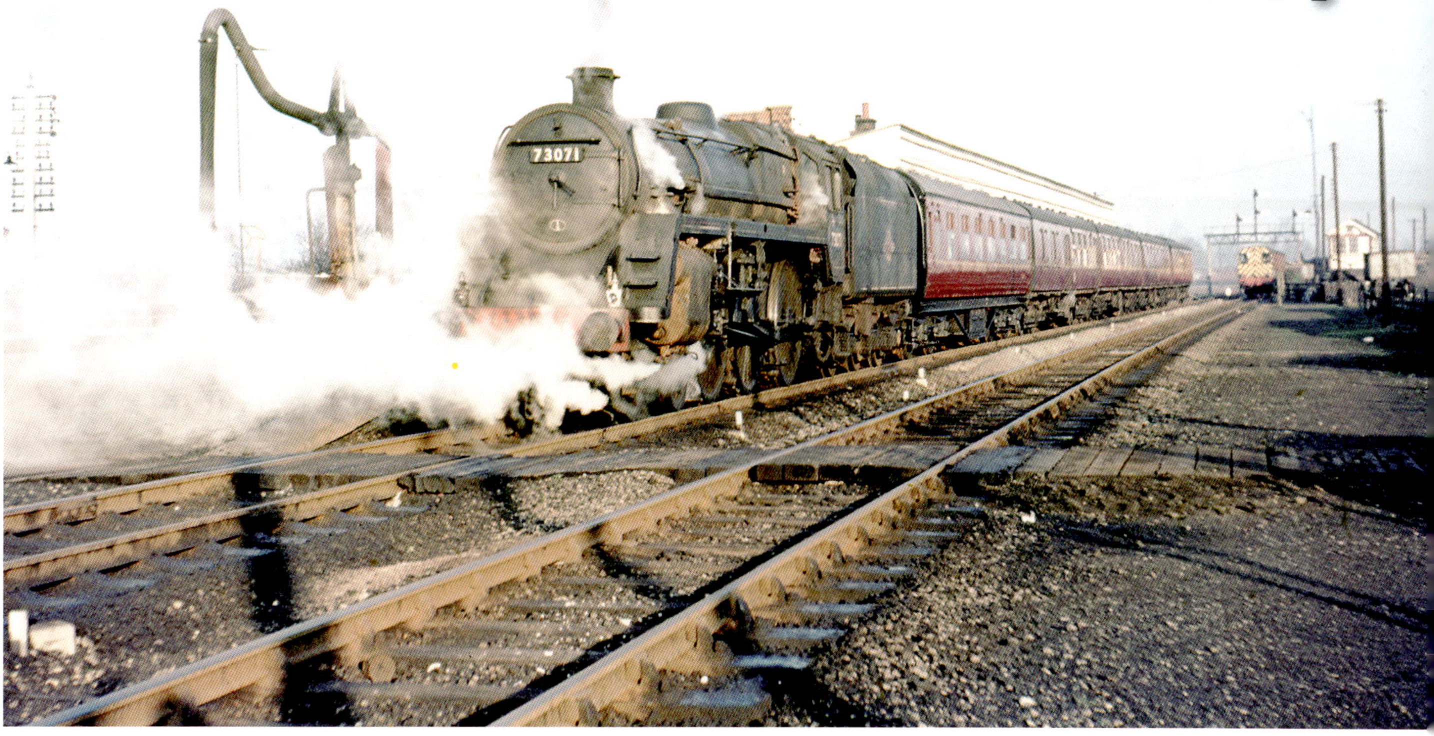

On 7 December 1963 the driver onboard Riddles 5MT 73071 throws open his cylinder drain cocks on departure from Woodford Halse with a service for Marylebone. ***Richard Icke***

The Rosebay Willowherb is going over at Woodford Halse on 23 July 1966 and this former Great Central route will follow in a few short weeks time when the new timetable is published, however this afternoon sees the 16.38 ex Marylebone behind Black Five 44920. ***Strathwood Library Collection***

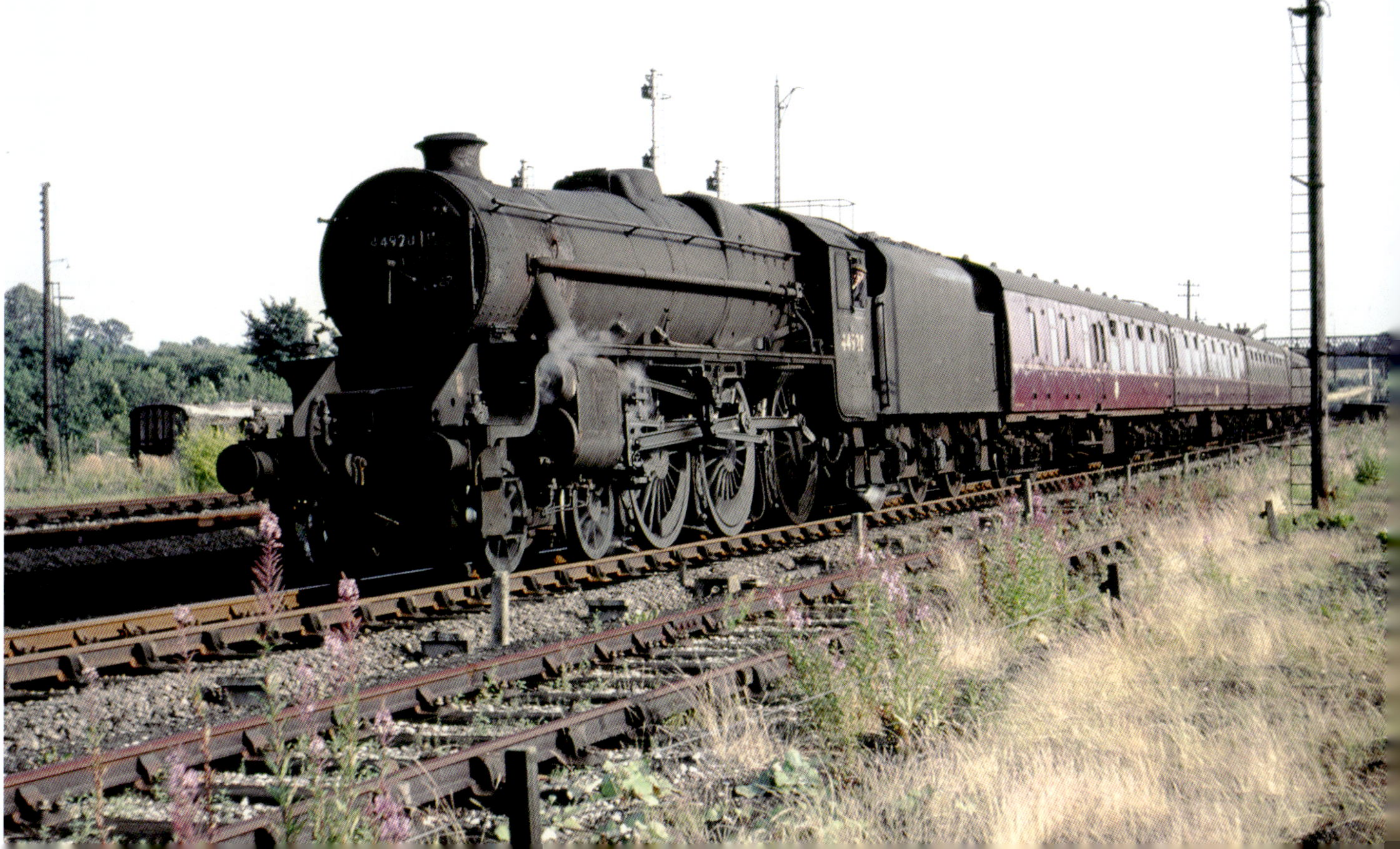

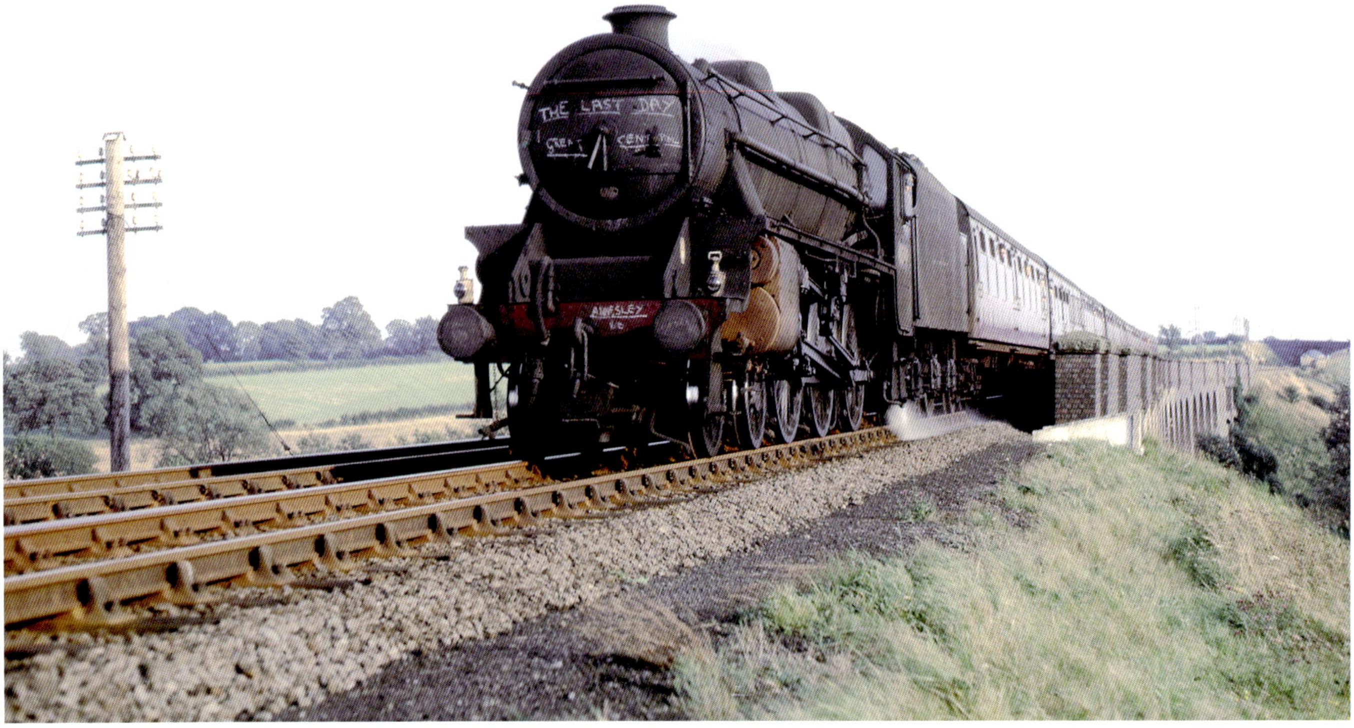

Steam on the southern stretches of the Great Central would come to an end on 3 September 1966 with Black Fives on the last two trains, 45292 worked the last down service at Brackley. Whilst the last up working was adorned with a wreath again at Brackley Central that evening. ***Both: Aldo Delicata***

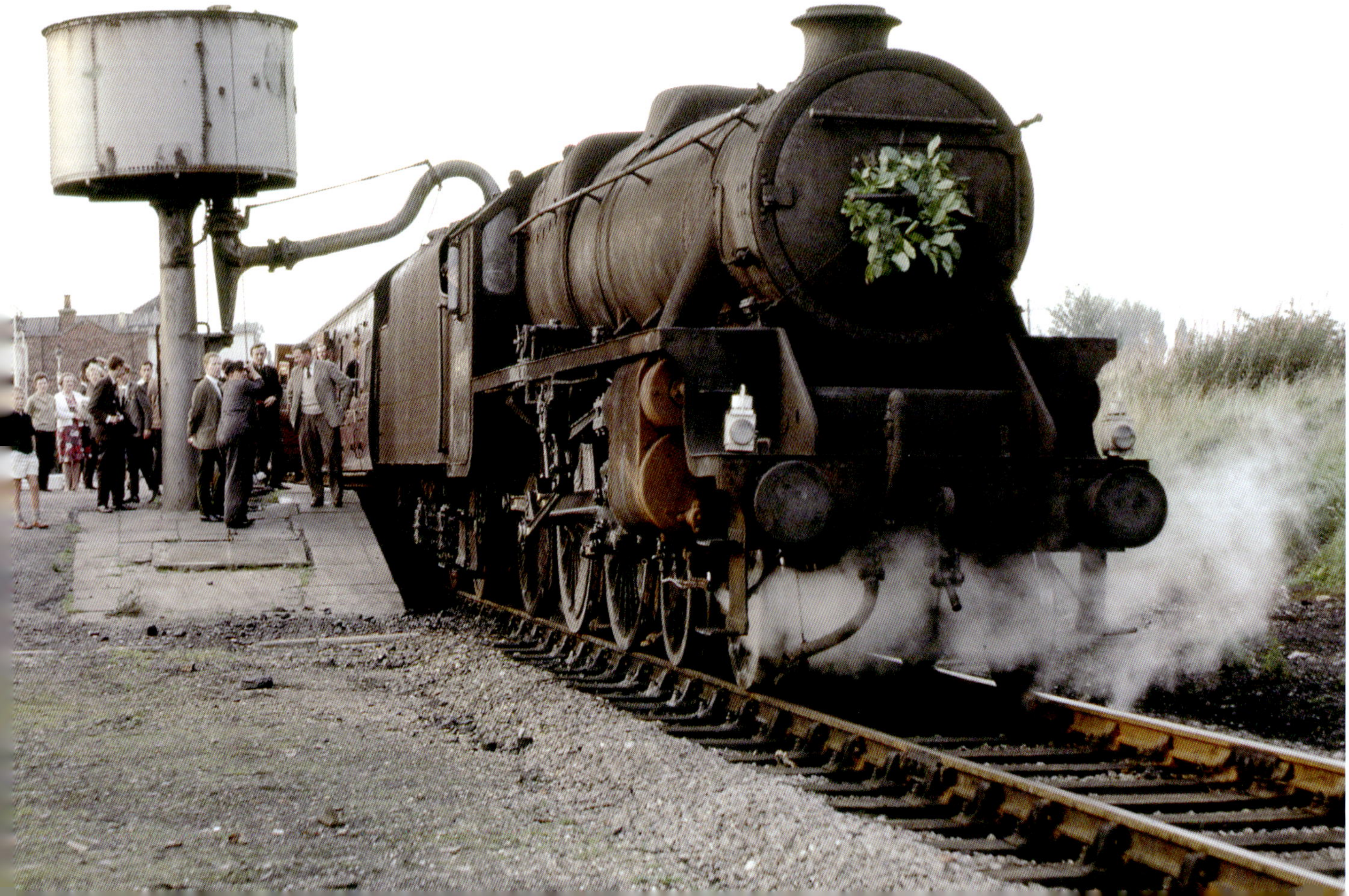

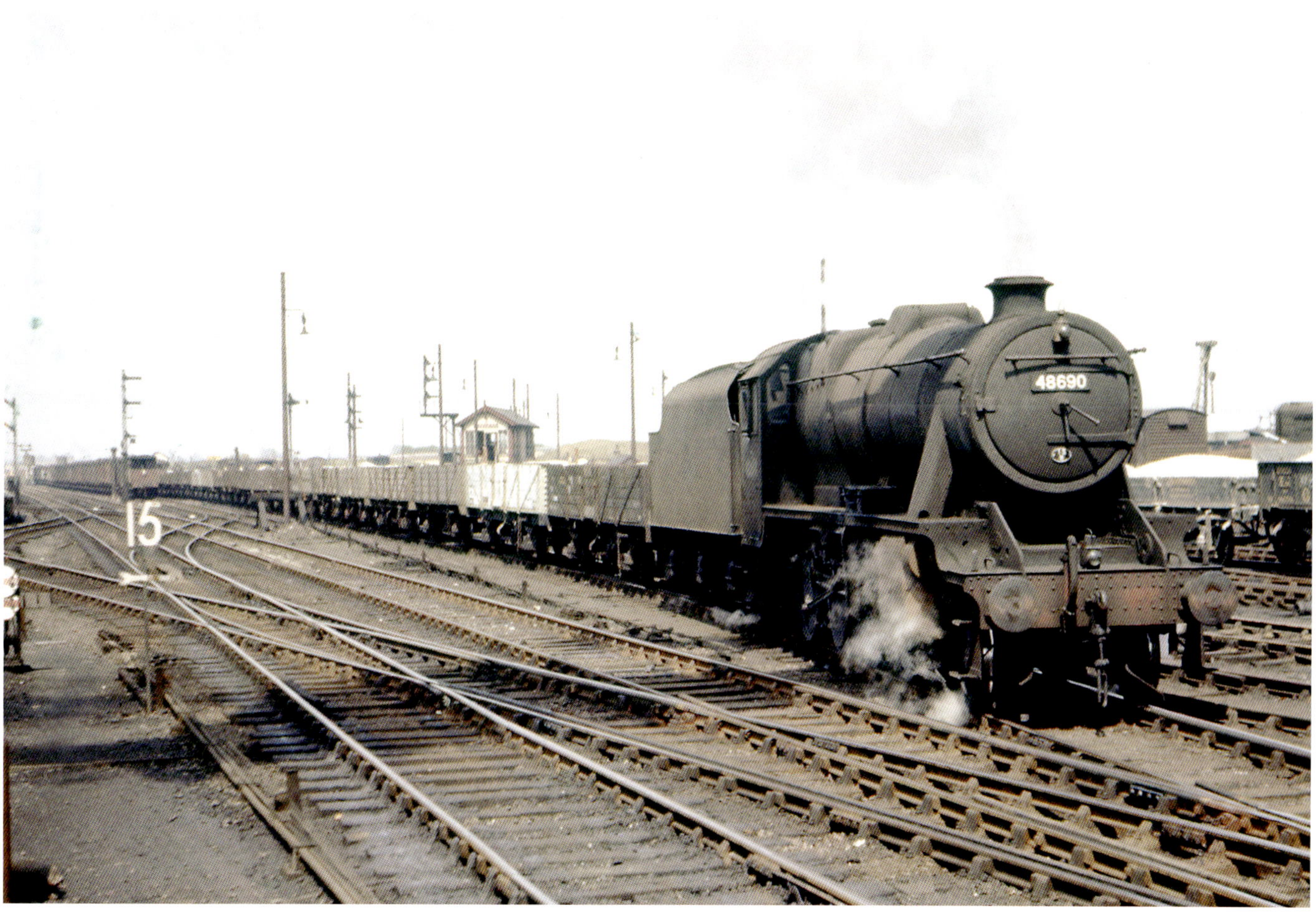

At the start of the decade there was a staggering amount of traffic on the West Coast Main Line, much of it freight such as this working behind Stanier 8F 48690 getting underway again at Bletchley on 30 April 1960. ***Frank Hornby***

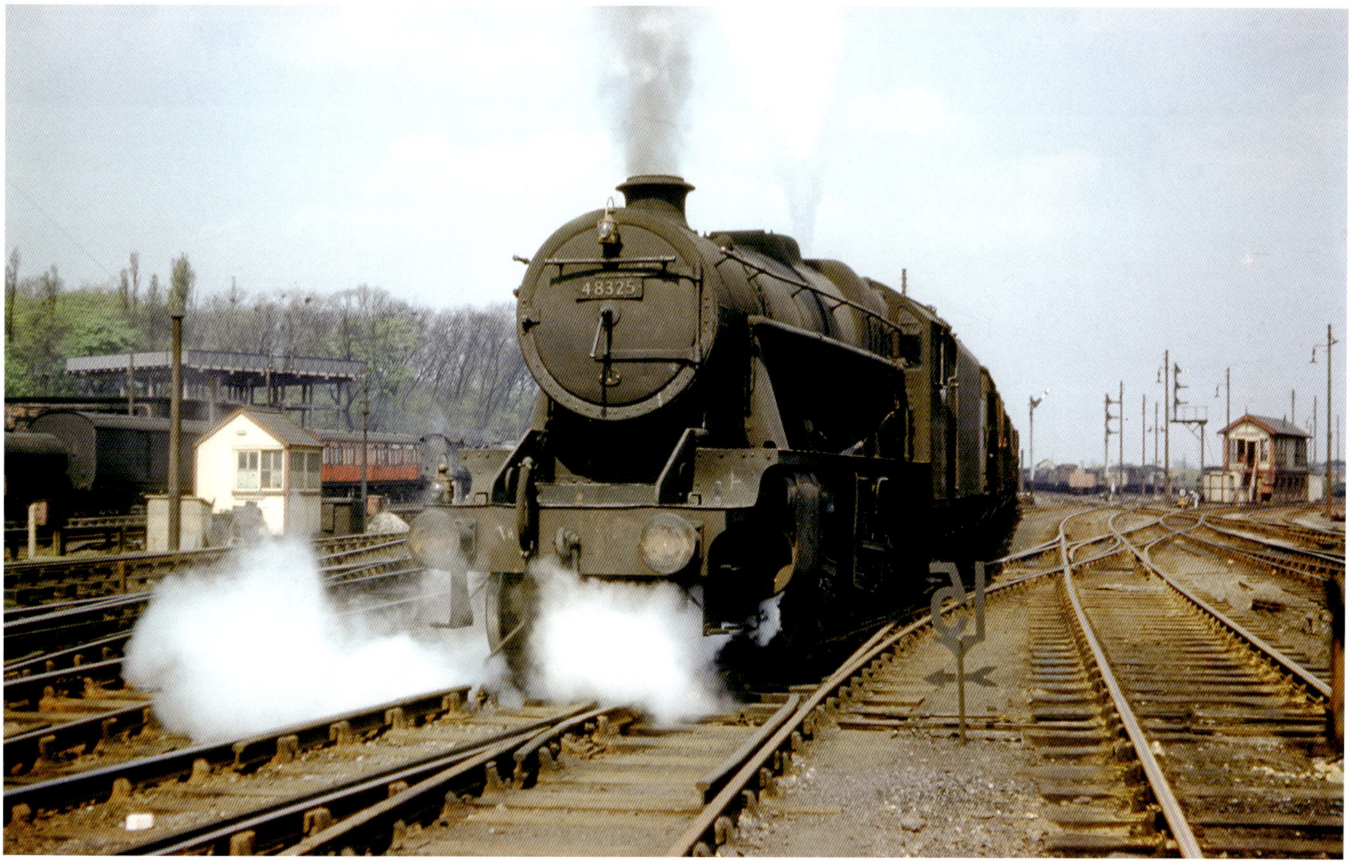

Another of the class 48325 heads out onto the up running lines at Bletchley with a further goods service the same Saturday. The Division One football season was drawing to a close that afternoon, and it would be Burnley who would be champions over Wolverhampton Wanderers a close second, whilst Leeds United and Luton Town would be relegated. ***Frank Hornby***

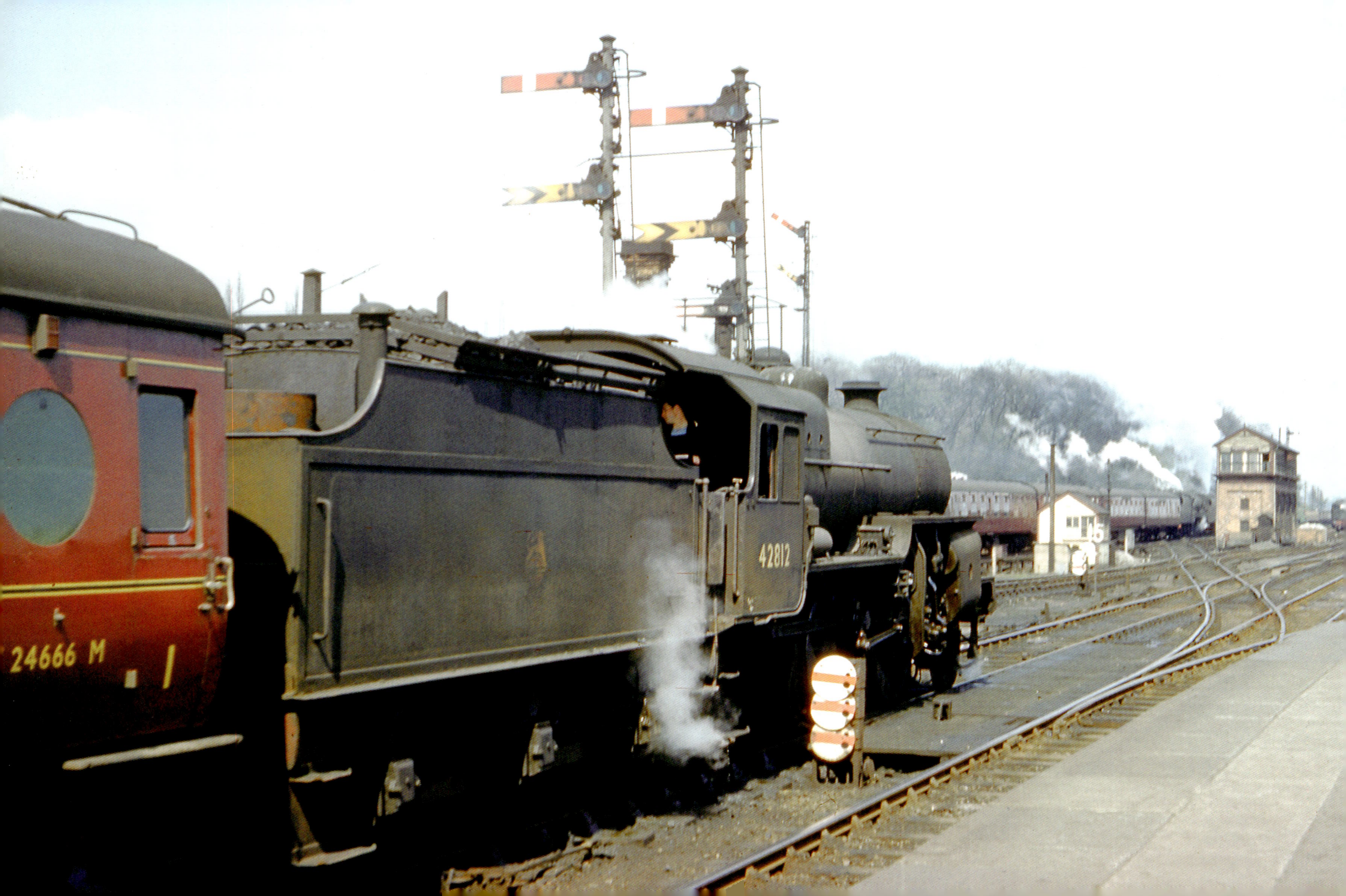

24666 M
42812

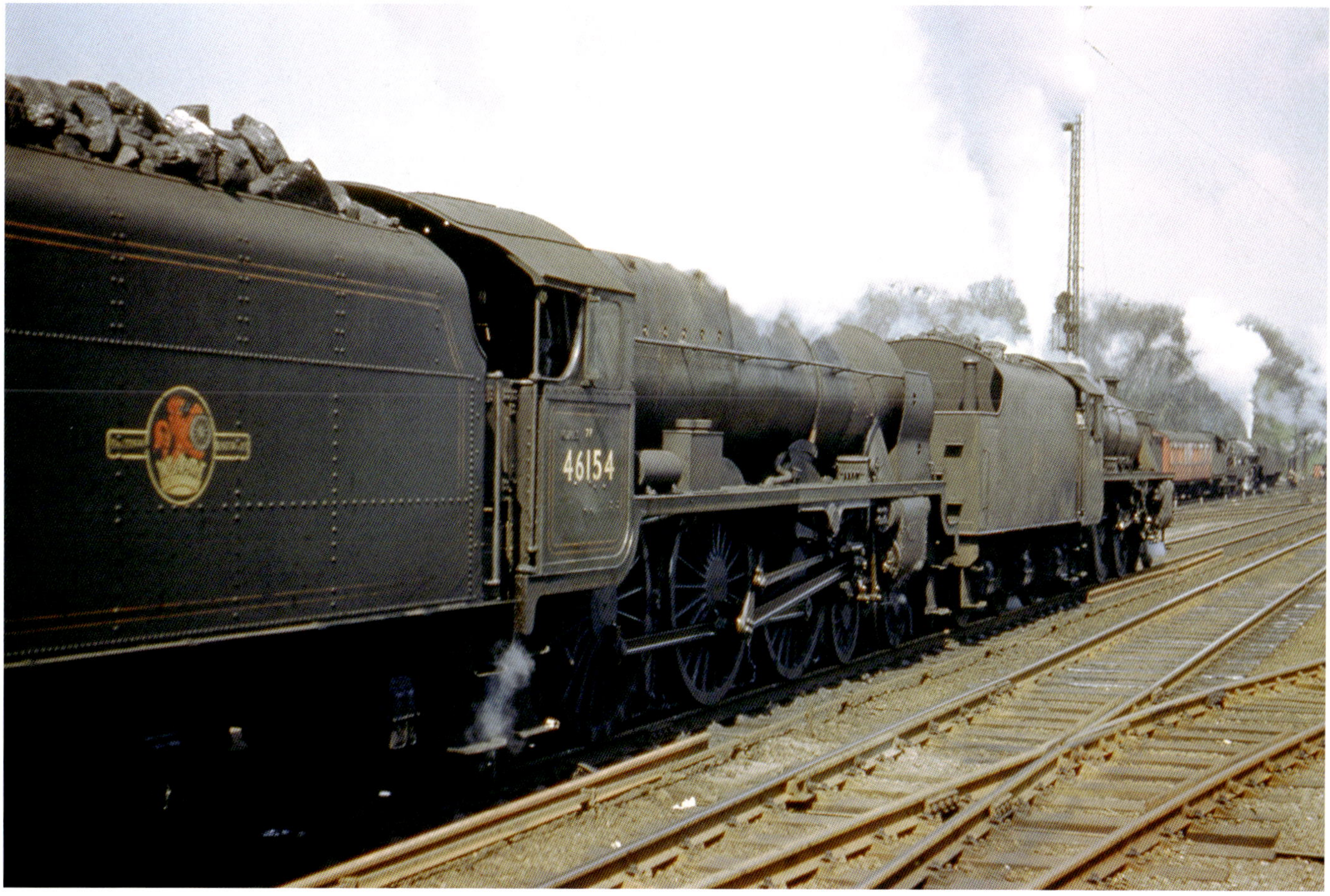

Two more views from 30 April 1960 at Bletchley with Crab 42812 waiting to be signalled away, whilst a Black Five pilots rebuilt Royal Scot 46154 The Hussar onwards. ***Both: Frank Hornby***

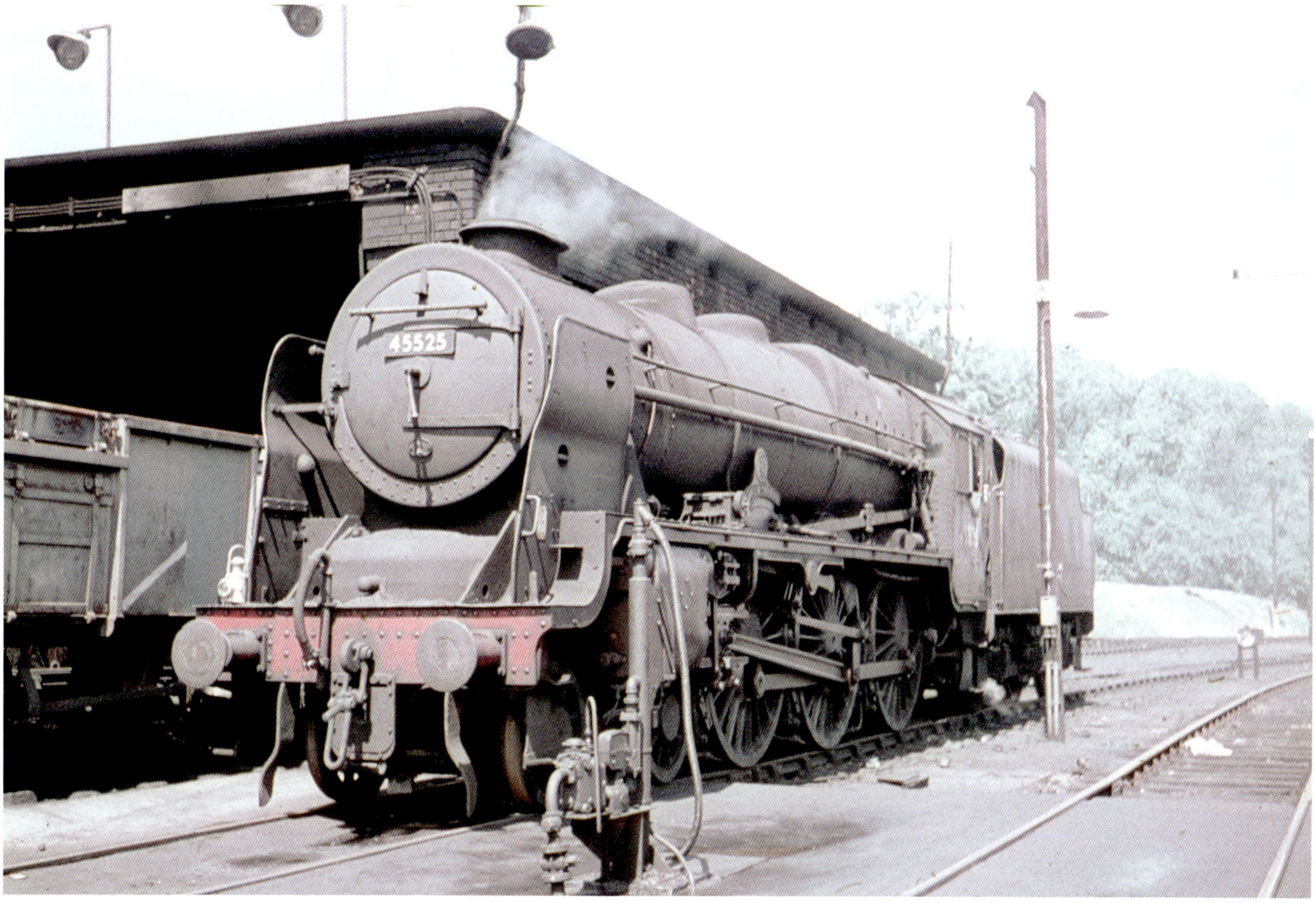

A visit to Bletchley shed coded 1E on 18 June 1961 finds an ash covered rebuilt Patriot 45525 Colwyn Bay standing by the water tower taking in the early summer sunshine. ***Late Vincent Heckford/Strathwood Library Collection***

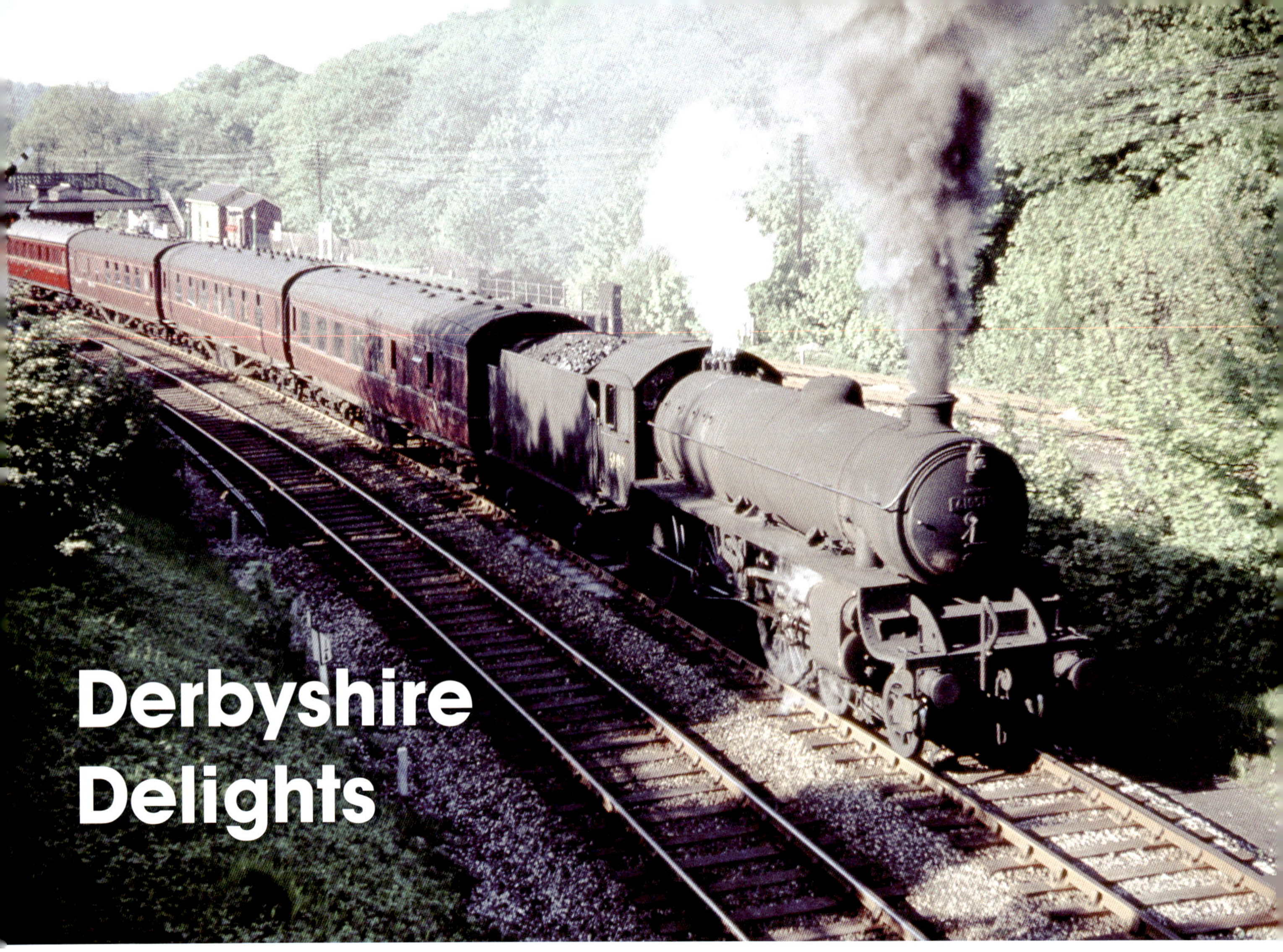

Derbyshire Delights

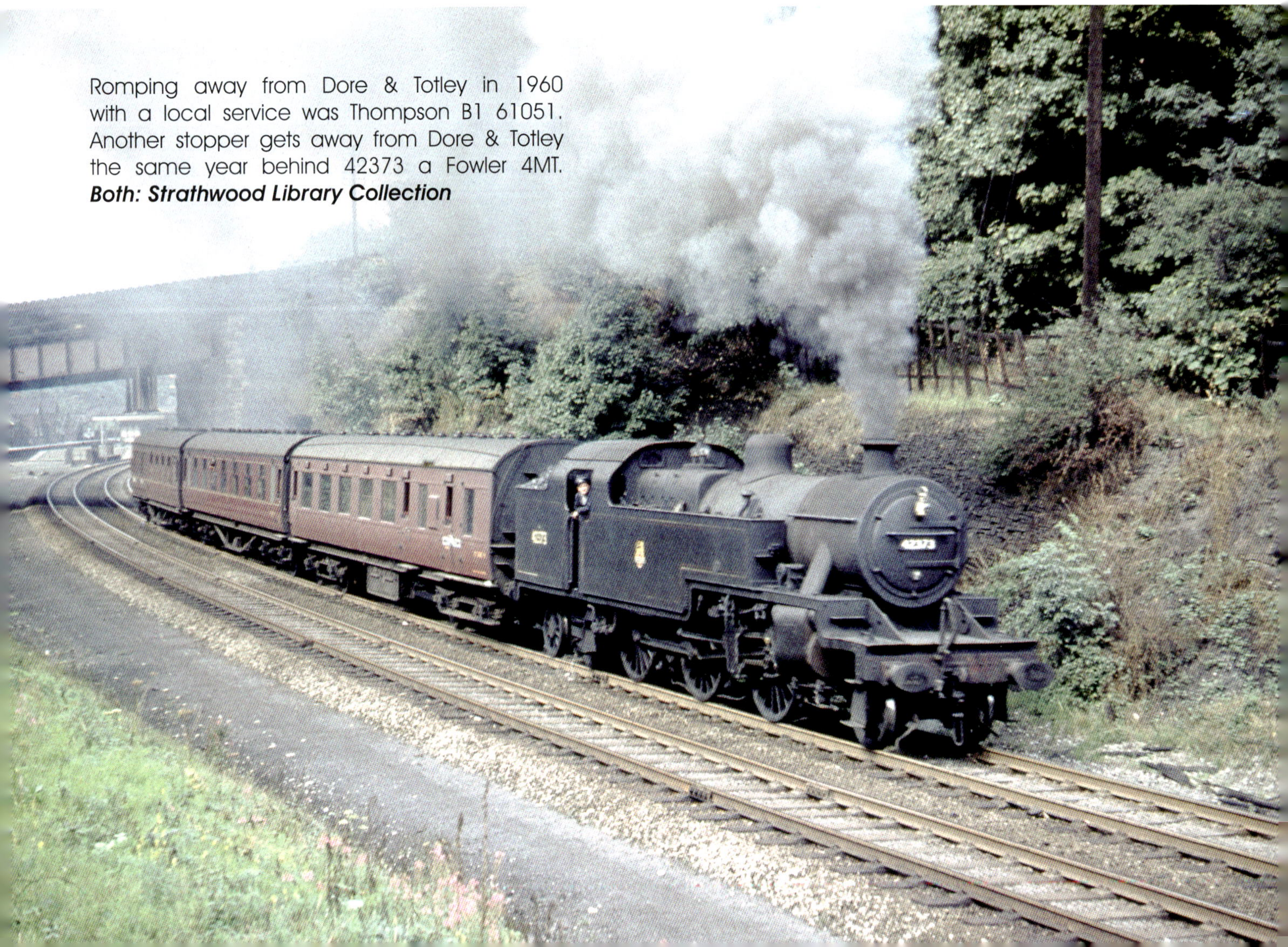

Romping away from Dore & Totley in 1960 with a local service was Thompson B1 61051. Another stopper gets away from Dore & Totley the same year behind 42373 a Fowler 4MT. ***Both: Strathwood Library Collection***

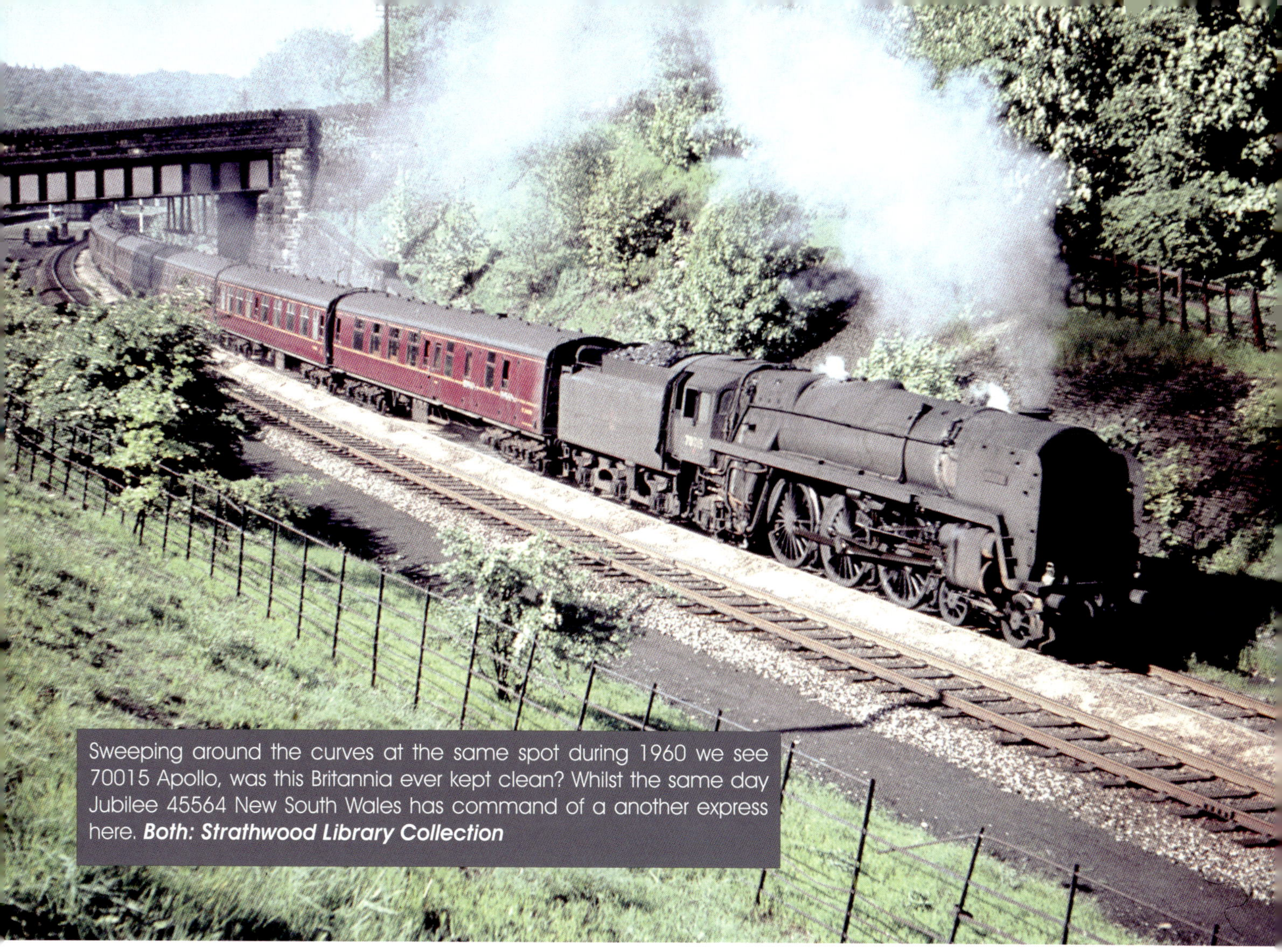

Sweeping around the curves at the same spot during 1960 we see 70015 Apollo, was this Britannia ever kept clean? Whilst the same day Jubilee 45564 New South Wales has command of a another express here. ***Both: Strathwood Library Collection***

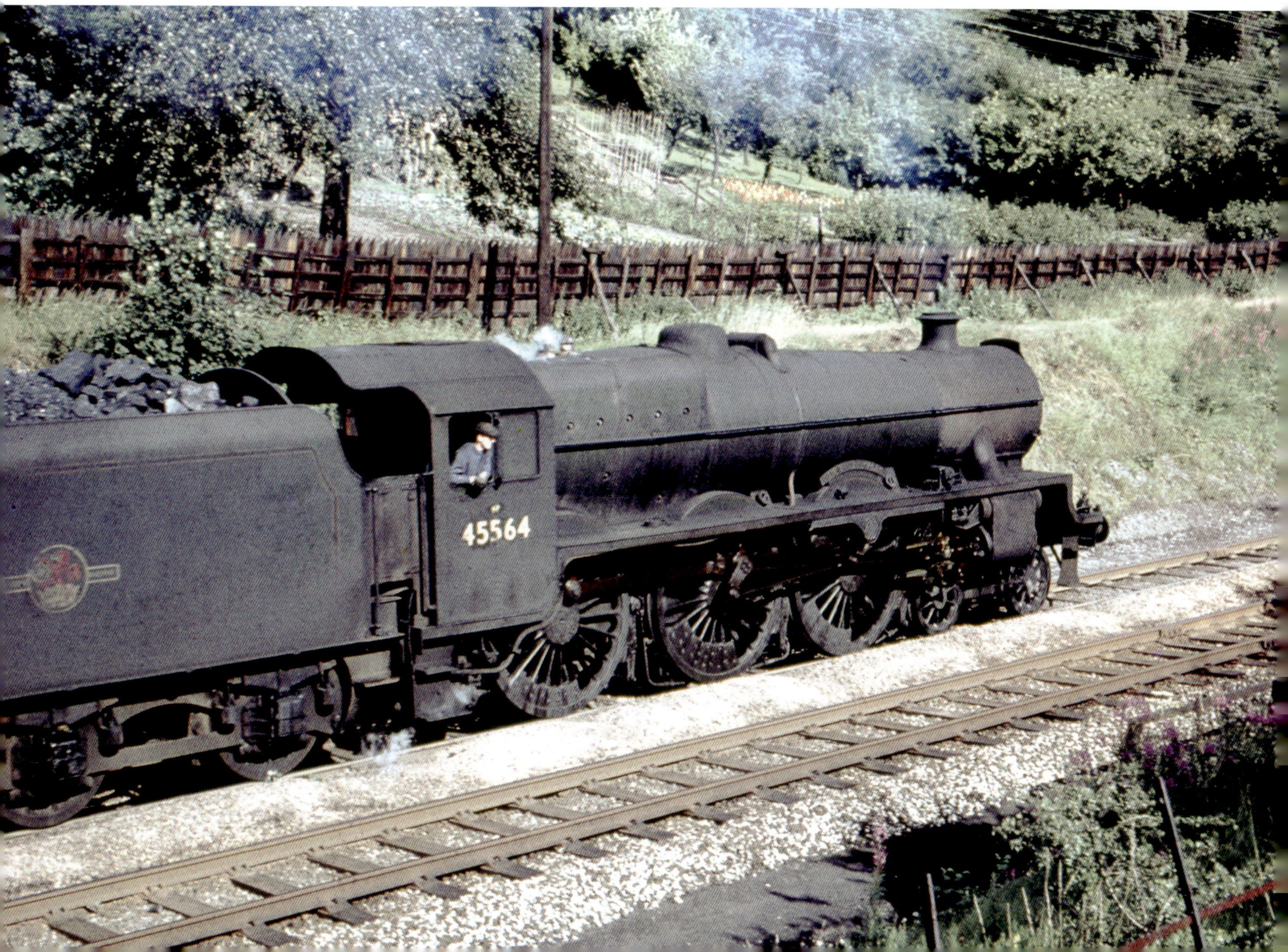

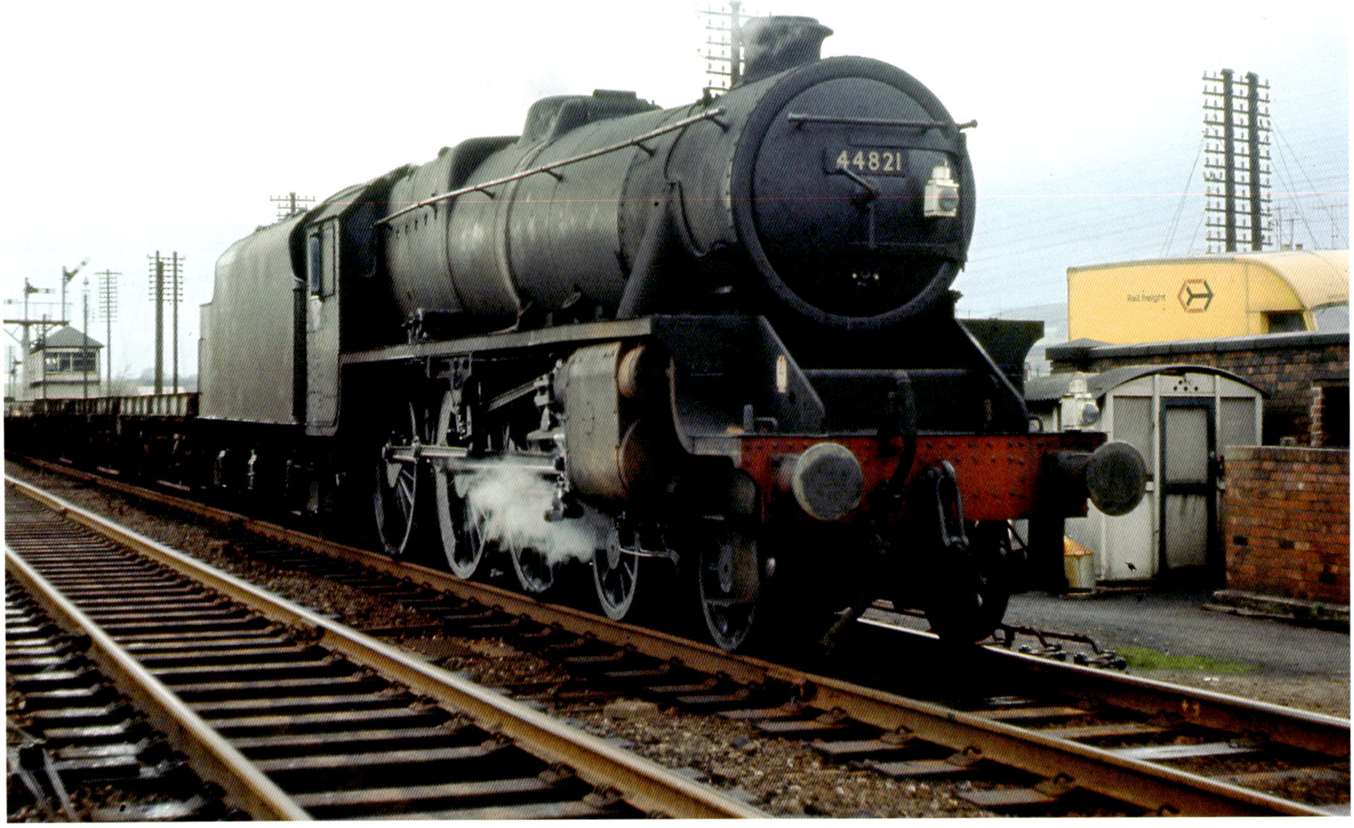

Pottering past Staverley with a short goods train was Black Five 44821 on 30 October 1965. At number one throughout the month was Ken Dodd with Tears, which took the Rolling Stones to knock the Diddy Man off his top spot after five weeks. ***Strathwood Library Collection***

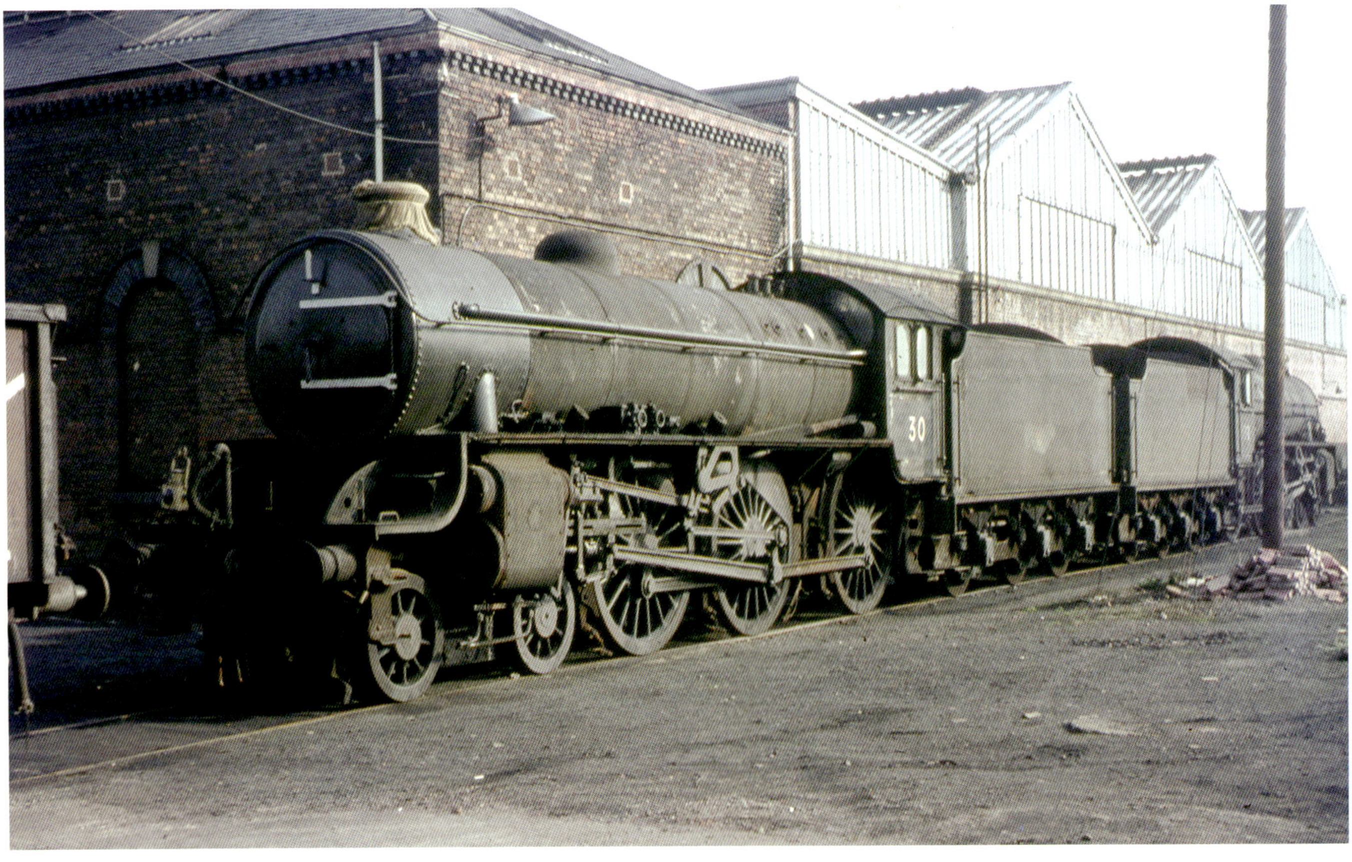

The Eastern Region found a use for a number of withdrawn Thompson B1s using them as stationary boliers for carraige heating or as depot boilers. Two of these found themselves tucked away alongside the roundhouse at Barrow Hill on 18 February 1968. Numbered 30 and 32 in Departmental Stock, they had been 61050 and 61315 in service days. The pair last saw use in 1967 and all that they could look forward to now were Sheffield's scrap merchants. ***Strathwood Library Collection***

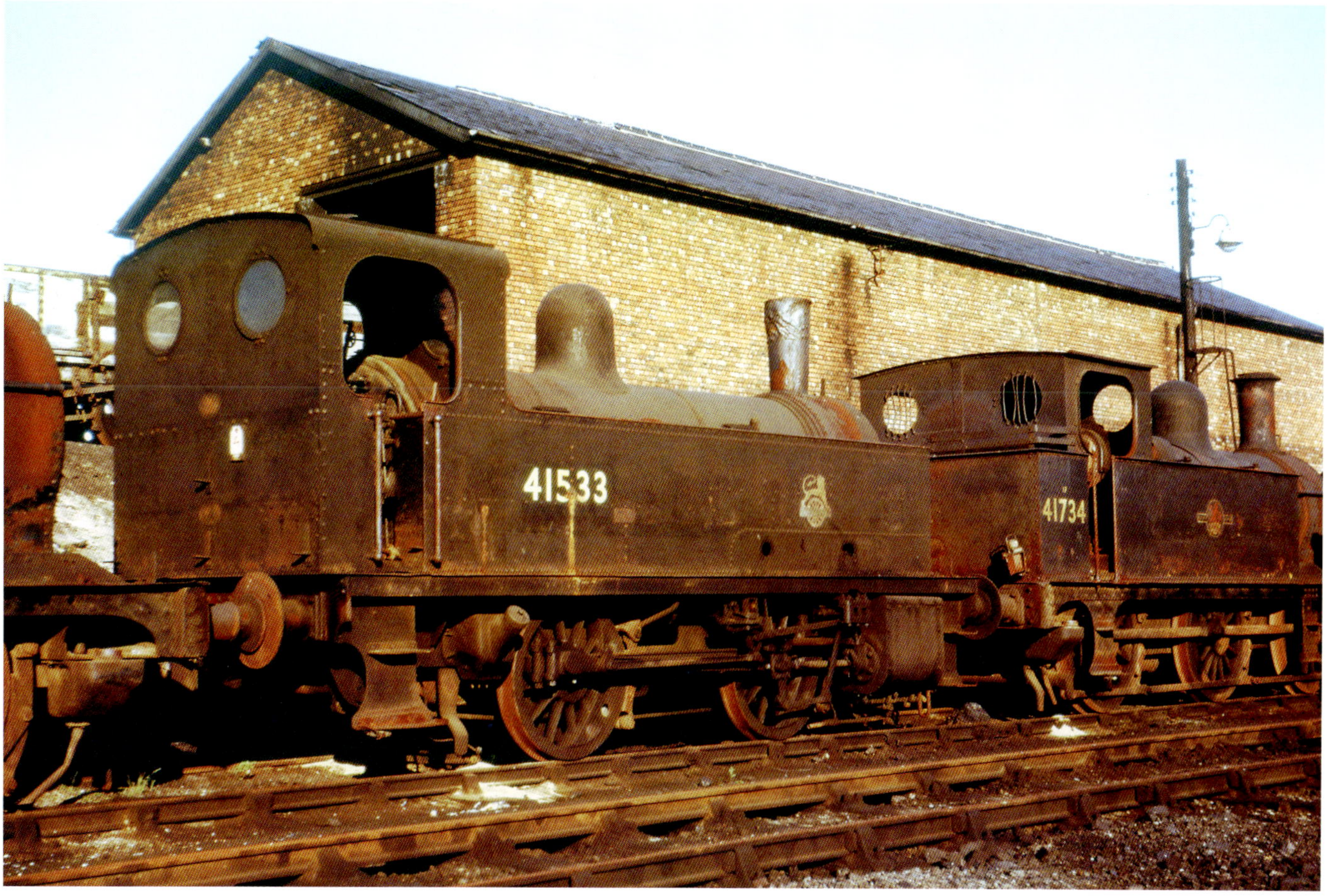

Among the line up of scrappers at Canklow on 17 July 1966 was Deeley 0F 41533 this diminutive 0-4-0T would not be posted as withdrawn until December that year, the shed here was coded 41D and closed on 14 June the year before. ***Strathwood Library Collection***

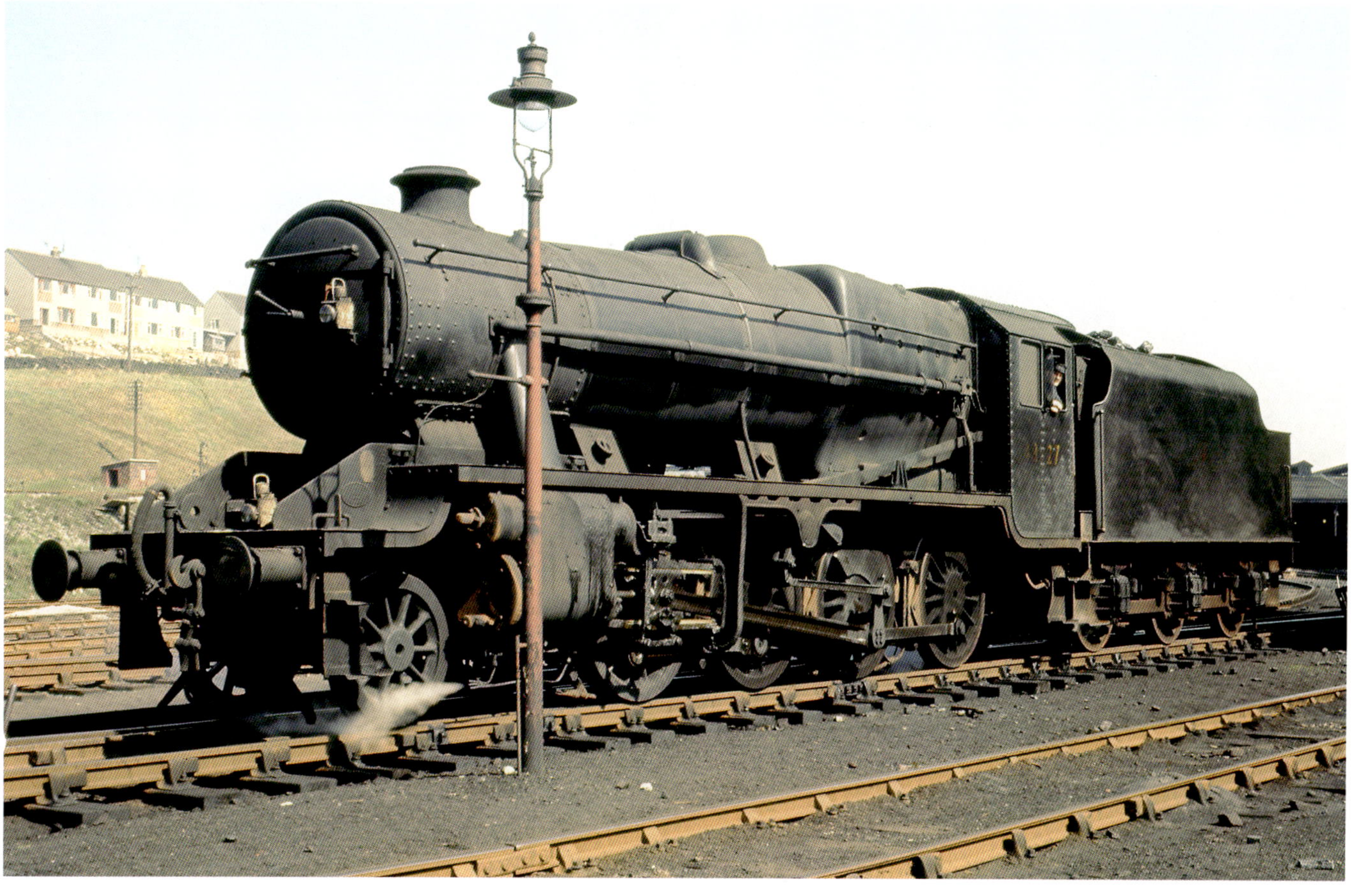

The Midland Railway had thoughtfully provided gas lamps to illuminate the shed yard at Buxton, they were still in good condition when this shot of Stanier 8F 48327 was taken on 1 May 1966. ***Win Wall/Strathwood Library Collection***

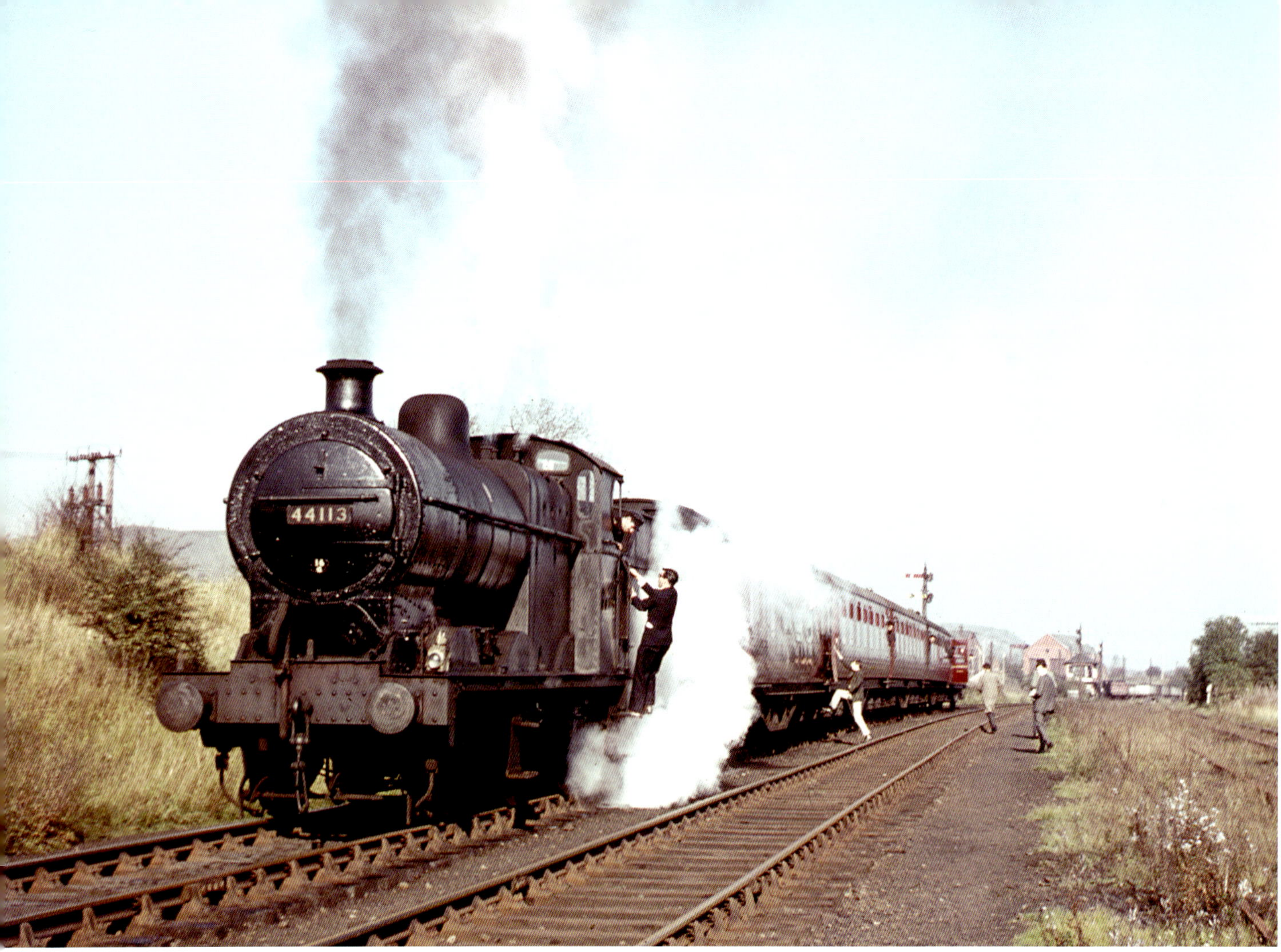

On 17 October 1965 the L.C.G.B. ran their Derbyshire Railtour headed throughout by Fowler 4F 44113 snaking its way around many once busy junctions and branches such as the one to Ripley where we find passengers being urged back into the coaches after a photo stop. ***Strathwood Library Collection***

The day before the R.C.T.S. had used another Fowler 4F 43953 for their Midlands Locomotive Requiem Railtour which was stopped at Ambergate during the afternoon. ***Strathwood Library Collection***

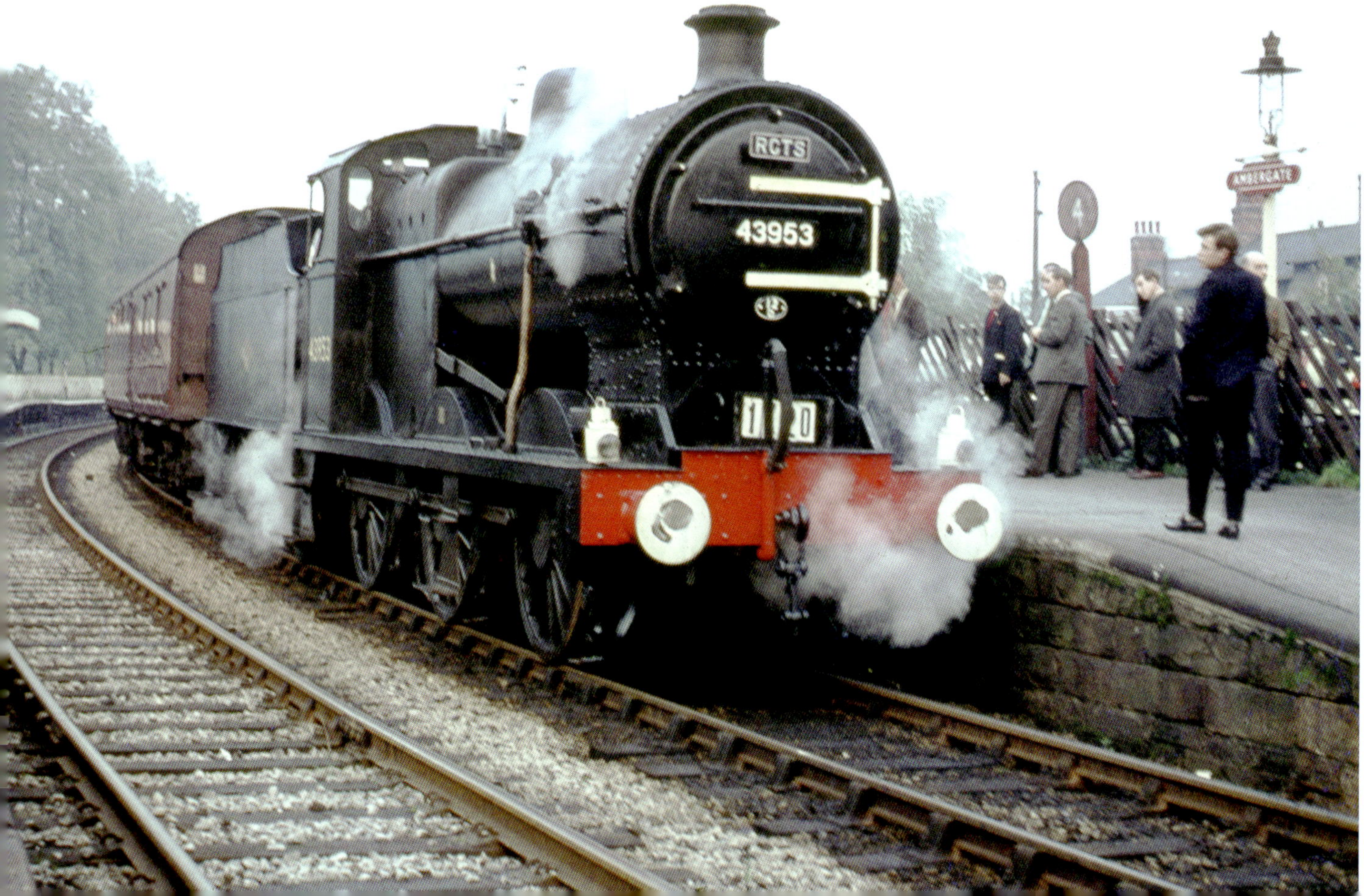

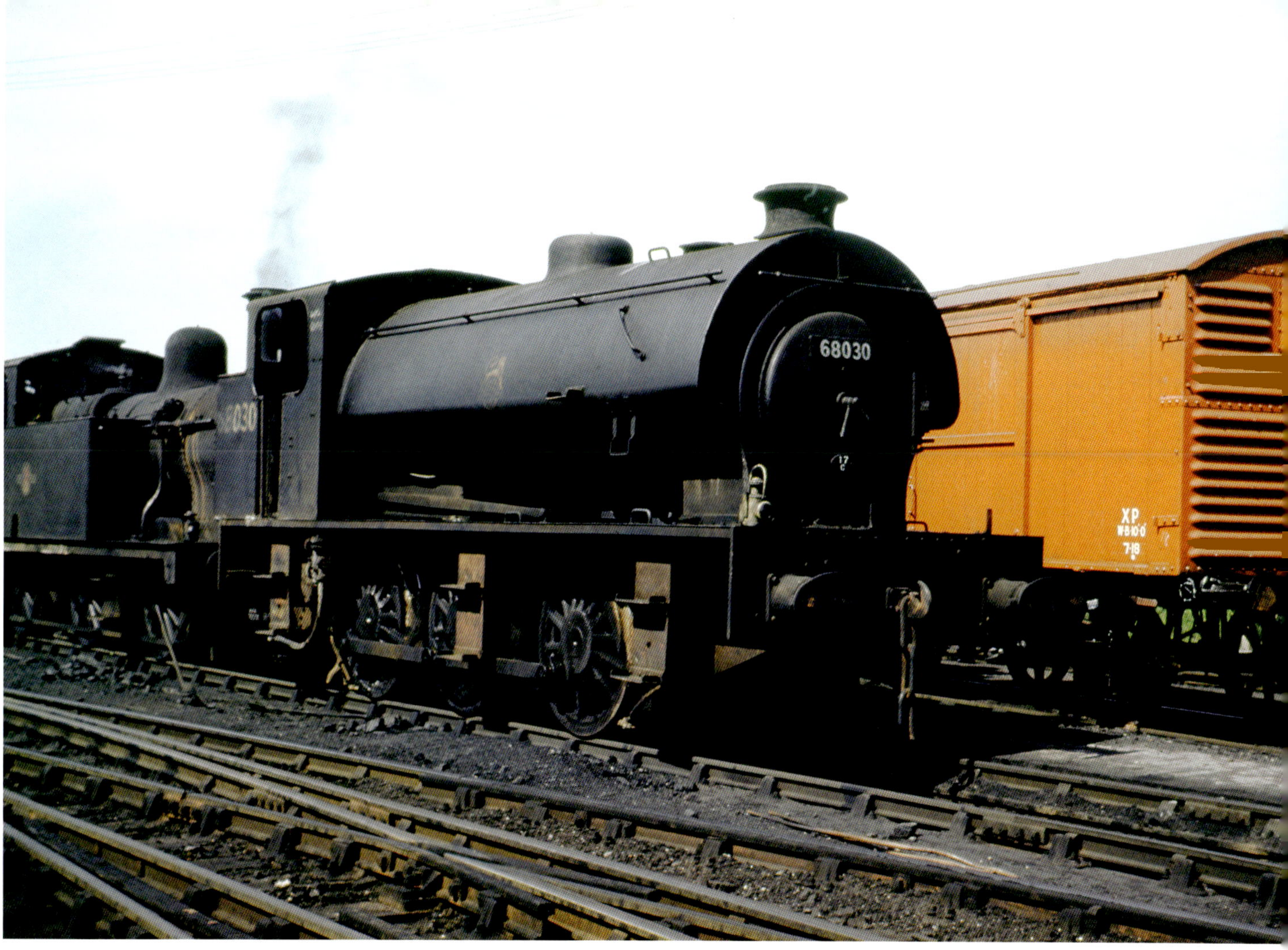

An ex works box van keeps company with a J94 Class 68030 on shed at Rowsley during 1960. ***John Gill***

Railtours to the Cromford and High Peak were popular with this one on 29 August 1964 making use of open wagons and 1953 Horwich built 47006 to carry the tour's participants. ***Strathwood Library Collection***

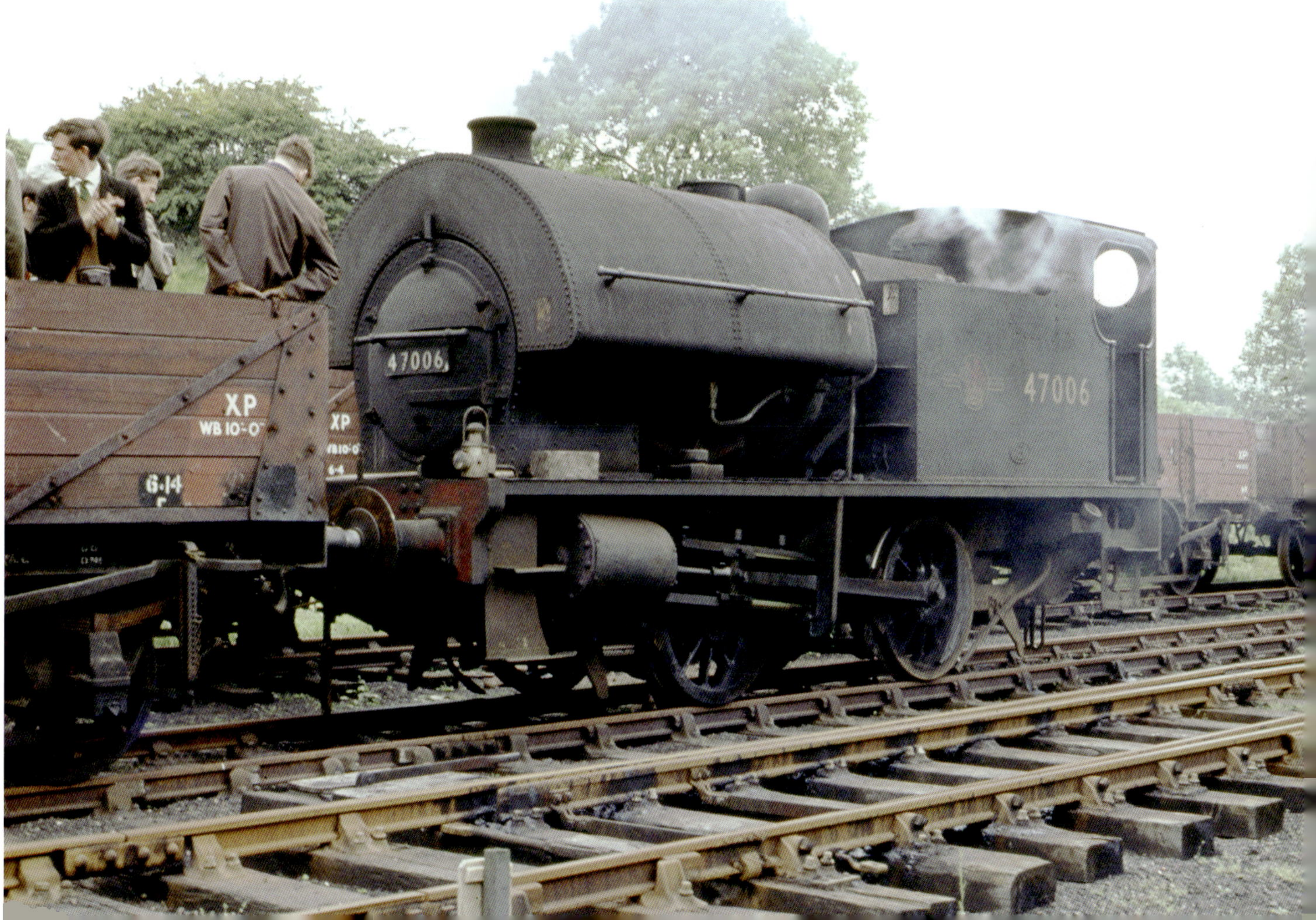

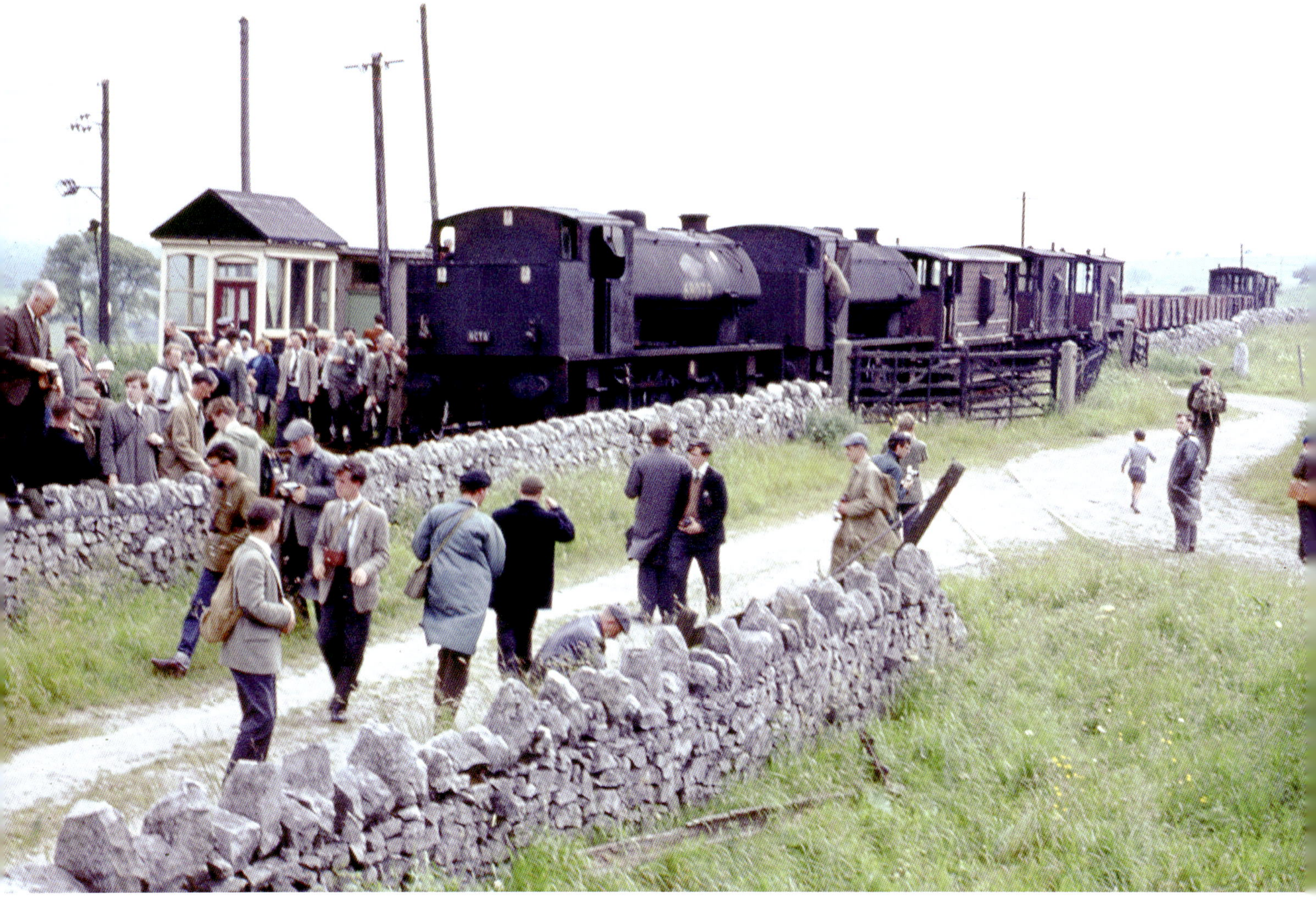

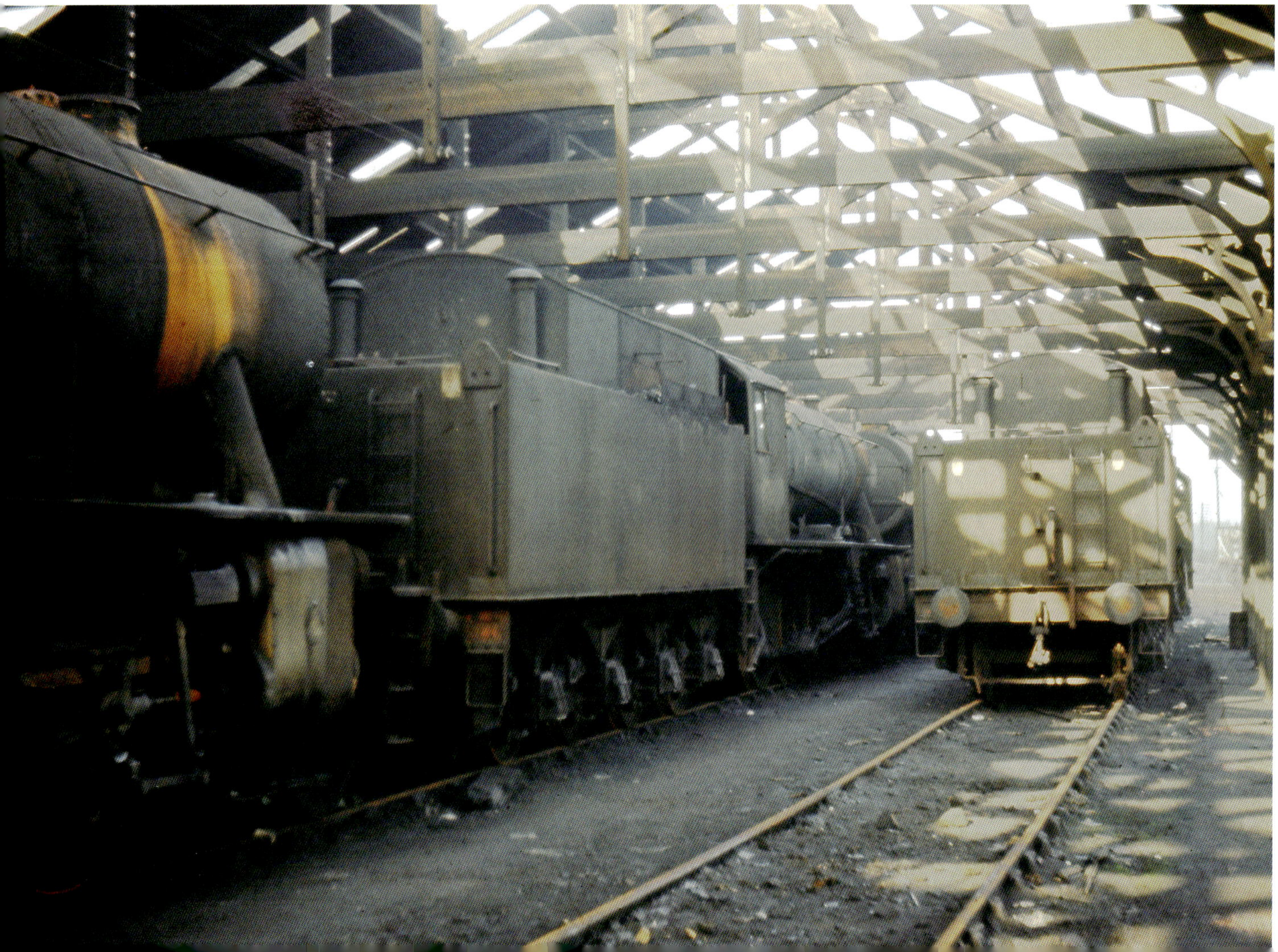

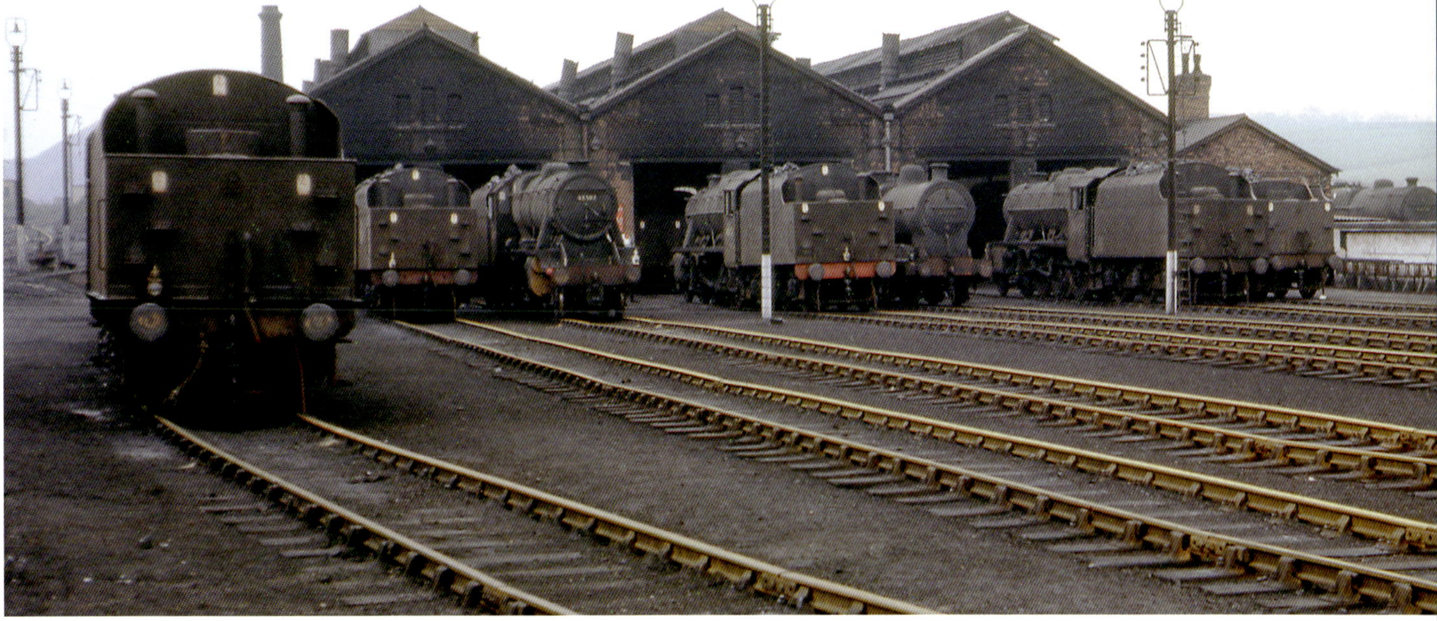

Opposite: Several trains were run on the line with Class J94 68079 leading a classmate the same August day. ***Strathwood Library Collection***

Opposite bottom: The open air shed roof at 41J Langwith Junction on 6 February 1966 was equally capable of letting the smoke out as letting the weather in. This would be the last day for booked steam here, the shed closed completely on 19 November the same year. ***Strathwood Library Collection***

Steam would remain active at 16G Westhouses until 3 October 1966, these scenes were taken the same day in April 1964. After closure to steam the location was used for stabling diesels for many years although the shed building was taken down shortly after closure to steam. ***Both: Win Wall/Strathwood Library Collection***

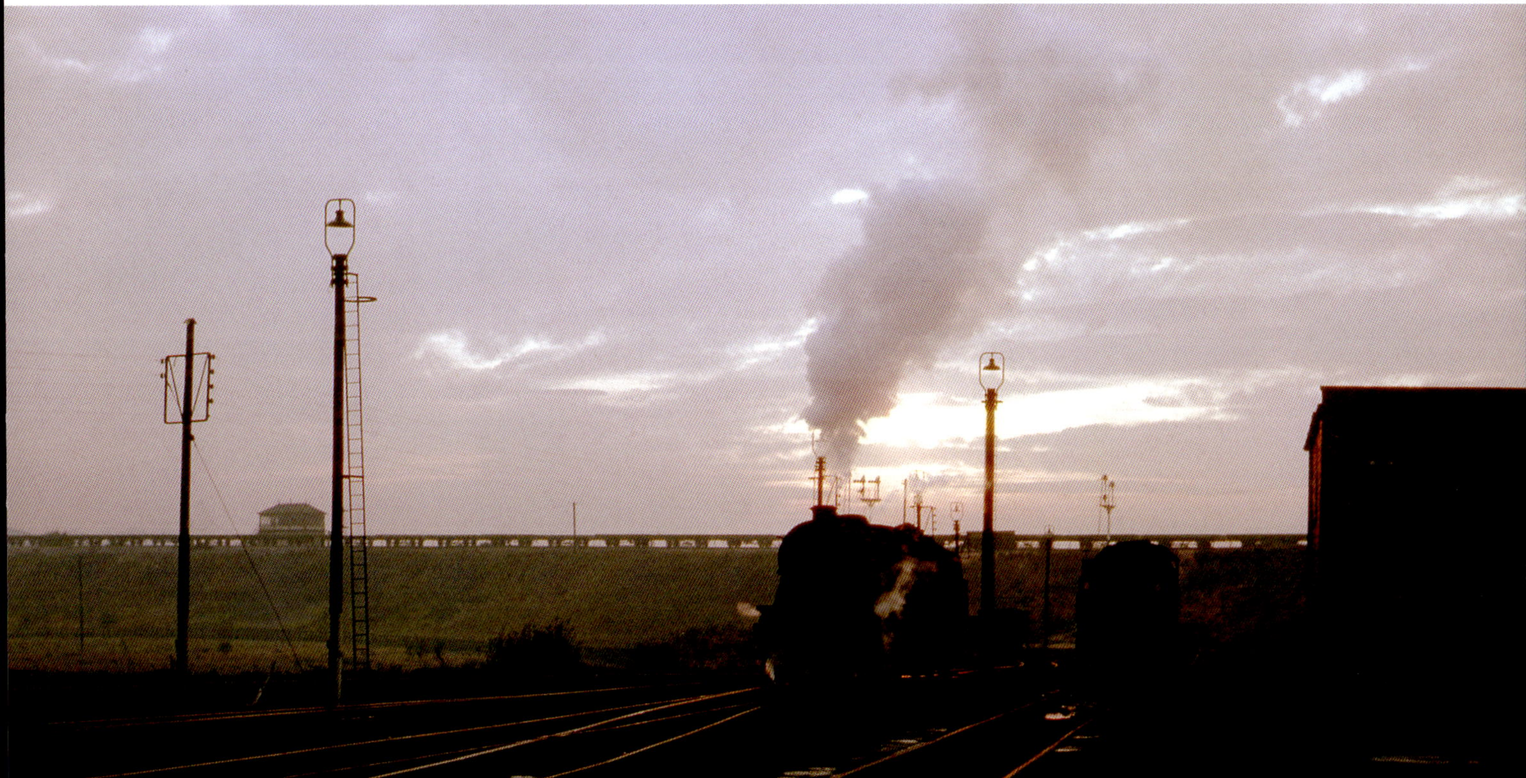

Specials

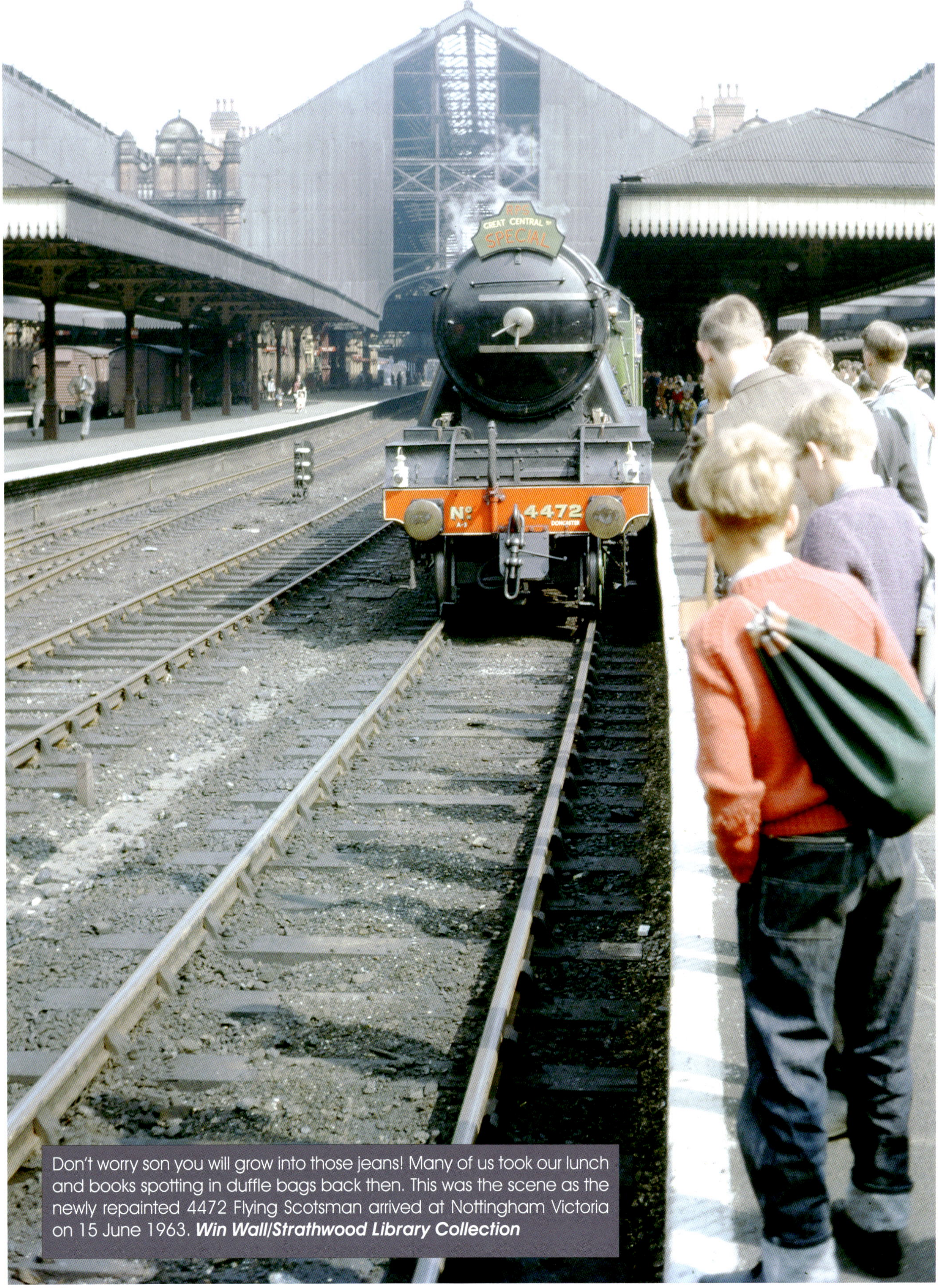

Don't worry son you will grow into those jeans! Many of us took our lunch and books spotting in duffle bags back then. This was the scene as the newly repainted 4472 Flying Scotsman arrived at Nottingham Victoria on 15 June 1963. ***Win Wall/Strathwood Library Collection***

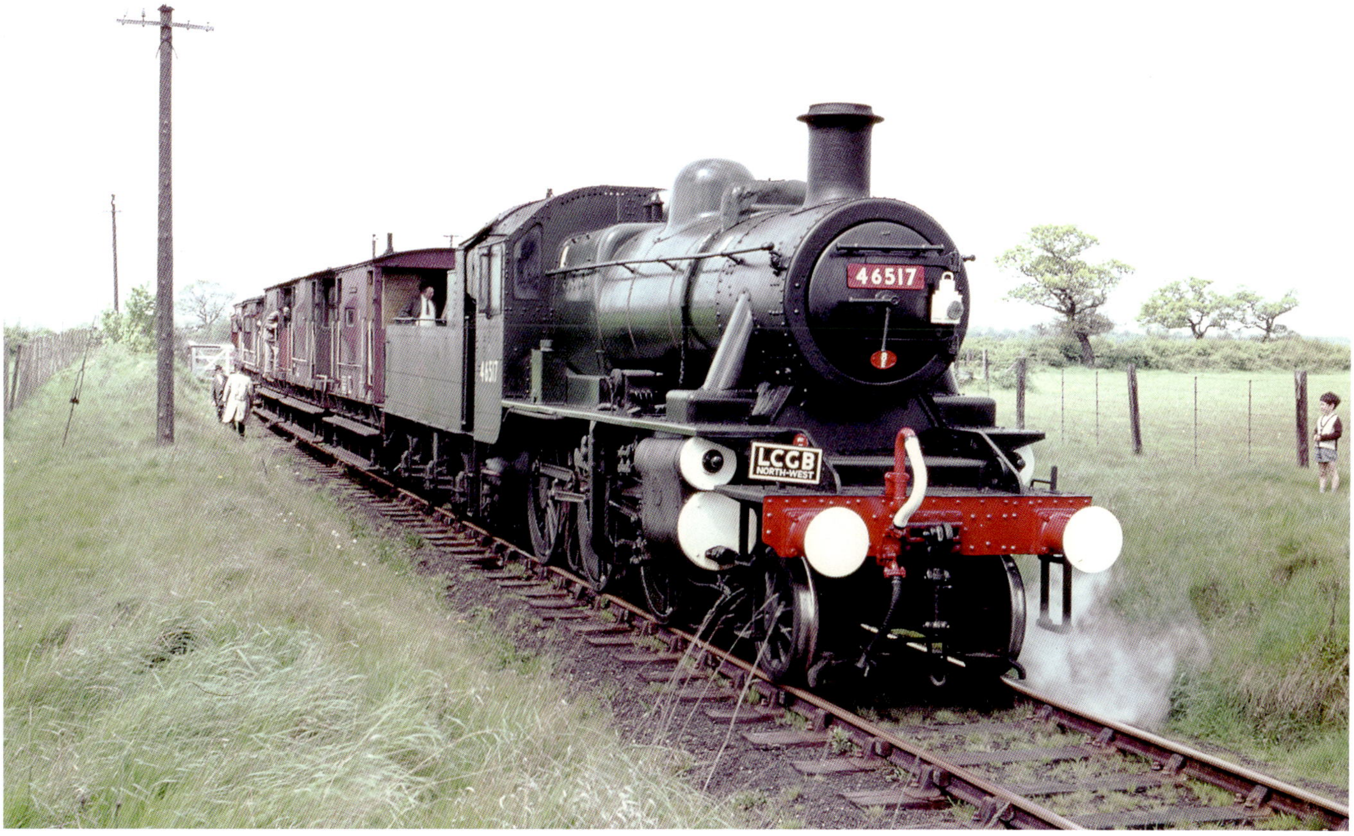

Having been bulled up for the day Ivatt Mogul 46517 saw use on the R.C.T.S. Cheshire Cat Railtour on 14 May 1966 covering the then limit of the Cheshire Lines Committee constructed Winsford & Over branch and the Salt Works branch with a train made up of a rake brakevans. ***Strathwood Library Collection***

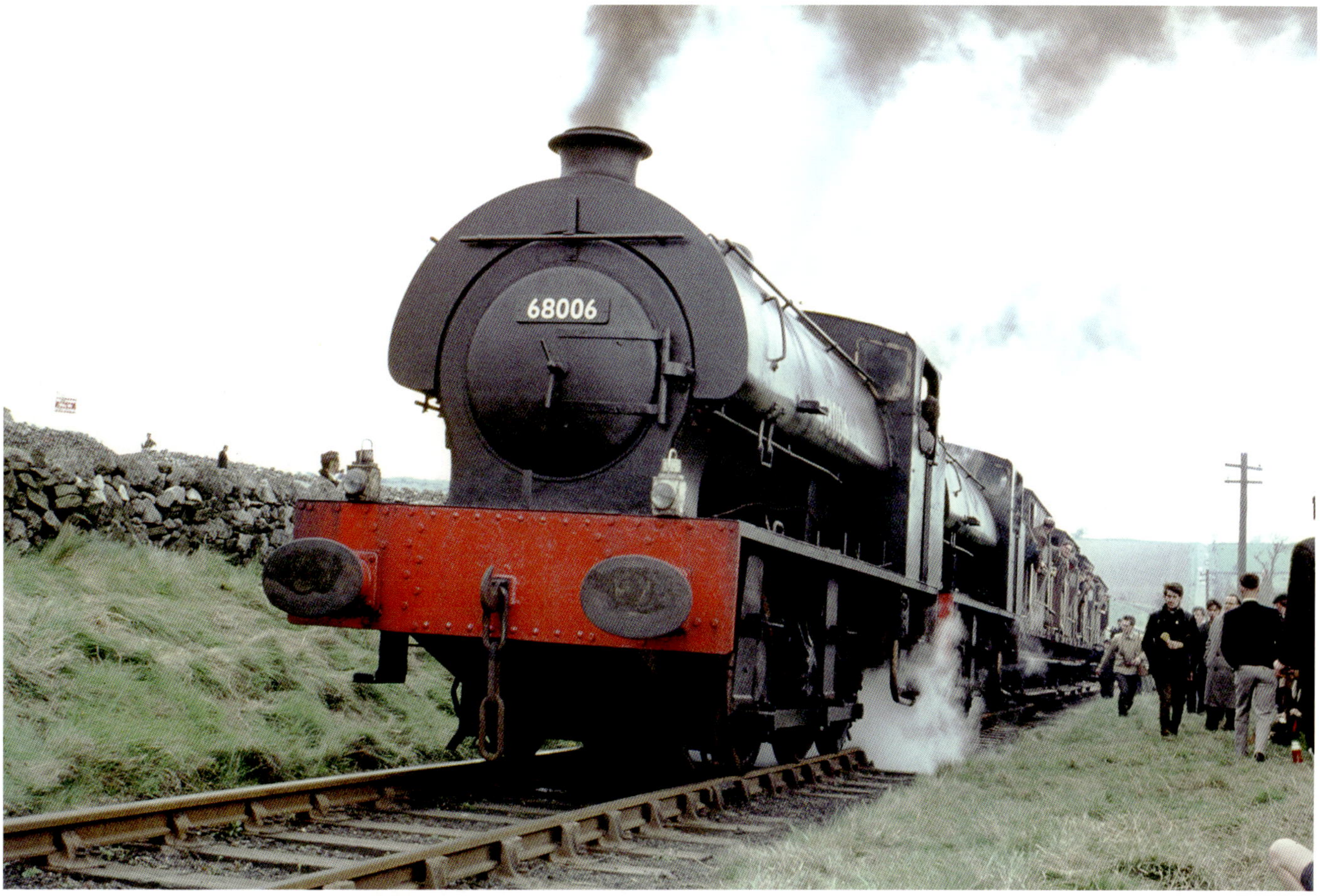

Enthusiats screwing down the brakes in at least one of the brakevans has caused Class J94s 68006 and 68012 to stall on Hopton Incline on 30 April 1967. Fortunately it all turned out well in the end, but it could just as easily have been a different story. ***Strathwood Library Collection***

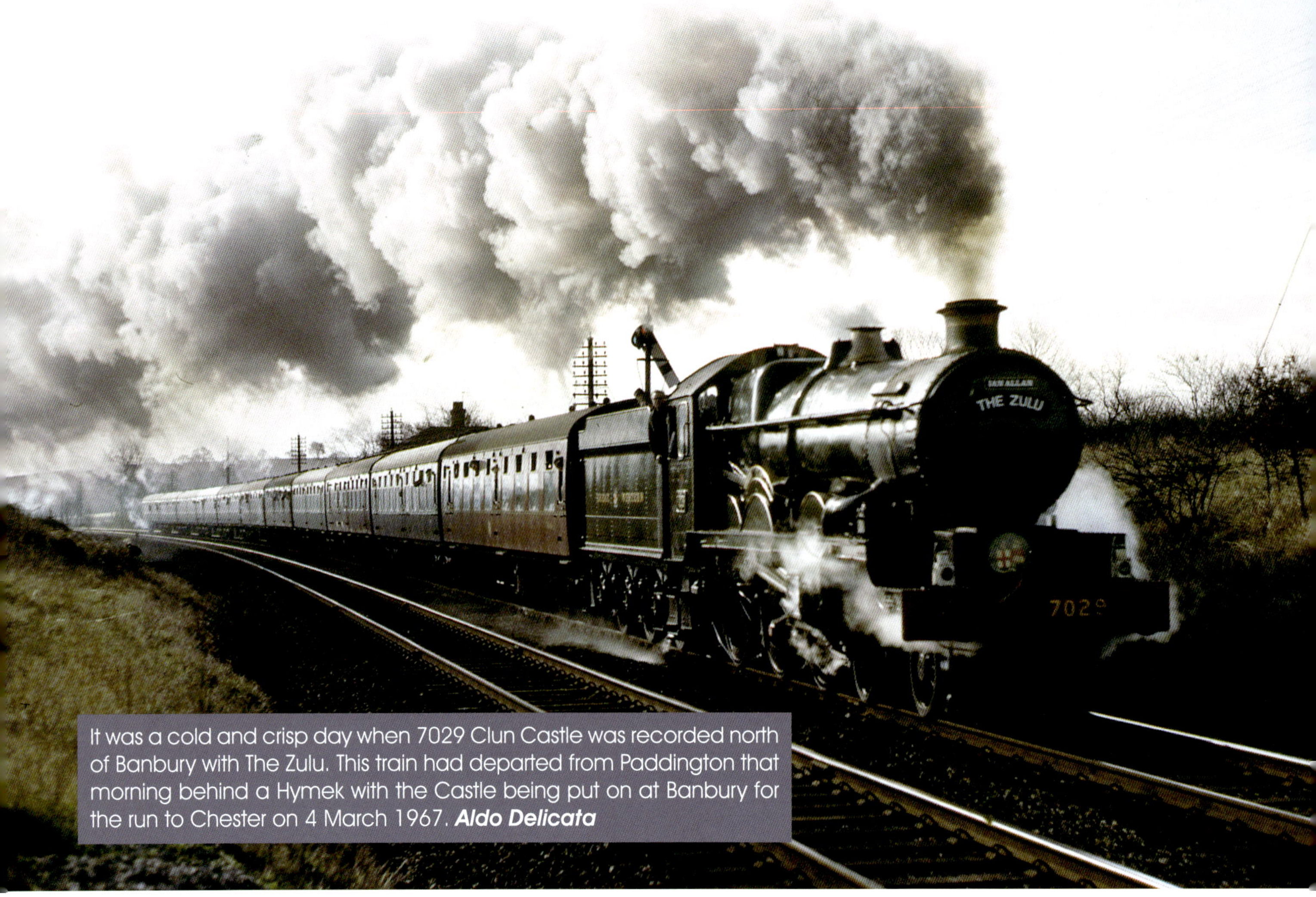

It was a cold and crisp day when 7029 Clun Castle was recorded north of Banbury with The Zulu. This train had departed from Paddington that morning behind a Hymek with the Castle being put on at Banbury for the run to Chester on 4 March 1967. ***Aldo Delicata***

Jointly arranged on 20 April 1968 by the Manchester Rail Travel Society and the Severn Valley Railway Society, The North West Tour came to a stand at Chinley behind Black Fives 45110 and 44949 allowing cameramen a chance to grab a photograph. ***Strathwood Library Collection***

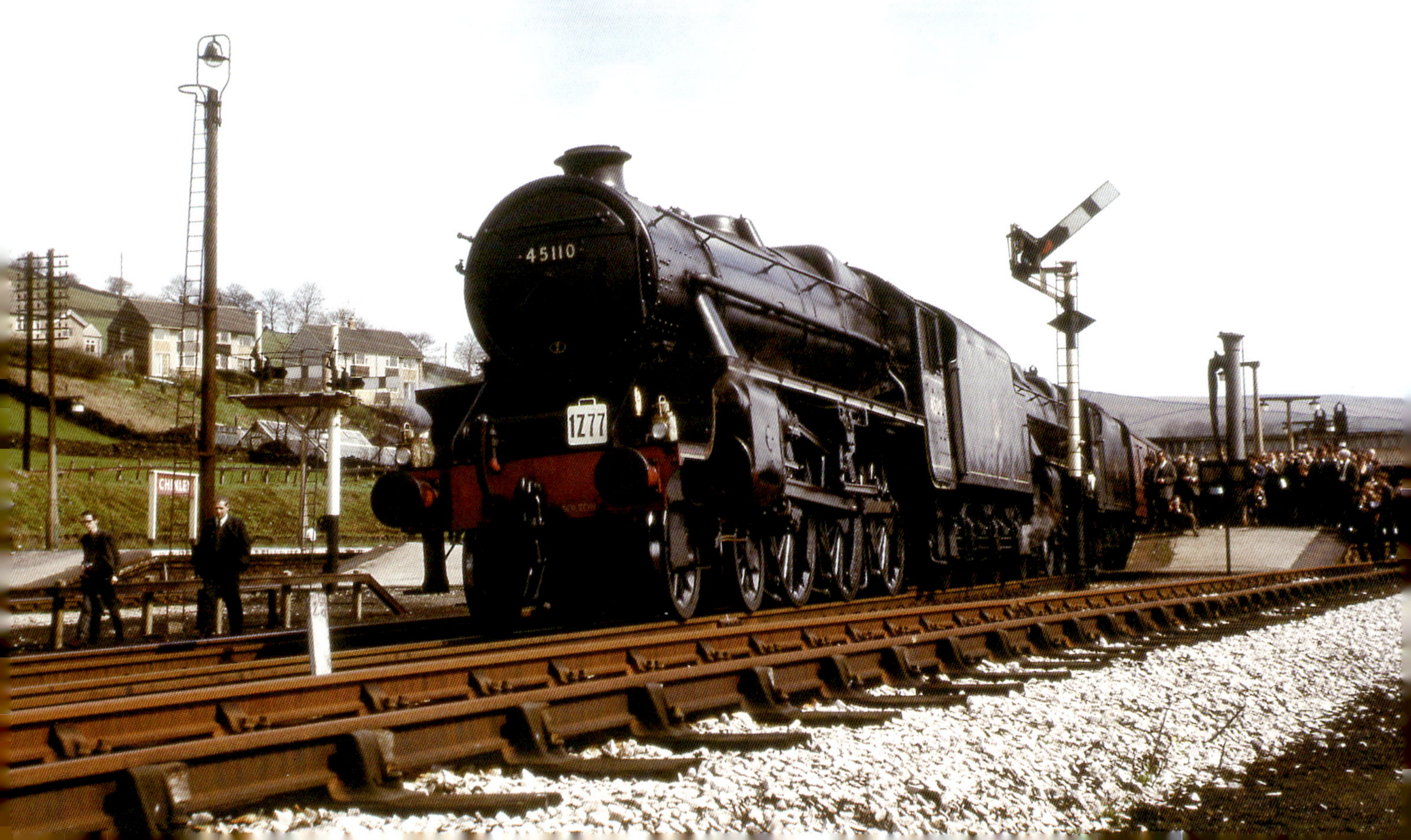

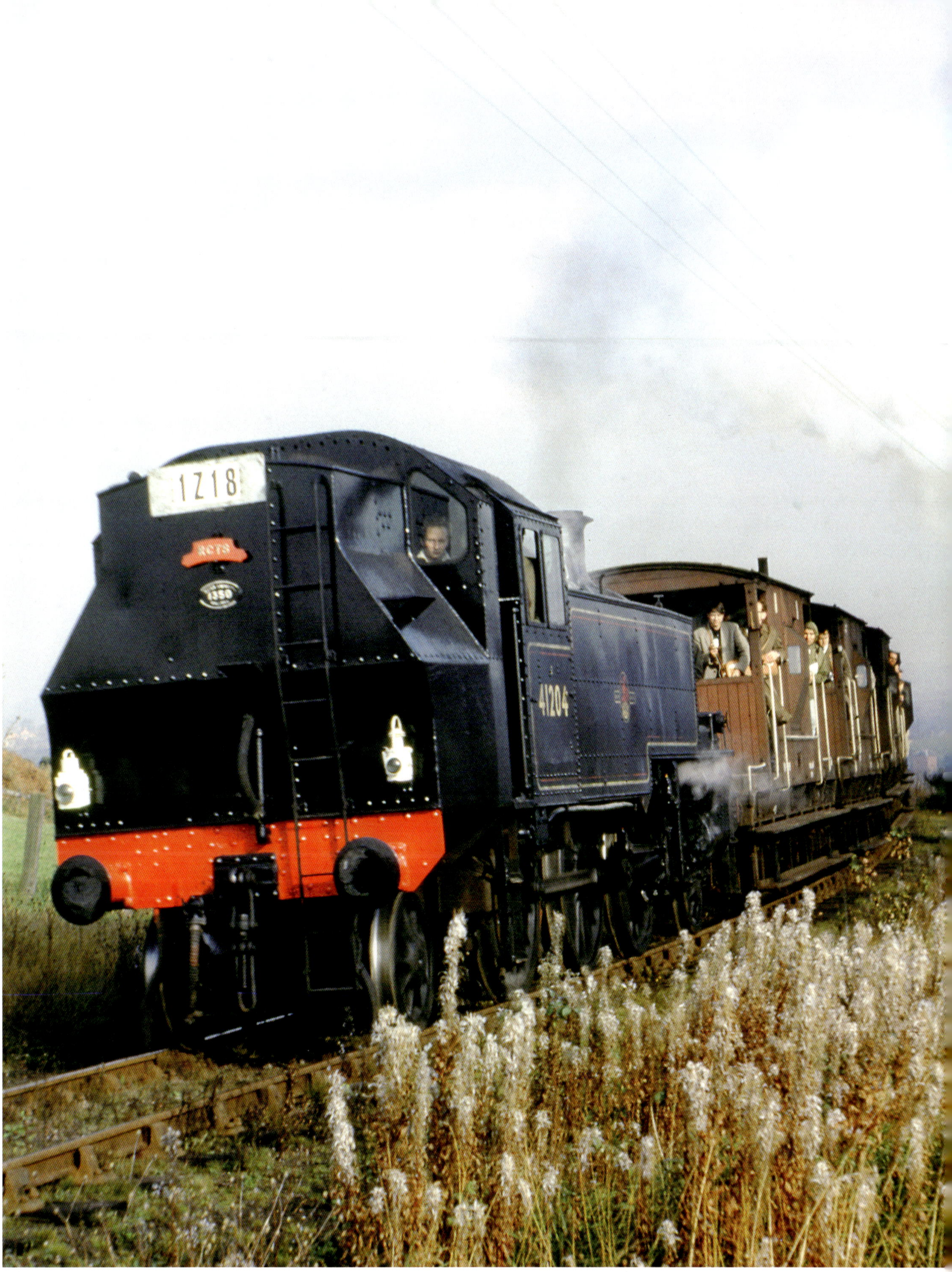

Once again the transport for passengers on the R.C.T.S. organised Stoke on Trent Area Brake Van Tour adds to the flavour of the day. The train engine throughout was Ivatt 2MT 41204 running bunker first on one leg near Cheadle on 29 October 1966. Whilst Carry On Screaming was already playing in the country's cinemas the team were making Carry On Don't Lose Your Head which would be released in time for Christmas. ***Jerry Beddows***

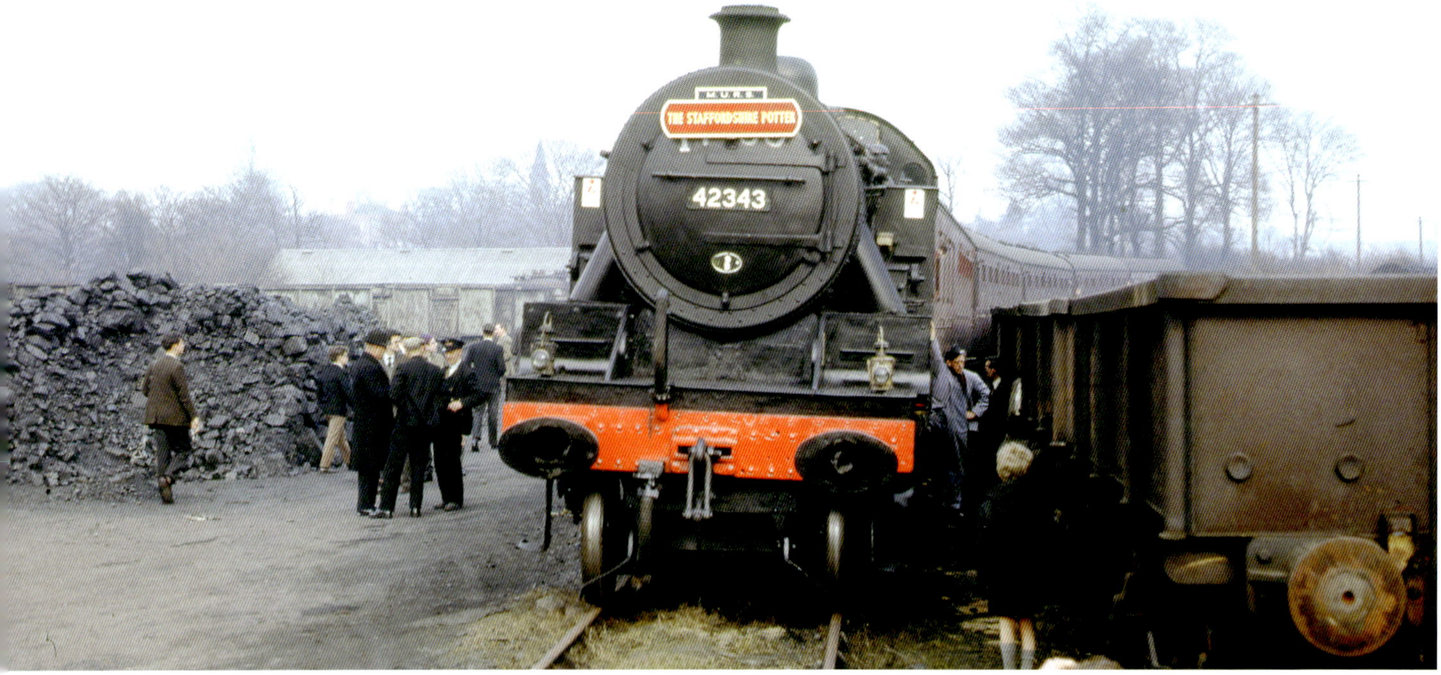

On 13 March 1965 The Staffordshire Potter tour was put together by the Manchester University Railway Society using Fowler 4MT 42343 as the main motive power. The tour traversed the branch to Congleton Brunswick Wharf where we see the train crew discussing how they are to back up as they could not run around and the train had to be split. ***Strathwood Library Collection***

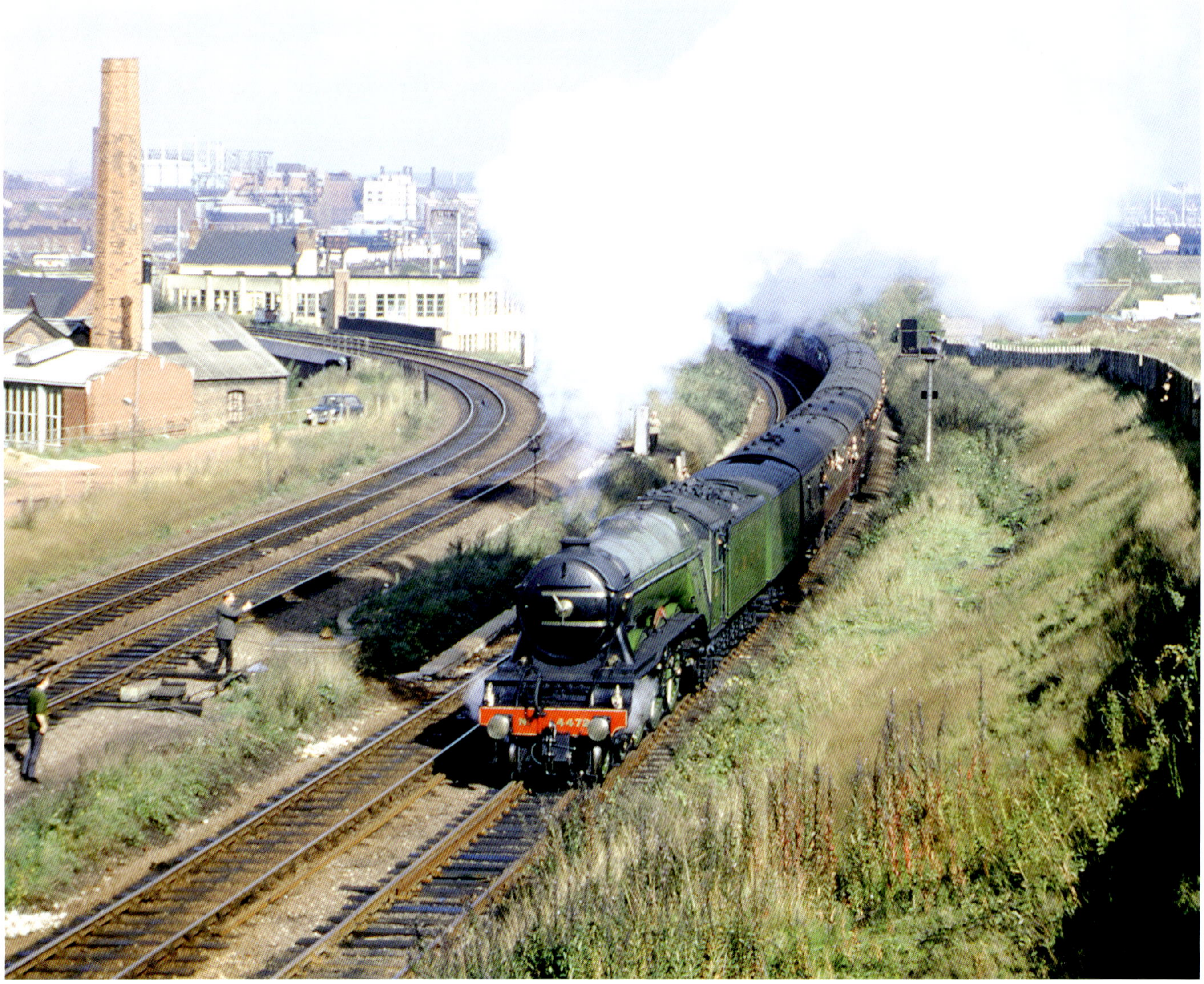

A well patronised enthusiasts special was run to Tyseley on 27 September 1968 hauled by 4472 Flying Scotsman now running with two tenders, for extra water capacity, when seen at St. Andrews Junction. ***Jerry Beddows***

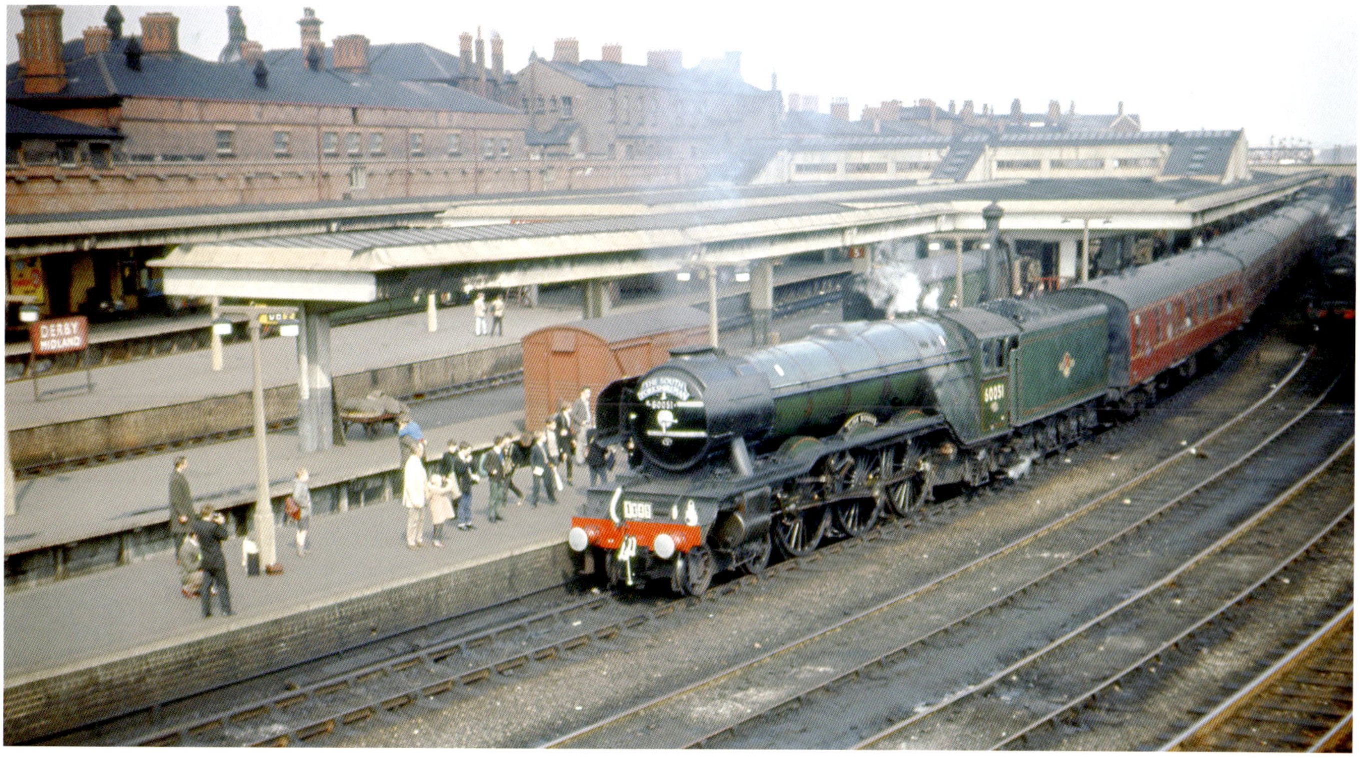

The South Yorkshireman No.2 railtour brought Gresley A3 60051 Blink Bonny to Derby on 18 April 1964, the passengers taking in visits to both Derby Works along with Crewe Works as part of their ticket price. It was reported during the month that Elvis Presley had sold 100 million records already. ***Len Smith***

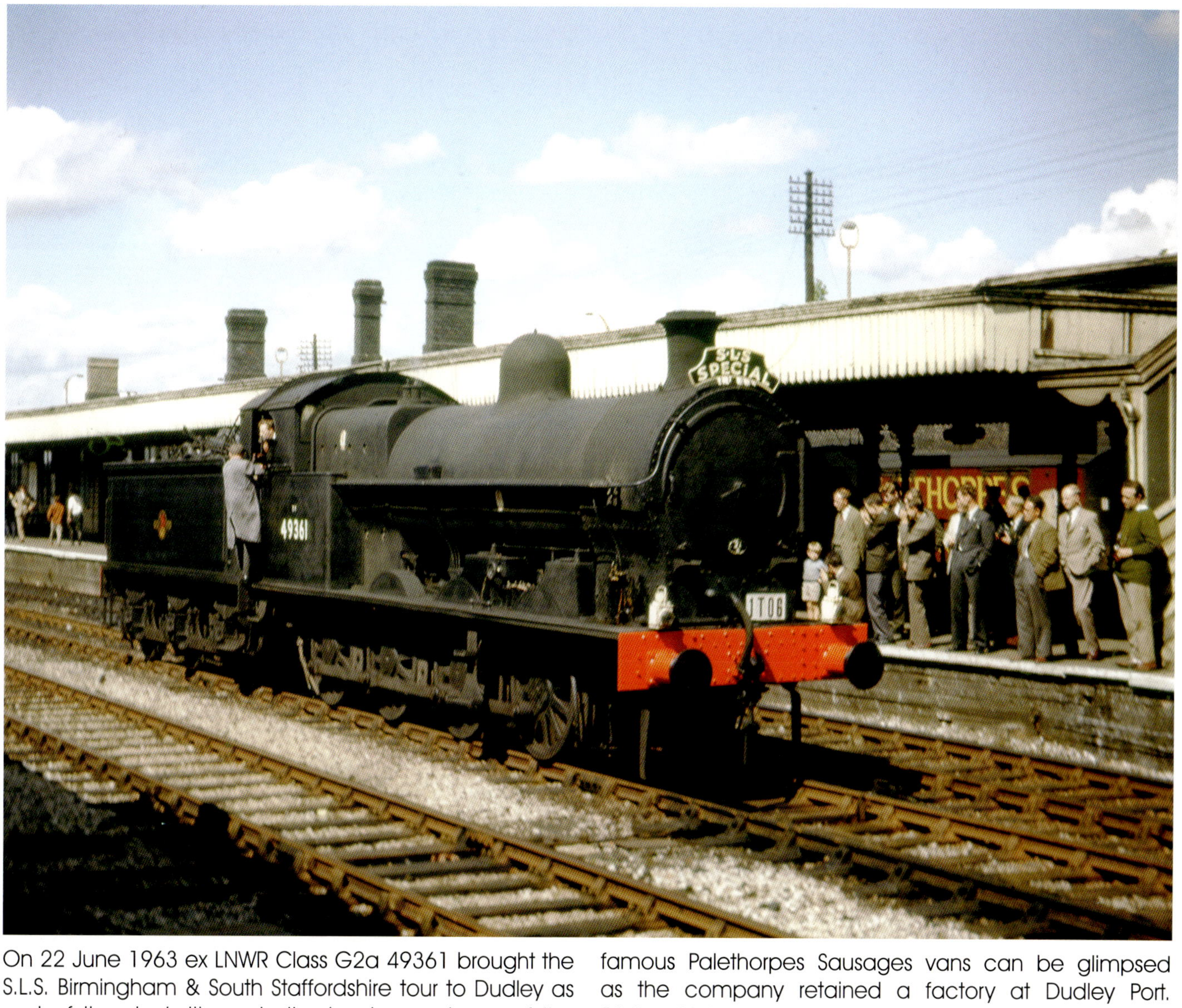

On 22 June 1963 ex LNWR Class G2a 49361 brought the S.L.S. Birmingham & South Staffordshire tour to Dudley as part of the day's itinery. In the background one of the famous Palethorpes Sausages vans can be glimpsed as the company retained a factory at Dudley Port. ***Richard Icke***

All Change at Crewe

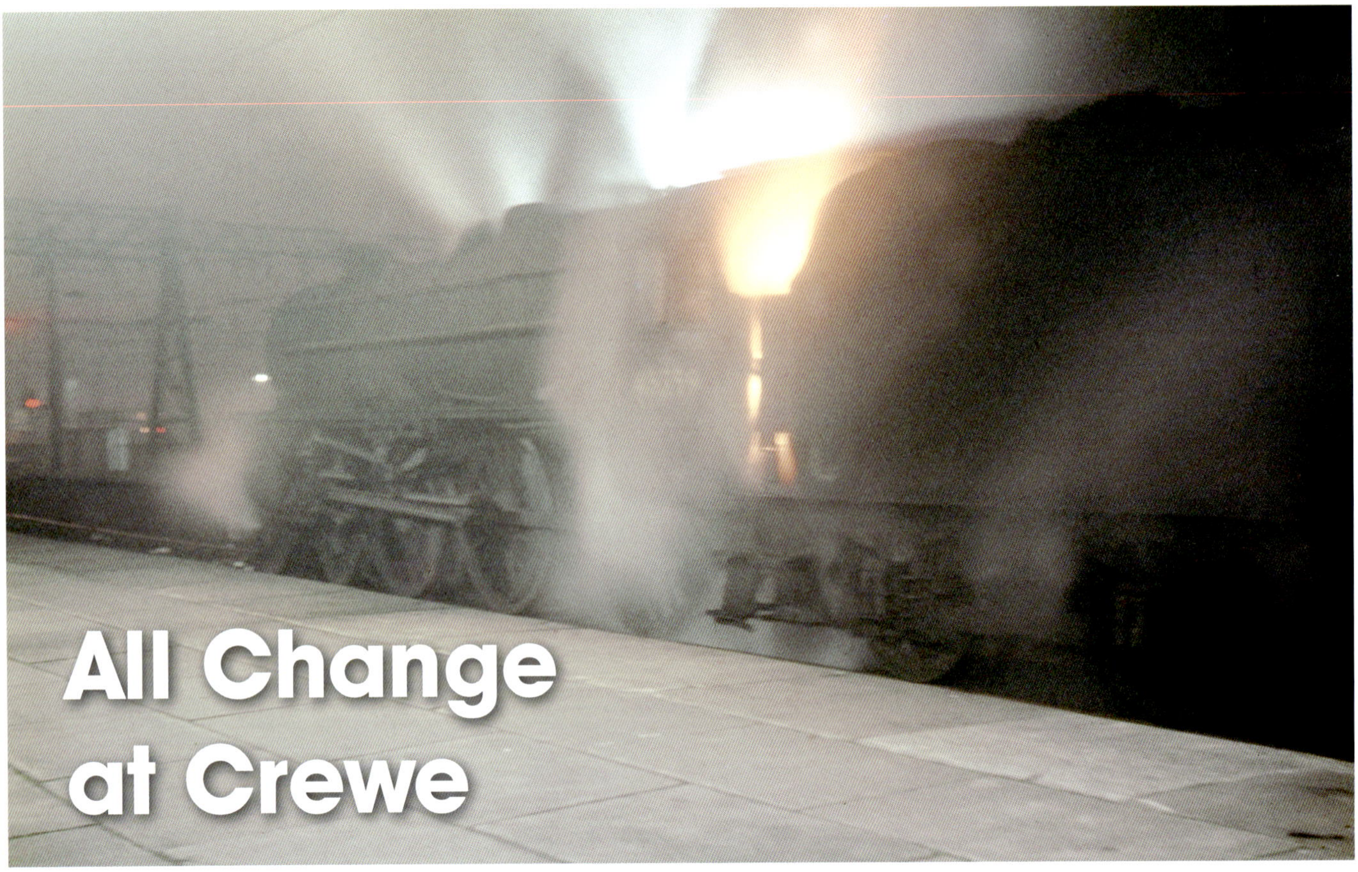

The glow from the firebox and the steam in the cool night air bring a sense of drama to this view of Black Five 45259 waiting to depart from Crewe in the winter of 1966 with a Euston to Barrow train. ***Strathwood Library Collection***

At first trains were only hauled by electrics from Crewe to Manchester and Liverpool involving engine changes and then as the wires progressed south to Stafford and Rugby the electric locomotives such as E3019 would enjoy longer runs. ***Tim Matthews***

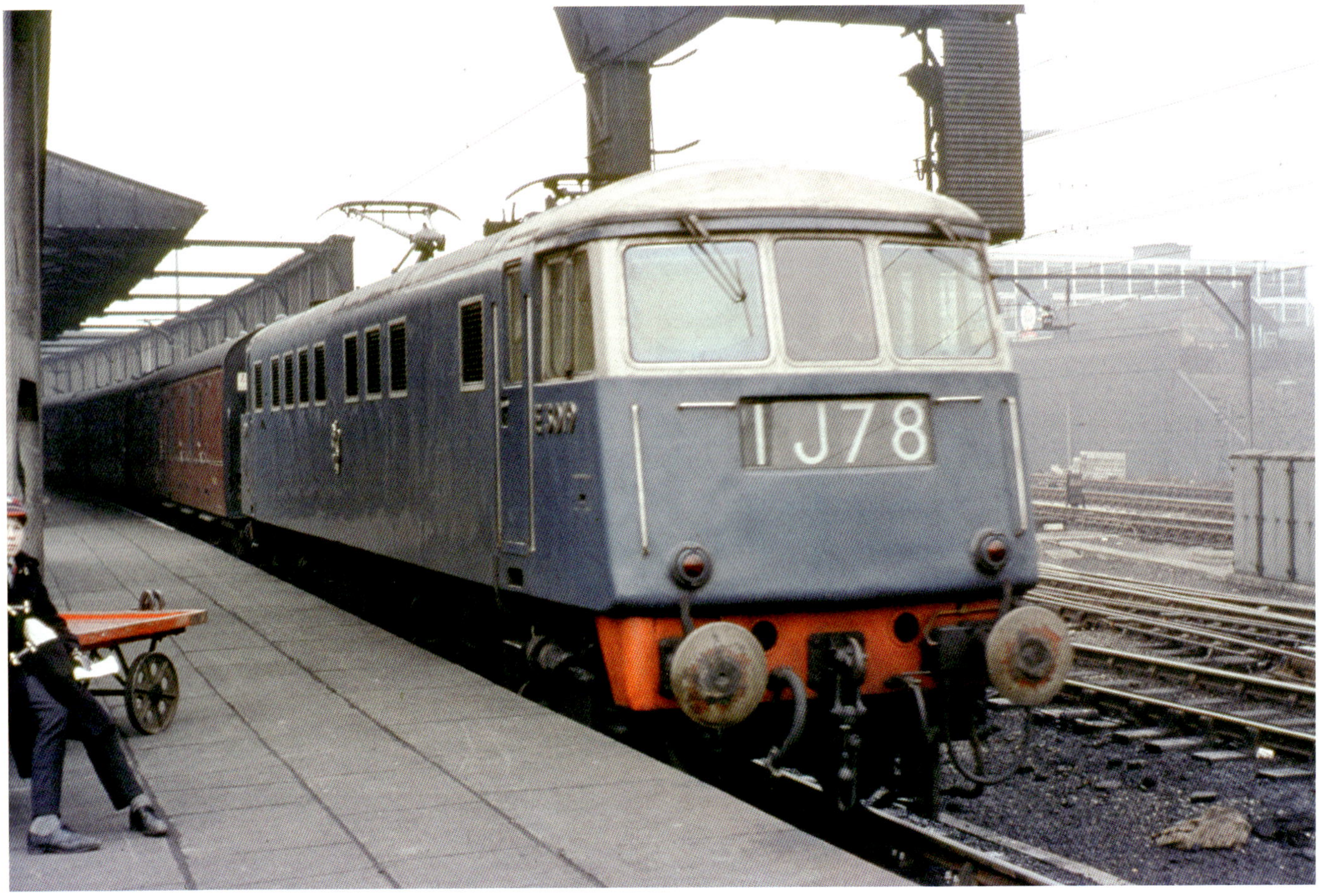

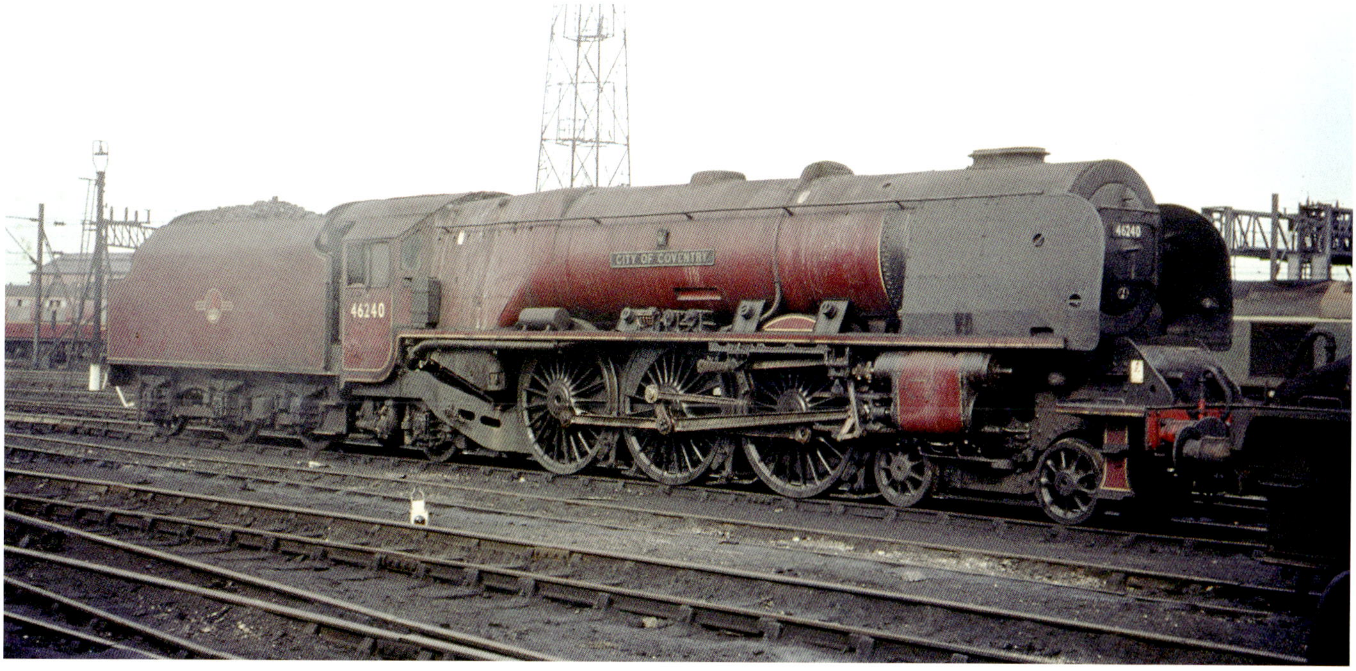

The overhead wiring gantries are in the background as 46240 City of Coventry is seen during its last year of service 1964. She had been one of the twenty four of her class originally streamlined until the programme of rebuilding began in 1946. ***Richard Sinclair Collection***

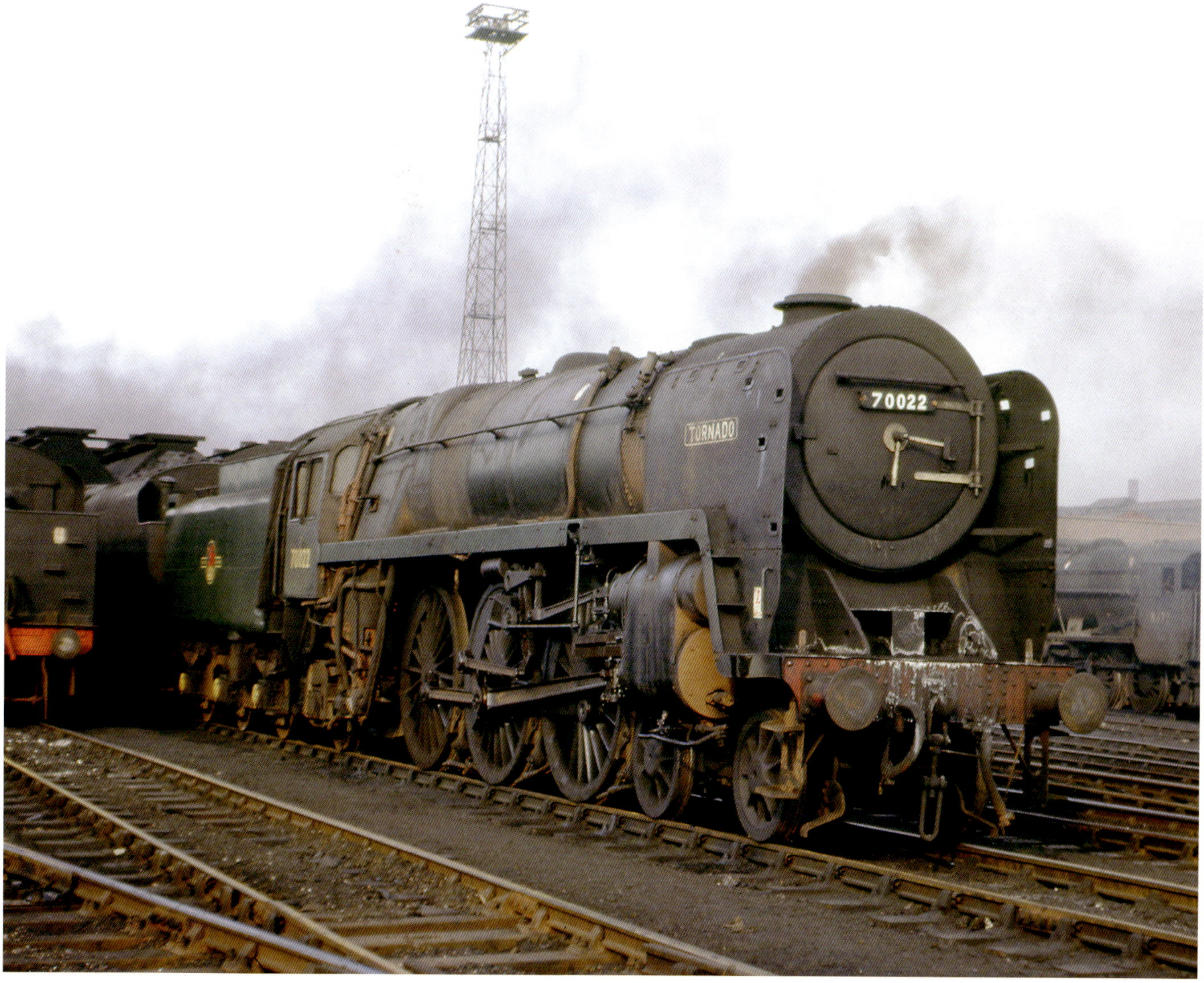

By 5 Febeuary 1967 when 70022 Tornado was seen at Crewe South, fifteen Britannias had already been withdrawn and six had even been cut up. Although some dignity was afforded again to the locomotive with a repaint into unlined green and a painted name to replace the nameplates proper which had vanished to see it through until December 1967. ***Jerry Beddows***

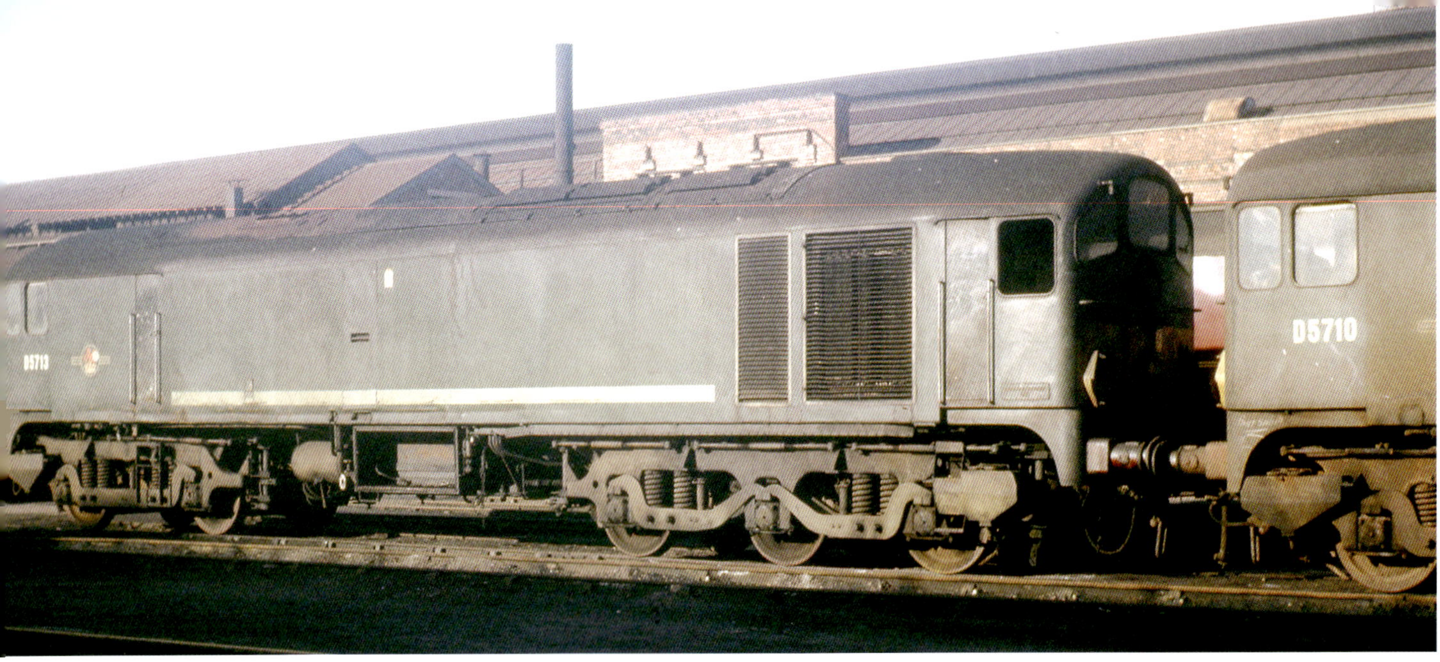

The track records of the Metropolitan Vickers Co-Bo's is equally short, but less distinguished as D5713 seen in Crewe Works on 19 February 1967 had been laid up since June 1965. ***Colin Rodgers/Strathwood Library Collection***

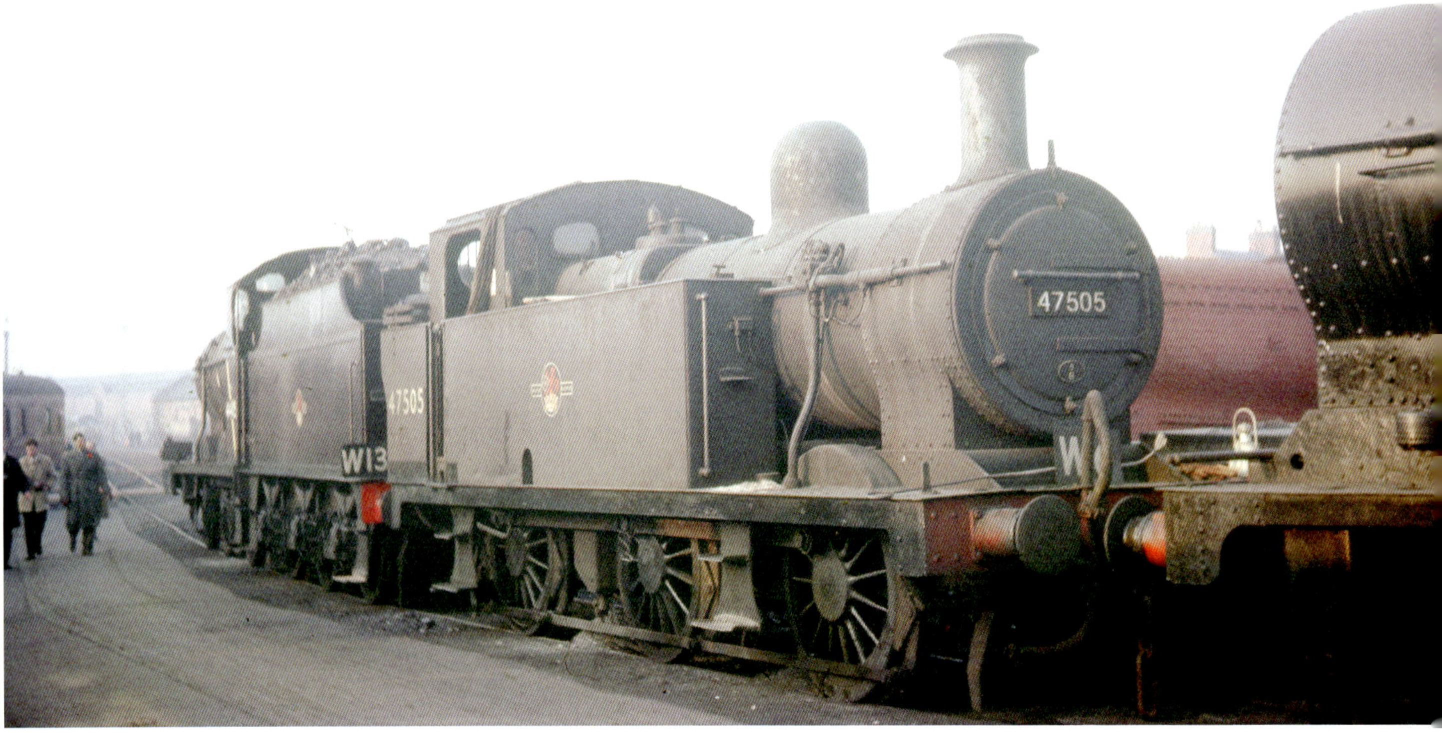

Steam was still in use as the works shunters when 47505 was recorded on Sunday 8 November 1964. ***Peter Coton***

Below: The numbers of ex Lancashire & Yorkshire Railway Class 27s such as 52218 seen within the works in 1960 had been thinned drastically throughout the 1950s. ***Strathwood Library Collection***

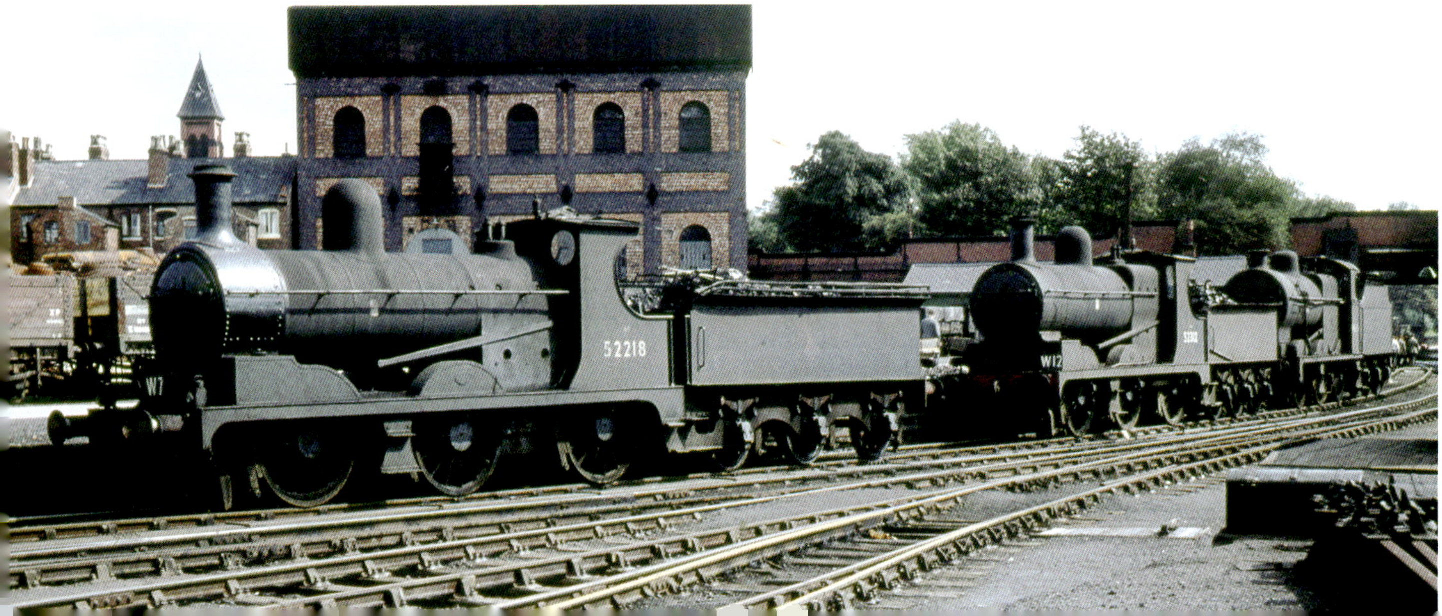

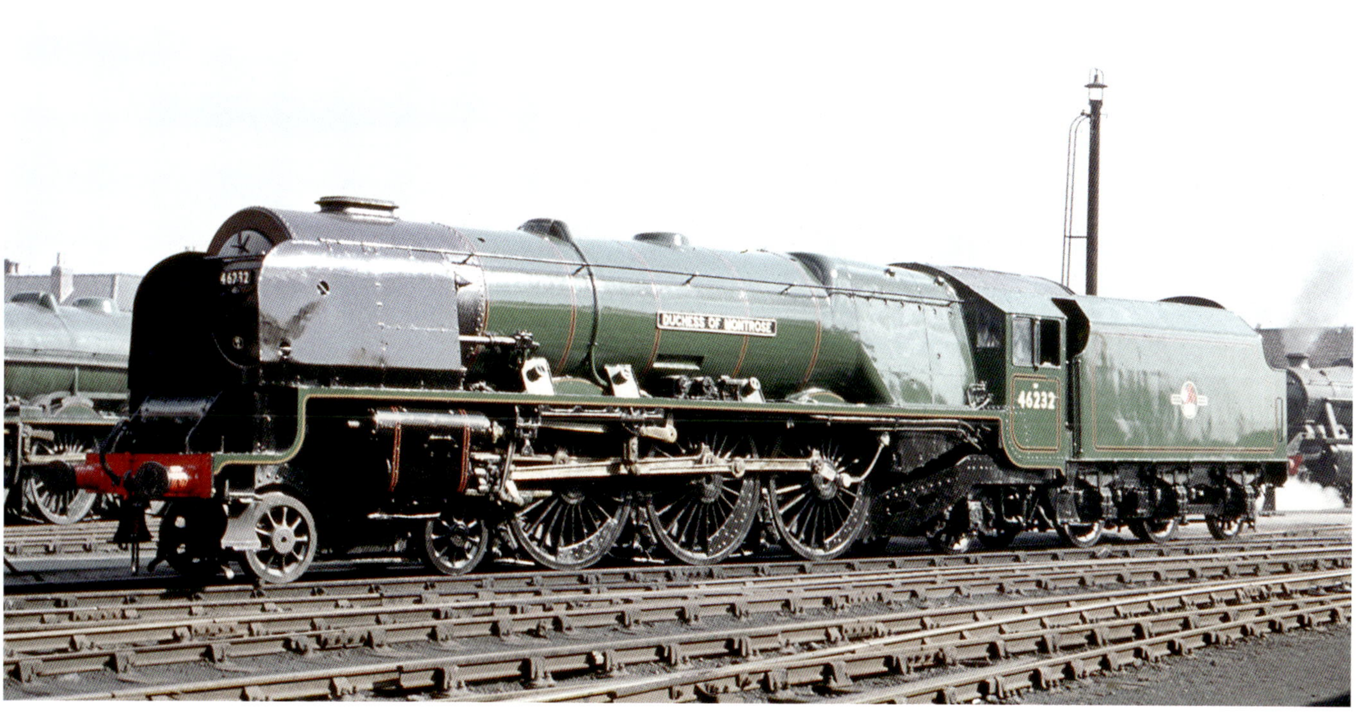

Just as the nineteen fifties became what would be later known as the swinging sixties Stanier's Coronation 46232 Duchess of Montrose was looking spick and span ready to return to traffic outside the paintshop at Crewe Works. ***Strathwood Library Collection***

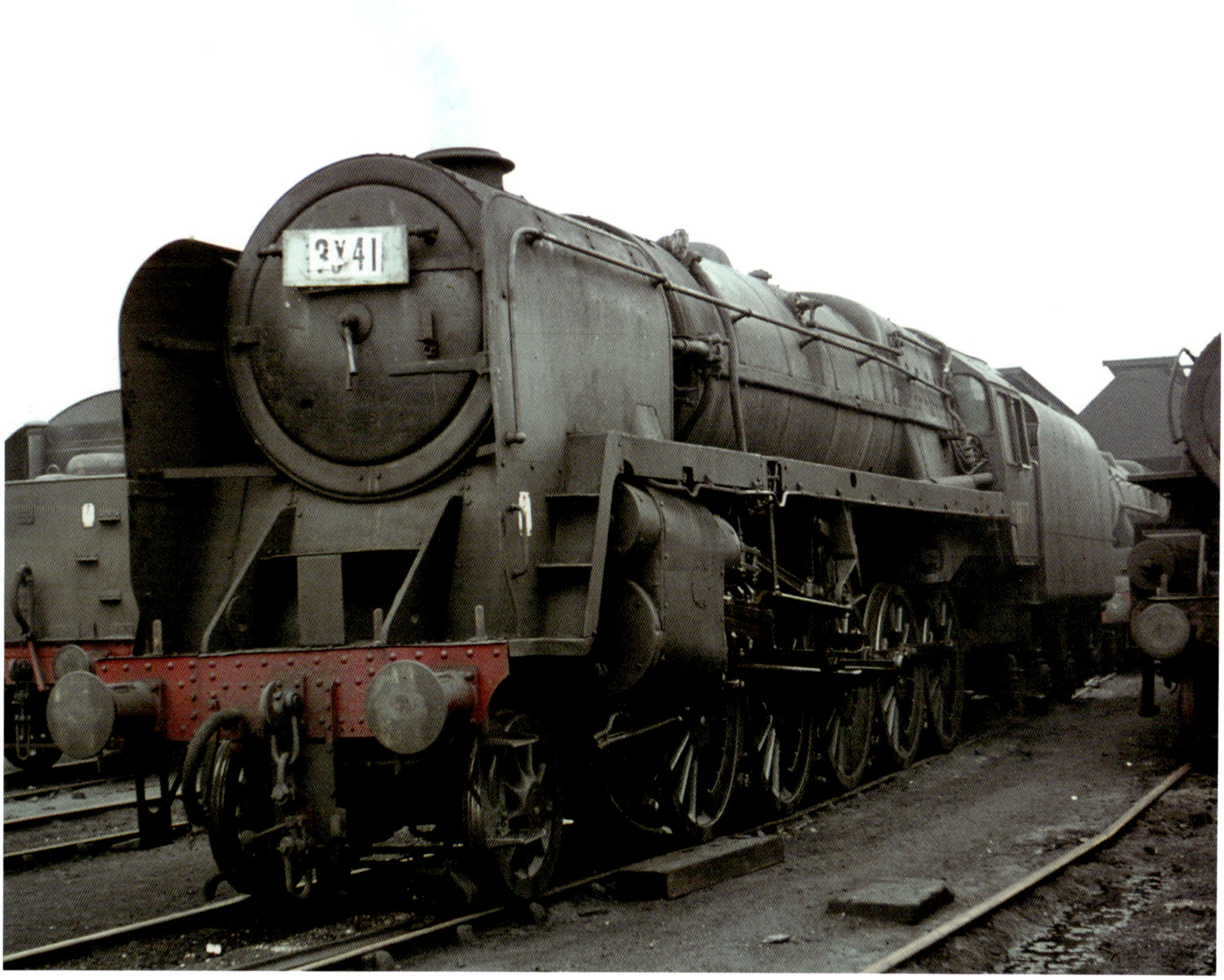

The same could not be said of Riddles 9F 92077 at Crewe South on 31 July 1966 two years away from being withdrawn. The train reporting number board affixed to the smokebox suggests the mighty 2-10-0 has seen some work on a summer passenger extra. ***Strathwood Library Collection***

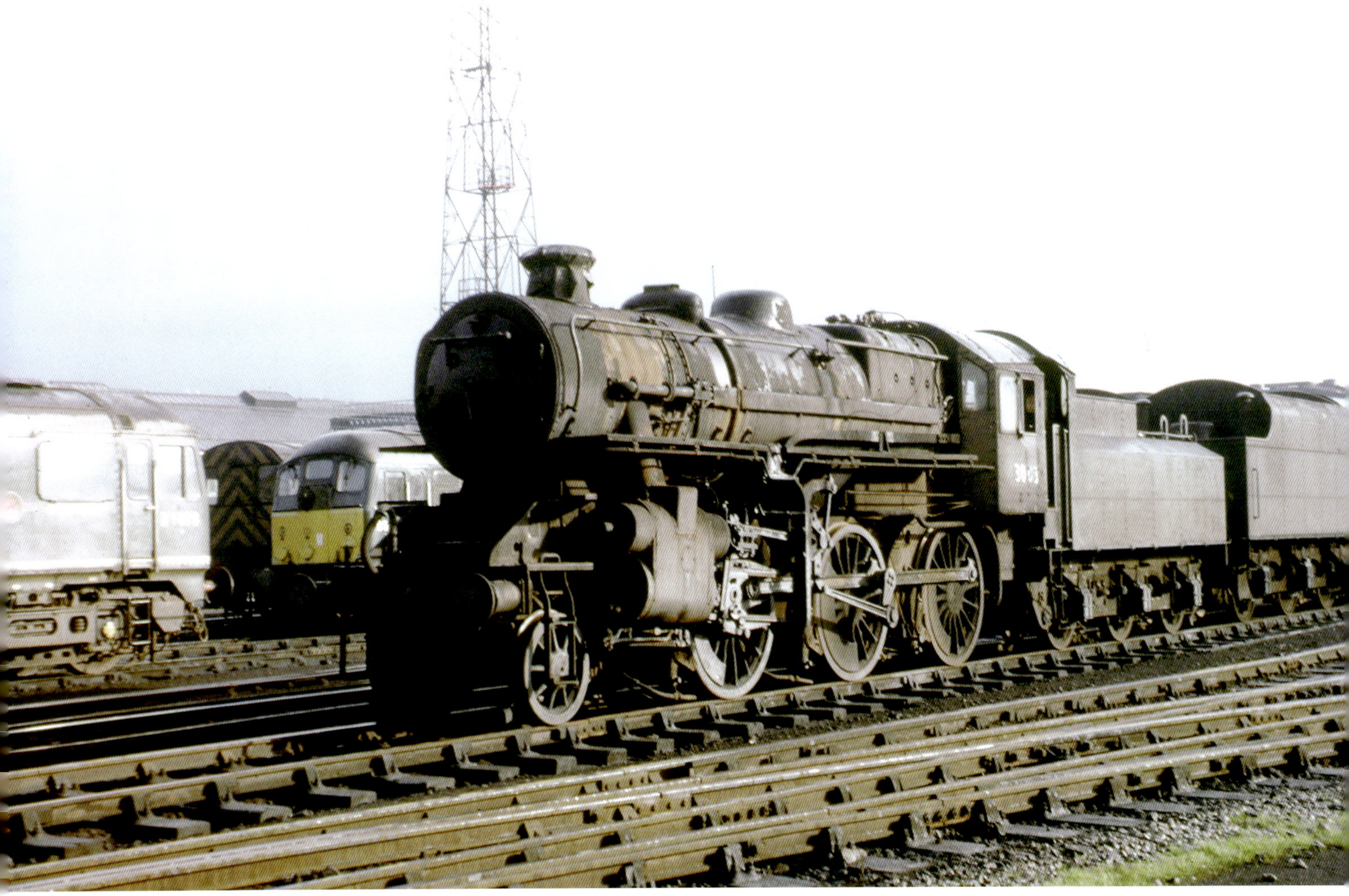

What would become Class 24s are being drafted to the Crewe area by 29 October 1967, some would take over duties previously performed by Ivatt Mogul 43003 which was taken out of service six weeks beforehand, although her chimney remains covered in the hope of a reprieve perhaps which was not to come. ***Strathwood Library Collection***

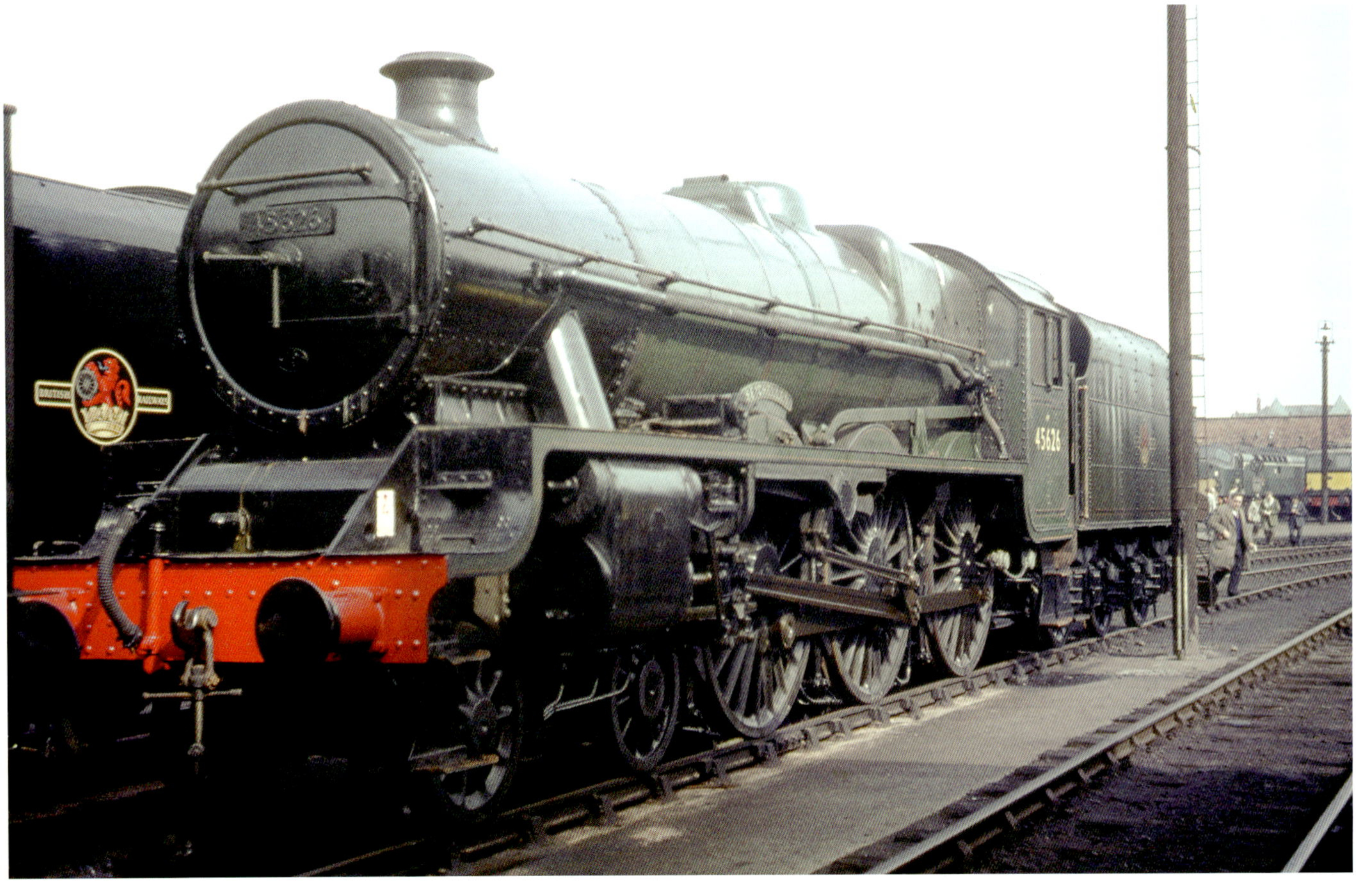

Many shots we have seen suggest that Crewe Works moved locomotives outside of the paintshops after full repainting but before their smokebox number plates had been picked out in white as here with Stanier Jubilee 45626 Seychelles in 1964. ***Richard Sinclair Collection***

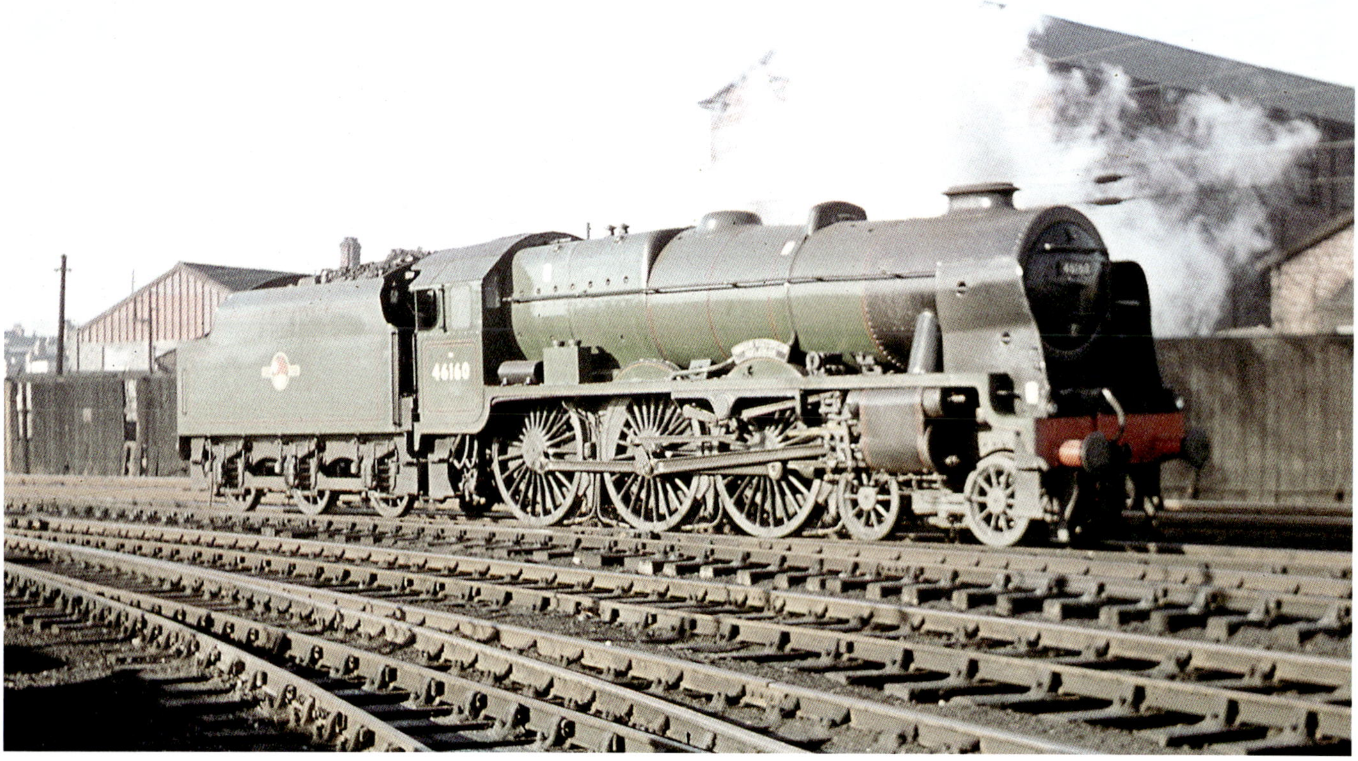

Running standrads were stiil pretty good in 1961 when rebuilt Royal Scot 46160 Queen Victoria's Rifleman was seen making its way off shed at Crewe North. ***Strathwood Library Collection***

The new generation in the shape of E3001 is framed by rebuilt Royal Scot 46118 Royal Welch Fusilier along with Ivatt 8P 46256 Sir William Stanier F.R.S. during 1962. ***Strathwood Library Collection***

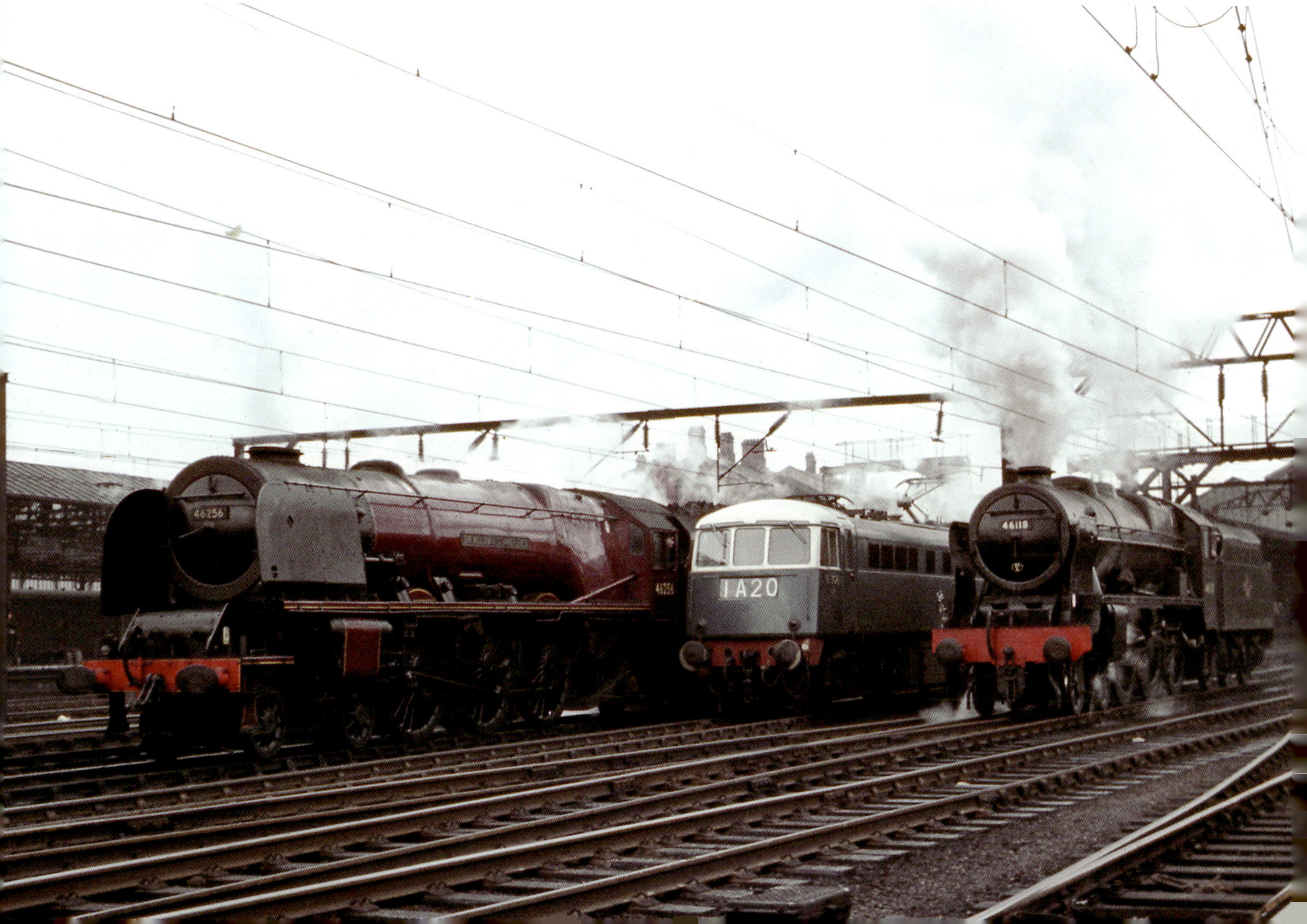

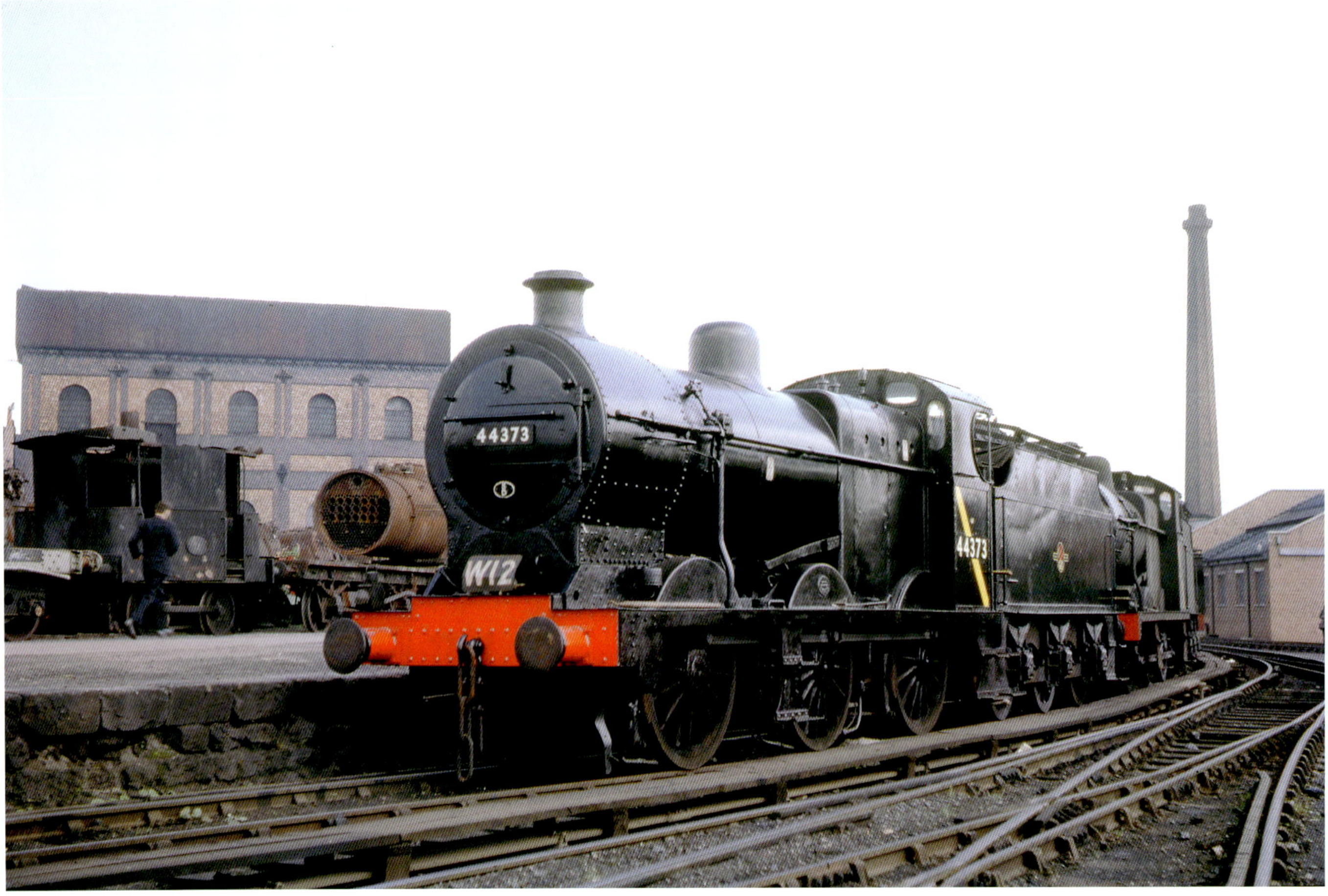

An ex works Fowler 4F 44373 carries one of the duty boards for Crewe Works shunters as another visitor skips past a relic from the LNWR awaiting disposal in the background on 30 August 1964. ***Strathwood Library Collection***

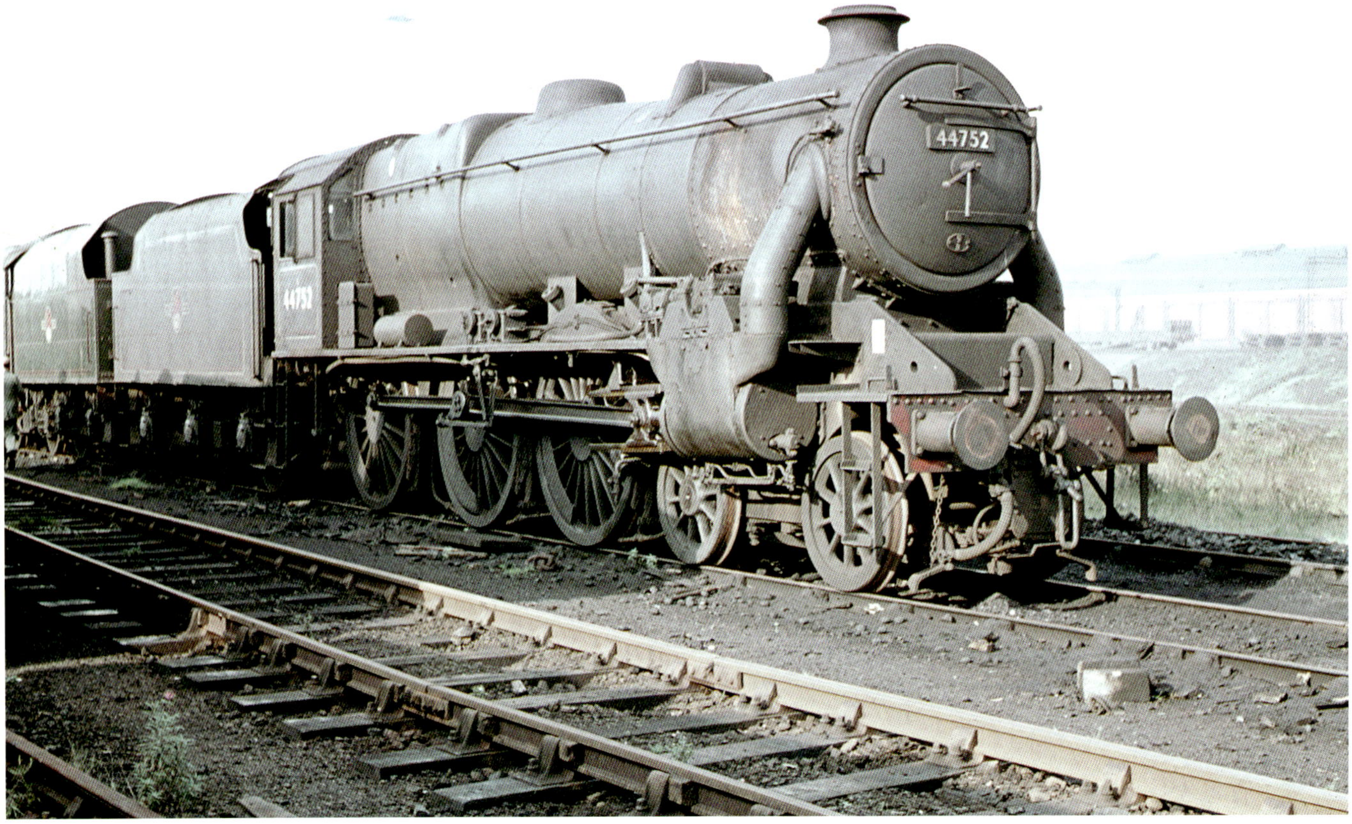

The Ivatt inspired Caprotti Black Fives such as 44752 seem to have spent some of their time in storage at Crewe South as here during 1962. Although they were built in the railway town they seem to have been unloved and did not accrue a good mileage record. ***Strathwood Library Collection***

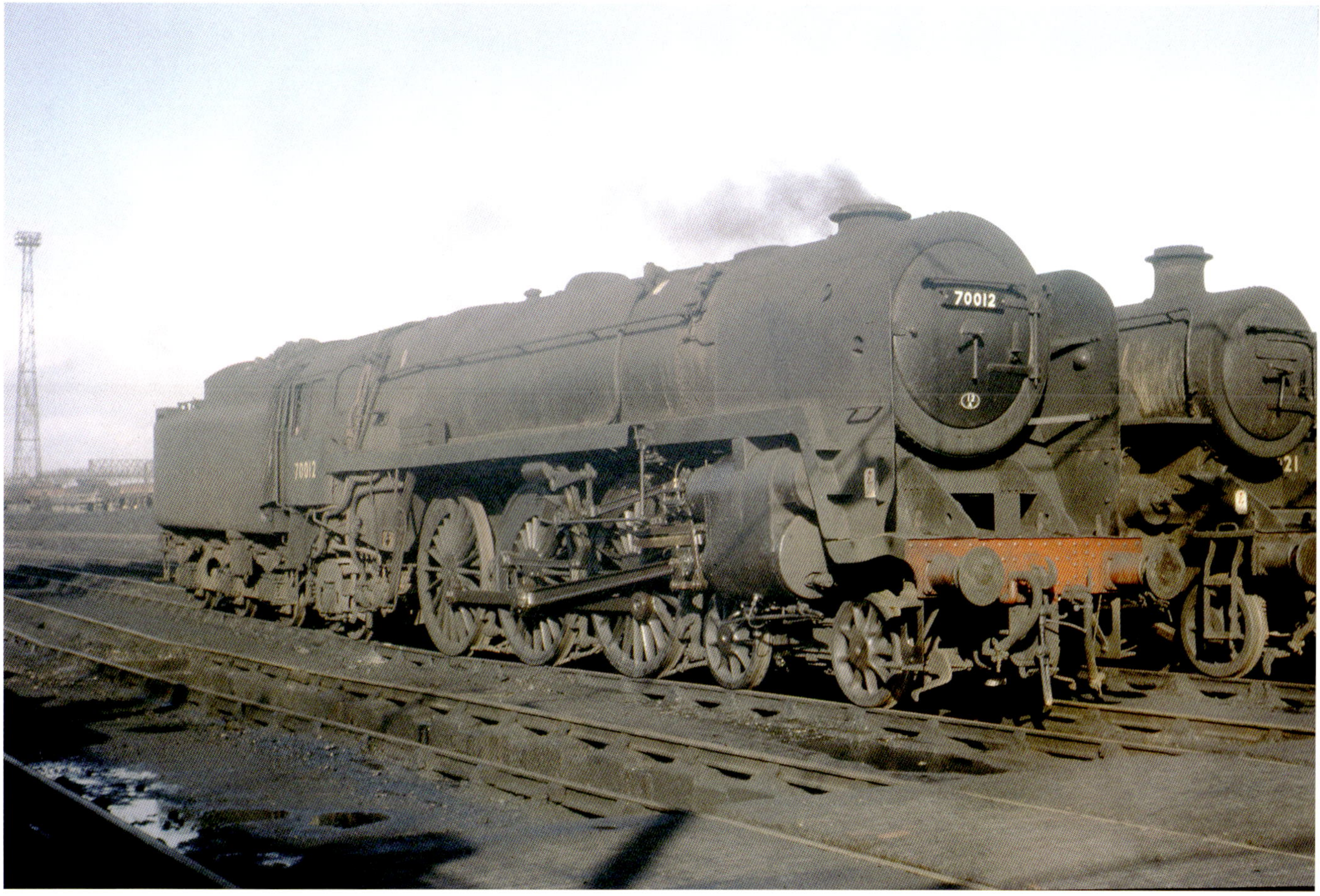

Another very sad and rundown Britannia 70012 devoid of it's nameplates as John of Gaunt and any respectabilty as a lined green express locomotive when seen outside the running shed at Crewe South on 19 February 1967. ***Colin Rodgers/Strathwood Library Collection***

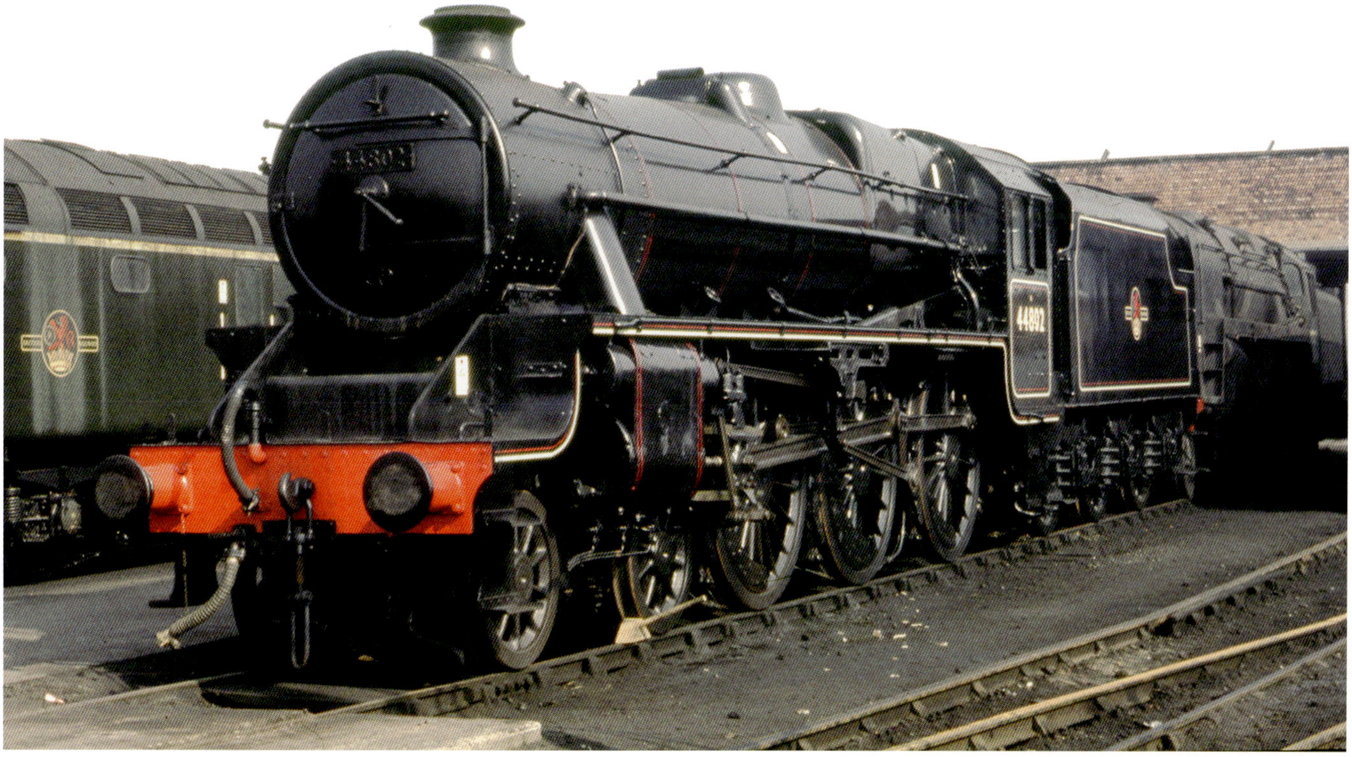

Crewe Works has done it again sending out of the paintshops Black Five 44802 with its' smoke box number still to be picked out in white for some curious reason in 1964. ***Strathwood Library Collection***

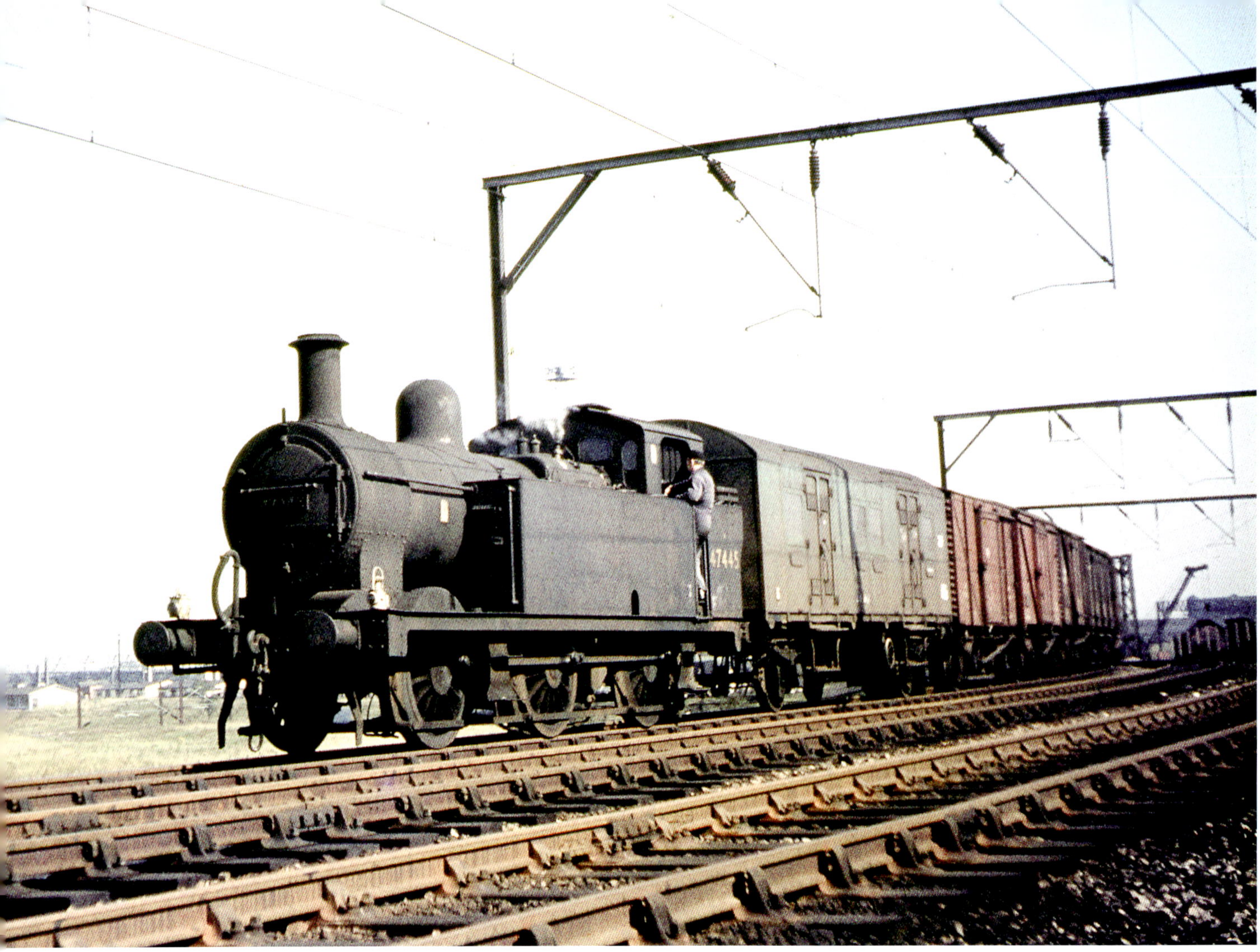

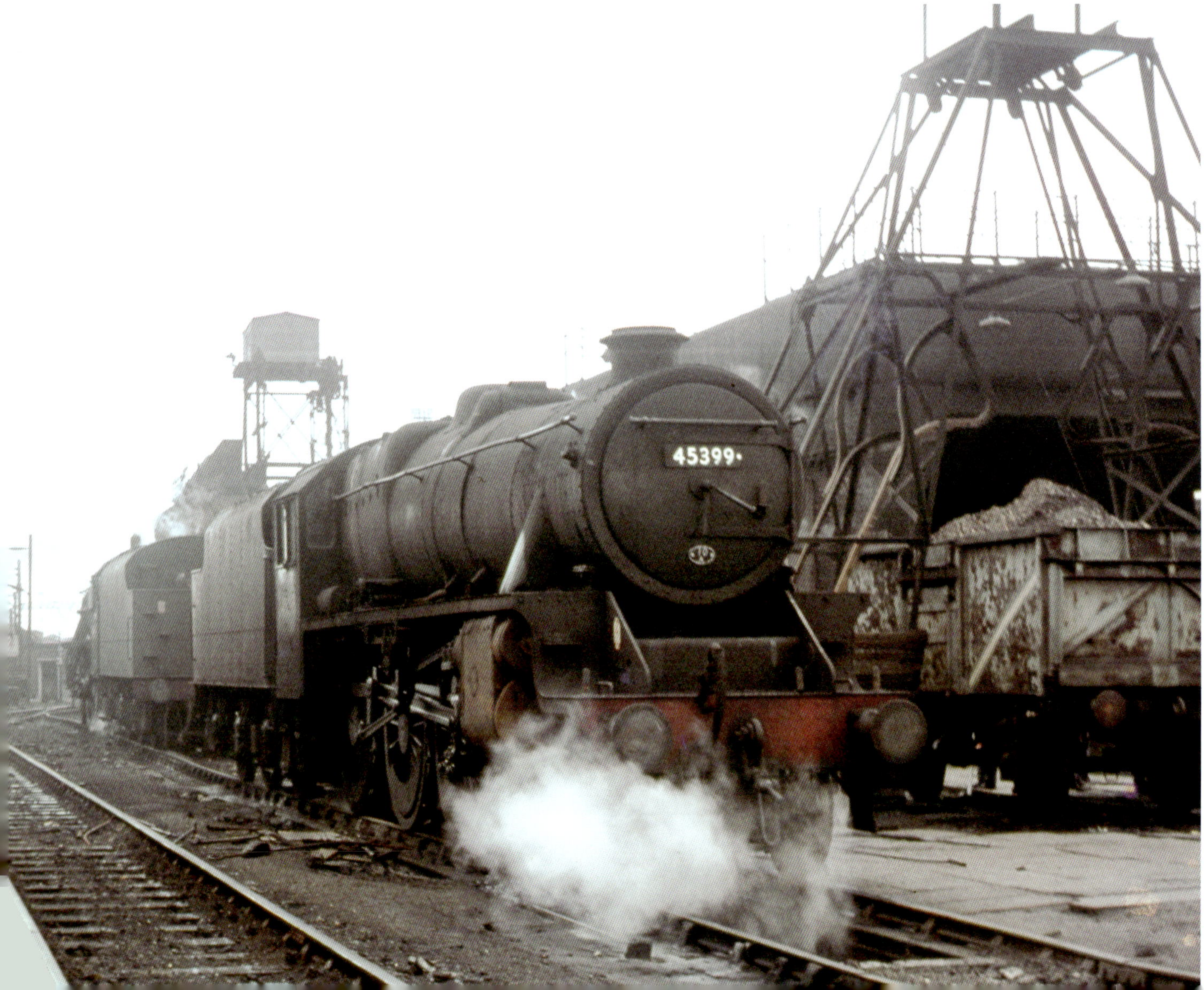
45399

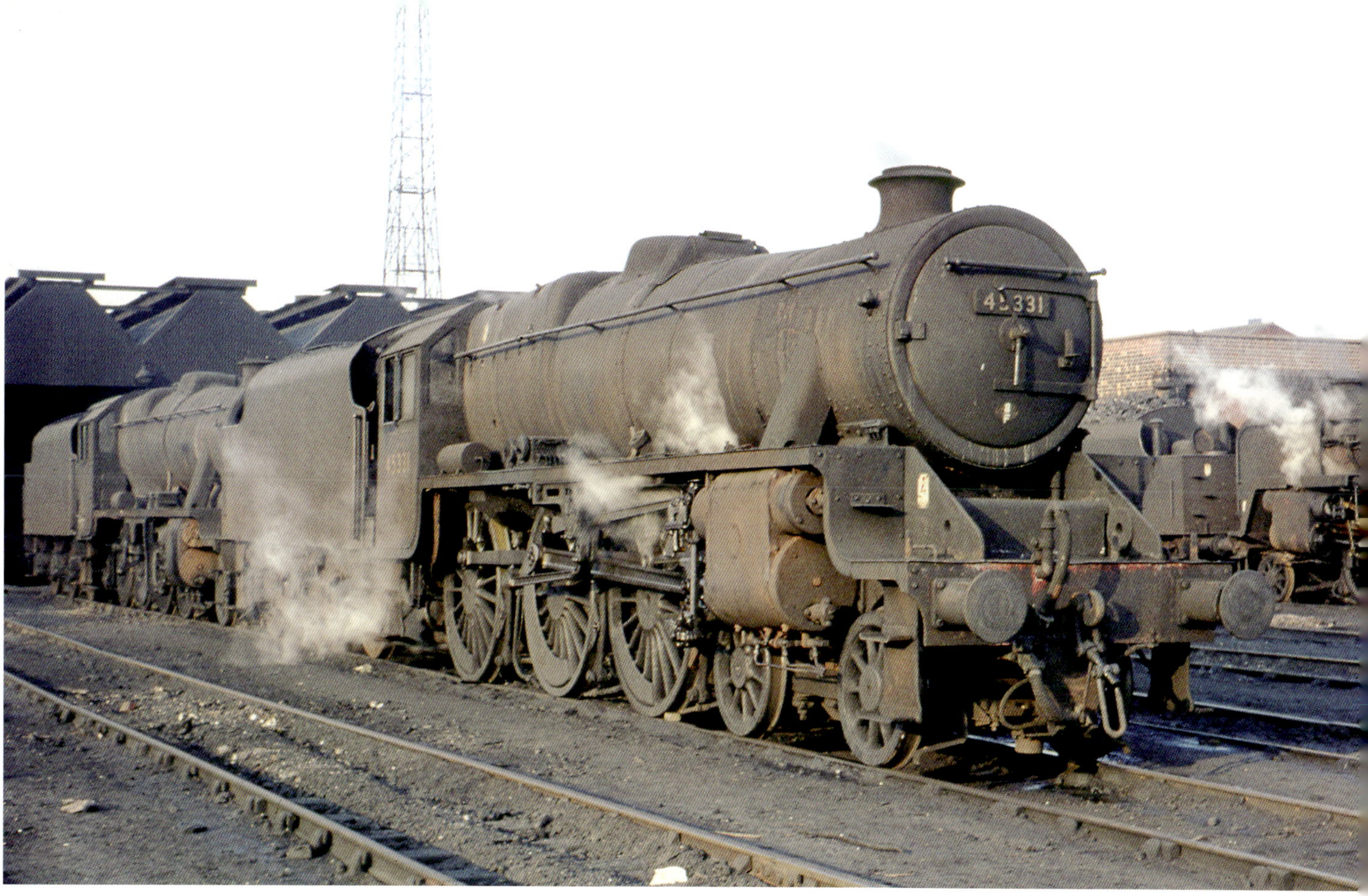

Opposite: A simplified style of overhead wire gantry was first employed on the electrification of the West Coast Main Line and various yards and bypass routes such as this one at Crewe. The design was typical of a type used on the Woodhead route previously. The Jinty numbered 47445 being tripped through Crewe in April 1965. ***Noel Marrison***

Opposite bottom: Crewe South services another pair of Black Fives including 45399 built by Armstrong Whitworth in August 1937. This would be the locomotive's final year in service as it would be posted as withdrawn later in December 1966. ***Strathwood Library Collection***

Above: Another Armstrong Whitworth locomotive from 1937 was Black Five 45331 in the winter sunshine of 12 February 1967 outside the sheds at Crewe South. ***Strathwood Library Collection***

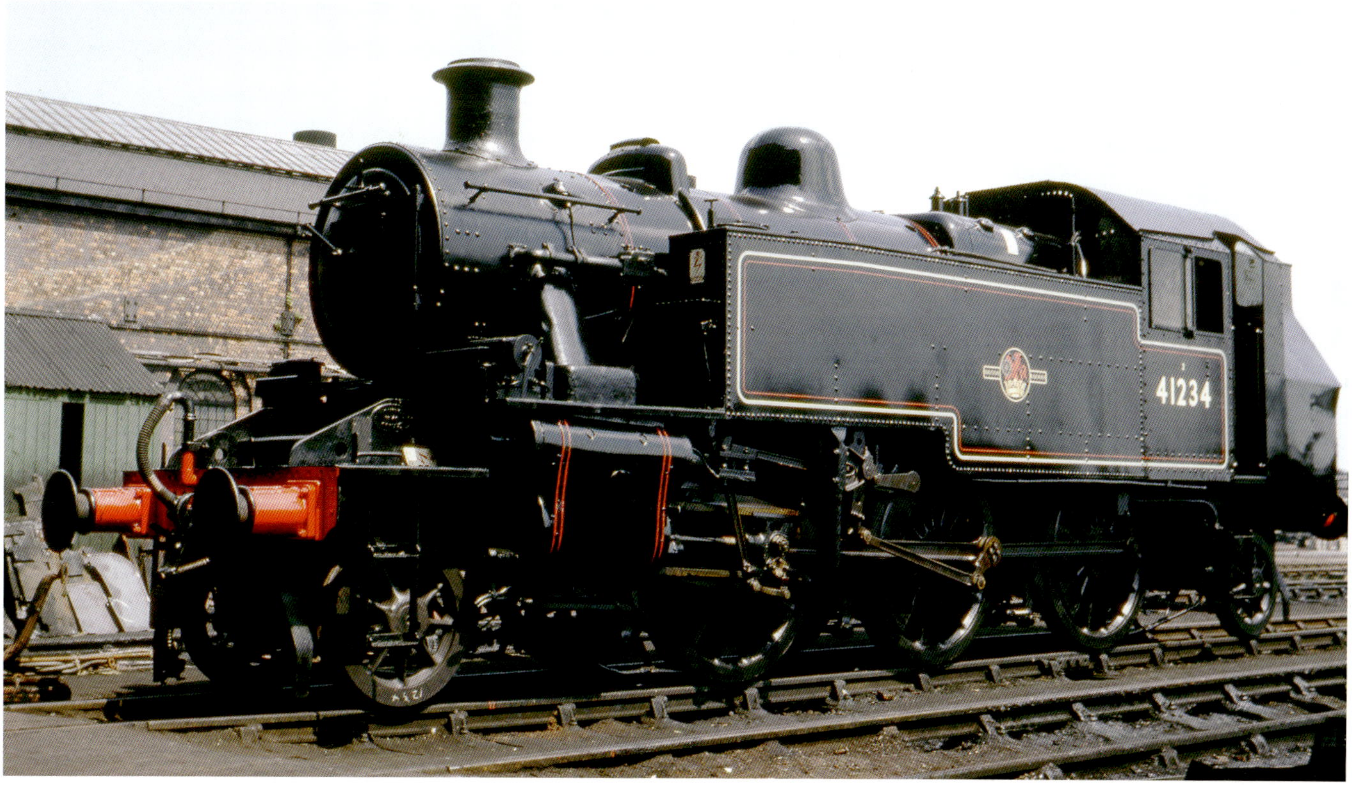

Here we go again Ivatt 2MT 41234 has been sent out by the Crewe Works Paintshop lacking that final finishing in 1964. ***Strathwood Library Collection***

East Midland's Variety

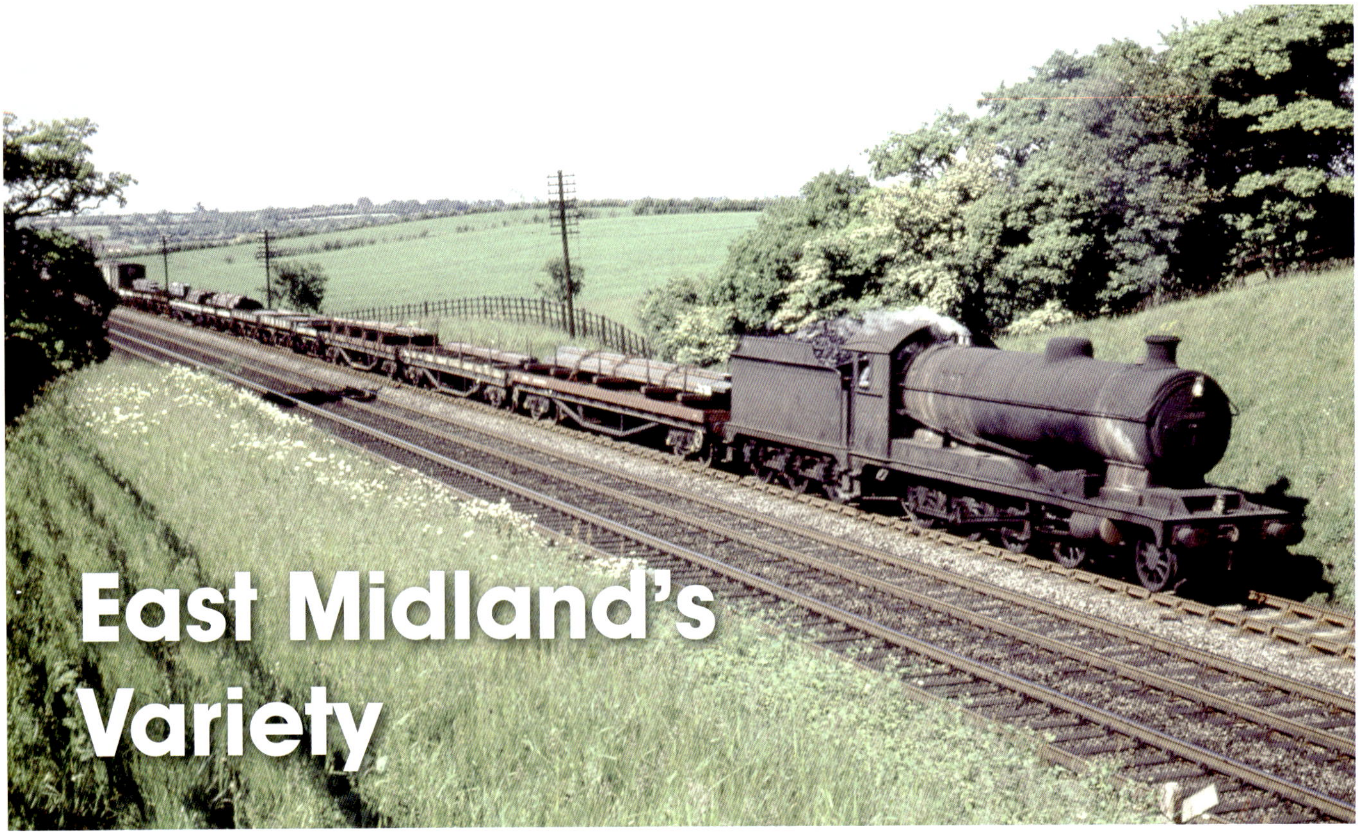

Running easily again near Retford in 1960 was Class O4/8 63647 in the late spring. ***Strathwood Library Collection***

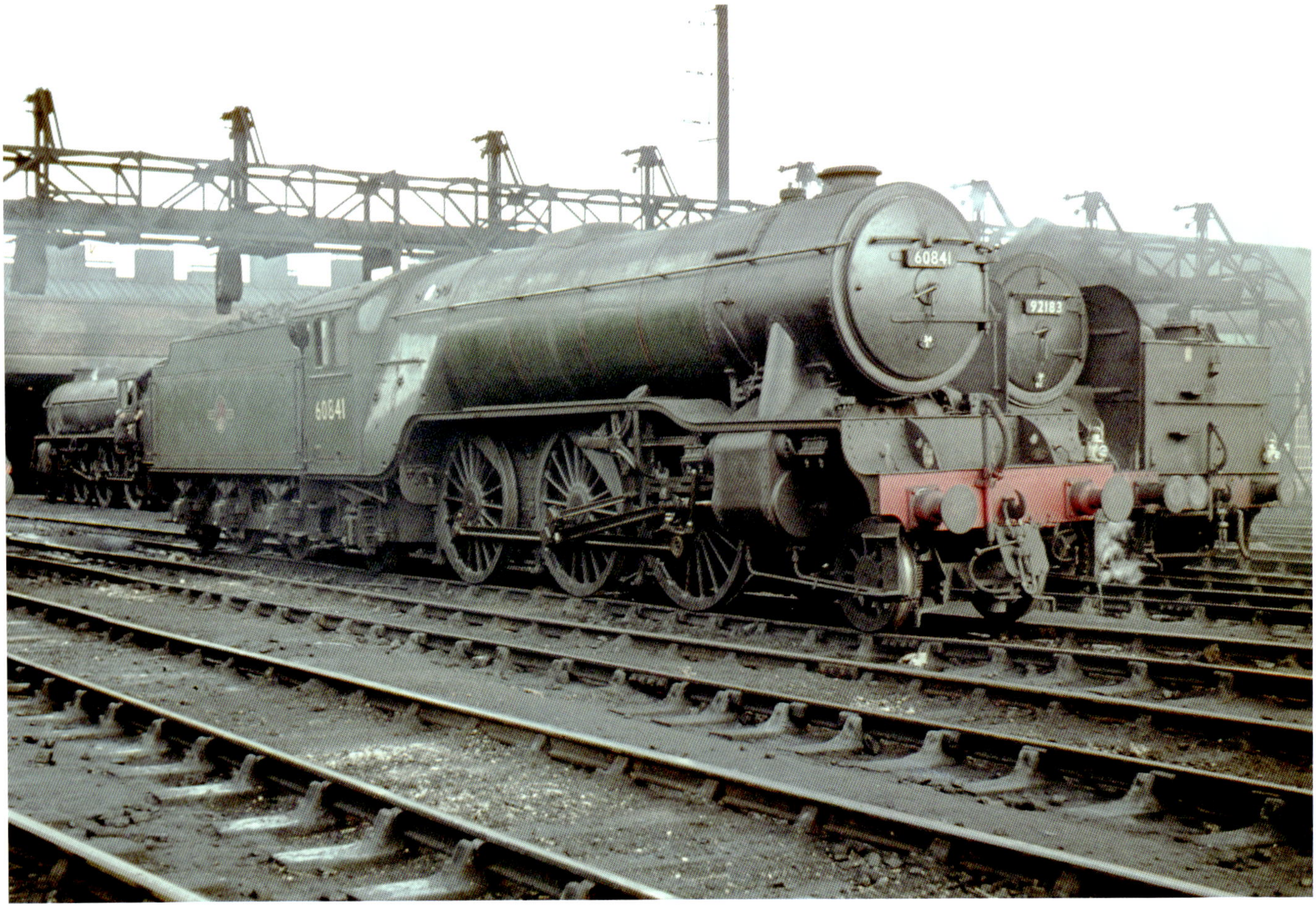

The overhead watering gantry at New England helps to frame the outline of Gresley V2 60841 during 1961. ***Strathwood Library Collection***

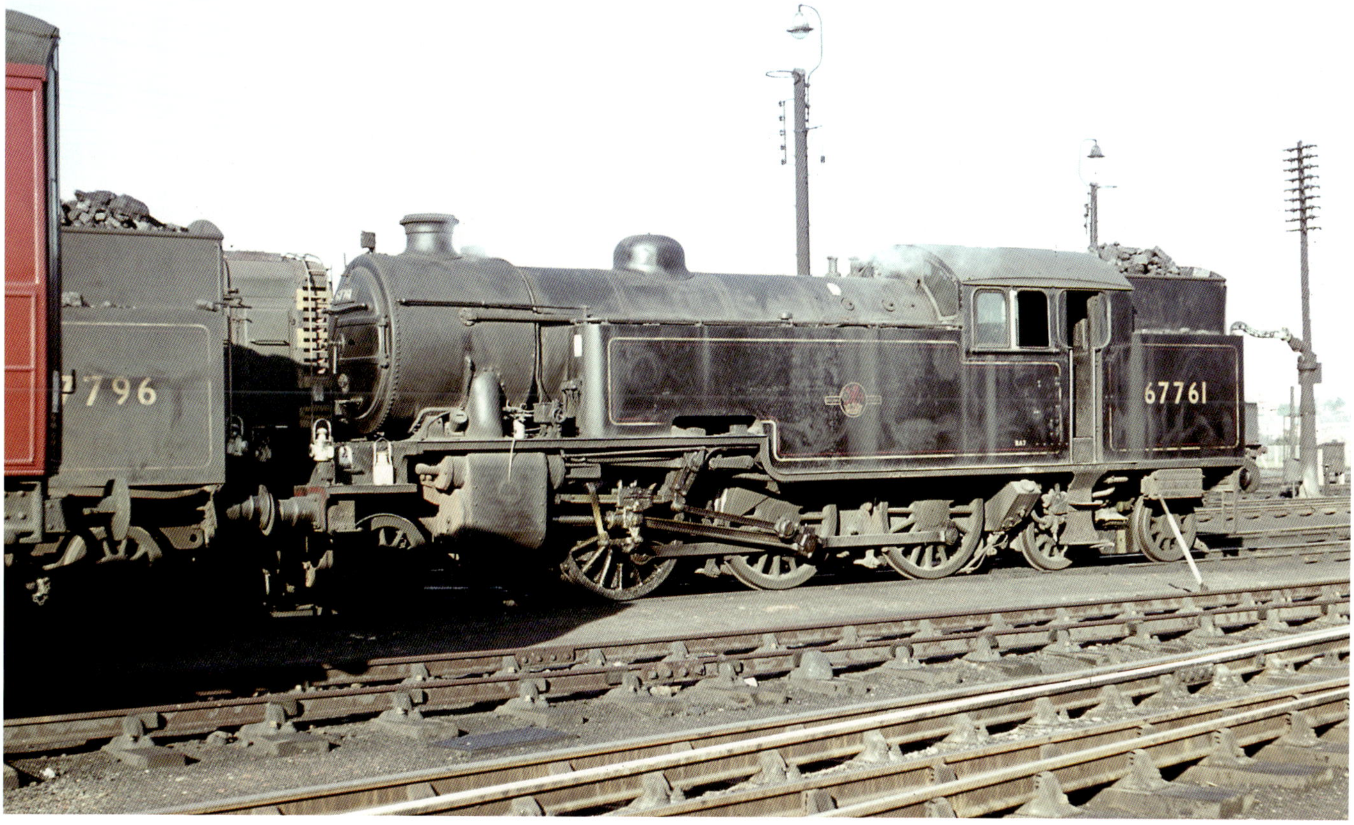

During the same visit one of Thompson's Class L1s 67761 was also to be found on shed and still in service, although their days were numbered as they fell prey to the introduction of DMUs and line closures by the end of 1962 very few survived. ***Strathwood Library Collection***

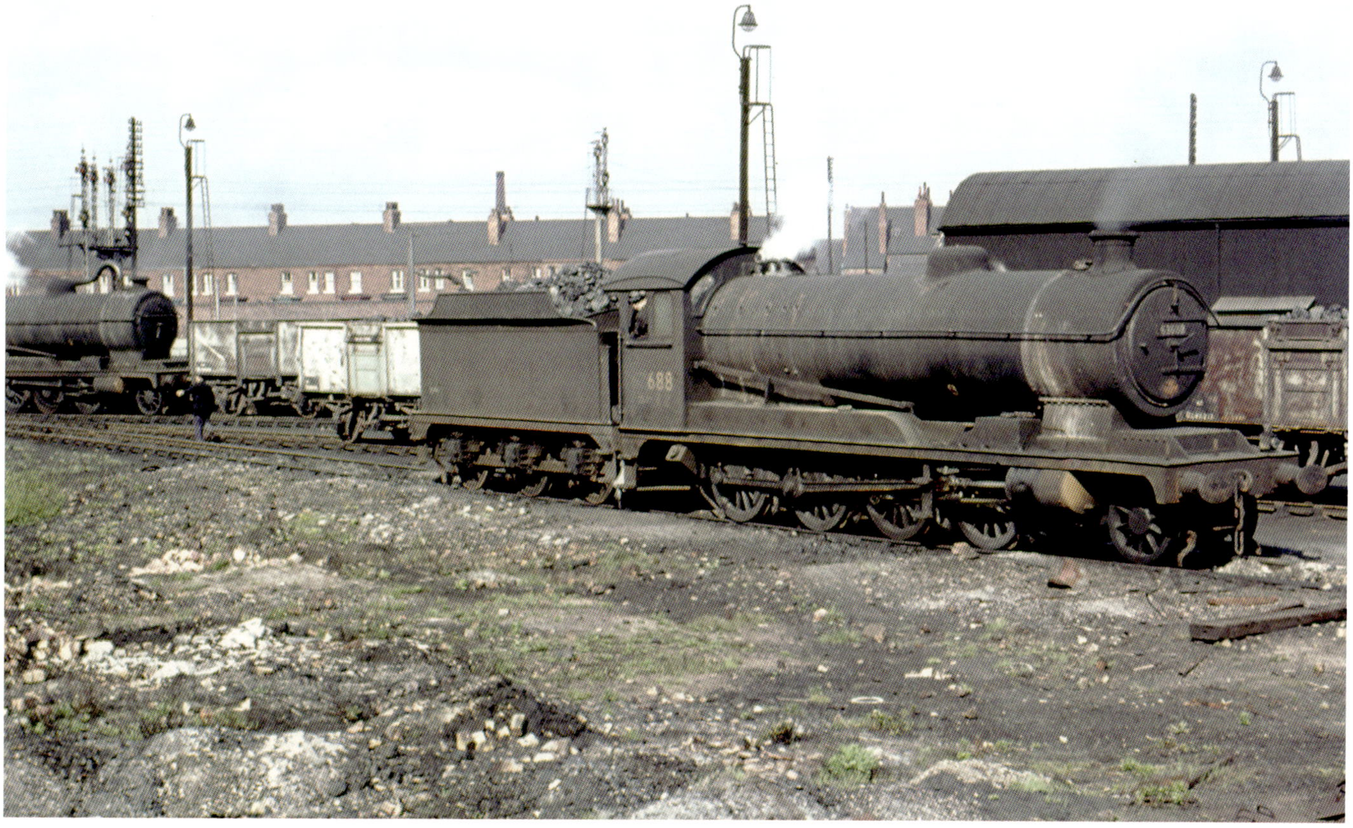

The rebuilding of Robinson 2-8-0s into Class O4/8s with Thompson B1 boilers continued through the 1950s, among their number was 63688 seen at Retford in 1960, this rebuild of a Robert Stephenson & Co. Ltd locomotive finding work until 1965. ***Strathwood Library Collection***

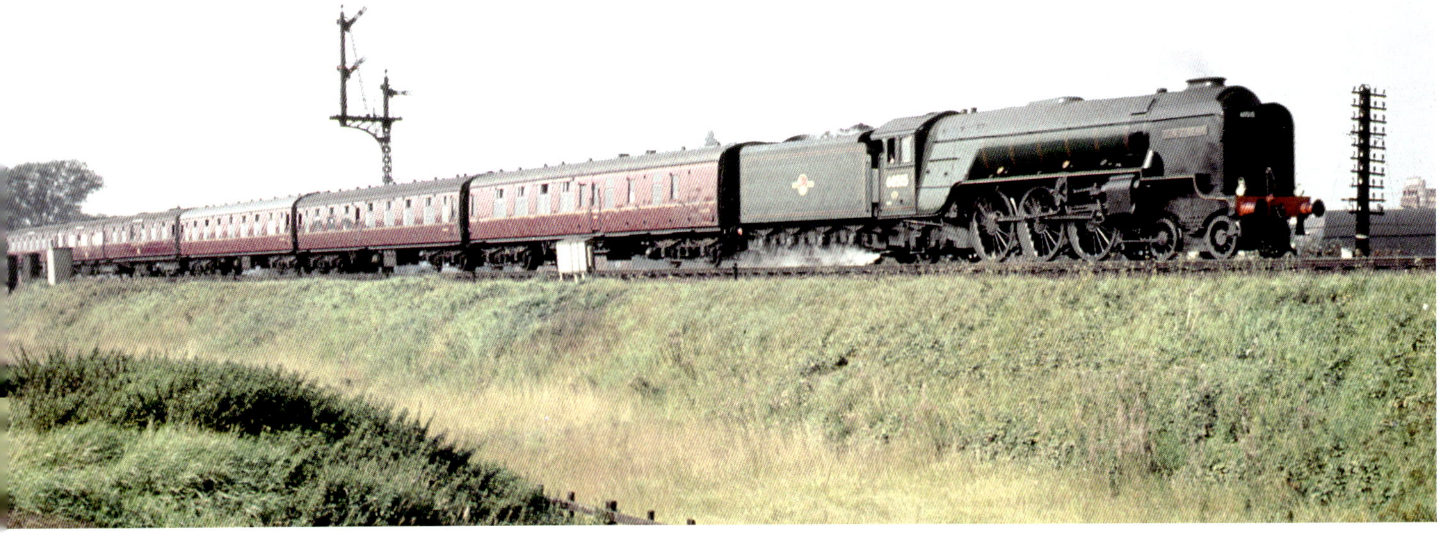

During 1960 the East Coast Main Line was stil dominated by steam and a fine array of Pacifics such as Class A2/3 60515 Sun Stream near Retford with her injectors working well. ***Strathwood Library Collection***

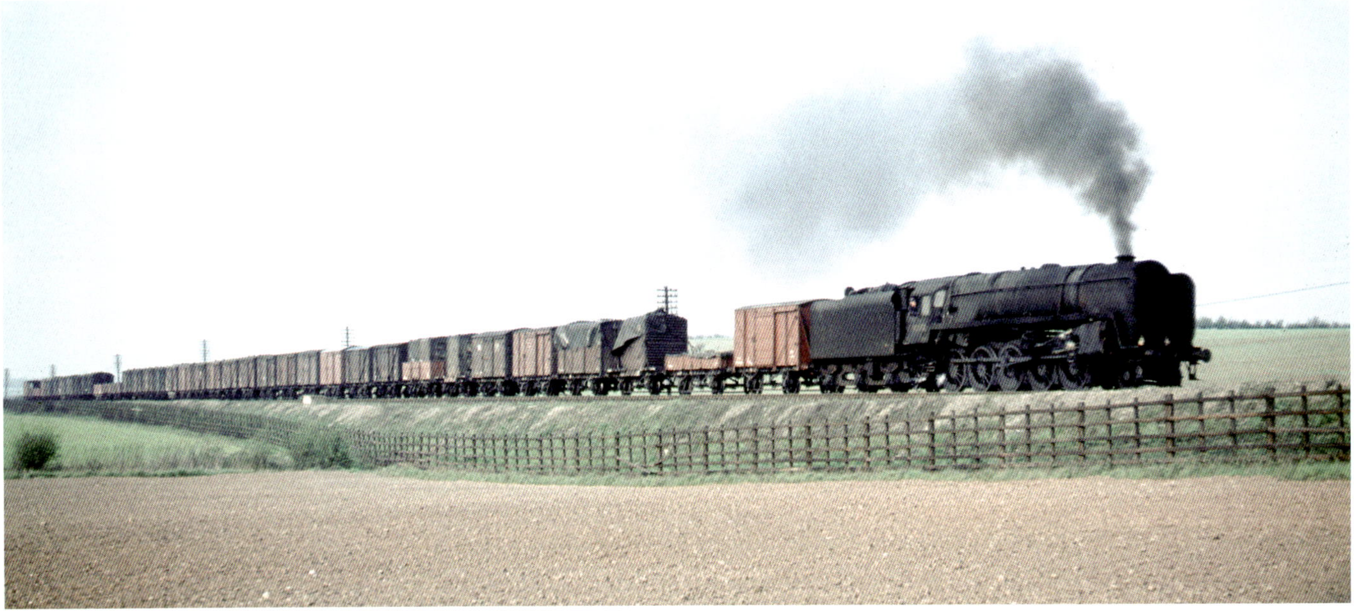

The driver of Riddles 9F 92182 keeps the couplings drawn out again near Retford during spring time in 1962. ***Strathwood Library Collection***

Below: An easy six coach load today for Thompson Class A1 60157 Great Eastern near Newark in 1960. ***Strathwood Library Collection***

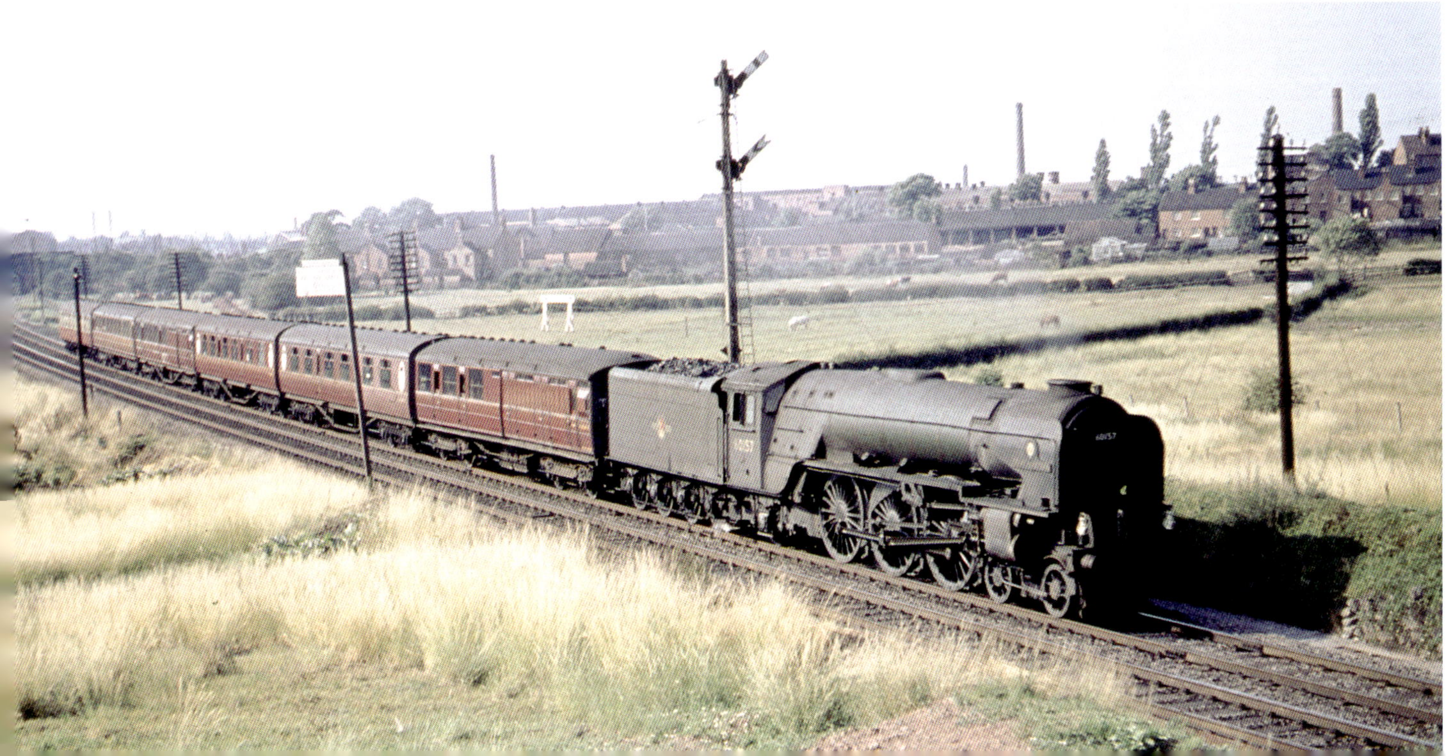

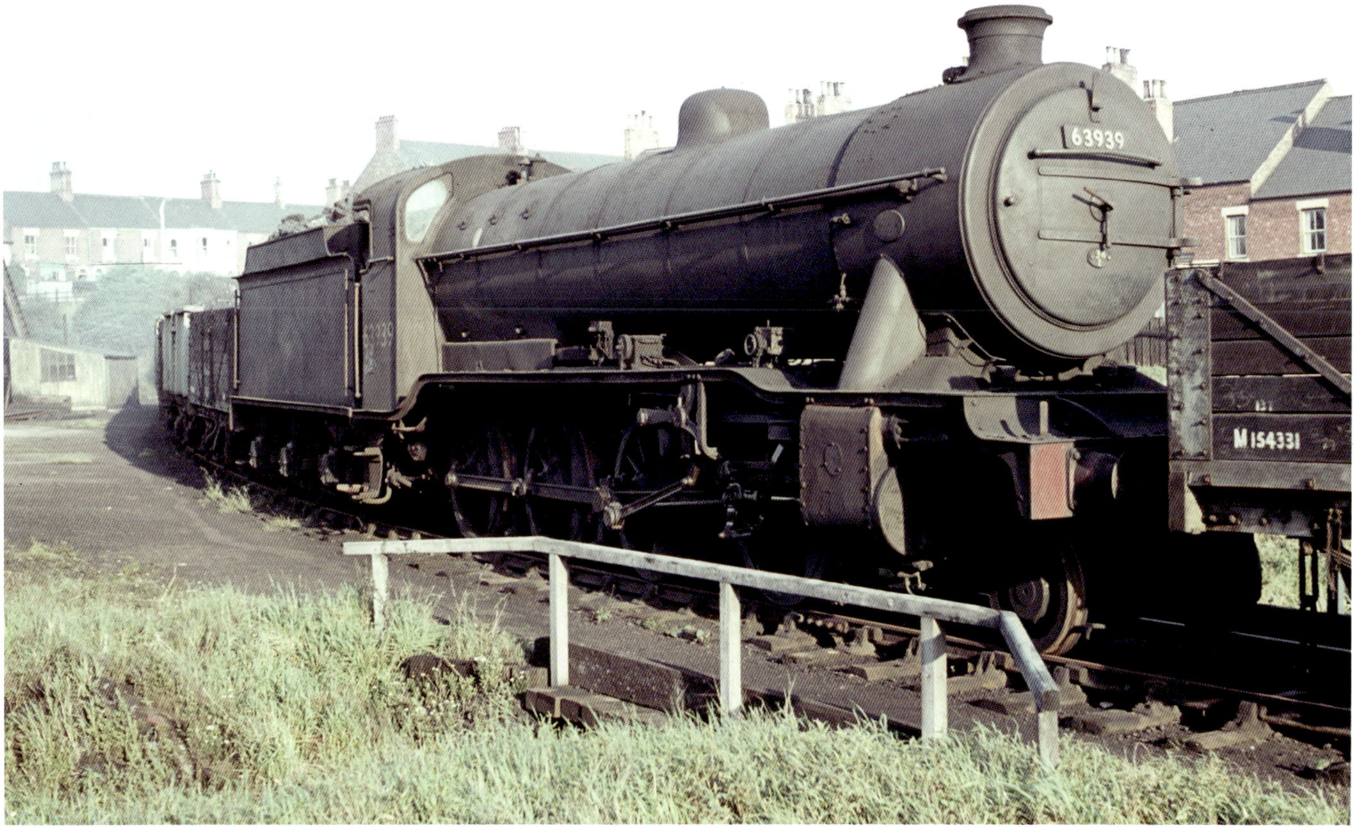

It was to be a day or two on shed at Retford during 1962 for Gresley Class O2/2 63939 penned in between a few wagons, possibly awaiting repairs from the fitters. ***Strathwood Library Collection***

Rounding the curves at Gainsborough in 1962 was Britannia 70011 Hotspur performing the work it had been designed for post war. ***John Rowe***

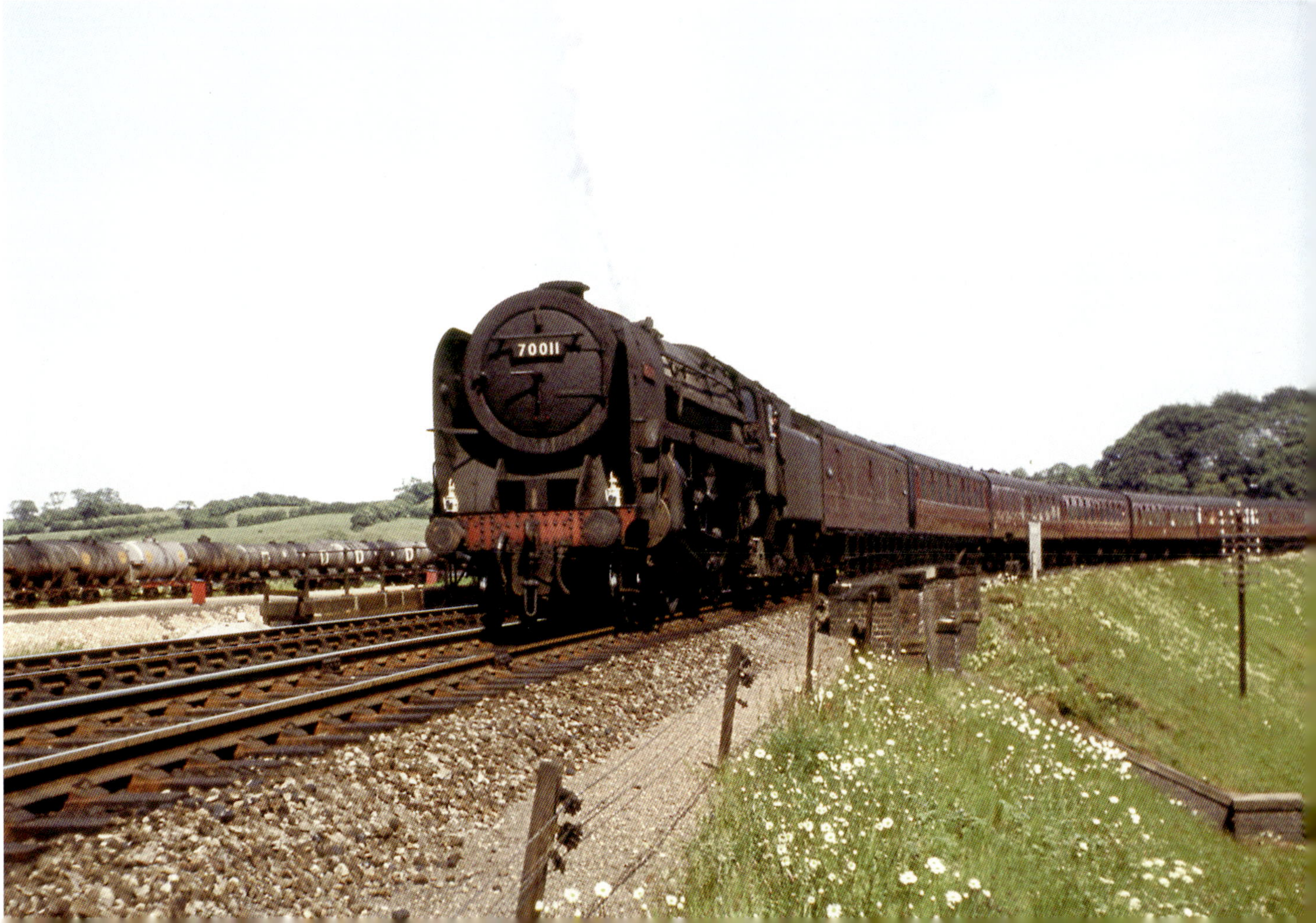

Rugby

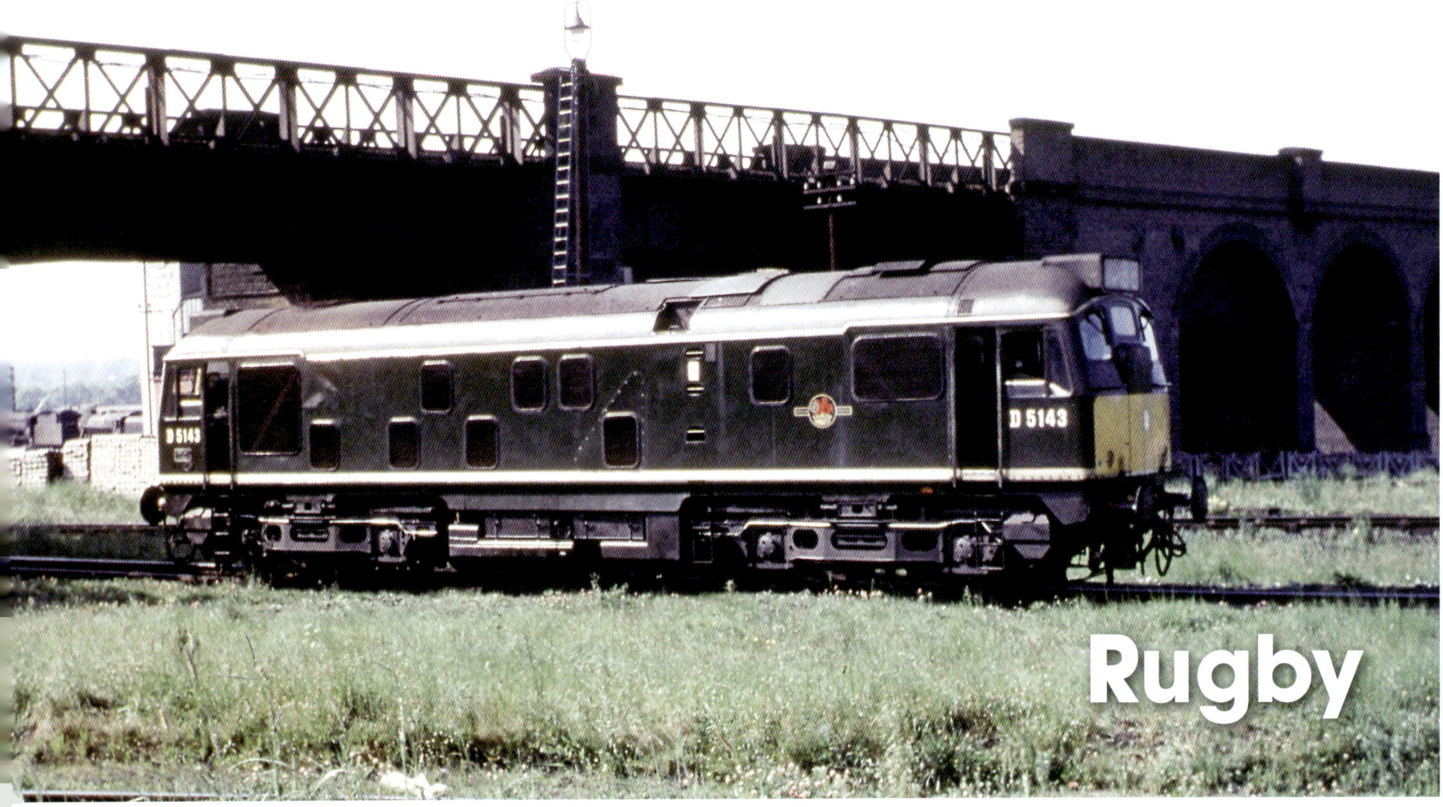

The first day in service for D5143 had been 26 November 1960 shedded at Willesden, by 1965 when this view was taken it had seen the passing of all of Stanier's great Pacifics from the mainline when it was seen at Rugby running light engine under the Great Central's route through the town. ***Tim Matthews***

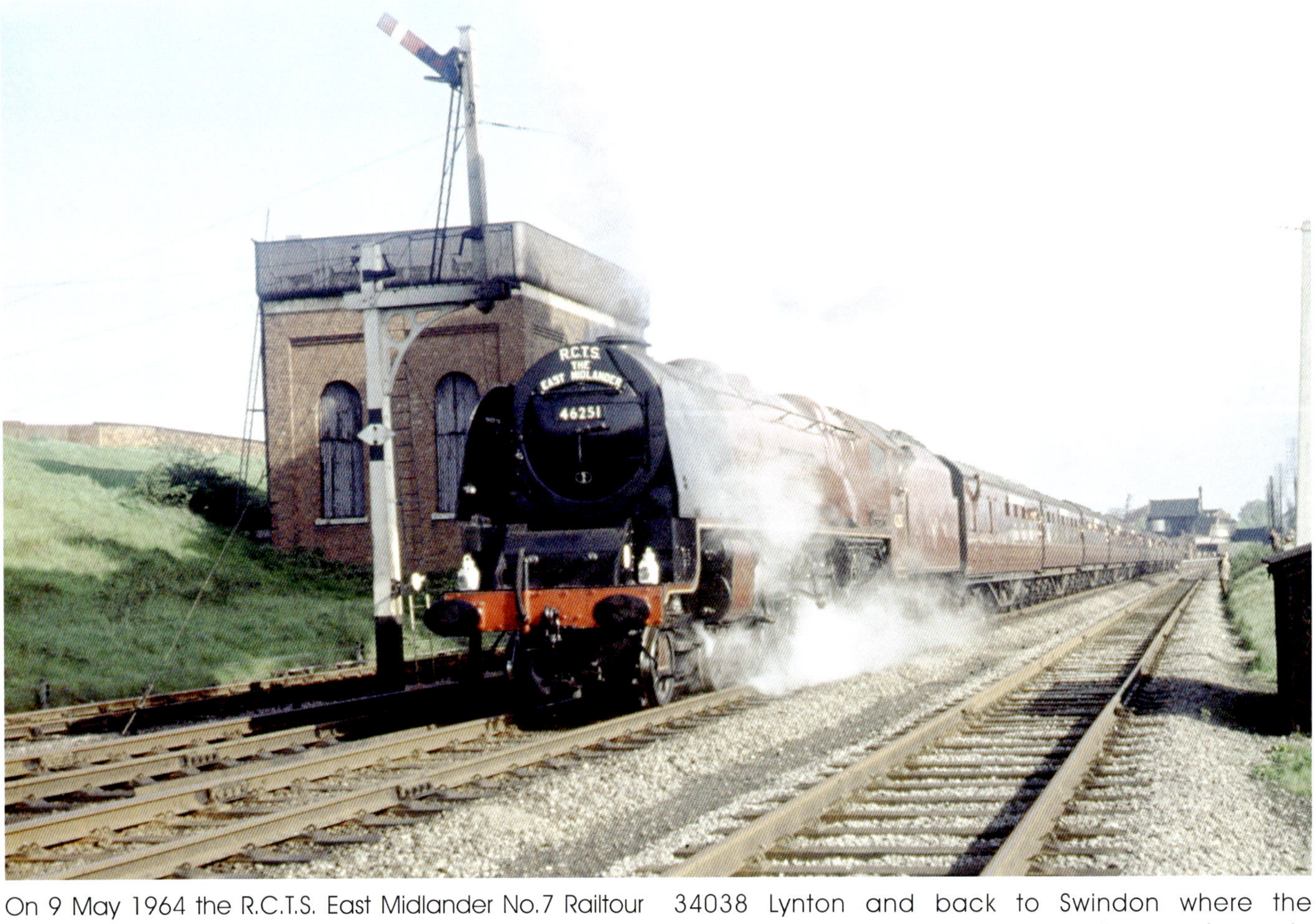

On 9 May 1964 the R.C.T.S. East Midlander No.7 Railtour was hauled through Rugby Central down the former GC mainline with a train full of spotters bound for both Eastleigh and Swindon Works behind 46251 City of Nottingham. The tour was worked from Didcot by West Country 34038 Lynton and back to Swindon where the Stanier Pacific was ready to bring the tour home to Nottingham Victoria. The shunt from Eastleigh station into the works complex was handled by USA Tank 30071. ***Jack Hodgkinson***

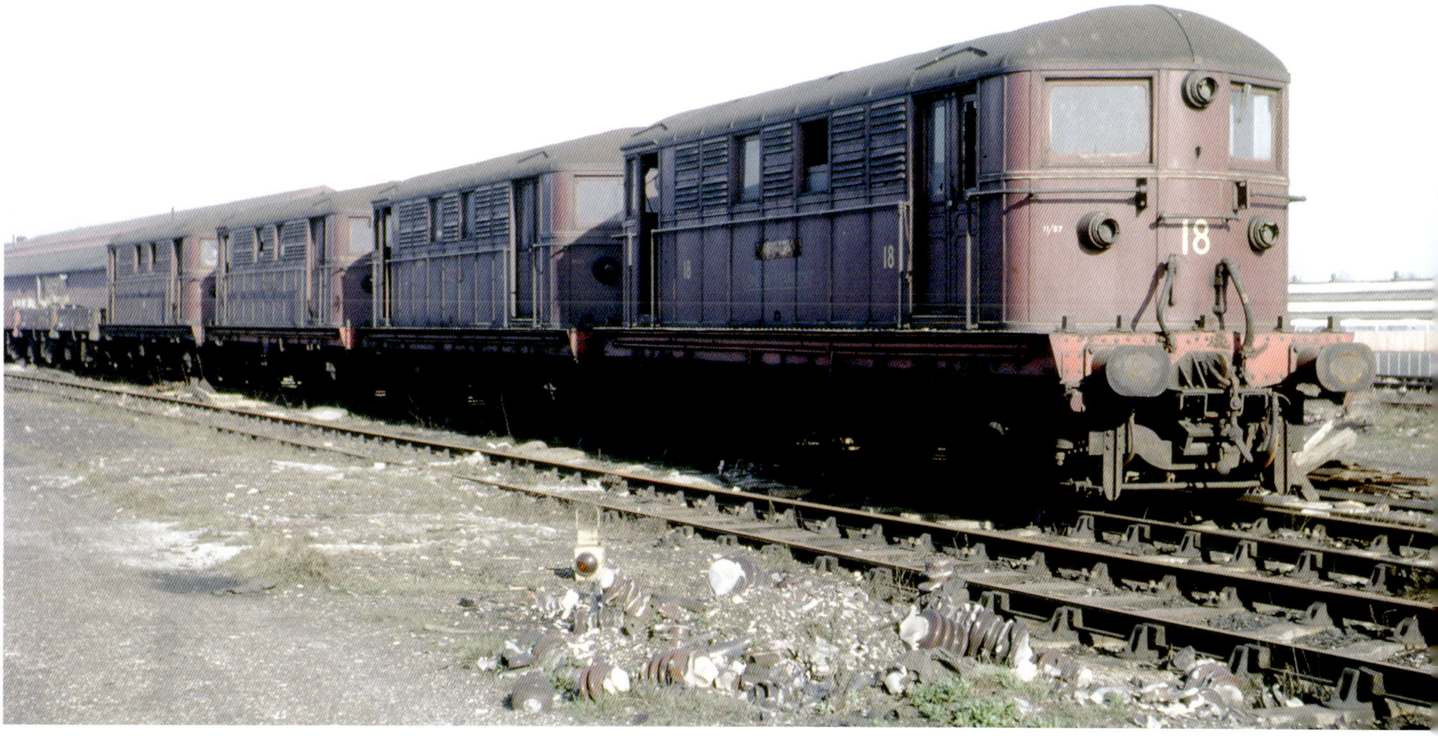

Captured stopping off on their journey to the breaker's yard for a while at Rugby shed on 28 March 1965 were this quartet of London Transport Bo-Bo's led by 18 once named Michael Faraday. ***Strathwood Library Collection***

Black Five 44711 had been built by British Railways at Horwich Works in October 1948 and when seen at Rugby in 1965 had another three years of service to put in. ***Tim Matthews***

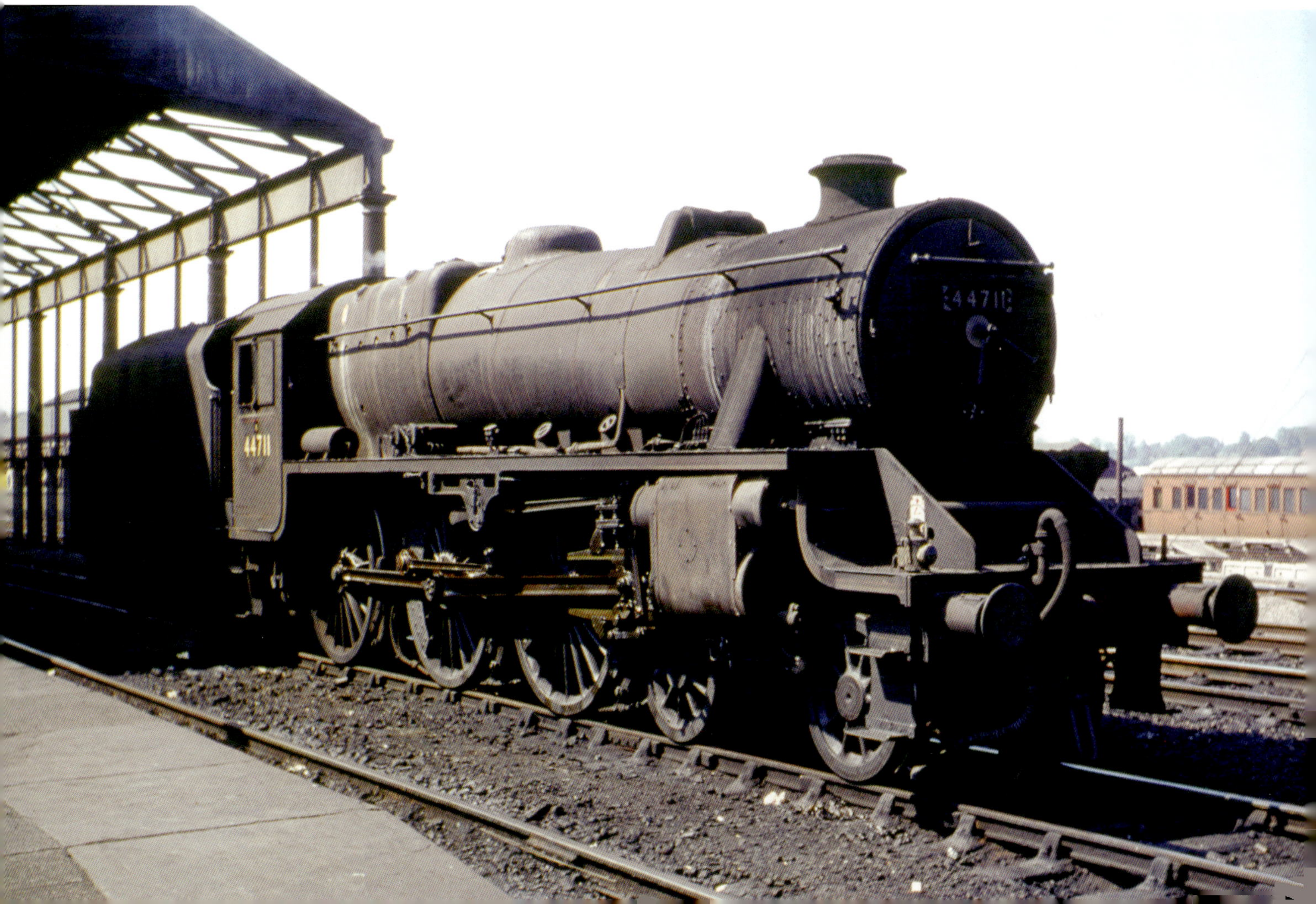

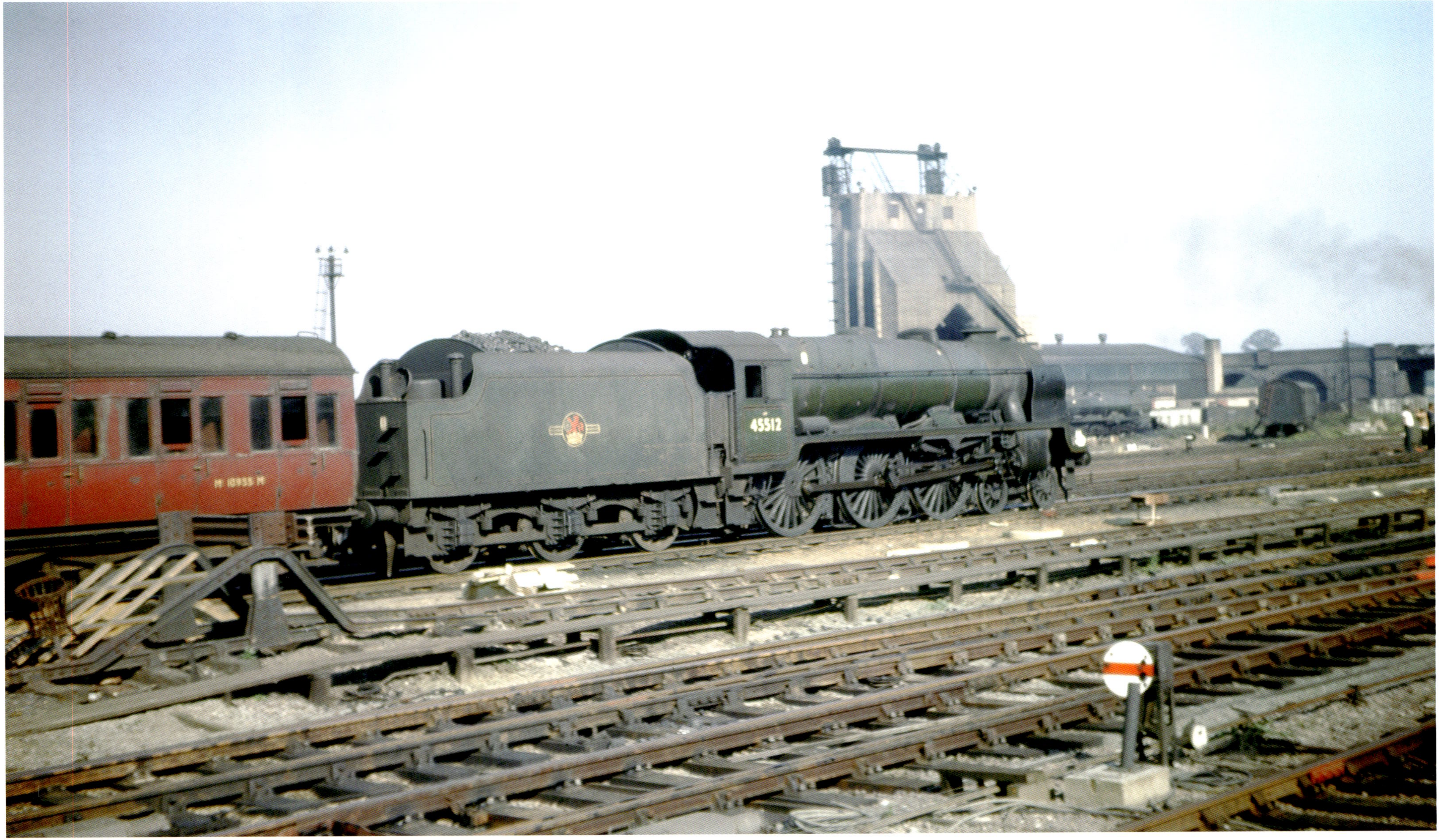

When Rebuilt Patriot 45512 Bunsen was photgraphed at Rugby in September 1963 the whole West Coast scene was changing with English Electric Type 4s already dominating passenger workings and very soon the overhead wires would bring hoards of electric locomotives south to take over completely the express workings.. ***Len Smith***

Page opposite: It will not be long now before steam is cast aside in the name of progress and 46245 City of London will have worked the 3A14 10.40 Crewe Willesden with 44244 set to work the 13.53 Rugby to Peterborough outside Rugby No.1 signalbox on 18 April 1964. ***Jack Hodgkinson***

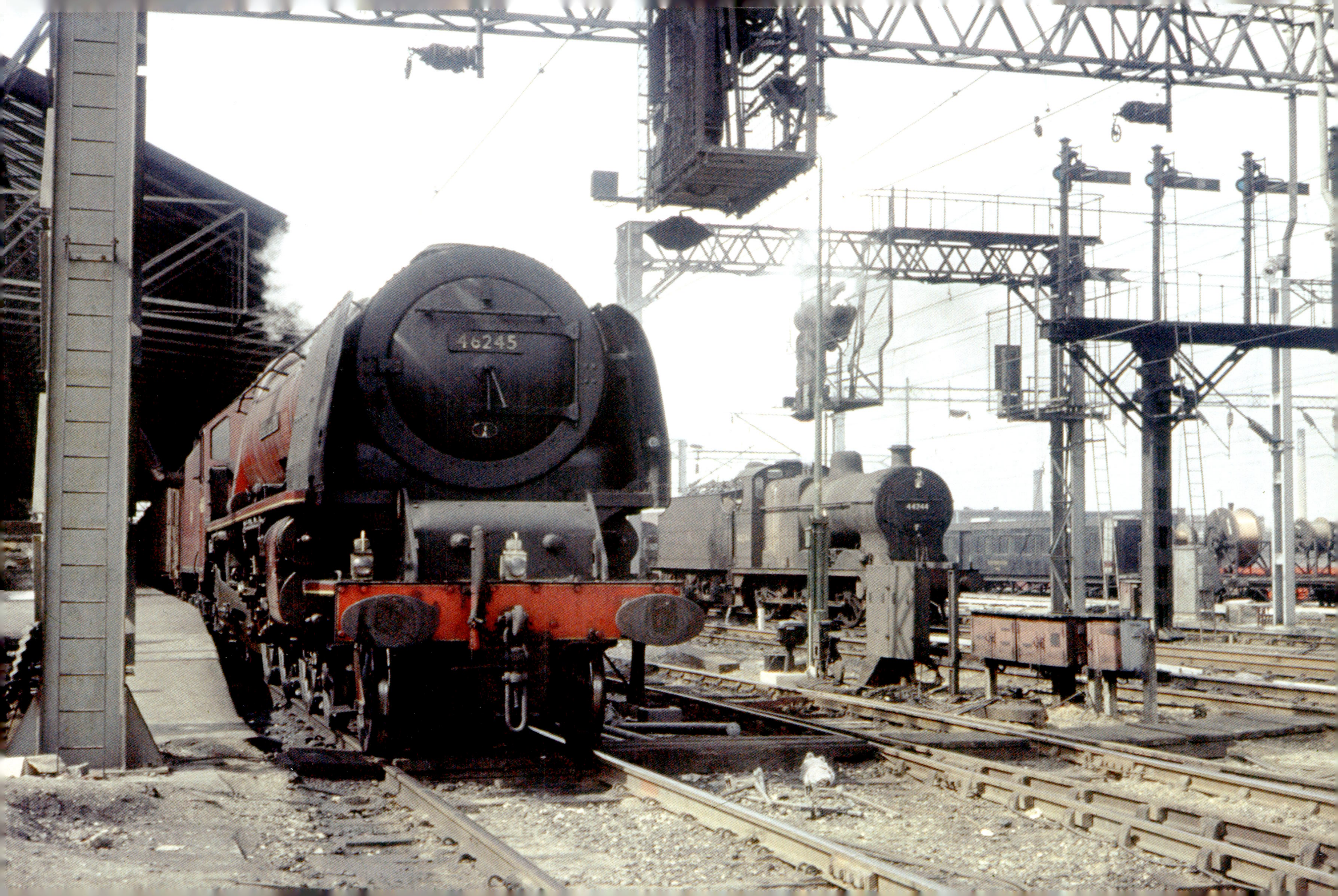
46245

Help To Preserve Our Railway Heritage

Strathwood not only publish books on our railway heritage but have also set up the Railway Photographic Preservation Association as a Charitable Trust to house an archive of images comprising over 200,000 photographic negatives and slides.

The archive was established to not only preserve the collections of over one hundred photographers both living and deceased, but to also make their work available to a younger audience for the future. To achieve this aim, we have begun an energetic programme to publish a considerable number of books. Allied to this we are making as many as possible of the photographs and slides we hold, available as copies to interested enthusiasts, individuals, societies and other publishers.

Many photographers have chosen Strathwood to care for their collections and to publish the best examples of their work for posterity.

If you have negatives or colour slides of transport subjects then we would like to hear from you. We purchase, accept on loan, or welcome donations of material to the archive. Photographers always receive recognition for their work when it is used by publishers (A N Other/Strathwood Library). To answer why so many images are just credited as Strathwood Library Collection in this volume, the reason is we do not know who the original photographer was. This is usually because their collection gets split up via auctions or collectors upon their death with no record of the late photographer for us to credit. Please do not let this happen to your collection. Make contact with us today to discuss what can be done to ensure your work is fully credited and recognised for both today and the future.

Please call us today if you would like to see your work in print, perhaps in a similar fashion to this publication. We also undertake publications to benefit charities and societies on behalf of our contributors. In addition we can store, and catalogue collections on behalf of clubs and societies by way of loan, thereby releasing such groups to concentrate on other aspects of their activities.

Strathwood Ltd,
Glenavon House,
Kinchurdy Road,
Boat of Garten,
Inverness-shire,
PH24 3BP.

Telephone 01479 831139

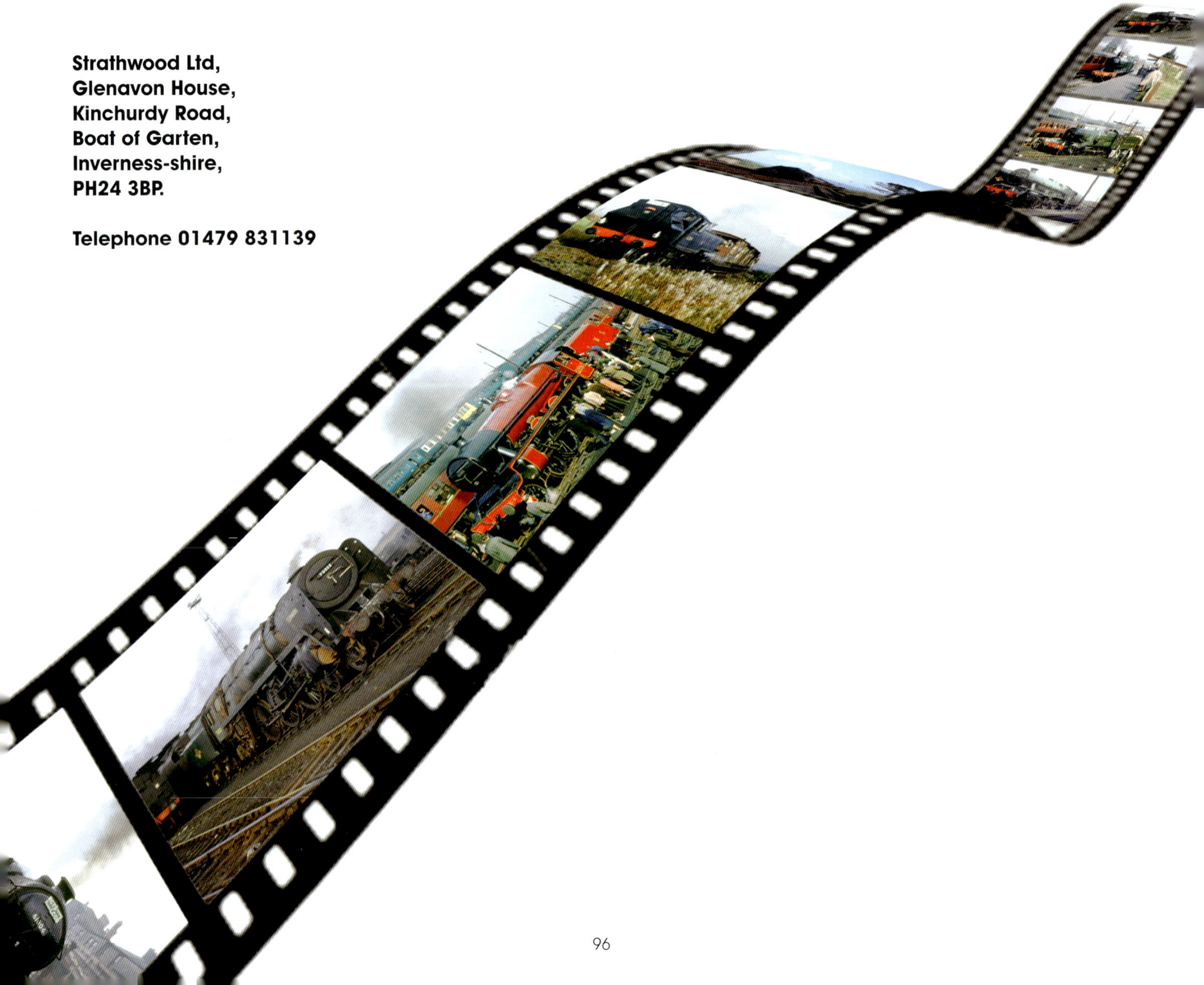